Political Philosophy

Political Philosophy is a comprehensive introduction to the major thinkers and topics in political philosophy. It explores the philosophical traditions which have formed and continue to inform our political judgements. Dudley Knowles introduces the ideas of key political thinkers including Hobbes, Locke, Marx and Mill and influential contemporary thinkers such as Berlin, Rawls and Nozick.

The individual chapters discuss and analyse the ideas of utilitarianism, liberty, rights, justice, obligation and democracy. As well as outlining central problems in political philosophy, Knowles encourages the reader to critically engage with all the issues discussed.

Political Philosophy is written in a fresh and easily readable style and is ideally suited to students taking introductory courses in political theory and philosophy as well as the general reader.

Dudley Knowles is Senior Lecturer in Philosophy at the University of Glasgow. He is the author of the *Routledge Philosophy GuideBook to Hegel and the Philosophy of Right*.

Fundamentals of Philosophy
Series Editor: John Shand

This series presents an up-to-date set of engrossing, accurate and lively introductions to all the core areas of philosophy. Each volume is written by an enthusiastic and knowledgeable teacher of the area in question. Care has been taken to produce works that while even-handed are not mere bland expositions, and as such are original pieces of philosophy in their own right. The reader should not only be well informed by the series, but also experience the intellectual excitement of being engaged in philosophical debate itself. The volumes serve as an essential basis for the undergradute courses to which they relate, as well as being accessible and absorbing for the general reader. Together they comprise an indispensable library of living philosophy.

Published:
Dudley Knowles
Political Philosophy

Piers Benn
Ethics

Alexander Bird
Philosophy of Science

Stephen Burwood, Paul Gilbert and Kathleen Lennon
Philosophy of Mind

Colin Lyas
Aesthetics

Alexander Miller
Philosophy of Language

Forthcoming:
Richard Francks
Modern Philosophy

Greg Restall
Logic

Suzanne Stern-Gillet
Ancient Philosophy

Simon Glendinning
Continental Philosophy

Political Philosophy

Dudley Knowles

London

First published 2001
by Routledge
2 Park Square, Milton Park, Abingdon, Oxon, OX14 4RN

Routledge is an imprint of the Taylor & Francis Group

Transferred to Digital Printing 2007

Typeset in Century Schoolbook and Futura by
RefineCatch Ltd, Bungay, Suffolk

British Library Cataloguing in Publication Data
A catalogue record for this book is available from the British
Library

ISBN 1–85728–760–6 (hbk)
ISBN 1–85728–550–6 (pbk)

To my mother, Margaret Knowles, and, in memoriam, GRK, DAK, AK, KC and EJC

Contents

CONTENTS

Preface

Political philosophy is a hard subject of study, but an attractive one, too. It is hard because the central concepts have been fashioned as much in the hurly-burly of political dispute as in the philosopher's study. These concepts have served as flags around which contending causes have rallied, banners for which opposing parties have fought – too often literally. Unlike many of the topics of metaphysics, say, they *always* have a resonance for issues of active controversy. They are the recognized currency of political argument and debate. This immersion in our practical concerns might be thought to contaminate the discipline, ensuring that no work in political philosophy is without the taint of allegiance. But this would be to suppose that there is a pristine science of political concepts waiting to be unearthed from the debris of interminable conflict, that the concepts can be scrubbed down and examined free of the scrapes and bruises inflicted by their rhetorical employment. There is no such science; there is no 'first philosophy' of political life. Yet it is vital that political philosophy be a careful academic discipline precisely because it is never merely that. It is vital that it be as scrupulous and transparent as its maker can manage because it will always be taken to be a contribution to struggles for power and campaigns for policies.

This makes it hard to do well. No one with a passion for political ideas can be detached from the circumstances of their employment. Political philosophy is attractive because it promises a deep understanding of the values at stake in daily strife, it promises a defence of causes that are dear to us. But careful thought may reveal that the defences are flimsy or that the values are confused. Most political philosophers will have a political agenda which governs their personal contribution to public affairs, and no doubt you will have worked out elements of mine by the time you finish this book. But philosophy is an open-minded discipline, so, para-doxically, personal commitments must be regarded as provisional, having no more credibility than is conferred on them by the strength of their supporting arguments.

I am particularly conscious of this since I have to report that my philosophical position has changed during the course of writing this book. When I began it, too long ago, I believed that the basic principles of liberal democracy should find universal acceptance. The grounding beliefs, that mankind is born free and equal, seemed to me to be basic elements of a common culture that have anchored themselves in the mind-sets of modern men and women. *We* think of *our*selves in this fashion, willy-nilly. These are the guiding principles history has bequeathed us. So I didn't think of liberalism as a radical point of view. I thought of it as mother's milk to the political sentiments of all good citizens. I believed, in the modern world, that the true conservative who is respectful of the traditions of thought that have formed us and our political environment, would be a liberal at least in the sense of accepting some story about universal freedom and equality, and distrustful of claims to authority. Of course, I recognized that values as loosely conceived as these require clarification and analysis, that tensions and confusions would be revealed as the grounding intu-itions were worked up into principles and theories of a specificity that could bear examination and assessment. But I didn't doubt that some cogent articulation of these values was the prospectus of philosophers and thoughtful citizens alike.

What I had ignored was the dire effects of religious belief, in particular the power of religion to corrode sentiments as crucial to peaceful social co-existence as mutual respect and relaxed tol-erance. The most noxious human capacities, agression, hatred and cruelty, seem to coagulate around religious beliefs which advertise their necessary distinctiveness, and then are transmuted into communal militancy. As the hatreds expressive of conflicts between political ideologies seem to have dried up, militant religion has stepped into the breach and now fuels murderous internecine conflicts worldwide – last year the former Yugoslavia, last month Indonesia, this week Nigeria. Doctors are murdered outside abortion clinics in the USA, and shoppers are blown up in Omagh. Hegel makes us shiver when he describes the mentality of the Terror in Revolutionary France as death, 'the coldest and meanest of all deaths, with no more significance than cutting off a head of cabbage'.[1] Rarely does a week go by nowadays without our seeing some TV footage of bodies piled into trenches, disposed of in the manner of waste vegetables.

So now I am a partisan, even militant, liberal. I despair of the prospect of finding common ground with those whose religious beliefs prescind from civility, from the task of seeking, minimally, a *modus vivendi* or, maximally, substantial agreement. I no longer see the sole task of political philosophy as the Hegelian enterprise of exploring and refashioning a consensus. Nowadays, we have to give as much attention to the dire task of drawing lines in the sand, marking off values which we recognize that only *some* of our fellows deem worthy of defence, values that are all the more crucial for being seemingly parochial.

When my efforts are set against this agenda, I don't claim to have accomplished much. On reflection, rarely do I reach definitive conclusions. What I do hope is to have placed some intellectual resources at the disposal of openly enquiring minds, raising questions, drafting lines of argument, provoking the kind of disagreement that challenges the reader to respond. I have concentrated on what I believe are the central areas of investigation. Though I am no card-carrying utilitarian, I examine the utilitarian theory in detail because I believe it is the most powerful, sophisticated and influential normative *theory* which is available to us, for better or worse. Next, I examine the core ideals of liberty, rights and justice in the distribution of goods. Next, I study the problem of political obligation, asking whether the state can make good its claim to rightful authority over its citizens. Finally, I look at constitutional issues, investigating the ethical credentials of democracy.

This self-directed focus has made it impossible for me to discuss many issues in political philosophy which have a direct bearing on practical and often urgent policy issues. So I don't discuss separately the politics of race, the particular injustice of racial discrimination or the legitimacy of affirmative action or reverse discrimination. I don't discuss justice between the sexes or the feminist contribution to political philosophy. I don't discuss the acceptability of nationalism, the ethical implications of multi-culturalism, or the proper conduct of international relations, except by way of example when other issues are in focus. I regret all of these omissions, but hope that those who are encouraged to tackle the questions I haven't raised may find in the book materials to help them in their efforts.

It is impossible to complete a work of this sort without accumulating debts. Some of them are acknowledged in the text, some unfortunately not. The bibliography furnishes a partial guide to my reading, but I should record the books I have had alongside my desk throughout the period of composition. Unsurprisingly perhaps, these have been Hobbes's *Leviathan*, Locke's *Second Treatise*, Hume's *Treatise*, *Second Enquiry* and *Essays*, Rousseau's *Discourse on the Origins of Inequality* and *Social Contract*, Hegel's *Philosophy of Right*, J.S. Mill's *Utilitarianism* and *On Liberty*, Rawls's *Theory of Justice*. Temperamentally, I don't seem to make much progress in political philosophy without first stepping back and studying what these giants of the discipline have to say.

My acknowledgement of personal debts must also be patchy. Students can always be relied upon to prompt their teachers into rethinking positions which would otherwise solidify into nostrums. Colleagues who, after reading students' work or listening to them in tutorials, stop me in the corridor and ask 'Do you tell them *that* ?', have similar effects – collapse of stout party and back to the drawing-board. Over the years, bits of this material have been read to philosophers in Glasgow and other universities, and I have welcomed and sometimes used their comments. Nick Zangwill read some of the manuscript material and I benefited from his advice. John Shand read early versions of the first five chapters, correcting errors and helping me clarify obscure material. Pat Shaw has read just about all of it; his criticisms, advice and encouragement have been invaluable. I am a duffer with a word processor and all things IT. My neighbours on the top floor of the philosophy department in Glasgow, Angus McKay and Susan Stuart, have responded kindly and patiently to my pathetic, panicky, pleas for assistance. John Shand, the series editor, and Tony Bruce and

Muna Khogali at Routledge, have been helpful and accommodating in the face of my prevarications and the anonymous referees they have recruited have improved the final version.

Since I expect that this book will be used largely for teaching, it is appropriate that I thank my teachers of political philosophy. I was first introduced to the subject at Kirkham Grammar School by Bernard Coates. There was no National Curriculum and political philosophy was certainly not on the examination syllabus, but Bernard thought it would be interesting for us to discuss the contract theories of Hobbes and Locke, so we did. I was so excited I immediately took the only valuable book in the house, a beautiful, many-volume work on *The Horse: Its Treatment in Health and Disease*, and swapped it for a tatty copy of Sabine's *History of Political Thought*. I suspect the booksellers, Messrs Halewood, of Friargate, Preston, are still laughing. This initial interest was rekindled in London, when I found myself preparing abstracts of material directed to questions my brother had spotted for his final exams at the LSE, but unfortunately had not had any time to study. It was fostered at Bedford College, London, by David Lloyd-Thomas, who had the wonderful, generous gift of finding good and interesting ideas in the most hurried and turgid essays I presented to him. My interests were further encouraged by Robin Downie when I came to Glasgow. It's a pleasure to acknowledge my debts to all of them and express my gratitude.

My wife, Anne, has had a lot to suffer in the preparation of this book. Mercifully she takes no interest at all in its contents, not having a philosophical bone in her body – so I thank her for the blessed relief.

Chapter 1

Introduction

Young children, we understand, are born philosophers. They ask exasperated parents such deep questions as 'Where is my mind?' or 'Is Granny living with all the other dead people in the churchyard?'. The spirit for philosophy which is born out of naïveté is soon extinguished, so the taste for philosophical reflection has to be rediscovered. I conjecture that it is an acquired taste, prompted by some strange contingency. Who knows the story behind your picking up this book? Still, some brands of philosophical enquiry are more likely to be prompted than others. An adolescent who found himself pondering the nature of numbers would be a splendid eccentric. By contrast, youthful rebellion can be relied upon to kindle low-level philosophical musings about the rules of behaviour. If parents say such and such is the right thing to do and the teenager insists that he does no wrong in not doing it, the conflict of views is likely to raise all sorts of philosophical questions: What is the nature and extent of parents' authority? What sort of respect is required for their rules? They can enforce their demands and prudence may dictate compliance, but does that make it right? If the question of who decides what behaviour is acceptable and what is not seems up for grabs, the question of how to decide will surely follow. Is it a matter of choice or preference or personal belief? And so on.

Such questions (and many more) comprise the subject of ethics, and I suspect that most people dip their toes into the water in the minimal sense of recognizing that there are questions to be answered, issues to be debated. Political life has the same character of putting philosophical questions up front. Authoritarian regimes prompt the same reflections as authoritarian parents. Democratic regimes conduct debates about competing policies in terms of the values such policies embody. Liberty may be opposed to justice. The public interest may require the sacrifice of persons' rights. This is the diet of editorials in tabloids as well as the broadsheet newspapers. Questions of ethics and political philosophy are ubiquitous, in the very air we breathe. The surprise for many is that the problems are not novel, that there is a rich history of careful deliberation about them, that the questions which seem fresh in 2000AD have often been recorded as debated for the last two and a half millenia.

We are heirs to this rich tradition of philosophical dispute. Though philosophical problems seemingly spring up afresh each day like mushrooms, similar problems have been worrying folks for as long as intellectual problems have been recorded. When we take seriously the philosophical questions posed directly in political life, we encounter immediately a vast literature organized around the problems mankind has encountered, the philosophers who have contributed to their solution and the theories that have been recurrently proposed as the means of tackling them.

The prospect can appear dismal. You ask: Do I have an obligation to obey the law? and one of nature's teachers gives you a reading-list – as they say, from Plato to NATO. In truth, this should be a source of excitement, since the history of philosophy does not parade itself as a progressive discipline in the manner of the history of science. You can learn from the Ancient Greeks, not least because the present is a small parish inhibited by parochial concerns. Escape into past ways of thinking, in philosophy if not in physics, can be a liberation. What a marvel it is to read Plato's report in the *Republic* of Socrates working out why might is not right, or Hobbes at the time of the English Civil War describing anarchy and arguing for the necessity of an absolute or unrestricted sovereign power. These are people you will want to argue with and you will find, to your pleasure, that it can be hard to do so.

Everyone who studies political philosophy has to know something about the history of the subject because that history is a priceless resource as much as it is an antiquarian interest. But this book will not address this history directly. Rather we shall concentrate on the central questions of political philosophy and the leading theories that have been employed to answer them. For the moment, I want to examine the methodology of political philosophy, to say a little more about the relationship of theory to judgement in the sphere of ethics – of which political philosophy is evidently a part.

The methods of ethics and political philosophy

A methodological impasse?

Let's begin our reflections with a hackneyed example. Suppose we have a sheriff who, along with utilitarian thinkers, believes the right action is the one that produces the greatest human welfare. Faced with a rioting mob, he decides a scapegoat is required to prevent widespread harm. He selects a plausible (but innocent) culprit for punishment and calm is restored. Harm and injustice is done to the poor innocent – but the greater evil is averted. The utilitarian sheriff defends his action as the right thing to do in the circumstances. A critic objects. The sheriff's action was wrong because it was unjust. No amount of benefit to any number of third parties can vindicate the punishment of an innocent man or woman. That principle is inviolable.

How are we to adjudicate the issue? On the side of the sheriff, supposing all the facts of the case are right, is a deep and plausible moral theory. The pity is that this theory of what constitutes right action commits him to doing what would normally be judged a wrong action. On the side of the critic is the principle ('intuition' is the term often used here) that it is unjust, and therefore wrong, to punish the innocent. The sheriff has a theory, which he can defend if pressed, which enables him to judge what is right in tricky cases like this. She (the critic) thinks that his theory is indefensible if it justifies him acting in a way that violates her principle. So – do we keep the theory and sacrifice the principle or do we jettison the theory because we cannot find it in us to reject the principle?

This question, often posed in the discussion of utilitarianism, is, at bottom a dispute about *methodology*. There are many ways forward and all of them are controversial since philosophical dispute reaches into the methods of ethical and political theory as well as the diet of problems which give rise to speculation about the appropriate method for tackling them. First, we need to understand the notion of a *theory* as the sheriff is employing it. The first, simplest, conception takes the theory to be a systematization of the moral and political judgements we are inclined to make. We find ourselves judging that this action is right, that action wrong, that this system is fair, that unjust. And we accord these judgements considerable status. They are not self-evident or absolutely unrevisable, but we are more likely to stick to them than we are to accept a theory which is inconsistent with them. We recognize that we operate with a great and complex stack of moral principles and reflection suggests that such judgements are the product of a deeper principle – in the case of the sheriff, the utilitarian view that actions and practices are right if they maximize well-being. We have explained the judgements we reach, but this explanation may serve wider purposes. It may guide us when we find ourselves in a difficult dilemma. In entirely novel circumstances, of the sort that medical advances seem to throw up daily, the theory may show us the way forward. Obviously, this conception of moral theory cannot help us if we review the above example. The sheriff and his critic differ precisely on whether the case represents a decisive example which should cause us to reject or qualify the theory. Since both agree that what is decisive is the authority of the particular moral judgement or rule, I shall dub this view 'particularist'.[1]

A different conception of moral theory regards the task of the theorist very differently. On this account, the task of moral theory is to validate or generate moral principles, to serve as a foundation for them. Utilitarianism may be viewed in this light, too, since, as we shall see, its techniques may be employed to assess not just specific actions and practices, but moral rules as well. If this is right, if some such theory finds conviction, whether it is utilitarianism, Kantian formalism which uses the test of the categorical imperative, contractualism or the theory of Divine Command, it follows that our intuitions regarding subordinate principles are all revisable in light of the theory to hand. Possession of such a theory would settle the dilemma posed by the sheriff's actions and the critic's challenge. We can dub this notion of theory 'foundationalist' – again with warnings about incautious use of the terminology. Unfortunately, I have no such theory to hand, believing that all attempts to delineate such an ambitous project have failed.

We have two different conceptions of moral theory and two different accounts of the status and revisability of the moral judgements and principles that such theories (in their different ways) encompass. It is worth noticing that these disputes about the nature of normative ethics find an echo in deep disputes about the appropriate methods of political philosophy. Hegel noticed that modern subjects claim what he described as '*the right of the subjective will*', a distinctively modern attitude which claims 'that whatever it is to recognize as valid should be *perceived* by it *as good*'. (Alternatively: 'The right to recognize nothing that I do not perceive as rational is the highest right of the subject.')[2] This stance may be dubbed 'individualist' or even 'liberal'. It echoes Kant's claim that 'Our age is the genuine age of criticism, to which everything must submit'.[3] In this context, the thought is that the individual who seeks the credentials of principles or institutions has detached himself from their moral 'pull' in order to conduct his investigation. He has placed himself above the mêlée, abstracting from all prejudice and allegiance in order to carry out a judicious review of what theory (in the guise of reason) requires. Suppose I find myself questioning the obligations I hitherto felt to a parent or a child. I see others behaving differently and wonder if perhaps I can legitimately do the same. It looks as though the only way I can examine these questions is by stepping outside of the institutions of domesticity and subjecting them to an external assessment. Or suppose I find myself breaking the law with

5

impunity and no sense of guilt – buying my under-age child a glass of cider in a country pub. Being philosophical, this causes me to wonder whether I have a general obligation to obey the law. Again, once prompted, once the question has been asked, I find myself at a distance from the press of what hitherto I had taken to be an obligation. Detaching myself from the moral force of the institutions that bind me by their rules, I can pursue my investigation as an outsider would. Should I subscribe to this general rule or should I modify or reject it in the light of the best reasoning I can command, the best theory at my disposal?

In the seventeenth century, for a variety of reasons, philosophers who reflected on politics began to question the grounds of their allegiance and the legitimacy of the constitutions of particular states. From what stance could this appraisal be conducted? It seemed obvious to some that the best way to answer the question of whether or not they had good reason to obey a sovereign power was to hypothesize that they had none – and then ask whether rational agents with a specific set of wants (Hobbes) or wants and values (Locke) would have good reason to establish one. They deduced that those without a sovereign power (as they said, in a State of Nature) would recognize that a sovereign ought to be instituted; those who found themselves already subject to the claims of sovereign authority should recognize it as legitimate. The reasoning which generated these conclusions could be advanced by (or expained to) each sceptical individual. Individualism of this methodological stripe has its origin in a sceptical impulse that subjects to scrutiny what many take to be the givens of one's moral and political regime. In order to conduct this scrutiny, it is evidently necessary to have some theory at hand that can serve as the test of the principles called for judgement. It is worth adding at this point that those who detach themselves in thought from the concrete demands of the institutions which govern them, seeking a rationale that should be good for any enquirer, generally attribute to all persons a moral status that endows them with liberty and equality as well as the universal ends of survival and 'commodious living'.[4] In a nut-shell, this is why individualism as I have described it may also be termed 'liberalism'. (And while we're charting the 'isms', this stance of the detached, disengaged, perhaps alienated, enquirer may be described as 'atomism' if a society is thought to comprise an aggregate of such individuals. But an intellectual health warning should be issued concerning the careless use of philosophical labels!)

By contrast, a different view will reject the possibility of this radically abstracted self. Call its protagonist the 'communitarian'. She will insist that we cannot, even in thought, strip off the lineaments of our personalities – for our moral constitution goes as deep as this. For better or worse, we are burdened by intuitions concerning the moral standing of ourselves and others and what it is for folks like us to live well. Our views on these matters are not optional extras; they will be embedded deeply in our language and the very ways we think. On an extreme view, we just find ourself located at a particular, specifiable, moral address. According to some feminists, humans are possessed of a socially constructed gender which has determined in a fundamental way their moral orientation – towards categories of rules and duties (men) or virtues of care and compassion (women). Most of us are enmeshed in families whose structures are describable in terms of rights and duties from which we cannot renege without doing wrong. These families may find their origins, sustenance and detailed regulation within a tribe or race, which may subscribe to a religion or worldview which gives point to its ceremonies and rituals. Such wider communities may inhabit a region with environmental exigencies which structure their domestic constitution. In the modern world they are likely to be regulated by a state whose history (and myths) deeply engage the allegiance of the people.

Our identities may be thick with attachments and emotional ties deriving from all of these sources and more; attachments and ties which cannot be repudiated or even questioned without the deepest personal loss and fragmentation. Such a dense moral address Hegel called our 'ethical life'. Its reality and the objectivity of the claims it makes upon us he called 'ethical substance'.

The modern debate between the individualist and the communitarian is not a fad of the moment. It echoes (in a distorted fashion, for historical purists) the contrasting views of Plato and Aristotle on the good society – Plato advancing a utopian vision founded on a conception of justice he worked hard to elaborate, Aristotle describing those institutions mankind has discovered to be necessary for the fullest expression of human nature. At the turn of the nineteeth century, battle was renewed again between another pair of near contemporaries, Kant and Hegel – Kant aspiring to a standpoint of reason which in ethics takes us right outside the phenomenal world of everyday experience into a noumenal world where principles of practical reason are disclosed to any dispassionate enquirer; Hegel, by contrast, finding this standpoint 'empty' and counselling us to seek a deep understanding of the principles and institutions which history has deposited as the framework of our social lives. To grossly caricature the contrast, the individualist seeks a perspective of reason whereas the communitarian articulates a description of ethical reality.

In the context of political philosophy, I am tempted to label the respective camps 'radical' and 'conservative'. The individualist position is *radical* because of the implicit commitment to subject *all* beliefs and institutions to review, according none a privileged status of critical immunity. The communitarian position is *conservative* in the sense that it accepts the validity of central categories of moral self-description which are entrenched within the practices and institutions of society. We cannot escape those dimensions of moral vision and feeling in which we have been enclosed by socialization. Outside of the sense of ourselves which the communitarian philosopher articulates, we would not employ the sharp vision of the detached critic; we would be altogether lost and aimless, without any sense of characteristic human ends or aspirations. We must begin at that place where we come *from*.

The issue is complex, but it should not be too hard to see how this dispute about the character of political theorizing reproduces the methodological disputes recorded earlier. The first should be obvious. In the first part of this chapter, I contrasted the respective approaches of the foundationalist, the theorist who wields a decisive theory, and the particularist, the thinker who takes her stand on principles or intuitions. The differences evinced by these two approaches reflect a pair of contrary dispositions – a top-down impulse to validate and a bottom-up need to explain and systematize. I believe that, in so far as the individualist/communitarian distinction is concerned with the *methodology* of ethics and politics, the same two dispositions are at work. The individualist, as I have characterized this position, is committed primarily to evaluation from a theoretical stance he endorses. Unless rules, principles, practices and institutions can be validated in the light of higher values to which he subscribes he will not authorize them, they have no claim to legitimacy. The communitarian, by contrast, is distinguished by what she takes as given, the values, principles, practices and institutions which constitute her historically contingent identity. She cannot, in fact, detach herself in principle so as to achieve a theoretical stance from which her commitments can be appraised.

Reflective equilibrium

Back to the sheriff's dilemma. Since we don't possess the quick fix of a theory which can review the situation and settle decisively whether the sheriff or his critic is right or wrong,[5] a first way forward is to expand the data available for judgement and hope that with more information to hand some agreement may be attained. We may amplify the detail of the example. The description already available is true, we have supposed, but that does not establish that it is sufficient for a correct verdict to be reached. In fact, the opposite is the case. The information given in the example is palpably insufficient for a consensus on the rightness or wrongness of what the sheriff has done. When more information is brought to bear – perhaps the critic can get the sheriff to agree that he can't keep secret his practice of framing innocents and so lots of citizens will become anxious that they may be selected as scapegoats – it may transpire that theory and intuition are brought into line as protagonists agree that the example has not shown that maximizing human welfare can require acts of injustice.

Second, we may review the theory. We may limit its ambitions, draw in some of its horns. We can supplement the restricted theory with another, different one which offers a better explanation or justification of the troublesome case. The resulting bunch of theories will be messier, an altogether less elegant intellectual structure and perhaps it will create boundary problems within the body of theory which has been yoked together. But this may be a price worth paying if the resultant structure promises an understanding of how we reach decisions in a disconcertingly wide range of cases. In the case of the sheriff, we may limit the scope of utilitarian reasoning and insist that independent principles of retributive justice apply.

Third, we may review the principle about which the critic was so confident. Perhaps we can get her to accept that there are circumstances, real or hypothetical, where it seems to imply conclusions which are unacceptable. An example which illustrates much the same point as that of the sheriff who lynches the plausible scapegoat, but which can trigger very different reactions, concerns the reality of systems of criminal justice. Let's all agree that in this world of fallible human beings it is quite impossible to devise a criminal justice system which can be guaranteed *never* to convict an innocent. Different mixes of procedural rules will generate different probabilities of innocents being acquitted or convicted. Now suppose we have to set up such a system or endorse a system which is in place. We *know* that sooner or later an innocent will be punished. We *know* that some unfortunate individual will have to pay for the utility (or justice) of our having instituted a workable system of trial and punishment to deal with criminals. Against this background – of having to establish *some* systematic procedures for responding to crime – the critic may come to recognize that, in practice, any such response will permit unintentional and undiscovered miscarriages of justice. Examples such as this may cause the critic who is confident in her intuitions of principle concerning the punishment of the innocent to register a doubt. In which case she, too, may be willing to enter negotiations when theory collides with intuition.

Let us review the conclusions of this discussion of the methodology of ethics. In my book there are two villains. The first is the philosopher who claims one can get nowhere in ethics until one has discovered, through *a priori* reasoning or the investigation of a sufficient range of moral judgement, some high-level theory of ethics which can serve the purposes of testing lower-level principles of action and generating verdicts of right/wrong, good/bad, just/unjust in respect of any particular action brought forward for judgement. The second villain is the philosopher (or ordinary moral agent) who believes himself endowed with a set of moral principles or intuitions which are in principle immune to correction, which brook no qualification or exception, nor require careful contextual elaboration.

What we are left with is a pair of propensities which draw away from and collide with each other in fruitful co-existence. The first is a bottom-up drive to gather together judgements made in particular cases and formulate principles which articulate the rationale of these judgements. We go further. Having to hand a set of principles, we can try to establish whether this exhibits any common features which we might employ to propose a still more general theory of ethics. Success in this endeavour would advance our understanding of a crucial range of human activities.

The second propensity is as powerful as the first and best thought of as a top-down impulse to cleanse our intellectual stables. It finds its beginnings in what may seem an incontrovertible insight into the nature of morality – and there are conspicuous modern candidates. For the utilitarian, morality is concerned at base with the promotion of human well-being and the relief of human suffering; for the Kantian, it expresses our nature as rational and autonomous creatures; for the contractualist, it elaborates and represents the employment of a need to find agreement if conflict is to be avoided and co-operation facilitated, or alternatively, it expresses the need we feel to justify our conduct to others. Whichever core insight we fix on is then developed into a theory of great generality, and is consequently used in a review of our judgements on actions and institutions, although again there will probably be an intermediate stage of assessment where rules and principles are subject to inspection.

I say both bottom-up and top-down strategies are propensities because we operate consciously and spontaneously in both ways, when we act, when we judge and when we theorize. We evaluate actions in terms of principles and we examine principles in the light of their verdicts in particular cases. We assess candidate principles by asking whether they can be derived from an overarching theory and we endorse or challenge theories because they entail principles we avow or repudiate.

This ideal – of satisfaction that our mix of theory, principles and judgements is in good order – has been dubbed 'reflective equilibrium' by John Rawls.[6] In the real world of imperfect information and variable judgement the picture breaks down. Reflective equilibrium will need to be created again and again as uncomfortable facts and the disturbing implications of our theories and principles are revealed to us. It is not surprising, given this conception of the task of ethics, that the subject has a long history and an assured future. Our contribution to this endeavour will be to display as comprehensive an equilibrium as can be attained in our reflections about politics.

We have sounded an optimistic note with the promise of reconciliation through the search for a reflective equilibrium. I want to continue in the spirit of optimism. Something akin to reflective equilibrium must be sought in reconciliation of the dispute between the individualist and the communitarian. My sketch of these two positions has been a caricature, too brief, too tendentious, to carry conviction although it may illuminate central elements of the work of distinguished philosophers. This will become evident as soon as we criticize these stereotypes. Against the communitarian we must insist that her account is vulnerable as soon as it is seen to defend the indefensible. Take your favourite example of an appalling practice with deep cultural and historical roots, the apologists for which seem blind to the iniquity: slavery, forced conversion, suttee, trial by combat, female circumcision, ethnic cleansing; there is no shortage of candidates! We cannot take the unreflective conviction of enthusiastic practioners, nor any amount of detail showing how firmly such practices are embedded in the belief- and value-structures of specific communities, to insulate them from criticism.[7] At the very least, we can attempt to show how far these traditions are based on false beliefs where this is evident. So we should be very suspicious of claims to the effect that subscription to moral principle or identification with institutions is somehow constitutive of the identity of potential villains. However deep their benighted views, they should be regarded as ripe for change.

But equally, our contempt for cruelty and wickedness should not convince us that we have attained the high ground of moral certainty. Some methodological modesty is in order. Individualism, as I have characterized it, presupposes *some* conception of the wants and values of typical individuals, once we discount the overambitious claim to algorithmic reason. Hobbes identified a universal propensity to avoid death and live commodiously. Even so sparse a conception of human nature as this offers a hostage to fortune. John Locke took these ends to be universal, too, and then bolstered his account by claiming that mankind could not act as trustees of the purposes God had ordained for them unless they were subject to the law of nature and recognized to be free and equal possessors of natural rights. These premises, too, are debatable. So just as communities may disseminate error, individualists may advance their critical positions on the basis of moral principles which can prove hard to defend. If communities need to find a place for bloody-minded critics, critics should not be surprised at the disclosure that their stance may be controversial and fallible.

As ever, some meeting of minds and temperaments must be sought. And a model suggests itself. We are the heirs to many centuries of careful moral philosophy – philosophy which both derives from and has contributed to a common social life structured by rules and institutions. We inescapably think of ourselves in terms of categories which carry moral potency. Thus we believe we are committed to and responsible for the well-being of others as well as ourselves. We insist on being respected as persons, as bearers of rights which command the duties of others. We claim to be autonomous and require a domain of personal freedom within which this autonomy can be exercised. We refuse to recognize any moral authority which can determine for us and dictate to us where our duty lies. Nothing shall be demanded of us which in principle is not available for us to endorse or reject.

At the same time, and equally inescapably, we find ourselves living within communities of fabulous complexity, our lives enmeshed with those with whom we associate in pursuit of domestic, economic, artistic, scholarly, religious and political ends. These pursuits, too, frame our severally rich conceptions of what is valuable to us and how we may live well.

My picture of our moral repertoire, which I acknowledge I have gathered from Hegel, is that of a structured cluster of principles of the kind listed above which are expressed in institutions, amongst which the law is dominant. We describe ourselves and recognize others in all of these ways – and more besides. The core terms of self-ascription have moral power in the simple sense that identification with them requires us to act towards others (and others to act towards ourselves) in ways consonant with the moral rules which constitute these patterns of identification. Thus to be a person, the most elementary of moral categories, is to claim respect for one's rights as one respects the rights of others. To be a parent is to have a duty of care to the children one has brought into the world – and much else. To be a citizen is to be an active creator of laws which demand the subjection of their creators. And so on . . .

I have stressed the complexity of this inheritance because this very complexity establishes the philosopher's itinerary. This is a house which very much needs to be put in order. We have to think through every element in it, elaborating the conception of the self which is prompted and articulating the associated values. We need to enquire whether this structure can hang together, whether we *can* be all things at once, to ourselves and our fellows. It is likely that we demand more of ourselves and others than can be accomplished, that roles and principles may clash and personal as well as social conflicts erupt.

This is the conclusion I wish to draw from these brief reflections on the methods of ethics and political philosophy. To advance in ethics (and particularly in political philosophy) we do not need to find some foundational touchstone to establish the credentials of all our beliefs at once – identifying this one as gold, that other as dross. But nor need we endorse all that prereflectively we find ourselves approving. There is plenty of work for us to be getting on with in describing, explaining, systematizing and inspecting for contradictions the set of political values our history has gathered together. We don't need to closet ourselves away from the demands of our communities – but neither should we assume that the moral demands our communities press upon us are in good intellectual order. A moderate scepticism, predicated upon suspicions of confusion and incoherence, is quite enough to get us started.

Political philosophy

One could divide up the subject of political philosophy in any number of ways, hoping that a systematic treatment will leave students with a solid grasp of the major areas of dispute. One could begin with foundational theories, enquiring how far they generate a set of principles which can be applied convincingly to a standard list of philosophical problems which our political life throws up. So one might study, in succession, say, utilitarianism, natural law and/or natural rights theory, Kantian autonomy-based theories, contractualist theories and no-theory theories. (I have in mind here that species of conservativism which argues that the political domain of political philosophy, and perhaps ethics generally, is a matter of practical wisdom and emphatically not susceptible to systematic, rational theorizing.) And no doubt there are more theories in the offing.

With our sights thus focused, we could investigate how well these theoretical perspectives deliver the goods, asking, for example: whether they can tell us whether we have good grounds for accepting the state (and, in particular, its powers to coerce us by threatening punishment) or whether we would do better without it, in a condition of anarchy; what is the optimal constitutional form of state authority (the rule of one: monarchy or tyranny; a few: aristocracy or oligarchy; the many: democracy, direct or representative; or some mix of these models); what is the proper extent of political power: Is there a private domain which can be invoked to limit the legitimate exercise of the states activities? Do these theories deliver an account of justice, telling us who should own what, how benefits should be allocated, which burdens should be accepted as due?

Suppose we take it that these problems have given rise to a range of clear answers prior to their theoretical exploration, we can then order our investigations differently. We can state the problem in appropriate detail, outline those answers which best encapsulate our intuitions, and seek out a theory from which these results could be derived.

In the chapters that follow, I shall use both of these approaches. In Chapter 1, I shall discuss the utilitarian contribution to political philosophy. I select utilitarian theory for close investigation for a number of reasons. First, because of its strength and the detail with which it has been articulated. Amongst philosophers, there may not be many card-carrying utilitarians nowadays, or not many utilitarians who accept the theory in an unqualified fashion. But utilitarianism has its classic sources in the work of Hume, Bentham and J.S. Mill, and the core theory has been refined and developed by countless thinkers since. It has many variants, each of which have developed responses to both sympathetic and relentlessly hostile criticism. As a body of normative theory it is

unrivalled in its sophistication. Second, from its Benthamite origins, it has been applied resolutely in the domain of practical politics. Its key insistence on computing the benefits and burdens of
all those who are affected by policy decisions has ensured its continued use by both politicians and those who criticize them.[8] This
practical influence has also ensured that it has been the target of
those who dispute its credentials, both generally and in the context of specific policy application. In recent years, for example, it
has been heavily criticized for its role in debates concerning
environmental policy.[9] Third, the criticism of utilitarian theory
has often been the starting point for those who have developed
alternative theoretical positions. In no case is this more conspicuous than that of John Rawls as he develops the argument of *A
Theory of Justice*. In which case, it is important that utilitarianism
should not be represented as a straw target; evaluation of these
competing theories requires that we understand the power and
plausibilty of utilitarianism at its strongest.

In the first part of Chapter 2 I lay out the structure and main
variants of utilitarian theory, signalling the most important lines
of criticism and detailing the utilitarian responses to them. If you
wish to skip this exercise in moral philosophy and proceed directly
to specific problem areas in political philosophy, feel free to do so.
In the second part, I look more directly at the political elements of
utilitarian theory, detailing classical or typical utilitarian
accounts of the central political values – liberty, rights and justice
in the distribution of goods. In two final sections, I examine briefly
the utilitarian account of political obligation and the utilitarian
case for democracy.

In the three chapters that follow we shall investigate in greater
depth the philosophical credentials of these central critical ideals.
In Chapter 3, I examine the value of liberty. This will prove a
complex, not to say exhaustive, task since liberty is the most
opaque of values. Although I shall be focusing on the questions of
whether or not liberty is a value, and if so, why so, the literature
has bequeathed us a complex task of careful analysis, examining a
number of influential explications of the concept of liberty. We
shall discover that these open up rather than settle the questions
concerning value and that a complex account needs to be constructed. At the heart of this is a controversial claim that liberty

as a political value can never require that citizens have the opportunity to do evil. Having clarified the conceptual background and stated why claims of liberty should be respected, I go on to consider what liberty requires in the way of institutional provision, how far the value of liberty supports democratic decision-making processes and what principles should govern the legitimate restraint of liberty by law and less formal social mechanisms.

In Chapter 4, I tackle problems raised by the notion of rights. Given the ubiquity of rights claims and the focus of political attention in both national and international contexts on human rights, philosophical attention could not be more timely. As with liberty, first there is a thicket of analysis and terminological distinction to be entered and much jargon to be clarified. We are assisted here by the work of jurisprudents who from Bentham onwards have been scrupulous in the definition of terms – which is not to say that their contributions are uncontroversial. We also look briefly at the question of group rights before tackling the vexed issue of the justification of rights claims. As citizens we are much better at claiming rights than defending them.

In examining the credentials of rights claims we shall explore a number of traditional approaches. Locke's theological account is a model, but the premises from which it is advanced are claimed to be too controversial to find widespread acceptance. Arguments from autonomy are more promising and, indeed successful over some of the terrain of rights. But some rights, I claim, are more evident than the justificatory apparatus proposed for them. Others, notably the political rights, are claimed to be a species of group rights for which support on the grounds of their promoting personal autonomy is inapt. Next, we re-examine, in more detail than hitherto, the utilitarian argument for rights. This, I maintain, is more successful than many opponents allow. But to be wholly satisfactory, utilitarian theory has to find acceptance. It may not be vulnerable to the charge that it cannot defend rights, but other objections may be harder to rebut. Finally, I examine a little-known view that I find persuasive – the no-theory theory. On this account, the success of appeals to rights lies in the fact that history has taught us to claim them and recognize that claiming them requires us to respect all persons as rights bearers.

In Chapter 5 we shall broach the questions of distributive justice: how may private ownership be justified; which criteria should
we employ in order to decide who should own, or be allocated,
which benefits and burdens? We begin with another common-
sense, no-theory theory, the 'entitlement' theory of Robert Nozick.
Here we shall see that presenting no theory to justify property
distribution is a handicap rather than an advantage, since claims
to property will be challenged, in the name of justice, by non-
owners and by the state which wishes to engage in the redistribution of wealth and earnings. The fundamental weakness of Nozick's theory will be exposed: if private property is so important a
value that claims of right to it should be regarded as sacrosanct, to
the point that taxation amounts to forced labour, shouldn't everyone have some of it? At this point, I shall discuss, too, F.A. Hayek's
rejection of a value of social justice.

Assume that justice dictates that everyone should possess some
property. This signals the need to find principles which determine
just allocations, and in what follows we discuss a number of traditional contenders. The first principle to be assessed is that of
need. Like principles of liberty and rights, we shall find that claims
of need require clarification by careful analysis and, job done,
command respect. Equality is a venerable (or disreputable) principle. Again clarification is demanded in order to answer the question: Equality of what? A range of candidate matrices of equality
will be reviewed. Desert is a familiar criterion of just distribution
– 'Folks should get and keep what they have earned' is an informal
way of expressing this principle. This view is examined, but in
large part rejected. Finally we look at one of the glories of
twentieth-century political philosophy – the theory of fairness
espoused in John Rawls's *A Theory of Justice*. Rawls's theory of
justices aims to solve more questions than who should own what,
who should be allocated which benefits and burdens, but we shall
review it principally as an answer to those specific questions and
try to measure its contribution.

Chapter 6 tackles one of the great chestnuts of political philosophy – the problem of political obligation. The central issues
here concern the legitimacy of the commands of government, the
authority which government claims when it addresses laws to the
citizens. From the perspective of the citizen, the question will

often be 'Do I have an obligation or a duty to obey the law, comply with the requests of the sovereign, or otherwise be a good citizen?'. In the literature of political philosophy, this clutch of related questions can be traced back to Socrates in his cell in Athens, deliberating whether to accept the sentence of death or escape with the assistance of his friends.

I put these questions in the voice of the state which makes demands of its citizens, and after some preliminary sparring discuss two approaches which reject the enterprise of justifying the authority of the state. The first of these, anarchism, insists that the state is an evil which cannot be justified; its use of coercive powers is immoral and unnecessary. The second attempt to reject the question comes from the communitarian who denies the citizen any perspective from which the questions can be properly raised. The authority of the state is beyond our critical reach. Unfortunately neither of these sceptical approaches carry enough conviction to disbar further investigation.

On any account of its powers, the state looks to be a nasty operation – this is the insight the anarchist just fails to exploit. And might is not right. This sets up the first and most obvious justificatory claim on the part of the state: however severe these powers may be in their application to citizens, if the citizens consent to the institutions which deploy them, the authority of the state is conceded. This argument is irrefutable – which is not to say the problem is solved, for it transpires that the phenomenon of consent is more easily charged than witnessed. Some persons consent expressly, some consent tacitly, but too many bloody-minded citizens can fairly repudiate the imputation of consent for these arguments to serve the purpose of the state which aspires to universal allegiance. The best argument from consent is addressed to citizens of a democracy who participate in the processes of making the decisions that bind them, but even this argument needs to be massively qualified and even then will not convince all dissenters.

Further arguments are needed by the state if it is to justify its powers to coerce dissenters. A promising approach develops the idea of hypothetical consent into a construction of a hypothetical contract, the terms of which conclude, on the basis of premises acceptable to all, that rational citizens ought to accept the authority of the state. Our judgement of this approach will be inconclusive. Despite the workings of the great dead philosophers – Hobbes, Locke and Rousseau – in this vein, a full modern statement of the case is necessary if it is to carry conviction. A related argument is offered by H.L.A. Hart, the Principle of Fairness, which claims that all who receive benefits from the co-operative efforts of others may be required to shoulder the burden of contributing towards the maintenance of the scheme that secures them – the state. Is there such a rule or convention of fairness? If there is does it govern the relationship of state to citizen? The responses to these questions are not obvious. The most direct answers exploit the notion of tacit consent which the principle was designed to articulate or replace. Finally we examine the most venerable of all arguments, the argument from gratitude. I shall rescue this argument from the appearance of silliness which it carries to the sceptical modern eye, but we shall see that the conditions required for its successful application impose severe limits on the constitution and laws of the state which can be said to deserve obedience by way of gratitude.

Finally, in Chapter 7, we broach the issue of the constitution directly. In discussing liberty, we claim that democratic institutions procure a valuable kind of freedom. On any account of human rights, the right of political participation will be central. The question of political obligation is easier to tackle, if not uniquely answerable, if the constitution is democratic. We bring all these threads together in our discussion of the claims of democracy. No wonder subscription to the values is just about universal.

We rehearse these values and explain their role in justifying democratic decision procedures through a presentation of Rousseau's contribution to democratic theory, which is not to say we are reciting uncontroversial truisms. His doctrine of the general will has been thought by many to be too opaque a mystery to serve as grounds for the legitimacy of democratic institutions, but we note that the clear utilitarian alternative – maximize satisfaction by implementing the desires of the majority – is deeply unsatisfactory.

Rousseau's arguments are directed to the justification of direct rather than representative democracy. For him, 'representative democracy' was an oxymoron; for us it may be a necessity as well as an improvement on the model of direct plebiscitary decision-making. But then, we may not be true democrats either. If we are not, if we recognize an imperative to draw in the horns of the enthusiastic democrat, this may be because we acknowledge the dangers of majority tyranny. Majority tyranny is as serious a problem as we are likely to confront in our lives as politically engaged citizens – and it is philosophically puzzling, too. We shall try to fathom the complexities.

Finally we discuss the claims of deliberative democracy to be the only ethically permissible method of settling deep moral disagreements. We shall conclude that these claims, in reaching for an ideal consensus, are overblown. There are good reasons for believing that substantial agreement concerning the issues put forward for political settlement may be unreachable. Moral pluralism fosters intractable debate. Differences in deep moral values, often the product of divergent religious beliefs, seem irresolvable. Agreement on a method of establishing policy, on reaching political accommodation, is often the best we can hope for. Sadly, we have no reason to believe that this best is good enough for the zealots of dangerous causes. The democrat will have to use coercion to defend his use of the ballot box.

Chapter 2

Utilitarianism

A good way to begin is by studying a deep and well-worked-out ethical theory which has commanded wide assent, reached clear conclusions when tackling the philosophical problems thrown up by our political life and produced unambiguous policy directives to settle practical questions. I select utilitarianism because I believe it has these features (or, at least, makes these claims). This has been recognized by many of the most impressive recent contributors to political philosophy. Few endorse utilitarianism – but most of them see the need to define their position against the utilitarian salient.[1] Utilitarianism should not be treated as a straw target; it has two great virtues which we should not lose sight of. First, it is based on a thought that ought to have universal appeal: when judging conduct, we should pay close attention to the consequences of human actions in respect of their contribution to the welfare of all those whom the actions affect. Second, (and this was a central preoccupation of the classical utilitarian thinkers, Jeremy Bentham and John Stuart Mill) that focus is particularly apt for fixing the purposes of government. We would do well to recapture the revolutionary impact of the claim that government, in particular, is in business to promote the well-being and reduce the suffering of all of its subjects.[2]

The foundations of utilitarianism

But first things first. Let me give a summary of the main elements of utilitarian theory, beginning with the simplest formulation of the principle of utility:

> Right actions maximize well-being.

This statement can be elaborated in many different ways, although it is worth mentioning now that the most familiar version of the principle, invoking the greatest happiness of the greatest number, should have been abandoned long ago. Recent commentators[3] have pointed out that a principle which requires the maximization of two independent variables will be indecisive over a significant range of cases. To use Evans's example, trying to rank outcomes in accordance with the greatest happiness of the greatest number is like offering a prize to the person running the furthest distance in the shortest time! Bentham, who first brought the phrase 'the greatest happiness of the greatest number' to prominence, used it as a kind of standing reminder that everyone affected by policies were to be counted and as a slogan redolent of democratic sentiments, but even he recognized that it was faulty in suggesting that the happiness of the majority only, the greatest number, should be counted. He saw that careless use of the principle in this formulation quickly leads the critic to charge that the utilitarian is prone to ignore the rights of minorities and to countenance other injustices so long as a majority is suited.[4] As we shall see, these questions cannot be settled quite as quickly as a faulty grasp of the principle suggests. For now let us just repeat that everyone's interests are to count equally in the calculations. As Bentham insisted and Mill repeated: 'Everybody to count for one, nobody for more than one.'[5]

Formal theory

Acts, rules and dispositions

There are two main elements to the utilitarian approach which need to be distinguished and reviewed separately – formal theory and value theory.[6] Formally, utilitarianism is a consequentialist theory. It requires that we compare alternative outcomes in point of their consequences, asking which realizes the maximum amount of some good. Which good is to be maximized is a matter for value theory and we shall examine candidate goods later. An important first question, then, which my account so far has concealed, concerns *what it is* of which we are to review the consequences. Three answers may be distinguished – and it is an important issue whether or not, or to what degree, they may be combined.

In the first place, and most obviously, we may review *directly* the consequences of alternative actions. The thought here is straightforward: we propose to evaluate the rightness or wrongness of actions by determining what the consequences of actions have been or by projecting what the consequences will be.[7] This position is often referred to as act utilitarianism. A second proposal is different. The rightness or wrongness of actions should be reckoned *indirectly* in terms of whether or not they are in accordance with moral rules; this is the basis of the rule utilitarian programme, the main burden of which will be the assessment of alternative rules (and systems of rules) to determine which *rules* will promote the best consequences. A different, and perhaps complementary, variety of indirect utilitarianism proposes that we evaluate actions in terms of the motives, dispositions or traits of character they exemplify, for example, praising a person who is honest or criticizing one who is mean. In this case the utilitarian will consider which qualities of character are likely to induce those who exhibit them to act in ways that lead to the maximization of well-being. This is evidently an important question for any moral theory which proposes to address issues concerning the formation of character in processes of moral education. And we would do well to remember that John Stuart Mill believed these issues were central to the utilitarian agenda.

So, we can be act or direct utilitarians, or indirect utilitarians investigating the tendencies of rules or dispositions of character. This way of putting matters suggests that these are alternative routes for the utilitarian to follow, whereas the correct position may be different. Note first of all, that there is no reason in principle why each of these subjects, actions, rules and dispositions, may not be susceptible to utilitarian review. We can examine separately the consequences of actions taken individually, of adopting and maintaining rules of conduct, of producing and promoting dispositions to act in various ways. In fact, any version of utilitarianism worth its salt will need to be able to appraise actions and agents in each of these ways. There will be problems for the utilitarian only if we have reason to think that assessment along these different dimensions will yield contradictions or dilemmas. Unfortunately there is reason to think that it might.

There are good utilitarian reasons for societies to introduce and stick to rules of property, determining who owns what, who may use what and much else. Conflicting claims are reduced, the possibility of co-operation is enhanced. Suppose we have in place a set of rules which will promote the best consequences for everyone if they are generally accepted. They include the familiar commandment: Do not steal. Suppose Sally needs to steal a few potatoes from Robert's field if she and her children are to survive. Robert, we might assume to make the case stronger, has plenty of potatoes to spare; he does not in fact notice the theft – and nor does anyone else. Sally, now well fed, finds work and can support her children. She is never tempted to steal again. Did she do right or did she do wrong? To the rule utilitarian she did wrong. The rule in play prohibits stealing and Sally broke it. The act utilitarian will judge differently. The gain to Sally and her children is evident. Robert's loss is negligible. More good has been achieved by the theft than by the family's starvation. We should conclude that act and rule utilitarianism reach different verdicts in this particular case.

The same conflict of views can be reproduced in cases involving act and disposition utilitarianism. Let us agree that a society which succeeds in creating compassionate and sympathetic dispositions in its members will better promote well-being than one which does not.[8] Carol gives money to a street collector who uses it to buy arms for a terrorist group. She was credulous in believing the money would be used to help wives and families in need of support and so contributes to the success of a damaging terrorist campaign. Since dispositions as deep as that inculcated in Carol cannot be switched on and off, her compassion as much as her credulity renders her vulnerable to evil solicitations. The disposition utilitarian will commend her display of compassion. The act utilitarian will say she did wrong if her act resulted in a great deal of suffering. Likewise, in cases where my compassion for others causes me to steal in order to prevent their starvation, the demands of disposition utilitarianism seem to conflict with a utilitarianism of rules.

Does this succession of cases reduce utilitarianism to incoherence – simultaneously condemning and endorsing actions from conflicting stances of judgement? Perhaps not, if we accept the main lines of the following characteristic utilitarian response.

What is the chief impetus behind our insistence that we should take into account the utility of rules and dispositions as well as, directly, the utility of acts? It is this thought: it is fantasy to suppose that the moral agent can be forever computing the respective utilities of all prospective acts in order to judge which is best. We haven't the time, we haven't the patience and, perhaps most important, we haven't the knowledge necessary to reach correct verdicts on what future consequences will follow a host of alternative interventions. This point may seem devastating to the act utilitarian but he has a swift response – which is to insist that if we take into account the utility of deliberating over what we should do we shall soon see that short-cuts are necessary. Why should the sailor start working out when high tide will be at Greenock tomorrow on the basis of what it was on a specific day last month if he can look it up in the *Glasgow Herald* or the *Nautical Almanac*?[9] Clearly we need some analogue of the tide-tables in morality and moral rules give us one. Instead of working our own way through the likely consequences of our actions, why not refer to a set of rules which provides accurate guidance?

If fallibility and the cost of calculation suggest an important place for rules, they also accord considerable weight to the cultivation of character. Some people do mental arithmetic well – and this disposition can be cultivated – but no one except Jeremy Bentham has suggested that the skills of utilitarian calculation ought to be widely developed.[10] But many utilitarians (and John Stuart Mill conspicuously) have accepted the importance of inculcating strong dispositions, believing that spontaneous and unreflective responses of generosity and honesty will more than compensate for our defects as calculators.

For the act utilitarian, then, rules and dispositions of character, far from comprising alternative dimensions of utilitarian assessment, must be employed in a practical and reliable calculus. Ultimately, of course, the only measure of right action is the goodness of the consequences of actions but this is not a measure that needs to be taken if we have to hand the right set of rules and a population with correct dispositions.

This account is plausible – but how does it help us tackle the problem caused by the examples of conflict given above? It suggests that we have to understand clearly the relation between actions on the one hand and rules and dispositions of character on the other.

Let us begin with rules.[11] Thus far I have been referring to rules as though these are simple phenomena with which we are well acquainted. In fact there are at least three different conceptions of rules in play.

The first sort of rule is the 'ideal' rule – a technical device unique to utilitarianism. We introduce ideal rules when we claim that actions are right if they are in accordance with those rules which would promote most good, were they to be generally complied with.[12] Ideal rule utilitarianism has been effectively criticized.[13] A first difficulty is this: Suppose our car is stuck just below the top of the last hill before we reach our destination. The rule for all five passengers to follow is clearly, 'Push', if pushing will see them over the summit and into a comfortable bed. Four passengers either don't work this out or don't follow the rule. If ideal rule utilitarianism were the best decision procedure to follow, the fifth passenger should push even if her solitary efforts will prove ineffective. This is clearly irrational. And it doesn't look like a utilitarian stategy either, since no benefits would accrue and the diligent rule follower will suffer for her efforts.

A second difficulty follows. Alter the scenario so that only the pushing of four passengers is needed to get the car over the summit. Why should the fifth passenger push? Isn't utility maximized if the fifth passenger loiters alongside rather than lending her shoulder to the task? Again ideal rule utilitarianism suggests that not pushing would be wrong, although it is hard to see how her unnecessary expenditure of effort could maximize utility. (I accept that other things might be wrong with her not pushing. Perhaps it is unfair of her not to shoulder her share of the burden. But now it looks as though fairness conflicts with utility.) The central point of both these examples is that real utilitarians would not stick to ideal rules if the circumstances dictate that utility is best advanced by breaking them. In J.J.C. Smart's terms, either one is a utilitarian or a rule worshipper – one can't be both.[14]

The second conception of rules identifies them as useful rules of thumb. A better example here than Mill's *Nautical Almanac* (which we should treat as infallible!) is a rule for hillwalkers such as 'If you cannot see the point to which you are heading, take a compass bearing and follow it'. Accepting such a rule will lead you to take a map and compass on your walk and generally help you to escape difficulties in route finding. But it is important to recognize that the rule should not be followed slavishly. It should be quickly broken if the bearing takes you to the top of a cliff. And if the compass veers erratically when you seem to be walking in a straight line, you should consider whether there might be magnetic rocks in the vicinity.

Are moral rules like this? There is good reason to think that they are. 'Keep promises', we say, but we recognize lots of cases where exceptions may properly be made. Sometimes we cite a specific qualification to the rule which suggests that the rule is more complex than the original simple formulation. We can add a clause: '. . . unless the promise has been extorted.' We can gather together exceptions, as when we say: '. . . unless disproportionate harm will be caused to some third party.' Or we can make exceptions on a case by case basis whenever exigencies seem to require the breaking of the promise. When these things happen, the utilitarian says we are justified if we can maximize well-being by breaking the rule.

It has been argued, successfully I think, that this rules-of-thumb variety of rule utilitarianism reduces to act utilitarianism since the bottom line in each of these calculations is that the right action is the one that maximizes utility. We can expect rules which we employ in the face of uncertainty to develop the force of inhibitions. We may be taught them in the secure expectation that they will develop this motivational power. But whatever the motivational push or pull exhibited by the rules we endorse, we should not expect them to be either immune to revision or privileged against exception wherever utility dictates. The utilitarian claims, with some justification, that the effects of spontaneous good judgement are so positive that we should be reluctant to break rules without compunction; the purposes served by having rules in the first place will not be easily subverted if the rules are strongly internalized. Thus although this variety of rule utilitarianism is consistent with (because it is reducible to) act utilitarianism, there remain strong reasons for supporting the induction of moral rules like 'Keep promises' in the consciousness of agents – just as there are strong reasons for getting walkers to make a *habit* of using a map and compass.

There is a third conception of rules which is of particular importance in political philosophy. This is the category of rules which are constitutive of institutions. Many of these rules will have the force of law and will be backed by legal sanctions although there are non-legal rules and non-legal sanctions. We can expect most societies to have an institution of private property. Such an institution is best understood in terms of an interrelated set of rules establishing rights, duties, powers and privileges. The core rules will be expressed in law, such as prohibitions against theft. But there will be associated non-legal or non-enforceable rules, too. 'Do not write in books that you borrow from friends' is one which I expect most readers to accept. Other institutions which comprise a mix of legal and non-legal rules include marriage and family life, arrangements for treating the sick and educating the young, and of course the political life of the community.

The 'ontology' of such institutions is complex and is not usefully clarified by the modern fad for issuing mission statements. I take an idealist view. Institutions as I describe them consist in rules which command the behaviour of members, rules with respect to which one may take an internal or external point of view. Internally, members (insiders) identify with institutions whose rules they recognize as valid. The external perspective is taken by observers (outsiders) who describe institutions on the basis of members' conduct. Of course, the same person may be both insider and outsider; these terms describe roles or perspectives and so all depends on the stance from which he is describing or evaluating the rules in question.[15]

Institutional rules differ from rules of thumb in two significant ways. In the first place, they will be justified as necessary for the effective functioning of the institution, serving as means to given ends. This is an oversimple way of describing a matter of great conceptual delicacy since it supposes that the purposes of institutions may be identified independently of the structure of rules which constitute them. But my point is this: suppose we recognize as *one* of the purposes of family life (or of alternative patterns of domesticity) the provision of a healthy and supportive environment for children. We shall then justify rules, both legal and non-legal, in terms of their conduciveness to this purpose.

Now remember that for the moment we are utilitarians. We have institutions characterized by rules which promote whatever purposes the institutions serve. It follows that we do not evaluate institutional rules one by one and directly, in terms of their several contributions towards utility. It will be the institution as a whole which is appraised. The utilitarian will tackle first the grand questions, for example: Should children be brought up in a nuclear family, an extended family or in a kibbutz? Having assessed the respective utilities of these different domestic arrangements, we can then go on to fix e.g. the rules for appropriate income tax allowances or whichever means we employ to support what we have concluded is the optimal domestic unit. Institutional rules differ from rules of thumb in that the primary focus of justification is the institution rather than the rule.

The second major difference is equally important. This concerns the justification of particular actions. Assume that we have in place a system for the regulation of private property which includes rules governing inheritance and bequest. My family are hard up. Am I morally justified in forging alterations to Donald's will so that his estate will give my family the security they deserve rather than support the drug addiction of Donald's intended beneficiary?

If the rules governing bequests were rules of thumb, immediately the question would be open: What does utility dictate in these circumstances? Matters are very different when we are thinking of institutional rules and it is important to work out just why this is so. Here is one immediate difference. In the case of rules of thumb, the rules have standing in the deliberations of the moral agent as ready reckoners which obviate the need for hard, often fallible, calculation – but where circumstances scream out for judgement outside the normal response of compliance, direct calculation of the appropriate utilities can be the only rational response. In the case of institutional rules, these have an authority quite independent of their service as guides to conduct for the unsure or hard-pressed. They are not open to scrutiny except as elements of institutions which find their justifications in terms of their operation as a whole. One may certainly question an institution, demanding whether or not it promotes utility. But if it does then the institution becomes entrenched, acquiring a social reality which cannot be dissolved by the exercise of deliberation. Similarly, one may seek to alter the institutional rules. Maybe different, better, rules will serve the institution more effectively. And this kind of tinkering goes on all the time, conspicuously in legislative activity. But suppose an institution promotes utility in the way its defenders claim and suppose the rules of the institution effectively secure this. If the utilitarian accepts these claims, it is not open to him to violate the rules in order to promote utility. If two people decide the most worthwhile way to spend their time is by playing chess, so long as the game is proceeding it is not open to one of them to cheat on the grounds that both of them will better enjoy subsequent play. It might indeed be true that it will make for a better game if the rules are changed, and this may prompt them to change the rules, giving a handicap to one of the players. But as the rules stand at the beginning of the game, cheating cannot be vindicated by rule changes it may be sensible to introduce later. The cost of subscribing to institutions which promote utility is that one sacrifices the opportunity of breaking rules on occasions which suggest that rule breaking promises utilitarian gains.

So, if I am caught out in my forgery of Donald's will, I should not expect the officials of the legal system to listen carefully to my utilitarian defence. They will follow the rules which utility has dictated should be followed in all cases. There is no great utilitarian ombudsman prepared to review all instances of individuals claiming they broke the rules in the service of some overriding utilitarian purpose. Nor should this kind of pleading persuade us that one should be installed. Readers can work out for themselves the disutility of introducing such an institutional role! This is not to say that in emergencies, in cases of disaster or catastrophe, the rules of institutions should not be broken. You may justifiably break the speed limit driving a badly injured person to hospital. But then you should not expect to get punished either, since an institution which is justifiable and maximally effective will make provision for such cases by, for example, specifying allowable defences against the charge of wrong-doing. If such defences are not in place, then the rules of the institution should be altered to permit them. Contrast this with the rule of thumb about following compass bearings. We don't alter or amend the rule when we find ourselves at the top of the cliff. We disregard it until we have circumvented the obstacle – and we pick it up later. We are not in the business of formulating optimal rules of thumb with guidance for each contingency; such rules would quickly become unwieldy and just as difficult to apply as pristine act utilitarianism. But we are in the business of designing and sustaining optimal institutions and there is something desperately wrong with institutions which cannot be remedied in the face of conspicuous disutility. Commanding officers, we are told, may decorate soldiers for bravery – then punish them, if their heroism involved disobeying orders. 'Change the rules', the utilitarian should insist.

Let us conclude, for the moment, that the utilitarian can endorse two different conceptions of rules: rules of thumb which pre-empt arduous and uncertain calculation and institutional rules which promote utility through the dynamics of some complex system. So rules have a place (or better, two) in utilitarian judgement. Can similar arguments be used to sort out the possible conflict between the utility of actions and the utility of dispositions?

I suspect that they can. It makes sense to cultivate in ourselves and others qualities of character which reduce the possibility of conflict and enhance the prospect of fruitful co-operation. It makes sense to subdue or eliminate tendencies which generate conflict or render it endemic. As utilitarian strategies these look eminently respectable – always supposing that conflict promotes suffering and co-operation increases well-being. Each of us can draw up our own list of favourite and suspect personal qualities. High on my list of admirable qualities, being in Nietzschean terms a typical modern wimp, would be compassion and sympathy, courtesy to strangers (especially beggars), tolerance and good humour.

One of the nice things about speaking of 'dispositions' in this context is the implication that there are no iron laws dictating rigid uniformities of response. Utility may determine that widespread good temper and equanimity may limit occasions of conflict, but the right thing to do in particular circumstances, again judged in terms of utility, may well be to erupt with rage. Once more, the utilitarian should recommend the cultivation of dispositions to counter the rigours and difficulties of judgement. Common sense tells us that those with a generous temperament are a social asset – but it also tells us that generous responses should be restrained if circumstances suggest that those who look to be in need of assistance would really be better off learning to cope with this kind of difficulty by themselves. In the case of rules of thumb we saw how rules could be of general use even though their application could not be justified in conspicuous cases where utilitarian calculation suggests otherwise. In the case of the utility of dispositions, the whiff of contradiction is more easily dispelled since we have no tendency to think of qualities of character as rigid determinants of action.

One interesting question remains. I suggested in respect of institutional rules that these do have an authority which defies the application of utilitarian calculation to particular opportunities for utility promotion. Is there any analogue with respect to qualities of character? I suspect that there may be. The category of institutions as I have employed it has been very wide,[16] comprising almost any congeries of rules, although I have suggested they will have some structure dictated by function or purpose. In fact, I doubt whether any institution can have the ethical force sufficient to motivate members or subscribers to develop the 'internal' point of view with respect to its rules, if it does not cultivate as qualities of character distinctive and appropriate styles of emotional response. There is something bloodless (and plain wrong) about any analysis of domestic relationships which focuses on rules and concomitant rights and duties as the essence. Capacities for love and affection should be in the foreground.[17] In which case, the utilitarian claim that specific institutions are conducive to general utility will require that participants display the appropriate emotional qualities – and we should recognize the force these may exert on individuals who exhibit them. Who knows . . . there may be occasions when in defiance of these institutions and their internally necessary sentiments, general utility requires the sacrifice of one's first-born son; unlike God, the utilitarian should not then expect obedience.

Aggregate and maximum average utility

A futher question in formal utilitarian theory concerns the matter of whether we are to maximize aggregate or average utility. For most purposes, computation in terms of aggregate or maximum average utility will give an identical ordering of different outcomes. If Policy A produces 100 units of utility and Policy B produces 50 units, Policy A is better on aggregate. If both policies affect the same number of people or apply over the same population, say 50 persons, A will again be better than B because the average of two units per person is greater than the average of one. So long as the number of persons over whom the average is taken is constant between the alternative outcomes, no issue of principle is raised.[18]

But this condition will not always hold good. We can all think of policies concerning housing, medicine, pollution control, traffic management even, which *themselves* determine, in part, the number of people affected by the policy. The possibility of population control, government action which is directed towards increasing or, more likely nowadays, decreasing the size of the population of a country, is a particularly obvious example of policy which gives rise to a new theoretical problem for the utilitarian.

Suppose two policies C and D effect the same aggregate utility – 100 units. Should we prefer policy C which distributes these units between 50 people (an average utility of two units per person) or policy D which leads to a doubling of the population and which then distributes the 100 units between 100 people (an average of one unit per person)? In point of aggregate utility the totals are the same; in point of maximum average utility the results are very different – C is superior to D. Whether the units measure resources or states of mind like happiness, it looks as though we should judge that policy C will make us better off. The cake is divided amongst fewer people. Children work out this principle at a very early age – just as soon as they find that times are harder with every addition to the family. With no more detail to go on, our intuitions favour Policy C.

But we should ask, if we strongly favour being amongst the lucky few, where are the missing 50 people? Do we have nothing to say about them? Have they no claim on us? These questions may strike you as silly, but there is a point to them. We do hypothesize such 'missing persons' and consider how policies will impact on them when we think through the consequences of what we do for future generations. I can start thinking now of saving for my grandchildren's education. I don't have any grandchildren at the moment and may never turn out to have any, but the idea of planning for these hypothetical descendants is not ridiculous. I must plan for my retirement, or so my independent financial adviser instructs, yet he knows no better than I whether I shall live to enjoy it. It makes sense to think of and plan for persons who do not now exist and may never do so, just as it does for persons who now exist but may turn out not to do so when the plans come to fruition. So, if our choice of policy determines that 50 people who don't presently exist will never do so, shouldn't we consider the consequences of what we do for them, what we have deprived them of or spared them from? If we select Policy C rather than Policy D haven't we denied them the prospect of a life with a positive sum of well-being? And maybe there is a Policy E in the offing which promises 150 units of utility spread between 120 beneficiaries. In this case there is a clear gain in terms of aggregate utility. Isn't this the best thing to do? This intuition conflicts strongly with the claim that the only thing that matters is maximum average utility. I shall leave this tricky problem unresolved. In what follows I shall be supposing that it is average utility that we are seeking to maximize – but you should note my reservations.

Maximization

One final assumption needs to be openly displayed and this is concealed in the unexamined use of the term 'maximization'. The standard utilitarian picture is that of agents, in their personal capacity or as policy-makers, charting the consequences of actions and then listing the positive and negative effects as these impact upon individuals. We 'maximize' utility by selecting that policy or action, amongst a range of alternatives, which promotes the greatest net utility – and the implication is that we decide on the best option by adding the utility scores in respect of each person affected to produce a sum of utility points represented by a cardinal number for each alternative outcome. Something like this practice was implicit in my discussion of the comparative outcomes in respect of aggregate and maximum average utility in the paragraphs above.

The questions begged by this construal of maximization as addition are many and deep and I cannot begin to explore all their ramifications – but here are a few.[19] Are the good (and evil) consequences of action susceptible of measurement at all? Can the consequences for one person be tallied as the sum of the varieties of ways in which persons may be affected? Suppose a policy both diminishes my liberty and improves my health. On what scale can these different effects find a common measure? If we agree that individuals may be able (somehow) to answer these questions for themselves, how are different individual responses to be compared and then registered in a common scale? To employ the familiar jargon, how are interpersonal comparisons and measurement of utility possible? Two things are absolutely clear: first, that a common denominator amongst a range of goods that will permit the arithmetical operations of addition and subtraction (as well as multiplication and division as soon as probabilities enter the calculations) will be very hard, if not impossible, to find; the utilitarian, for all Bentham's talk of a 'felicific calculus', may well have to manage with instruments of calculation which do not permit the operation of arithmetical functions. Second, just what is possible in both individual and interpersonal cases will depend upon the description of the goods in question – and so it is to utilitarian value theory that I now turn.

Value theory

Utilitarian value theory tells us what to look for when we assess actions, rules or dispositions in the light of their consequences. It tells us what it is that we are measuring when we set out to compare alternative actions or states of affairs and judge which is best. Thus far, I have described the good to be assessed as utility (the weakest formulation), well-being or welfare. I have been supposing that we have a rough idea of what these terms connote, but in truth I have been issuing blank cheques, trusting the reader to fill in the value in a plausible fashion. It is an open question whether the utilitarian has the philosophical assets to redeem them. In this brief survey of different accounts of the value to be maximized I shall highlight issues which have a bearing on the agenda of the political philosopher (although the prime concern of the utilitarian who wishes to contribute to debates in political philosophy will be to give the *correct* account of value!).

Hedonism

The classical utilitarians, Bentham and John Stuart Mill, thought of value, the human good or the good of sentient creatures, as happiness and explained happiness as pleasure and the absence of pain. This identification of the good with happiness is the doctrine of hedonism. For Bentham and Mill it was an empirical claim about human nature that human beings desire happiness – and Mill went so far as to claim that, at bottom, happiness is the *only* thing they desire.[20] Mill's strategy in this proof has two elements: happiness is a good, he claims, because everyone desires it, and happiness is the only good because any alternative candidate good can be seen to be either a means to happiness or a part (or ingredient) of it.

Mill's arguments are not easy to evaluate. It is clearly a hedonist position; what is hard to see is whether Mill has successfully disengaged himself from the egoism of Bentham, as he believed. He thought it obviously true that agents desire the happiness of others. They may be kind, helpful, generous and compassionate – and the sensible utilitarian will acquire dispositions of these sorts and encourage them in others. And having dispositions of these sorts may cause their bearers to act in ways that reduce or sacrifice their own happiness. Mill must insist, at this stage in his proof, that these qualities of character, which we may call virtues, following his account, must be, in some sense, elements of the agent's own happiness. Their life must be going better for the exhibition of them. The virtuous person must be frustrated and diminished if no opportunities arise to be virtuous, since their virtue is a part of their happiness. Minimally we must suppose that the virtuous person enjoys the exercise of virtue, but if we are to steer clear of egoism (and retain some sense that the agent is acting truly virtuously) we must detach the enjoyment from the motivation of the agent.

In fact, this is quite easy to do. I guarantee (unless the circumstances are somehow peculiar) that you will gain pleasure, sometimes great pleasure, from acting virtuously. Many recipes for attaining pleasure are unsound given the ways human beings differ. The sources of pleasure are a matter of self-discovery rather than expert tuition. Nonetheless, the satisfaction of having done something worthwhile is as universal a phenomenon as any that may be attested in this area. And yet it is clear that those who achieve it do not act in order to gain it. It is not a satisfaction that can be actively sought, a sensation that one can pursue with forethought and diligence – and without hypocrisy. It is a very special kind of moral creep (a kind I have not encountered in either real life or fiction) that will react with pleasure at the prospect of someone desperately in need of assistance. 'Oh good!' such a one might exclaim, 'another opportunity to gain that unique kind of satisfaction which I experience when helping others!' I hesitate to generalize over the peculiar sphere of human motivation, but I don't see how the sense that one has acted virtuously can co-exist with the knowledge that one has sought and attained a kind of personal pleasure which one prizes. The fact is that although the feeling of pleasure is just about universally *consequent upon* the genuine exercise of virtuous sentiments, the actions themselves will not be *motivated by* the prospect of attaining it.

Mill knew this very well. But if it is true, what remains of his claim that actions performed by agents who desire to act virtuously are explained by or exemplify the desire for happiness? Of course virtue can contribute to happiness – I have argued that it always will in the sense of producing in the agent an invariable sense of satisfaction in having acted well – but this is not the same as claiming that virtue is a part or ingredient of happiness. (Cheerfulness and a feeling of content that one's life is going well: these are the sorts of states of mind that can be recognized as ingredients of happiness.) I conclude that the virtues only contribute to our happiness when it is not our happiness that we seek by their exercise, and hence that acting virtuously is something that we desire independently of the prospects for our happiness, however good these prospects might be as a result. If this is accepted, it follows that happiness is not the only good we seek. We also recognize the good of a virtuous life.

We now have two distinct goods – happiness and the pursuit of a virtuous life. Perhaps there are more. The standard way of developing a list of distinct goods is to give examples of conflict. A famous example, discussed by Griffin,[21] is that of Freud who was prepared to suffer a great deal of pain during his terminal illness in order to continue being able to think clearly. So one could claim on this basis that knowledge of one's affairs and one's surroundings is a good independent of the absence of pain. Amend the example slightly and we can describe cases where a suffering patient is prepared to undergo great pain in order to retain control over those aspects of her life which she judges to be important. This will introduce a separate value of autonomy.[22] A slightly different patient may undergo great suffering in order to accomplish some task which has been central to her aspirations – designing a house, planting a forest or writing a book. And we may applaud those who risk their lives climbing mountains, diving caves, undertaking arduous sea voyages – all in the grip of ambitions which cannot be described as the pursuit of pleasure. So it looks as though a sense of achievement is a characteristic human good. Health, too, is distinct from pleasure (and these other goods). I may sacrifice my health in the pursuit of pleasure – and give up pleasurable activities if these threaten my health. I may risk my eye-sight painting miniatures and keep up skiing at the cost of further damage to my knees. The list of distinctive human goods throws up dilemmas at every turn.

In the face of these difficulties the utilitarian may continue to insist on hedonism, but it is quite clear that he can do so only by continuing to insist that all of these separate goods are desired as the means to happiness or as constitutive of it – parts or ingredients, in Mill's terms. I suspect however that whatever cogency the argument can gather is achieved by stipulation because our concept of happiness is so ragged. Defined as pleasure and the absence of pain, the concept is operational but, as I suggested above, we are forced to recognize other conflicting goods. If we are to include these competing goods in the account we give of happiness, then happiness becomes little more than a cipher, collecting together all of the distinctive objects of human desire. What threatens, of course, is incoherence since happiness is no longer a value in terms of which we can appraise alternative outcomes which promote happiness along these different dimensions. We have lost the sense of happiness as a common denominator which can be employed in the calculation of what is the best thing to do.

Desire-satisfaction

The utilitarian is still not without resort. He can claim, still with an eye on Mill's proof, that we have overlooked one important unifying feature, that these goods are each of them the objects of characteristic human desires. In which case, why not identify the satisfaction of desire as the distinctive good to be employed in evaluating outcomes?

To many this has seemed a very attractive proposal. Desires (or preferences) are revealed in human actions. Our actions serve as the mark of their strength; indeed the prices of goods, determined by how much we are prepared to pay, may quantify their intensity and register the degree of our satisfaction. At this point ethics and political philosophy join hands with economics and all the powerful mathematical tools of that discipline are liberated for application outside the conventional boundaries of the dismal science. No longer will we have to pretend to be 'weighing' the pleasures and pains in prospect as though these could be put on the scales with fruit and vegetables. Welfare economics is at the disposal of the consumer with a spreadsheet who wishes to take a voyage of self-discovery, as well as being the resource of the policy-maker concerned to implement those policies which maximally suit those affected by them. Bentham's antiquated apparatus of the 'felicific calculus', computing the intensity, duration, propinquity, fecundity, etc. of pleasures and pains can be consigned to the same museum of primitive scientific instruments which houses the first slide-rule.

It is difficult to overestimate the importance in policy-making of this line of development of utilitarian theory, although the harms caused by its application as well as the dangers in prospect may be considerable. Environmentalists rail at the application of the techniques of cost–benefit analysis to questions involving the conservation of wild nature or beautiful countryside. How can these goods be weighed in the balance?[23] At the moment, however, we are considering its theoretical underpinnings – and these are not secure. There are two initial difficulties which both point in the same direction. In the first place it is obvious that desire-satisfaction may not be a good where the desire is ill-informed or ill-judged. A sick child who hates the taste of medicine may have her strongest desires satisfied when she pours it down the sink, but if the child is ignorant of the properties of the compound or judges that its taste is of greater importance than its curative effects, this preference should be discounted. Its satisfaction is not a good. So we modify the account, seeking value now in *informed* desire satisfaction. Other desires should be subject to scrutiny as well – and this leads us to the second major difficulty. Take the desires of the sadist. It looks as though our evaluation of sadistic behaviour will require us to give some weight to the satisfaction of his desires, with the utilitarian registering these in the balance with the desire of the victim to avoid the pain the sadist is keen to inflict. A squeamish desire-satisfaction utilitarian must hope and pray that the dissatisfaction of the victim is greater than the satisfaction in prospect for the sadist. But surely the satisfactions of the sadist should not count *at all* in the evaluation of his conduct. That his preferences are satisfied when he succeeds counts towards the evil rather than the good of what he does. So again the account needs to be amended; the good to be registered is now the satisfaction of desires which are both fully informed and legitimate; illegitimate as well as ignorant and poorly judged desires should be discounted.

The difficulties are obvious. How much knowledge and rational capacity do we need for our desires to count as sufficiently well-informed? We need more than the child who believes that nothing which tastes awful can do her good – but do we need as much knowledge as the best science makes available before our desires are sufficiently well-informed? How much good judgement do we require, supposing all relevant information is to hand? Again, we shall need more than the child who believes the avoidance of nausea is a greater priority than good health. But how much more is not easy to determine. Smoking, one is told, reduces life expectancy by five years on average. Is there something defective in the judgement of the well-informed doctor who continues to smoke despite the risk to her health?

The response to the sadist example is even trickier. Defects of knowledge and judgement subvert the natural authority of the desires they generate and so there is more than a whiff of normativity in the requirement that desires be well-informed and soundly judged. There must be, in prospect if not in place, canons for the appraisal of desires from these perspectives. And these canons cannot derive from considerations of utility upon pain of circularity in the account. This difficulty is even more evident in the case of the requirement that desire-satisfaction be gained legitimately, since the utilitarian needs a non-moral argument to show that the desire for another's harm, and the satisfaction gained from achieving it, should be entirely discounted.[24] The most dangerous tack here would be to distinguish as legitimate desires which are normal or natural, alluding to some spurious hybrid of folk biology and religious dogma, of the kind that powerful churchmen are prone to sell.

I do not believe that the utilitarian has the philosophical and anthropological resources necessary to breathe life into the claim that the fulfilment of desire is the root of all human value or that desirability is the basis of a formal account of the good which collects together all the qualities of life which humans value. If we can describe separately, and vindicate as plausible, a range of human goods, I see no point in adopting a theoretical apparatus which collects them together under one label – as desirable or as ingredients of happiness – if that apparatus does no work in the ranking of outcomes as better or worse. In some cases we may judge this action is best in respect of happiness, that in respect of autonomy and so on. We may weigh the different appeals and claim some action is best all things considered. But we shall not be able to justify this latter claim by finding some secret ingredient or common denominator which serves as an overall measure of utility. Instead, we shall be left with an 'objective list' account of the good, making a case separately for each of the different elements. Happiness, knowledge of one's situation and affairs, sound personal relationships of love and friendship, good health, autonomy and liberty, a sense of accomplishment, the recognition of beauty in human works and nature: all these and more are candidates to be explored. The major difficulty for the utilitarian will be to explain how different mixes of these goods can be compared with one another to the point where a verdict of 'best outcome' can be delivered. But what the critic describes as a difficulty, the utilitarian worth his salt will see as a challenge!

Review

I do not intend my review of utilitarianism to have the status of knock-down criticism. Utilitarianism is in need of repair in several of the areas I have mentioned and in others, too. But the dialectic of philosophy reveals the major theories to have very great resilience in the face of damaging attacks and utilitarianism is no exception. As critics propose refutations of greater and greater depth and sophistication, advocates find within their theories resources hitherto unrevealed which serve for a time to repel boarders and limit the damage of the assault. Thus far, I have been examining the groundwork of utilitarianism, the basic elements of the theory. I want to continue by looking at utilitarianism at work, by reviewing the utilitarian story in respect of core political values. This will serve not only as a basis for assessing the utilitarian contribution to political philosophy. It will also introduce problems which we shall discuss in more detail in the chapters which follow.

Utilitarian political theory

Liberty

There is a good historical reason why we should expect the utilitarian to have things of interest to say about the value of liberty. The greatest of the classical utilitarian thinkers, John Stuart Mill, has also been the most influential advocate of liberty. In *On Liberty* he argues mightily for civil liberty, for the opportunity to act without interference from the state or, equally important, from the intrusive pressures of busybody neighbours. So it would be surprising if the arguments he advances on behalf of liberty did not have a utilitarian cast. And, despite the incorporation of distinctively perfectionist appeals claiming that liberty advances mankind in the development of characteristic excellencies, Mill's utilitarianism is evident throughout. Liberty is argued to be essential to the well-being of both individuals and society.

One defect of Mill's argument should be made clear from the start, although it is perhaps anachronistic to point it out in a critical spirit. Moreover it is a defect we shall attempt to remedy later. I am thinking of his lack of, or carelessness in, analysis. We ask what does 'liberty' mean in the arguments and slogans of its advocates and detractors. Mill took it that both his supporters and critics had the same things in mind and that, because his (and their) understanding was equally capacious no harm was done. As we shall see in the next chapter, this was a mistake. For now, we shall suppose that our understanding of the ideal of civil liberty is sufficiently well articulated for us to follow Mill's defence of it.

The first strand of Mill's utilitarian defence of liberty is developed in the chapter of *On Liberty* dealing with freedom of thought and discussion. The main drift of the argument is uncompromisingly utilitarian.[25] There are benefits to be had from the propagation of true opinions, false opinions and opinions which contain a mixture of truth and falsity. These benefits derive from the contribution made by a strong and uninhibited intellectual life to the progress of society. The cost of censorship and other controls on the media of communicating ideas is the stifling of progress through ignorance of opportunities for betterment. On the other hand, we may be able to identify kinds of circumstance in which the costs of freedom of speech are excessive. Incitement to damage (denouncing corn dealers as starvers of the poor to an angry mob outside a corn dealer's house, is Mill's example),[26] libel and slander, and no doubt other sorts of action, may be legitimately prohibited. The costs, we must suppose, outweigh the benefits.

We thus have an argument for a specific structure of institutional protection. To procure the suggested benefits, a society should establish or respect a network of positive rules, which will be a mix of constitutional, legal and non-legal permissions, prohibitions and defences. We can each of us think of the most effective way this strategy may be implemented and review our institutions in the light of such a prescription.

Mill believed, plausibly I think, that freedom of thought and discussion was a crucial means to social improvement – but I don't want to discuss this case here. Instead we should focus on the structure of the argument, since Mill himself believed that in defending this particular network of freedoms he was showing us how arguments of this sort should be conducted. The first thing that is necessary is that we make out a case for the usefulness of a specific practice, showing how conspicuous benefits may be attained if it is promoted and protected. If public speech and debate are valuable, freedom to engage in them is necessary to realize the benefits. The same case could be made in turn for all the major liberal freedoms; religious worship, secular association to promote common interests, finding occupations one wishes to pursue, engaging in political activity: each of these can be defended on utilitarian grounds and institutions devised to enable and secure citizens' engagement in them. And as with freedom of speech, limitations and qualifications can be put in place where utility dictates.

Notice that this is not an argument for liberty *per se*. Each pattern of activity must be vindicated separately with the case for liberty falling out of the value of the activity described. The second element of Mill's utilitarian defence of liberty explains how liberty is a value independently of the value of the activities liberty permits. This is his argument for individualism as necessary for the well-being of both individuals and society in Chapter 3, 'Of Individuality', of *On Liberty*.[27] Again the argument is a straightforward application of utilitarian principles. Mill explains how the happiness of individuals is enhanced when they are free to make their own decisions on how to act. Our happiness depends upon the exercise of what he called our distinctively human endowment. This comprises capacities for perception and forethought, reflection and judgement, capacities which are employed most fully in the exercise of choice. To anchor the utilitarian credentials of this argument, we should note that the use of these capacities is conspicuous in those activities which yield the 'higher pleasures' Mill famously (and controversially) defends in *Utilitarianism*, Chapter 2. We shall be dwarfed and stunted creatures if decisions are taken for us, nothing like as happy as we could be if we were our own masters. And if we were conscious that opportunities for such educative decision-making were being denied to us, we would experience a good deal of frustration as well. Explicitly, Mill is drawing a contrast between societies where choice is heavily circumscribed and individuals live spiritually impoverished lives and open societies which encourage individuals to draw upon and develop capacities which are necessary for them to flourish by creating for them maximal opportunities to work out how best to live their lives.

Each individual is better off for having the opportunity of decision-making created by the space of liberty because the very act of decision-making brings its own rewards. It uses (and trains and cultivates through regular use) mental capacities central to our overall well-being. But individuals will be better off, too, since the decisions taken are likely to be better than those which other individuals take on their behalf. Individuals are most often the best judges of what is in their own interests, of what constitutes for them a full or rewarding life.

Think of a well-stocked newspaper shop with rack upon rack of magazines catering for interests of highly specialized sorts – not just one magazine for fishermen, but three or four on trout and salmon fishing, the same number for coarse fishing, a few for sea-anglers, together with weekly newspapers for fishermen of all kinds. And then multiply the number as dozens of interests parade themselves on the shelves. The thought is that just as we can select any magazine to suit our interests, so, too, must we select these interests ourselves. It's hopeless to think of anyone, parents or close friends even, still less Big Brother, dictating where our interests shall be directed. We make better decisions when we choose for ourselves how to live because we are the best judges of where our happiness lies.

So, not only are we happier because of the way we develop when we make choices, we are happier for having the opportunity to get what we know best to be good for us as individuals. And this is not the end of the benefits accruing from widespread liberty. Each life, conventional or eccentric, will be an experiment in living from which all stand to gain as enthusiasms give rise to expertise and excellence produces role models as well as inventors. Mill's vision of society as a mutually supporting cosmos of independent centres of excellence is inspiring.

But, as with all utilitarian appeals, it is no stronger than the facts allow – the facts upon which the projections of utility are based. And the facts of the matter cloud the vision. In my newspaper shop of alternative lifestyles, no consumers collide. Each seeks out what they have decided they most want to be without interfering with other prospectors. But the real world is not so harmonious and well-aligned. Individuals get in each others' way, deliberately block off each others' chosen paths, do harm to each other out of malice as well as in the pursuit of conflicting interests.

So liberty generically identified has significant costs as well as undoubted benefits. Can we keep the benefits while limiting the costs? Mill thinks we can. He believes he has established a presumptive (or to use some useful modern jargon – a *pro tanto*) case for freedom. Some weight must always attach to claims for freedom since benefits will accrue whenever individuals are in a position of choice: minimally to themselves, maximally to others. But these benefits may be outweighed when the exercise of liberty imports excessive costs to others. Liberty may then be limited, for good utilitarian reasons, in the case of actions which harm other persons. The utilitarian can respect the presumption in favour of liberty, yet limit liberty in cases where that presumption is defeated – when one person's exercise of liberty harms others.

We can give this qualified case for liberty expression by endorsing a harm principle which circumscribes intervention by the state and society at large in the lives of members to those kinds of activity which cause harm to others. This is Mill's version of such a principle:

> The sole end for which mankind is warranted, individually or collectively, in interfering with the liberty of action of any of their number, is self-protection. That the only purpose for which power can rightfully be exercised over any member of a civilised community, against his will, is to prevent harm to others.[28]

Note finally, that as a good utilitarian, Mill believes he has established a necessary condition on legitimate interference. Whilst the case for the prevention of harm to others must always be made good if interference is to be judged legitimate, the fact that such a case *can* be made does not of itself justify interference. There is a simple reason for this. Interference carries its own costs. If the only way the prospective harm could be prevented would be to authorize a massive extension of police powers, for instance, the costs of this extension might well exceed the benefits promised by the prevention of harm.

This is the utilitarian case for liberty at its strongest. We shall return to the discussion of liberty in the next chapter.

Rights

The utilitarian defence of rights is obviously closely linked to the utilitarian defence of liberty. Conceptual analysis is required, to link as well as to distinguish claims of liberty from claims of right, but at first sight the right to free speech is at no great conceptual distance from the ideal of freedom of speech – and the same goes for other characteristic liberal freedoms. What talk of rights signifies for many thinkers is a distinctive mode of justification for freedom, a mode of justification which is to be sharply contrasted with the use of arguments from utility. I shall take up these questions in appropriate detail later. For the moment I am content to signal the leading elements of the utilitarian case for rights. And once again, John Stuart Mill provides as good a starting point as any.

We cannot complain that Mill does not attempt an analysis of the concept of rights. To have a right is to have a legitimate claim against other persons, a claim necessary for the promotion and protection of vital interests.

> When we call anything a person's right, we mean that he has a valid claim on society to protect him in the possession of it, either by the force of law, or by that of education and opinion. If he has what we consider a sufficient claim, on whatever account, to have something guaranteed to him by society, we say that he has a right to it . . . . To have a right, then, is, I conceive to have something which society ought to defend me in the possession of. *If the objector goes on to ask, why ought it?* I can give him no other answer than general utility.[29]

Claims will be protected and promoted by rules and policies. Again, these may be legal and/or non-legal rules and protection and promotion will require the actions of the state, lesser associations and individuals.

The pattern of argument in defence of rights is thus beautifully simple. Take a candidate right – the right to bodily integrity – and spell this out minimally as a claim on the part of individuals that they be neither physically assaulted nor raped. In defence of this claim, the utilitarian will cite the suffering caused to victims of such assaults and the anxiety created by insecurity to vulnerable persons. Any society which is concerned with the well-being of its members will identify as near-universal its members' interest in security. It will protect this interest through legal (and other social) structures which deter and punish violators. So: to have the human right to bodily integrity is to be in a position to advance strong utilitarian arguments in favour of claims that interests in personal security be promoted and protected by whatever institutional means are most efficacious. Whatever human rights we claim can be assessed according to this procedure. The utilitarian has told us what human rights are and how they can be justified; he will have available strong empirical studies to determine how they are best defended in practice. What more does the advocate of human rights require? We shall return to these questions in Chapter 4.

Distributive justice

Every society needs principles which allocate resources to members, principles which adjudicate conflicting claims and distribute the benefits produced by co-operative activity. It has long been thought that utilitarianism has a special problem in formulating principles to do this work. This thought is uppermost in the mind of the critic: utilitarianism ranks outcomes in terms of maximization of the good, but different outcomes may yield the same amount of utility, differing only in respect of the distribution of that good between individuals. Most of us, however, believe that some distributions are morally superior to others in point of fairness. They are more just. Some believe that equality in distribution is morally desirable. How can *any* principles of distributive justice be registered within utilitarian theory?

We can present the problem schematically with the aid of some figures. The numbers represent units of utility, but it does no harm to think of them for the moment as measuring wealth in £'s.

		Persons	
		A	B
	(1)	50	50
Outcomes			
	(2)	70	30

In both cases, utility scores are the same: aggregate utility = 100 units, average utility = 50 units. Thus far, the utilitarian has no reason for favouring (1) over (2); the egalitarian, of course, will disagree. And consider:

	(3)	150	0

(3) is better than both (1) and (2) in respect of both aggregate and average utility. But if we can imagine a society altering the rules which determine who commands which resources so that the outcome shifts from that represented in (1) to that represented in (3), wouldn't we judge the new outcome radically unjust, although it is

productive of more utility? The utilitarian requires that we maximize utility, making the society of A and B, taken together, better off overall. Our intuitions tell us that this would be unjust.

For many, this objection serves to refute utilitarianism; for others, it signals a need that utilitarianism be supplemented by an independent principle of justice in distribution. A utilitarian worth his salt will try to reply – and a number of replies are available which I shall sketch briefly.[30]

Hume's argument

The utilitarian wants to draw us away from simple models of the kind we have been discussing. He is particularly concerned to dispute the claim that utilitarian theory can find no place for principles of distribution. To review the case for the defence, a good starting point is Hume's account of justice.[31] Hume argues (and I summarize his views to the point of caricature) that human society needs to establish rules of property (justice) which fix who can make legitimate claims on which resources if universally destructive conflict over scarce resources among folk of limited generosity is to be avoided. If resources were infinite and available upon request, there would be no problem – but they are not. If persons were predominantly generous, again there would be no problem – but generosity is strictly limited. Our natural sentiments cannot be relied upon to steer us clear of mutually damaging confrontations. We have to devise institutions which secure co-operation.

Which institutions do we select? To answer this question, Hume's focus shifts from a perspective of individual problem-solving to a speculation about the history or genealogy of institutions. We must suppose history to have been a proving-ground for different solutions to the problem of justice. Rules of property have been established – and gone under as they proved to be inadequate. The enormously complicated residue of rules that have stood the test of time have remained in place because they represent the most satisfactory collective settlement. They are justified because of the security they confer and the benefits they promote. A system which spreads its benefits sufficiently widely will enjoy stable support; those sympathetic feelings which lead citizens to approve the good which others receive transform one's personal interest into a virtue.

At the heart of this argument is a utilitarian claim. Distribution is just when it effectively ameliorates the human condition and gathers the support of those subject to its standards. These standards will be a dense thicket of laws and moral rules, intricately interwoven, the bequest of mankind's history to a specific society. The reality of justice in operation cannot be reduced to a simple model which bears comparison to other simple models. We are grateful for what we have received – and properly so.

This is a conservative argument, endorsing institutions which are fixed in place because they have served utilitarian purposes.[32] It suggests a cautious approach to reform in the name of improvement. Since we *know* the contribution made to human well-being by institutions as they stand and can only speculate about the benefits to be gained from introducing changes, we should be reluctant to pursue revolutionary ambitions, contenting ourselves with a continuing programme of small-scale tinkering and adjustment in the service of greater utility.

Equality

The utilitarian need not be entirely conservative or radically opportunistic in the search for improvement. Well-known principles may indicate fruitful directions to take – and the articulation of such principles comprises further elements of the utilitarian ideal of justice in distribution. The first subsidiary principle is likely to be a principle of equality, defended by the use of a law of diminishing marginal utility much discussed by economists. Imagine we have six persons dividing up a cake. Which division will produce maximal utility? We can contrast an egalitarian division with each person receiving an equal slice with inegalitarian proposals by noticing that consumers will get so much satisfaction from a first portion of cake – and some degree less from each subsequent slice. The satisfaction to be gained from further portions at the margin will diminish the more one has already consumed. If three get two slices each and the other three none, the lucky three will get less satisfaction from their additional slice than the unlucky three would have gained from their first. We can imagine that satisfaction may even become a negative quantity for the person who makes himself sick gorging the lot! Another way of making this point is to argue that those who receive less in an unequal distribution than they would receive were the good to be distributed equally lose more from the movement away from equality than is gained by the individual who receives more of the good than equality dictates. This line of argument suggests that our six cake-eaters should each receive an equal share if we wish to maximize overall satisfaction.

This is a notoriously difficult argument to assess. I spoke of diminishing marginal utility as a 'law', but I cannot claim to have much evidence for it – and it should not parade as an *a priori* principle of practical reasoning. There are too many counterexamples for this to be plausibly claimed, as we shall see when we discuss the criterion of need. The example I discussed only gains whatever plausibility it has by making assumptions which may strain one's credibility in more realistic cases. We must suppose for example, that the claimants are all equally hungry or equally satiated, that they all like cake to the same degree. At bottom, we must suppose that we can both measure and compare, not only the portions of cake which we distribute, but also the satisfaction which the different recipients derive. There is a technical debate here which is crucial but which I shall leave once more unresolved.[33] The principle of diminishing marginal utility may well be the kind of common sense which is nothing more than the theory of some defunct economist, but it does retain a point which is easy to recognize although difficult to apply with any precision. I surmise that if you were the executor of a will instructing you to allocate the bequest to whichever charity you believed would do most good, you would not spend long investigating the claims of Eton College.

Need

Diminishing marginal utility furnishes one (very rough and ready) principle. Another principle which is widely recognized cuts across it. To return to the example of the cake-eaters, suppose one of the six is starving, the others are well fed. In this case, we may judge that the starving person has claims of need which require that she be fed first with as much cake as would satisfy her hunger. The utilitarian believes that he can account for the strength of claims of need, trading on a feature of utility that we have encountered already when discussing diminishing marginal utility, namely that a distribution of utility cannot simply be mapped on to a distribution of resources. There we noticed that those with more goods than equality dictates were poorer transformers of extra goods into utility than those who had less. In cases where individuals are identified as needy, we are supposing that these are efficient transformers of goods into utility, converting a given input of resources into a better than average utility score. Thus in the case of the cake-sharers, the benefit to be gained by apportioning all or a large measure of the cake to the one who is starving realizes more utility in sum than more egalitarian distributions. And in fact we can imagine cases in which principles of equality and principles of need can be combined to achieve maximal utility. We may be able to save the starving person's life by giving her half the cake. The rest may be divided equally to preserve utility against diminishing marginal returns.

This argument has great appeal. Claims of need – for food, shelter, physical mobility, medical and educational resources – have an urgency which is widely respected. The utilitarian can register this urgency in terms of the suffering of the needy and the degree of satisfaction achieved when relief is provided. And he can justify policies which systematically cater to need in terms of their output of utility, which will be characteristically higher than average. There are many who take responsiveness to need as an intuitive constraint on accounts of just distribution. No theory of justice is satisfactory if it cannot explain this constraint and endorse principles which respect it. The utilitarian believes he is on strong ground here.

Again this is a difficult argument to evaluate fully – and full evaluation would take us far off course. It will in any case be taken up later in Chapter 5. Let me limit discussion by making just two points. The first concerns the concept of need.[34] This has proved notoriously difficult to analyse. Discussions have focused on whether needs are identified objectively or subjectively and whether some needs are universal or all needs are relative to the circumstances of time, place and community standards. The most plausible answers to these questions propose that needs are object-ive in a sense that desires, however deep and strong, are not. Some needs may be universal – sufficient food to sustain expenditures of energy may be one – but most will be relative to standards of well-being which are regarded as acceptable minima within particular societies. These matters need not be pursued further since I think the utilitarian is essentially an observer rather than a protagonist of these debates. Whether needs are objective or subjective, whether the criteria for identifying them are universal or relativ-ist, the utilitarian can pick up the results of the discussions and explain how principles which promote utility defend the provision for need. One can see how it might be argued that families in West-ern democracies need a wide range of consumer goods which their grandparents regarded as luxuries. Possessing (or having the option of possessing) a TV set may be necessary for a sense of self-respect which is damaged by one's inability to watch and converse about the most popular soap operas. A dismal thought – but if it were true, if the lack of such possessions *were* the source of great misery, the utilitarian would take account of these facts.

The second problem concerning the utilitarian account of needs provision also arises from considering the facts of the matter, the facts on which the utilitarian bases his strategy. Implicit in the concept of need is the thought that needs represent thresholds of necessary provision. A person's life cannot go well *at all* if that person's needs are not met. *In extremis*, he may even die for the lack of the necessary good. Meeting the claims of need thus seems discontinuous with satisfying the claims of persons who desire goods over and above the threshold of needs. We might put this point by claiming that a person who is in need of some good would not rationally forego its provision in favour of any amount of alternative goods which are above the need threshold. If I need some medicine to recover from cancer (in normal circumstances) I would not welcome the offer of a Porsche from a health service manager who judges that this would be less costly, however much I might have wanted the sports car hitherto. This sort of fact is what makes needs provision an attractive policy for the utilitarian.

Unfortunately, the facts of the matter are not within the utilit-arian's control and this may be a case where he is hostage to them.

If claims of need are strictly discontinuous with any amount of above-threshold desire satisfaction, we may be led to endorse any amount of expenditure in cases where needs can only be met by extremely expensive treatment. The value of a child's life is inestimable, we are often told, and mercifully a popular newspaper campaign will induce some generous millionaire to fund the necessary course of treatment. But who would endorse the systematic provision of all necessary resources to achieve some low probability of meeting dire medical need?

The utilitarian can go two ways on this. He can bite the bullet and insist that overall gains do require whatever is necessary to provide goods that are genuinely needed and on this basis call for a radical redistribution of resources. Or he can revise his view that the claims of need are discontinuous with non-needy claims. But this threatens his belief that he has principles of justice that reflect our prereflective intuitions about the strength of claims of need. The utilitarian faces a genuine problem here – but perhaps he can console himself that it is a problem that no theorist of justice can easily avoid.

Desert

We have established that the utilitarian has something plausible, if not definitive, to say about distributions of resources that favour equality and the meeting of needs. Another important principle, which many prereflectively endorse, is that goods should be allocated to those who deserve them, in particular to those who have worked hard in the production of goods and services. Can the utilitarian accommodate any principle of desert?

The traditional utilitarian strategy has been to reduce claims of desert to the provision of incentives. First, there is the piece-work argument: if I cut down twice as many trees as you, working harder, I deserve more financial reward than you do. You could have worked as hard as I, but you took a longer lunch break and sunbathed for a couple of hours in the afternoon. Behind this claim, it is suggested, is the thought that greater productiveness requires the incentive of greater reward. Second, it is often claimed that some skills need a good deal of effort to acquire –

extra years at school, the rigours of university education and possibly a further poverty stricken period of postgraduate training. How can one induce youngsters to undergo these hardships – necessary if society is to have architects, doctors and lawyers – unless subsequent salary levels provide the incentive?

I am deeply sceptical of both of these arguments and invite readers to penetrate for themselves the smokescreen of unrealistic, self-serving rationalization which they throw up. But if it is true that the incentives argument is often unconvincing, the utilitarian can hardly be faulted if he doesn't endorse it. If, on the other hand, this is how the labour market works to the advantage of all, the utilitarian can use these facts to justify incentive payments. There may be more to desert as a principle of distribution than my discussion of incentives has intimated, so I shall take up the issue later.

The state

I shall bring to a close my survey of utilitarian political thought by outlining a utilitarian view of the state. Once again, my contribution will be brief to the point of caricature. But again the discussion will serve to introduce some of the central topics of political philosophy.

Political obligation

One such – perhaps *the* central topic of political philosophy – is the problem of political obligation. Can the state make a legitimate call on our obedience? Do we have a moral obligation to comply with the demands made by the state through its legislation?

The utilitarian tradition has a very strong answer to these questions. One clear reading of Hobbes identifies a profound utilitarian strain in his arguments. Hobbes describes a condition in which we have no government – the state of nature – which is so awful that we would find good reason to institute a government if we were in this condition and good reason to preserve one if a government were already in place. Without government, in circumstances technically described as anarchy, there would be no stable property, no investment in industry or agriculture, no commerce, no arts and sciences, no building of bridges or arts of navigation. The life of man would be 'poore, solitary, nasty, brutish and short', to quote his famous phrase.[35] This argument touts the benefits of government as the antitheses of the evils of the natural condition, evils so evident and widespread that everyone has good reason to avoid them in the only way possible – by accepting an obligation to obey the law of the sovereign.

I said that Hobbes's argument bears a utilitarian reading because its conclusion would be welcome to the utilitarian who seeks to justify sovereign authority. Such authority, we are told, is necessary for everyone to be happy, to get what they want, or to promote other independent values. But it is important to recognize that Hobbes himself was *not* a utilitarian, he was an egoist, accepting a theory which identifies the good as relative only to the agent who experiences it.[36] So we should recognize a coincidence rather than a conflation of views. Hobbes's case is that sovereign authority can be justified severally to each rational agent concerned to promote his or her own best interests; it procures their mutual advantage. The best outcome for each coincides with the best outcome for all since each, distributively, has good reason to endorse that institution which maximizes benefits for all, collectively. The utilitarian can accept Hobbes's conclusion and much of the argumentation which establishes it without endorsing the egoism on which it is based.

This was noticed by David Hume. Hume insists, time and again, that the reasons we have for allegiance derive from the 'public utility' of government: '. . . government binds us to obedience, only on account of its public utility' (and public utility is the only satisfactory defence for disobedience, 'in those extraordinary cases, when public ruin would inevitably attend obedience').[37] Government is necessary for justice, justice is necessary 'to maintain peace and order; and all men are sensible of the necessity of peace and order for the maintenance of society'.[38] Hume does not deny that self-interest can give us a reason to obey the government, and this reason is buttressed by our fear of the coercive powers which governments exert, but self-interest can also give us grounds for disobedience. Our original, Hobbesian, interests must be checked and restrained by reflection on the universal benefits of peace and

public order. 'The observation of these general and obvious interests is the source of all allegiance, and of that moral obligation
which we attribute to it.'[39] Hume has no doubt that reflection on
the widespread benefits of government will give rise to a sense of
obligation rooted firmly in an 'opinion of interest'; 'the sense of
general advantage which is reaped from government; together with
the persuasion, that the particular government which is established is equally advantageous with any other that could easily be
settled'.[40]

Perhaps it is better to see this as a utilitarian *form* of argument,
rather than a convincing utilitarian case. The anarchist, for one,
would not accept it since he would reject the skimpy account of
the facts of the matter. The Hobbesian groundwork – the description of anarchy in the state of nature as impoverished and dangerous – would be immediately challenged by the counterassertion
that mankind lives well without the state. Masterless men do not
fight, they co-operate amicably. It is men under government who
are the real moral dwarfs: used to being ordered about, under constant threat of punishment for non-compliance, willing to disobey
the law and harm each other as soon as they see an opportunity of
personal advantage with impunity. Such creatures contrast poorly
with moral agents unconstrained by the chains of government.
These paragons – and it is important for the anarchist that this is a
moral status which we are all capable of attaining – would determine what is right and follow the rule, showing no interest in what
they could get away with.[41]

At this point in the argument it is important to locate the debate
between the pro- and anti-government camps as an issue of fact.
Hume and his followers believe a little knowledge of history, a
small measure of experience, taken with a moment's reflection,
will establish that government is justified in terms of the advantages it so obviously brings. The utilitarian anarchist begs to
differ. Government diminishes our well-being. I do not wish to
adjudicate this dispute now, being content to signal the quality of
the debate amongst utilitarians concerning whether or not we do
have an obligation to obey sovereign authority. Supposing that
right is on the side of Hume, we can go on to the next question,
which concerns the best form of government.

Democracy

Continuing his argument concerning the optimal rules for property distribution, the system of justice, Hume believed that, apart from some small opportunities for limited improvement, the best form of government is likely to be the one we have got in place. Whatever its form, we can accept it as a most suitable response to local problems in local conditions, given the history of the population in the locality. It will be some mix of monarchical and republican traditions, incorporating elements of authority and freedom. Bentham, writing shortly after Hume, regarded this sort of complacent conservatism as the defence of the indefensible. First principles are available from which we may deduce that the only legitimate form of government is democratic. Leisurely rumination in a comfortable armchair, scholarly allusions to Thucydides and Tacitus – these are no substitute for rigorous theory where appropriate theoretical techniques are to hand. If we are genuine utilitarians, we can inspect the mechanisms of the different forms of government – monarchy, aristocracy, democracy, plus a host of mixed and qualified forms – to see which of them best facilitates utilitarian purposes.

Bentham thought institutions were legitimate if they maximized happiness. Government is necessary to constrain the worst effects of rampant self-interest and to engineer co-operation. These purposes are effected by law, and the test of good law is whether it maximizes the happiness of all those who are affected by it. How can we tell, of two proposed remedies for a social problem, which is the best? One answer is to call in the wisest utilitarian calculator you can find, the expert in this domain of economics, sociology or futurology. Mercifully, we do not have to inspect credentials in these spheres since a short cut is available. Policies can be appraised by working out how they impact upon the happiness of the target population. Why not assume that each member of the population is the best judge of his or her own happiness and leave it to them to declare, on this basis, which policy they favour? If the declaration is made in a ballot, and if each contribution is weighted equally in the process of counting, then a majority decision will suit more members of the population than it frustrates.

The policy favoured by the majority will produce more happiness than any alternative.[42]

This argument is blissfully simple. It is also plausible given the wealth of circumstances in which we recognize its application. It is my turn to make the arrangements for a holiday with five friends. Do I book a fortnight of sun, sand and surfing or do I arrange a holiday visiting art galleries, cathedrals and fine restaurants? It would be quite wrong to foist on my friends my own heavyweight conception of what would be in their best interests, all things considered – isn't the best policy just to ask them what will please them most and go along with the majority decision? That way we maximize satisfaction; and even the frustration of the minority will be tempered by the thought that they prefer the company to a solitary trip to their first-choice destination.

The obvious objection to this argument attacks the source of its immediate appeal – its simplicity. What is obviously best policy when arranging holidays is not necessarily wise for a legislator. We shall look at democratic theory more closely, later, but for the moment we should mention some of the assumptions that are made when this argument is used in a political context.

First, the argument applies most conspicuously to direct democracies where ballots are taken on specific proposals as they arise. If the question to be answered is: Which party shall form the next government? it should not be assumed that each policy subsequently enacted by the elected party promotes the welfare of the voters who mandated the party to govern. Representative democracy is a different creature from its directly democratic cousin, and the differences deserve the closest scrutiny – which is not to say that the utilitarian cannot make a contribution to the defence of representative institutions.[43]

Second, the argument assumes that the utility of each democratic decision can be computed independently of the utility of other decisions, taken before or after. This assumption may be false. Persons may get increasingly dissatisfied as they find themselves in the minority party on successive occasions. 'Win some, lose some', fairly represents the democratic temper, but one who finds himself losing all or most decisions, may experience incremental increases in displeasure. It has been shown that it is technically possible, within a democracy, for a majority of persons to be in a minority on a majority of occasions.[44] Over the longer run, when the outcome of a number of democratic decisions is reviewed, it may be that the tally of good achieved is not a simple sum of the good these decisions would have produced had they been considered separately. If there is a large but solid minority which votes together over a wide range of issues and attracts a sufficient number of different floating voters on each occasion of voting, the frequently disappointed majority will get increasingly fed up. The workings of the system will induce measures of frustration independently of those produced by specific decisions. If a majority is entrenched because of religious or ethnic affiliations this dissatisfaction will turn into the anger of perceived injustice. In which case, the majority principle will be rejected.

Third, the argument assumes not only that interpersonal comparisons are possible, but that the impact of decisions for and against is equal in respect of all those who implement or suffer them. Again, this may not be true. A majority may be lukewarm in favour of the winning policy. The defeated minority may be rabidly hostile. The utilitarian democrat must just hope that partisans of the opposing sides experience an equal average degree of satisfaction and dissatisfaction, each side being composed of protagonists hostile or in favour in roughly equal measure of intensity. Maybe, with a large enough population, this assumption is realistic. But the phenomenon, recognized daily, of the passionate minority interest group pursuing policies which would impact in a mildly inconveniencing fashion on large numbers of puzzled or cynical opponents, equally suggests that this assumption is complacent.

These are technical difficulties which it would be a mistake for the utilitarian to discount. Nonetheless, it would be quite wrong to dismiss wholesale the utilitarian instinct to ask people to register their preferences, then judge as right the policy which results from the ballot. We all know that majorities can be mistaken and that counting heads does not settle the matter of truth in a controversy, but we should remember that these truisms give strength to the elbows of those with something to gain from deciding issues for us. Bentham thought the arguments for democracy were perfectly straightforward – to the point where he suspected any rejection of them was motivated by class- or individual self-interest. 'Sinister interest' was the term he employed to characterize the motives of those who advance claims for greater power under the cloak of greater wisdom. If the message of the utilitarian case for democracy, direct or indirect, is, 'Beware of sinister interests', we should be wise to heed it.

Conclusion

In this chapter I have introduced utilitarian theory as a powerful and influential project in ethics. I make no claim to have investigated the foundations of this theory in any depth. My main interest has been to show how utilitarianism finds application in the study of central problems in political philosophy. I hope, as a result, to have introduced the reader to issues which will be explored in greater depth later, with the utilitarian treatment of these issues in place as a foil.

Although I have mentioned difficulties in the utilitarian story, it would be fair to say that my emphasis has been on the strengths of the account, detailing the contribution which utilitarian thought has made to our understanding of the problems which emerge as we think philosophically about our political life. Let me end this discussion with a few remarks about what I see as utilitarianism's greatest weakness. I do not locate this in the foundations of the theory. For some, this is the source of its deepest flaws. Utilitarianism, we are told, does not take seriously the separateness of persons. It can give no satisfactory account of the importance to all agents of their individual projects and the sense of integrity which is challenged when these deep aspects of an agent's personality come into conflict with the greater good. It threatens the importance to us of claims deriving from particular relationships, claims of friendship, love and allegiance. These are strong objections [45] – and where they resonate in political philosophy I shall take them up later. But as one might expect, the utilitarian is putting up a robust defence.[46] The worry I have with utilitarianism is quite different and can be simply stated. It concerns the possibility of calculating the greater good. Here I suspect the utilitarian is caught between two stools. The first is the tendency towards conservatism which we identified in Hume's thoughts about justice in the distribution of property, the legitimacy of government and the duty of obedience. Take any firmly entrenched institution or practice, or any generally accepted moral rule. How does the utilitarian evaluate these? Hume supposes that the lessons of history have taught us, over the long run, that the institutions and practices have proved themselves to be maximally beneficial. John Stuart Mill offers a similar account:

> As men's sentiments, both of favour and aversion, are greatly influenced by what they suppose to be the effects of things upon their happiness, the principle of utility ... has had a large share in forming the moral doctrines even of those who most scornfully reject its authority.[47]

Again,

> ... mankind must by this time have acquired positive beliefs as to the effects of some actions on their happiness; and the beliefs which have thus come down are the rules of morality for the multitude and for the philosopher until he has succeeded in finding better.[48]

Mill is not a conservative thinker. He is not suspicious of proposals for reform. If utility is promised, even the most radical reforms should be implemented. What I am emphasizing here is the assumption that utility *supports* existing rules and practices until utility dictates that reform is due, that present practice is the default position. And this assumption is grounded in nothing more than the thought that utility has guided history in the generation of optimal rules and practices. How could we possibly know this? The very necessity for radical reform in some instances – a thought more accessible to Mill than to Hume – shows that history may have taken a path away from that which utility shows to be optimal.

The utilitarian's readiness to consider that existing institutions, practices and rules maximize utility *by default* seems tailor-made to achieve a reflective equilibrium between theory and moral beliefs. The insight should not be dismissed, but it should be recognized that there are challengers in the field. Some philosophers, Rousseau for one, have claimed that history is the record of the degeneracy and immiseration of the species.[49] The utilitarian appeal to history for vindication seems to reflect, by contrast, a belief, if not in providence, then in the progress of mankind towards the best possible condition.

One thing is for sure – the utilitarian has not done the work his quasi-science suggests should be undertaken if he is content to make the sort of grand gestures towards history we have seen in Hume and Mill. Furthermore, the critic will not be surprised at this omission. How could this work be accomplished? What sort of facts do we have available for a genuine contrast of government and anarchy, liberty and authoritarianism, private and common property, societies with promises and societies without them? Experiments are impossible and historical episodes are too cluttered with the particularities of time and place to permit ready generalization.

Utilitarianism on the grand scale might therefore seem an exercise in rationalization or wishful thinking, depending on whether its focus is on the present collection of rules and institutions or on future alternatives. But perhaps utilitarianism works successfully when its focus is narrowed to the judgements of specific acts or policy proposals. Again, I have my doubts. The most ambitious attempts to quantify outcomes are the work of welfare economists, and it is fair to say that this work has not been widely persuasive. I remember listening to E.J. Mishan describing the work of the Roskill Commission. Their task was to find the optimal site for a third London airport and different sites had advantages and disadvantages which required evaluation and comparison. The whole audience was doubled up with laughter as Mishan listed the factors the Commission had solemnly taken account of. These included prospective damage to the black-bellied race of Brent Geese who migrate each winter to feeding-grounds at Foulness on the Essex coast, the destruction of medieval churches in Hertfordshire and the provision of non-seasonal employment for citizens of Southend-on-Sea who were overly reliant on summer migrants from the East End of London.

Of course, the cost–benefit analyst does not suppose that there is an easily identifiable common denominator which will permit a ranking of alternative policies. Radically different goods such as those I have mentioned are assessed in terms of the preferences consumers express with respect to them, and preferences are signalled by willingness to pay as signalled by questionnaires and opinion polls where no money changes hands. 'Shadow prices' are worked out for goods, like the Brent Geese and medieval churches, which do not have a market price.

I am persuaded by critics of these methods that the enterprise is misguided, particularly in respect of environmental goods. From my study window in the centre of Glasgow I can see the mountains of the Isle of Arran, fifty miles away, whenever there is some north in the wind. Fifty years ago, factories cast a smokescreen over the city which was dispersed only rarely, on Sundays and public holidays. My life is better for the view – but how can that be quantified?[50] I conclude (after too little argument) that when utilitarianism abandons the assumptions of a providential history and gets down to the brass tacks of policy appraisal using the techniques of welfare economics, it is likely to fail here, too.

There may be a middle road – of common-sense evaluation of outcomes in terms of an objective list of values that we are used to comparing and trading off in familiar dilemmas.[51] This will have to be worked out in detail. We can properly reserve judgement on the success of the utilitarian enterprise, even as we keep in mind its systematic contribution to the problems of political philosophy.

Chapter 3

Liberty

Introduction

One enjoyable, though probably fruitless, way to spend an afternoon would be to discuss which is the most prominent or important political value, which ideal carries most clout in political
debates – in public bars or parliaments. Candidate values might
include justice (more particularly, human rights or equality), democracy, and certainly, liberty. It is hard to think of a political manifesto that does not trumpet the prospect of liberty – and it is easy
to think of fractious political disputes where freedom[1] is a contender on both sides of the issue. Freedom in education requires
the provision of educational opportunity for all, free at the point
of service, some say; others, that it signals the parents' freedom to
choose the education they judge best for their child. These different aspirations may collide if resources do not permit them both to
be fulfilled.

Liberty, liberalism, libertarianism

We shall examine the different ways in which liberty may be appealed to, but one thing is sure: whoever makes such appeal is attempting to claim the moral high ground. Just why this is so is a matter of delicate analysis, not least since 'the meaning of this term is so porous that there is little interpretation that it seems able to resist',[2] as Isaiah Berlin notes. Before we proceed in this direction, however, it will be useful to distinguish the value of liberty from a couple of other terms closely associated with it – 'liberalism' and 'libertarianism'.

Of the two, 'liberalism' is the hardest to capture in a nut-shell definition. As with other '-isms' in the domain (conservatism, socialism . . .) it signals a cluster of political ideals advocated (and put into practice) within a tradition of political thought and political activity. Major contributors to the literature of liberalism include thinkers as diverse as Locke, Montesquieu, the Federalists, Constant, de Tocqueville, J.S. Mill, T.H. Green, Karl Popper, F. Hayek and latterly, John Rawls and Joseph Raz – and this is a very selective list. Probably the only thing that unites members of this list is that they all subscribe to a strong value of individual liberty – and even then we should note that they speak in different voices when this value is canvassed for our endorsement. For some, the heart of liberalism is captured in Locke's claim that all men are born free and equal; others shudder at the commitment to equality. For still others, liberalism requires the opportunity to participate in democratic institutions; some liberals discount this, insisting that democracy represents a separate or subordinate value, or no value at all, or even a threat to liberty.

Conspicuously, liberalism amounts to a different political agenda in different places. In Britain, liberalism as a political movement is a halfway house between conservatism and socialism, shifting in policy content as these other political movements veer away from or move towards the middle ground. In the United States, liberals have bleeding hearts, and for many 'liberal' has become a dirty word. Anyone who advocates welfare programmes, indeed much public spending beyond what is necessary for defence and law and order, is likely to be castigated as liberal.

Key liberal themes include the right to private property and advocacy of the rule of law as well as defence of the traditional freedoms – freedom of speech and artistic expression, freedom of association, religious freedom, freedom to pursue the work of one's choice and freedom to participate in political decision procedures. 'Liberalism' is a poor, but indispensable, label, perhaps best understood when one has a clear idea of the movements or ideologies which most conspicuously oppose it in its different manifestations.

Libertarianism is a much less amorphous creature. It is the theoretical stance of one who strictly limits the competence of government to collective defence, the protection of negative rights, rights of non-interference, and enforcement of contracts. The state on this account has the two tasks of the night-watchman – to guard the city walls against outside attack and to patrol the city streets, ensuring that citizens are not murdered, raped, robbed or defrauded. The state has no role in the provision of education, health-care or social security payments, no duty to redistribute resources amongst citizens for purposes other than the rectification of violations of rights. We shall study the libertarian agenda in Chapter 4. In the meanwhile we shall try to understand better the concept of liberty.

Analysis

Philosophical analysis promises clarification, but with a concept as diffuse and battle-scarred as liberty, we should not expect quick results. We shall soon see that there are many concepts of liberty, as Berlin suggested. It is not that the term is ambiguous in any straightforward way. 'I sat by the bank and wept' is quickly sorted out, but a dictionary won't tell us what Patrick Henry had in mind when he cried 'Give me liberty or give me death!' If there are indeed more than two hundred senses to this word, I would rather someone else took on the job of charting them. We need to put some limits on the enterprise of analysis.

In the first place, we shall focus on liberty as a political value. There are two aspects to this demand: we can ignore obviously non-political usages and we shall insist that a proper analysis makes clear why proponents of liberty have claimed it as a value.

The former point is perhaps trivial; political philosophy has no interest in explaining why liberty bodices are so called or in relating freedom of speech to newspapers which are free, gratis and for nothing (as against frank, fearless and free!). The latter point – that freedom is a value – is of considerably more importance, since there are clear accounts of freedom which can be criticized and rejected on the grounds that they offer either no account of why freedom is a value or an account that is plainly defective. One way of arguing for this conclusion is to claim that liberty is not a value-neutral concept, it is always normative, always accompanied by a positive ethical charge. Thus to describe a condition as one of liberty is to attribute a positive value to it and hence to begin making out a case for it. On this account, it would be self-contradictory to disvalue a liberty or to describe a condition of liberty as wrong or evil. John Locke clearly employed the concept of liberty in this way when he made a sharp distinction between liberty and licence, claiming that the state of nature as he describes it, is 'a State of Liberty, yet it is not a State of Licence',[3] since man is governed by the law of nature.

I am inclined to think this is right, but there are plenty of reasons to give one pause. 'Is liberty of the press a good thing?', ask pundits and parliamentarians, anxious that they might be found out. This question would only make sense if the use of 'liberty' here does *not* imply that liberty is a positive value, if the usage is in some way non-standard – which it may well be, finding a purely descriptive meaning in terms of the specific institutional practices of a particular state. My own view, which could not be defended without some measure of stipulation, is that this debate may indicate the only distinction that can be drawn between liberty and freedom. The concept of freedom, I believe, is thinner than that of liberty and carries less evaluative baggage. 'Ought citizens be free to . . .?' is a perfectly straightforward question. We have no difficulty in thinking of some freedoms as worthwhile and others not so. If I could tidy up the language, I would do so, distinguishing two kinds of freedom: that which we approve I would designate liberty; that which is disreputable I would call licence. Sadly, I am impotent in these matters, so let us leave this matter of terminology unresolved.

This does not mean, however, that the connection between

liberty or freedom and value is indeterminate. Whilst it may not be a conceptual truth that liberty is valuable, it must still be required that philosophical accounts of liberty explain why it has generally been accepted as valuable and why its advocates regard it as valuable. Of course the political philosopher need not endorse such accounts – they may bear witness to widespread illusion – but if so the error must be comprehensible.

Second, despite my insistence that we focus on liberty as a political value, we must not draw the lines of conceptual demarcation too tightly. John Stuart Mill begins his essay, *On Liberty*, with a disclaimer in the first sentence: 'The subject of this Essay is not the so-called Liberty of the Will, so unfortunately opposed to the misnamed doctrine of Philosophical Necessity; but Civil, or Social Liberty.'

Mill may be right to separate these philosophical questions. It may turn out that the metaphysical question of whether or not there is such a thing as free agency is quite independent of issues concerning political liberty. But we cannot *begin* our enquiries with such an assumption in place since it may turn out that an account of the value of political liberty which is successfully embedded within a wider account of free action will be deeper and more satisfying. A link between a satisfactory account of free agency, considered generally, and political or social freedom may also help us with our first objective – to see why liberty is of value to its protagonists.

Mill's specific objective limits the range of the concept of liberty in another way, since it ought to be an open question whether, as he believes, the question of liberty is exhausted when we have investigated 'the nature and limits of the power which can be legitimately exercised by society over the individual' (as the quotation above continues). Mill imposes this latter restriction deliberately because he believes that, in his day, democracy poses sharp threats to civil liberty. He has in mind the possibility of majority tyranny and the levelling spirit of democracy which may lead to an intolerance of social experimentation and personal eccentricity. He believed de Tocqueville's reports of democracy at work in America: give a measure of power to everyone at the town meeting and conformity will soon become a parochial priority. These dangers are real, but as we shall see, liberty may require democratic institutions just as surely as democratic institutions require strong liberties.

Isaiah Berlin: negative and positive liberty

Isaiah Berlin's Inaugural Lecture, 'Two Concepts of Liberty', has proved to be one of the seminal contributions to political philosophy in the twentieth century. It is remarkable for the resonance of its analytical apparatus and the depth of its historical foundations. It is also notable for the strength, and perhaps dogmatism, of its conclusions. Berlin distinguishes negative and positive liberty and, on his account, these different senses of liberty are elicited as the answers to two different questions.

If we ask, 'What is the area within which the subject – a person or group of persons – is or should be left to do or be what he is able to do or be, without interference from other persons?' we characterize an agent's negative liberty. 'Political liberty in this sense is simply the area within which a man can act unobstructed by others.' If we ask instead, 'What, or who, is the source of control or interference that can determine someone to do, or be, this rather than that?'[4] we aim to describe the agent's positive liberty. This is summarized later as 'the freedom which consists in being one's own master'.[5]

Negative liberty

Let us look more closely at negative liberty. The clearest exponent of the simplest version of negative liberty was Thomas Hobbes, who defined a free man quite generally as, 'he, that in those things, which by his strength and wit he is able to do, is not hindered to do what he has a will to'.[6] Negative liberty is often glossed as the absence of coercion, where coercion is understood as the deliberate interference of other agents. In recent times, the most rigorous version of negative liberty, 'pure negative liberty' has been articulated by Hillel Steiner, but since it is an implication of Steiner's analysis that not even the most draconian laws can inhibit liberty, because they render acts ineligible rather than impossible, I judge that it has little relevance to political philosophy, despite its influence.[7] Negative liberty, of the Hobbesian kind that is compromised by coercive threats as well as other modes of prevention, is often contrasted with theories (if there are such) which imply that mere inabilities inhibit liberty. Berlin quotes Helvetius to make this point: 'It is not lack of freedom [for people] not to fly like an eagle or swim like a whale.'[8]

The evident truth of this conceals a difficulty, nonetheless. Suppose I can't walk because my enemy has tied me up or broken my leg. Here, too, there is a straightforward inability but we would judge this to be a case of freedom denied because the inability is a direct result of another's action. But suppose that my inability to walk is the result of a medical condition – and this condition can be remedied by an operation which I cannot afford. Am I unfree if others fail to pay for my treatment? The case differs from my inability to fly like an eagle in two ways. First, humans can walk in normal circumstances but they will never be able to fly like eagles. Second, the condition is remediable whereas human flightlessness is not. Do these differences count? Before we tackle this question, let us see how this problem arises within Berlin's account of negative liberty.

Berlin insists that we should distinguish between the value of (negative) liberty and the conditions which make the exercise of liberty possible.[9] Thus there may be freedom of the press in a country where most citizens are illiterate. For most, the condition which would give point to the freedom – literacy – does not obtain. In these circumstances, Berlin would insist that illiteracy does not amount to a lack of freedom. Clearly something is amiss in a society which fails to educate its citizenry to a level where they can take advantage of central freedoms, but that something need not be a lack of freedom. A basic education which includes literacy may be an intrinsic good, or it may be a human right. Its provision may be a matter of justice, its denial, transparent injustice. But however this state of affairs is described, we should distinguish a lack of freedom from conditions under which it is hard or impossible to exercise a formal liberty.

Berlin has his own reasons for insisting on this point. He has a laudable concern for clarity; obfuscation and confusion result if different values are elided by careless argumentation. More importantly, he wants us to recognize that different fundamental values may conflict. The demands of justice or security may require the truncation of liberty, or vice versa, in circumstances of moral dilemma or irresoluble tragedy. There is a natural tendency to seek escape by assimilating the strong differences, by attempting to redescribe the awful circumstances as having only one value at stake – in which case we can take whichever course of action maximizes the unifying value or minimizes its violation. For Berlin, these are strategies of self-deception. They lead to 'absurdities in theory and barbarous consequences in practice'.[10]

It is hard to dispute this claim. The twentieth century is replete with examples of regimes which have instructed their subjects that solidarity or the service of the state comprise true justice, real freedom, genuine democracy or the greatest happiness, wrapping up all tensions and incipient conflicts in a totalitarian cocoon which silences the clamour of otherwise inescapable debate. This tendency is the chief target of Berlin's philosophical endeavours and we should endorse his aims. However, it is difficult to relate this general caution to the issue concerning liberty and its conditions.

In the first place, it is worth noting that Berlin himself cannot maintain the distinction wholeheartedly. Negative liberty *has* been curtailed by 'social and economic policies that were sometimes openly discriminatory, at other times camouflaged, by the rigging of educational policies and of the means of influencing opinion, by legislation in the sphere of morals'.[11]

It would seem that the key to determining whether such policies inhibit negative freedom is whether the limiting condition on the exercise of liberty was either an intended limitation or, if unintended, a limitation which it is possible to abolish. Policies which are openly or covertly discriminatory are likely to be unjust, but if they restrict opportunities available to others they offend against freedom as much as justice. Berlin is quite correct to insist that we should keep separate values distinct. But we do not confuse or conflate different values when we condemn a practice that offends two or more of them – we strengthen the criticism.

There is another error induced by Berlin's emphasis on the clear-minded discrimination of different values. No one could object to the distinction between liberty formally achieved and the satisfaction of conditions which are necessary if the full value of liberty is to be attained. It is important that both be implemented and vital that breakdowns or shortcomings be accurately identified if remedies are required. Nonetheless, if it is true in a particular case that the full value of liberty is not obtained, because of remedial illiteracy or physical handicap for example, then the prime reason for reforming the inhibiting conditions will be liberty itself. If we *have* identified social conditions which frustrate the achievement of a recognized good, then that good itself serves to vindicate efforts to eliminate these conditions. Suppose we discover that a system of land tenure has become a cause of famine; we don't need any reason beyond the abolition of famine to tackle the conditions which created it. And the same is true of liberty; if freedom of the press is worthwhile, being necessary if citizens are to be informed participants in the democratic process, this is reason enough to secure the condition of widespread literacy which enables citizens to make use of it.

What is really at stake here is an issue of political rhetoric. If we are concerned to effect reform in health provision or education or social security, it may well be that we have a choice of values that we can cite in order to gain support for our proposals. We can advance our cause under different banners. Social justice and freedom may both serve; in which case, it is a matter of practical, strategic judgement which value we highlight in our campaign. The temper of the times, signalled by the success of an opposing party, may favour an appeal to liberty. The astute politician may then argue that liberty requires obvious conditions on social provision to be met if the proclaimed value is to serve as more than a shelter for the privileges of the rich. This rhetoric may succeed or it may fail. The electorate may judge the argument which has been advanced as too elaborate to be convincing – and vote against. Having learned his lesson, the astute politician will try a different route and rediscover social justice.[12] I stress that this process of selecting values in which to couch political rhetoric is philosophically respectable. We do not equate or confuse the different values of liberty and social justice when we recognize that a case for specific reforms can be supported by either or both. Which value we choose for a particular campaign is not a matter of philosophical propriety. Both could be advanced together if this were thought to be effective.

We have reached a capacious understanding of negative freedom by exploiting materials furnished by Isaiah Berlin. The most obvious difference between his proposal and ours is that we are more ready to countenance as hindrances or obstacles, conditions which limit persons' opportunities; which conditions may not have been imposed by human agency, but if they can be eliminated, they ought to be.

How do we identify conditions which ought to be eliminated? On the account, thus far, I am unfree with respect to any opportunity which I cannot presently take, but which I could take advantage of were others to resource me. I am therefore unfree to visit the moon, whereas I am not unfree to fly like an eagle. Does this fact, of itself, establish a claim on my behalf against those individuals or governments which could furnish me with the necessary resources (as they have found them for some fortunate others?) If claims of freedom are moral claims, as I insisted at the beginning of this chapter, we need some further account of which opportunities *ought* to be available to persons, since I take it that no one would identify a case of unfreedom in my inability to make a moon landing.

I have in mind a condition of freedom which has been described by Ralph Wedgwood as *social empowerment*. [13] On this account, the ingredients of freedom will comprise 'the social conditions that confer favourable prospects with respect to wealth, income, and the knowledge and skills that can be acquired through education', [14] as well as the standard list of liberal freedoms – so long as those social conditions are attainable. But again, not all social empowerment is of value. We should not empower potential bank robbers by reducing legal limitations on their access to weapons or by granting them resources to purchase them. A principle of liberty which is going to be useful must enable us to identify *justifiable* claims for empowerment – and I don't think this can be achieved within the framework of the negative concept of liberty. In order to advance, we need to specify the opportunities that *ought* to be available to claimants. This requires the development of a positive concept of liberty.

Positive liberty

This is how Isaiah Berlin introduces the concept of positive liberty:

The 'positive' sense of the word 'liberty' derives from the wish on the part of the individual to be his own master. I wish my life and decisions to depend on myself, not on external forces of whatever kind. I wish to be the instrument of my own, not of other men's, acts of will. I wish to be a subject, not an object; to be moved by reasons, by conscious purposes which are my own, not by causes which affect me, as it were, from outside. I wish to be somebody, not nobody; a doer – deciding, not being decided for, self-directed and not acted upon by external nature or by men as if I were a thing, or an animal, or a slave incapable of playing a human role, that is, of conceiving goals and policies of my own and realizing them. This is at least part of what I mean when I say that I am rational, and that it is my reason that distinguishes me as a human being from the rest of the world. I wish, above all, to be conscious of myself as a thinking, willing, active being, bearing responsibility for my choices and able to explain them by references to my own ideas and purposes. I feel free to the degree that I believe this to be true, and enslaved to the degree that I am made to realize that it is not.[15]

This is a capacious nut-shell. But we shall see that the notion of positive liberty is more expansive yet. As Berlin develops his historical-cum-conceptual story, a sequence of ideals, initially attractive then progressively more sinister, is charted. To summarize, in cavalier fashion:

(a) *Self-control and self-realization.* This involves my working on my own desires – ordering, strengthening, eliminating them – in line with a conception of what it is right or good for me to do or be. This is a complex notion, with its heart in a sophisticated account of freedom of action. In modern times the development of this account can be traced through Locke, Rousseau, Kant and Hegel. It has re-emerged in the recent work of Harry Frankfurt and Charles Taylor.[16] We are well used to the idea that we exhibit self-control when we resist temptation. Freedom of action consists in our ability to appraise the desires which prompt us to act and to decide whether or not to satisfy them. On this account, the paradigm of freedom consists in our going *against* what we most want, doing what we think best. But as Hegel pointed out, the best of all worlds for the free agent is that in which what, after due reflection, we believe is the right thing to do is also what we discover we most want.

(b) *Paternalism.* Suppose I am not able to exercise this self-control. I may be ignorant of what is best for me. I may not understand the full value of alternatives. Like the child who does not wish to take the nasty-tasting (but life-saving) medicine, I mistake my real interests. In such circumstances, the wise parent will not be squeamish. She will force the medicine down. Might it not be justifiable, then, for *you* to exercise the control over me that I am unable to achieve or sustain? Might not my freedom require whatever control over me that *you* can exercise – absent my own powers of self-control? This thought is particularly apt where your paternalistic intervention creates for me or sustains conditions of autonomous choice that my own activities thwart. This is a deep issue, which we shall examine later, but it is hard to see how some varieties and instances of paternalism can be rejected. And it is hard to deny that my freedom is promoted when you liberate me from temptations that I would reject were I in a calmer, saner or more knowledgeable condition, when you empower me to act, despite my self-inhibiting dispositions.

(c) *Social self-control.* But if I exercise my freedom through self-control, and if you promote my freedom by appropriate paternalistic intervention, may not my freedom be further enhanced by institutional measures that I endorse? In the republic of Rousseau's *Social Contract*,[17] citizens achieve moral and political liberty by enacting laws, backed by coercive sanctions, which apply to themselves as well as to others. If, as an individual, I cannot resist a temptation which will likely cause me harm, wouldn't it be a wise stratagem to devise some social mechanism which will bolster my resolve? If I realize that the threat of punishment against me will keep me on the straight and narrow path which wisdom alone cannot get me to follow, shouldn't I institute and accept social restraints which are more forceful than my unaided moral powers? And in doing so, don't I expand my true freedom? Ulysses tied himself to the mast to resist the Sirens' call. As a result, he gained a freedom lost to his unfortunate shipmates. Addicts of all sorts can seek the discipline and social order of the clinic or self-help group as a means of liberation. A wise citizen in a democratic state will establish laws and voluntarily submit to the regulatory power of the state where self-control cannot suffice, and thus achieve freedom – or so the argument goes.

(d) *State servitude.* An unwise citizen, unable to exercise immediate self-control and insufficiently far-seeing to enact or endorse devices of social coercion, can nevertheless attain freedom indirectly and at second hand if the state effects the necessary control, notwithstanding his disapproval or lack of participation. The state can control us in the service of our real interests – and thereby make us free. This is a recipe for totalitarianism – in four seductive philosophical steps!

This is a brief, analytic summary of Berlin's potted history. But I think it carries the drift. More importantly, it shows the complex dialectic whereby a plausible and historically influential understanding of freedom of action can be elaborated into a doctrine of social freedom. Second, and equally important, it illustrates how the doctrine of positive liberty acquires its moral content. The central thought – that liberty is the opportunity or capacity to achieve something *worthwhile* – is explicit at the first stage of the argument in the ideal of self-realization. This canvasses one's freedom as the control of her desires in the light of some conception of the good life, some account of the virtues, some principles of right action.

Berlin himself favours the sparse, negative concept of freedom, believing this can accommodate all political aspirations to the core liberties and enable us to locate liberty within a range of potentially conflicting values. His chief criticism of positive liberty is that the sequence of ideals we have just canvassed represents a slippery slope. If we endorse the initial equation of freedom and self-control, we shall be unable to arrest a fall into the

embrace of the ideals of totalitarianism, whereby the state pro-
mulgates a conception of the good life and yokes everyone into its
pursuit. The most potent criticisms of Berlin deny this. But before
I discuss this response, I should deal with another influential
objection to his analysis.

MacCallum's response

Gerald C. MacCallum, Jr proposes an alternative analysis. For
him, freedom is best understood as a triadic relation between
agents, opportunities and preventing conditions. Thus each statement of freedom (and unfreedom) can be unpacked in terms of this
schema: x is free (unfree) from y to do or be z. This analysis of
freedom statements carries the implication that all freedom is both
negative and positive – freedom *from* as well as freedom *to*.[18] Joel
Feinberg has argued for a similar analysis, finding additional variables through, for example, a distinction of internal and external
constraints: an inhibiting neurosis, such as agoraphobia, can
restrict my freedom as strongly as a locked door.[19]

How can one adjudicate this dispute? Berlin, himself (and one of
his recent defenders, John Gray)[20] claims this is mistaken; a person
in chains may wish to rid themselves of their chains without having any clear idea of what they wish to achieve through their freedom. This strikes me as a possible but most unusual case. It is
certainly not a paradigm of negative freedom, since, in the standard case, McCallum's analysis not only will apply but must apply if
we are to identify the demand for freedom. Taking the example
literally, one will generally suppose that the prisoner wishes, at
least, to move around unshackled, but there may be more at stake.
The demand that I be unshackled may be predicated on a case for
freedom of assembly, freedom to attend church, freedom to engage
in any activity from which I am effectively disbarred – and it is as
well to know which freedom is at stake.

Gray's objection to Feinberg's more sophisticated analysis is
equally unpersuasive, viz., that since the admission of internal
constraints allows 'as *constraints on freedom* constraints and evils
(such as headaches, disabilities) that are not unfreedoms at all'
freedom is obliterated as a distinct political value.[21] Feinberg can

reply directly that the distinctness of freedom as a political value is best captured by investigating which constraints do, and which do not, inhibit *political* freedom. Headaches may cripple personal freedom. They are not likely to figure amongst the constraints that politicians either impose or could alleviate, but if they do so figure, they limit political freedom, too.

I conclude that, so far as the analysis of the language of freedom is concerned, the criticisms of McCallum and Feinberg must be well taken. Linguistic analysis does not permit us to draw the distinction which Berlin employs. But this is not the end of the matter. McCallum goes further, arguing that the use of analytically unsound labels will lead to confusion and error as we affix them to inappropriate positions. He thinks we should avoid dubbing Smith a theorist of negative liberty or Jones a proponent of positive liberty since most philosophers of historical significance will advance complex doctrines which are best viewed as a combination of the two. I think this caution is timely, too.

However, I don't think that Berlin has made this mistake; despite the grand sweep of the historical materials he surveys, he is remarkably sure-footed. Moreover, I suspect that Berlin is right in his claim that much of the literature on political liberty can be fruitfully placed within one or other of two major traditions within the history of ideas. Berlin's chosen apparatus for identifying the different traditions – distinguishing two leading questions – is certainly clumsy, but the distinction he draws captures a very real difference.

We can pinpoint this difference by considering a problem concerning freedom of action. Take the case of the addict. What I want most now is a cigarette – and so I smoke one. I don't, however, want to be a smoker. When I smoke, do I act freely? On that starkly negative conception of freedom elaborated by Hobbes, my freedom is attested by my getting what I most want. No one has stopped me doing what I please. On the alternative conception of freedom, described above as the first step on the road to positive liberty, I have not acted freely. If I don't want to be a smoker, if I want to be in a condition where I don't want cigarettes, if I view myself as a pathetic appetitive creature whose desires have got out of control, the experience of doing what I most want to do will be the very experience of unfreedom, a personal slavery to obnoxious desires.

What is distinctive here is that I disvalue getting what I want. We shall discuss this view, most familiar perhaps from Kant's moral philosophy, later under Rousseau's rubric of 'moral liberty'.[22] This dispute cannot be adjudicated here, but notice how sharp the conflict is. The one example gives rise to diametrically opposed verdicts concerning the smoker's freedom of action and the difference between the two verdicts derives from the applicability to the judgement of whether I act freely of normative considerations concerning whether what I do is best. On the Hobbesian account of free action norms concerning what I ought to do are irrelevant. On the Rousseauian or Kantian view, they are central.

We can shift the discussion towards an analogous political dispute. Do all coercive laws limit my freedom? The coercive instruments of the state, generally the police, may just stop me from getting what I want, but in the usual case the whole apparatus of the criminal law (police, courts, prisons) works by raising the potential cost of illegal activities – a cost specified by the conventional tariff of punishment. There are two views one might take. On the first, I am unfree whenever the criminal law proscribes what I want to do. Suppose what I most want is to eliminate my rival for promotion. The bad news is that since this is illegal, I am unfree to kill her; severe penalties are prescribed for murder. Judging that the possible gains are not worth the risk, I refrain. The good news is that the disvalue of my unfreedom is outweighed by the value to her of her survival.

A very different (positive) analysis of freedom requires that the option variable, what it is that I am not forbidden to do when I am free to do it, is not satisfiable by an action that is morally wrong. Suppose I make a very bad moral mistake and think that all is permissible in love and war and business, including the killing of rivals for promotion. On this positive analysis of freedom, my error is compounded. Since it is wrong to murder rivals, murdering rivals is not the sort of thing one could logically (or conceptually) be free to do. It follows that one's freedom is not impugned by laws that threaten punishment for those who are convicted of murdering their rivals for promotion. Extrapolating from this example to the common case, one's freedom is not limited by coercive laws which prescribe punishment for wrong-doing. It is, in Locke's phrase, licence, not liberty, that is curtailed. It is not a case of the bad news (my freedom's being limited) being outweighed by the good news (less murder). There is no bad news when I am stopped or inhibited from doing what is wrong in any case. Opportunities to do wrong with impunity do not enhance my freedom. If I am inhibited from doing what I most want by what I believe the state demands of me – and hence resist the temptation to murder the competitor – my freedom will not be abrogated. As we saw above, citizens should welcome the power of a state which constrains them to keep to what they know is the right path. If we think of freedom as the condition of social empowerment canvassed above, almost paradoxically, we can recognize the coercive agency of the state as enabling us to do what we believe to be right, refraining from wrong-doing and pursuing the good life.

I have outlined two opposing positions. Which is best? The question is still open despite my biased exposition of the differing claims they make. A theory of freedom developed in recent years takes a very clear view of the issue.

The republican theory of freedom

The republican theory of freedom has its recent origins in the work of Quentin Skinner and has been developed in some depth by Philip Pettit and Jean-Fabien Spitz.[23] The republican theory has classical foundations in the ideal of liberty proposed for the Italian city-states of the Renaissance. Historically, it was an aspiration for both states and citizens, celebrating both their independence from potentially dominant neighbours and a constitution which was republican, with citizens (generally, some portion of the adult male population) taking up public offices and living under the rule of law. Such a constitution contrasts notably with despotic or monarchical regimes; citizens have a robust moral and civic standing – they are not slaves or the ethical subordinates of arbitrary rulers. This way of thinking about liberty is the product of a distinctive tradition, with respectable classical sources. It incorporates a specific conceptual analysis and is claimed to present an attractive political ideal.

It is glossed by Pettit as 'non-domination':

someone dominates or subjugates another, to the extent that

1. they have the capacity to interfere
2. on an arbitrary basis
3. in certain choices another is in a position to make.[24]

Non-domination is to be distinguished from non-interference, from self-mastery and from that collective self-mastery which is exhibited in participation in directly democratic decision procedures. It is a *status* concept, expressive of the equal comparative moral and legal standing of all citizens. So, against those theorists who value negative liberty, it is claimed that one can be subject to dominion without interference. If a woman has a gentle master, a master, perhaps, who is susceptible to her wiles, if he will not interfere so long as, like Sheherazade, she can spin out his entrancement, she is free according to the negative theory, but not on the republican account. As a dancing girl, *raconteuse* or slave, or, in modern times, a clever wife with a doting husband but no legal rights against his possible molestation, she is unfree even if, *de facto*, in charge.

Further, we may be subject to interference but not dominated, by just coercive laws. These will be laws that are not arbitrary – and non-arbitrariness comes in two forms: the laws are enacted by the processes of a proper constitution and they are in accordance with citizens' interests as informed by their values. In the first form, we have the 'empire of laws, and not of men'.[25] This wonderful slogan is more perspicuous for what it excludes rather than designates. It excludes the caprice of monarchs and the whim of suspicious dictators. It includes (probably) a host of constitutional devices intended to protect the innocent citizen from this sort of unpredictable intervention in her daily business. Laws must be enacted by the citizens or their representatives, promulgated widely and comprehensible universally; offices should be open to all on the basis of ability and popular endorsement.

Second, the laws which direct citizens' conduct and legitimize sanctions against criminals should be fully in accordance with their interests and values. It is possible that laws which are ideal in point of their provenance can still get it wrong. In which case, an aberrant majority, say, will still prescribe arbitrarily. Such laws, impeccable in point of their source, will infringe freedom. So, we may conclude that arbitrariness in two distinct fashions must be absent if laws (or other coercive social instruments) are to leave freedom intact.

This is a complex and wide-ranging theory of freedom; what holds it together is the idea of non-domination. I have my doubts about this. Non-domination is an important and central personal and political value, and the republican theorists deserve great credit for giving it new life. It is related in clear ways to liberty. The difficulty, to my mind, is that the theory gives the concept of non-domination too much work to do. Non-domination can be understood narrowly, embracing differences of status or quasi-moral authority; here what is vital is a *capacity* to interfere in the actions of others solely on the grounds of differential status. Slave-owners best exemplify this model of domination. Their interference in the lives of the slave will be arbitrary in that the slave will have to do *whatever* the slave-owner wishes. His demands may be more or less onerous in fact, but it is clear who is the master and who is dependent on the master's requirements.

The slave's debilities are twofold: she is subject to the master's commands and dependent on his graces. She is both biddable and vulnerable. For Rousseau, dependency was the great vice of economic systems which foster inequality; differences in property holdings are soon magnified into differences of social status which are then entrenched as differences of political power. Strikingly, dependency becomes symmetrical. Everyone suffers, though not plausibly in equal measure, when the masters become dependent on their slaves.[26] In *The Phenomenology of Spirit*, Hegel amplifies this criticism of human relationships which are marked by domination and subordination.[27] In disbarring the possibility of mutual recognition, they distort the self-images of the protagonists to the point where they are both incapable of fulfilling their potential as equally human self-consciousnesses. This material, which stresses the psychological damage inflicted in unequal power relationships, has been used to criticize all manner of social dependencies: men/women, husband/wife, employer/employee, imperial power/colony. At its heart is a thesis concerning the personal and social importance of reciprocal, mutual recognition and the necessity of various forms of equality in achieving this.

I concede that this thesis has strong implications for politics; it calls directly for some version of equal citizenship, most evidently that of equal participators in a democratic decision-making procedure. Non-domination, thus construed, amplifies that strand of thinking about liberty which stresses self-control in both its personalized and social versions – important elements in the positive conception as described by Berlin. It is hard to see how non-domination, identified in this narrow fashion, can be used to place limits on a sovereign power which comprises a body of equally powerful citizens.

And yet Mill, famously, and Pettit, latterly, insist that it must. To be fully non-dominating on the republican account the laws must track the interests and values of the citizens.[28] Legislation, however non-dominating its source in democratic institutions, must be non-arbitrary in its content as well. Mill's solution was to insist that legitimate legislation should respect the harm principle – 'the only purpose for which power can be rightfully exercised over any member of a civilised community, against his will, is to prevent harm to others'.[29] Other philosophers have stressed the role of human rights in delineating the proper competence of the sovereign power, howsoever democratic it may be. These are issues we shall broach later. For the moment, let me conclude simply that I cannot see how such restrictions on the content of law-making can be derived from non-domination in the narrow sense that I have sketched. Perhaps a wider one will serve, but we should be wary of losing the clear content of the concept of non-domination as we extend its application. The real lesson we should learn from the republican theory of liberty is the necessary complexity of any persuasive account of the value of political liberty.

The value of freedom

In what follows, I shall attempt to give such an account. First though, let us review our progress so far. We have on the table versions of the ideals of positive and negative liberty charted by Berlin, together with an example of how (and how not) to construct a hybrid theory. All three are candidates for our philosophical allegiance; they have sound analytic credentials. How do we select between them? My suggestion is that we accept as an anchor the thought that political liberty is a value and endorse that account, or construct a fresh one from the assembled ingredients, which best explains why it is precious to us, *in extremis*, why so many have been prepared to die in its cause.

This approach requires us to strike out negative conceptions which stress the intrinsic value of our being able to get what we want without being stopped. Unless what we want is itself of some value, the freedom to pursue it is just about worthless. Contrariwise, and this is the lesson of one way of thinking about positive liberty, the value of liberty is the instrumental value of whatever worthwhile opportunities liberty grants. So, freedom of thought and discussion is valuable because thought and discussion is valuable. Freedom of worship is valuable because religious worship is valuable. And so on. These would be poor liberties, though, if their exercise was compulsory. We would value being able to speak up at Hyde Park Corner a good deal less if we were required to do so once a year. So the *whole* value of liberty cannot be instrumental. In the most impressive recent work on freedom, Joseph Raz suggests that freedom is of value since it is defined as a condition of personal autonomy.[30] But personal autonomy turns out to be a very complex personal and social condition. Whilst acknowledging my debt to Raz's work, I want to develop from scratch – or at least from more classical philosophical material – an elaborate account of freedom which does justice to a range of persuasive views about the value of the condition. In so doing we shall interweave some of the doctrines that have been outlined above.

A theory of freedom is no doubt tidier if it can encompass the traditional problems of free will and free agency as well as the issue of political liberty. Theorists who attempt a unifying theory – Hegel, amongst the great dead; Stanley Benn in modern times[31] – are ambitious, but for many, including John Stuart Mill, confusion and muddle are the intellectual cost of this synthesizing ambition. I have no brief for tidiness against truth, but I do believe that those strands of the positive liberty tradition which emphasize the link between freedom of action, generally considered, and political liberty contain an important insight. To make this point, I need to outline in more detail that strand of thinking about the nature of free action which I mentioned as the first ideal of positive liberty and labelled 'self-control'. Readers who are properly sceptical about my conclusions are invited to pursue the literature on these difficult issues. Readers who are knowledgeable of the literature on free will will recognize what follows as a tendentious gloss.

Freedom of action

We do not act freely when nothing or no one stops us getting what we want, if we have no control over these wants. For many, as we have noticed, the experience of unfreedom is most acutely felt when one pursues the satisfaction of desires he despises himself for suffering. If I know my hands are clean, accept that no good purpose is served by washing them for the umpteenth time this morning, recognize that my obsession disables me from other, better, projects, and still find myself going to the hand-basin – since that, it appears, is what I most want to do, for reasons that are unfathomable to me, I get what I want, but act unfreely. To act freely, reason, in some fashion must be brought to bear on my desires. At its simplest, I must want to want what I try to get, appraising the first-order desires which assail me in the light of second-order desires which operate on them.[32] But not just any second-order wants will serve to establish my freedom. What if I am uncritical, a 'wanton', in respect of my second-order desires?[33] True freedom is realized when actions are determined by desires which are ordered in the light of some conception of the good or are expressive of qualities of character (virtues) produced by strong evaluations of how it is best to live.[34]

This account of free action is not new, although it is certainly fashionable. Important elements of it can be traced in Locke, Rousseau, Kant and, most thoroughly, in Hegel's *Philosophy of Right*. It captures one strand of thinking about autonomous action – we are free when we are in control of what we do, acting against what, phenomenologically, are our strongest desires when this is called for by reason or morality or the ethical demands of communities we recognize as authoritative.

This ancient and modern way of thinking about free action raises many difficult questions which I shall sweep aside for present purposes. There are two central points which I want to lift from these discussions: the first can be expressed in positive or negative fashion; I act freely when I am the author of what I do, when my actions issue, in recognizable fashion, from my own deliberations. Reversing the coin, my freedom is evinced in actions that are not the product of brute nature working through me by prompting desires which I blindly follow. Further, if I follow rules or ordering principles when I oppose, control or select amongst the heteronomous forces that assail me, these are rules which *I* select or endorse. They must pass some test or filter imposed by my capacity for reason, most famously the Kantian rule of the Categorical Imperative. Negatively, they are not alien impositions. They may have been taken on board at the command of some superior authority, be it parent, priest or politician, but such commands will be legitimate only if the commands directly or their putatively authoritative sources have passed some test of rational legitimation. (Some have asked, concerning Kant's Categorical Imperative: Where is the freedom in following rules which are the product of quasi-algorithmic calculation? One answer to this hard question is that the rules which pass the test are not the commands of anyone else.)

The second point we should notice is that freedom of action, far from being constrained by rules or principles of conduct, requires their positive endorsement and efficacious employment. There is a danger that this point may look overly restrictive and overly moralized. Do I not act freely when I select the colour of toothbrush I wish to use? What rules or principles are in play here? Most choices that we make can be effected absent of any moral considerations. When did *you* last take a decision that hinged on scrupulous moral deliberation?

A plausible response to this objection is to claim that free actions must be *sensitive* to appropriate moral considerations when these are in play. The free agent has a moral gyroscope, finely balanced and firmly set. He will be alert to circumstances in which principles of conduct may impact. Suppose there has been trouble and strife in the family caused by careless use of toothbrushes (and what issue is in practice too trivial to disturb domestic harmony?). If Fred has promised that he won't buy a pink one again, alarm bells should ring as he approaches the supermarket shelf. If he is insouciant and thinks only of what colour would match his razor, something has gone wrong. If the alarm bells *never* ring for Fred – and this sort of moral blindness is chronic – we have a case of someone who is not fully in control of his actions. Contrariwise, if Fred thinks through what colour toothbrush to buy in the light of the agreements that he has made and the principles which dictate fidelity to those agreements, his actions are not unfree simply because they are constrained by his moral scrupulousness.

I don't think an acceptable account of political liberty can be *derived* in any thoroughgoing fashion from insights such as these concerning freedom of action. But they are suggestive. They are likely to colour the story told by one who accepts them. They may delineate the contours of the favoured account, as we shall see.

Autonomy

A different starting point can take us towards a similar conclusion. On the starkest conception of negative liberty, that of Hobbes, we act freely when we are not hindered in getting what we want, given that this is physically achievable. Mill, in a careless moment, endorses this account: 'liberty consists in doing what one desires.'[35] The value of freedom can be swiftly inferred. It is the value of getting what we want, doing as we please. Thus put, the value of freedom is instrumental; it amounts to the value of whatever we want, which our freedom is instrumental in enabling us to get. If we are unfree in a given respect, we either cannot get, or can get only at too great a cost or risk (of punishment, generally) whatever is the object of our desire. This account of the value of freedom has the great virtue of being simple and straightforward. Moreover it enables us to rank freedoms in respect of their value to us. This will be a function of the value of the activities that freedom permits. The more important is the object of desire, the more important the freedom to get it, the more serious the restriction in cases where we are made unfree.

The weakness of this account should be evident from our consideration of freedom of action. Although I am prepared to admit the general importance of getting what we want and, *a fortiori*, the freedom that permits us to achieve it, we cannot assume that this is true across the board. What the agent wants may be plain evil – the thrill of causing pain and suffering to someone else – or harmful to the agent himself. In such cases, since the satisfaction of his desire is not itself a good, neither is the freedom to achieve it. We should conclude that freedom is an instrumental good only where there is some positive value to the agent's satisfaction of his desire. If freedom is an intrinsic good, good *per se*, its goodness must be at least, in part, independent of the value of the opportunities it makes available. So even where the choice is that of doing something evil or refraining, the news is not all bad, since there is some positive value to the agent in being able to actively select amongst the options available.

This idea has to be treated very carefully, since it has great intuitive appeal. What is the value of choice? Minimally, choice is just plumping, going for one alternative rather than another with no grounds to guide one's selection. Do I choose heads or tails when you toss a coin, do I put my chips on the red or the black at the roulette table? No doubt I would feel (and be) deprived if you were to both toss the coin and choose heads for me. It would be a funny roulette table were the croupier to place the bets! So the value of choice even in this minimal situation is not negligible. Nonetheless, the value to me of just plumping is not great. The lottery punter who goes for the Lucky Dip rather than selecting her own six numbers has forgone little of value.

But not all choices are as experientially bereft as these. Mill himself dwelt on the value of choice to the chooser. He described what he called 'the distinctive endowment of a human being' as 'the human faculties of perception, judgement, discriminative feeling, mental activity, and even moral preference' and claimed that these 'are exercised only in making a choice'.[36] What sort of choices did Mill have in mind? Clearly it was not choices of the 'heads or tails' variety, nor even more challenging ones, concerning the texture of the anaglypta wallpaper, perhaps. He was concerned rather with choices amongst alternative plans of life.

Again, this is a point which must be advanced carefully. It is not sufficient that we have in mind something like big moral decisions. This is the Kantian value of autonomy. It is realized when human agents deliberate about the right thing to do. They apply the rational will, a transcendental capacity to employ reason to test or generate moral principles in the light of which they thereupon act.

We can grant that Kantian autonomy is exercised under conditions of freedom which permit agents significant opportunities to work out what is the right thing to do, but if this is the core value of freedom we may find that freedom does not provide the best circumstances in which autonomy may be developed. In the aptly named 'Kantian Gulag',[37] Flint Schier points out that

> autonomy can flourish under the most oppressive and despotic regimes. Poets like Mandelstam and Akhmatova continued to produce their own poetry even in the darkest moments of Stalinist terror and repression. Bruno Bettelheim has told us how communists and priests in particular were able to maintain their moral gyroscopes even in the grotesquely convulsed circumstances of Nazi concentration camps.

Schier noticed how survivors of the camps could *fear* freedom, anticipating that the free life would not have the moral density experienced in surroundings where daily life was fraught by decisions concerning how best to live a life of moral integrity. It can be a hard decision that one should look one's captors in the eye. And to do so continually can be a hard and risky policy. It is no surprise that those who left the camps, especially those who took up a comfortable life in the USA, Western Europe or Israel, were prone to deplore the superficiality of the culture they embraced, contrasting it unfavourably with the horrors they had escaped in respect of the opportunities it afforded for a life of deep moral seriousness.

What is missing from life in the Gulag is the freedom to live one's life in accordance with goals of one's own choosing.[38] Mill's notion of a plan of life is central here, so long as we do not read his prescription in too literal a fashion. Encouraged by talk of agents as authors of their own life, constructors of their own life-narrative, one may construe this ideal in implausibly dramatic terms. Politicians, writing their autobiographies, encourage us to do so when they portray the happenstance of a successful climb up the greasy pole as the successful implementation of youthful designs executed on the back of an envelope. We can write the story for them. Success at school is to be followed by an Oxford Scholarship. Stunning reviews for her role of Portia in a garden production of Merchant of Venice will accustom her for future glory as President of the Union. After a few years in the city or at the bar, having earned a fortune, she will stand for Parliament in a by-election. Swift promotion will see her as Prime Minister at the door of 10 Downing Street – and out come the family photographs of her posing with policeman and proud parents in the same doorway, thirty years before.

This should *not* be our model of an autonomous life. Mostly, autonomous agents will see their lives as a muddle, but their *own* muddle, a series of advances and withdrawals meeting with moderate success and some (perhaps frequent) failure. Far from being a blueprint resolutely followed, the autonomous life will be identified retrospectively as the agent claims *responsibility* for the courses she has followed and the streams down which she has drifted.

We must not make the autonomous life too heroic an aspiration. The modest measure of autonomy I have described requires a societal framework where pathways are available for exploration even if the traveller is likely to take a wrong turn or get lost. Negatively, gates must be open; positively, capacities must be developed as agents are empowered to select amongst realistic or challenging options. We know well the sort of blocks to autonomy that our fellows can meet. Parents may project their own ambitions on to a docile child and go to their grave unsuspecting that their doctor son hates his patients and his profession. Schools may go about their business educating their charges to be the workforce of the mine or mill, long after the mills and mines have closed, unsuspecting of the talents they ignore and so fail to foster. The conformist traditions of a well-disciplined community may induce social paranoia in otherwise generous and outgoing souls. And states, following the middle road to electoral success and hence pandering to perceived majorities, may suffocate what Mill called experiments in living. The widespread achievement of a sufficient measure of even that modest variety of autonomy I have described requires a tolerant public ethos as well as strong liberal institutions. It should not be authority's grudging tribute to mankind's natural bloody-mindedness.

'A poor life, but mine own' characterizes the sort of autonomy a society can realistically aspire to on behalf of its members. It need

not educate them to be career planners of business school proportions. Does this do justice to the generous liberal ideal? Is this a
morally worthy goal?

It must be confessed that it falls short of one well-known model –
that of the life organized around an individual ideal.[39] Ideals of the
sort I have in mind may be thought to give meaning to the lives of
their proponents and hence, though they do not prescribe universal ends, they do have a moral tinge to them. Any account of the
phenomenon of ethics which ignored them would be incomplete.
Thus we might admire a life devoted to public service or religious
devotion. We may recognize as worthy practices of asceticism and
stoical self-discipline. A life devoted to art, as practitioner or as
connoisseur, may command a similar respect in many quarters.
And we should not ignore the value of loyal domesticity. Such
ideals fade into pursuits which may be equally demanding but are
barely ethical except perhaps for their display of executive virtues
– intelligence, foresight, resolution, indeed many items on Mill's
list of distinctive human endowments. Thus one may be fully committed to a career or a club, or both together in the case of political advancement. We see the shadow of asceticism in the pursuit
of good health, organic vegetables, personal trainers and the like.
We are well used to the idea of lifestyle choices, having glossy
embodiments of them paraded daily in newspapers and magazines.

Respect for autonomy demands acceptance of others' devotion
to a range of moral ideals to which one may not subscribe – and to
which one may be hostile. (I shall discuss the issue of toleration
later.) But the pursuit of an autonomous life need not involve such
all-consuming aspirations. Self-realization need not be so strenuous an exercise as liberals have portrayed it.[40] An autonomous life
single-mindedly engaged in the pursuit of a great ideal evidently
requires appropriate freedoms – but so does that species of autonomy which is displayed in less exalted enthusiasms, stamp-
collecting or bird-watching, perhaps, or a range of enthusiasms
conducted by Jack-of-all-trades. So, too, does the unsettled and
wide-ranging pursuit of fancy, trying this and that as a means of
occupying leisure time, a different evening class every winter, none
producing true mastery. In each case we find humans balancing,
compromising or sacrificing conflicting demands on their active
attention and fashioning a life out of the debris.

On my account freedom is justified as instrumental to the worthy activities it permits and as the necessary precondition of an autonomous life. Why is autonomy a good? We shall have more to say on this question when we discuss rights in the next chapter. But as a hint to my way of responding to it, I invite readers to consider whether or not, after due deliberation, they desire it and believe, in consequence, that the demands of others for it should be respected. If this question seems too abstract, focus on the denial of autonomy, and consider whether you are averse to that in its characteristic manifestations. If your philosophical temperament inclines to a more ambitious and more soundly anchored way of thinking, you will see autonomy as a *jewel*, as expressive of mankind's rational will, the transcendent capacity to reach beyond the trammels of our natural state towards a spiritual, even Godlike facility of self-creation.

If so, a *Philosophical Health Warning* should be issued. Think of the man who is mistaken. He believes that humans should adopt something akin to the sexual lives of pygmy chimpanzees. He accepts the Freudian story about infantile sexuality and believes that children are a legitimate target of his desires. He accepts that his community excoriates his attitudes and so takes them underground. Gathering appropriate degrees and diplomas, he works his way into positions of responsibility, say, manager of a children's home, and expresses his sexuality by the physical and mental abuse of the children in his care. He then lives a life of appropriate, careful, pleasure. Absent of any considerations about the sources of his sexual appetites, this is an autonomous life – indeed it is unusual in respect of the cleverness and forethought that has been invested in its plan. Is this a model of the good life?

It would be, if the executive virtues were all that is necessary for its success. A denser exhibition of the executive virtues would be hard to find, excepting the prescient politician I described above. Still, we should accept that autonomy, without its Kantian overtones of sound moral judgement, may be the source of the greatest evil. There are two ways forward here: either we can *moralize* the notion of autonomy so that the autonomous agent does no wrong (the Kantian route) or we can accept the possibility of autonomous evil.

We should stick fast to the insight that freedom is a good. In which case, we should modify our understanding of autonomy or accept that its connection with freedom is contingent. If autonomous action can be evil, freedom cannot be vindicated as the expression of an autonomous will. If we take the Kantian route, we need to say more about autonomous action to disbar the possibility of autonomous wrong-doing. Why not return to our sources in Rousseau, try to work out what moral liberty requires and develop a more robust theory of positive liberty?

Moral freedom

On Rousseau's account, this is the freedom which is attained by those who can control their own desires. It is developed further in Kant's account of autonomous willing which stresses how we bring to bear our resources of rational deliberation in the face of our heteronomous desires, those desires which we are caused to suffer by the nexus of our (internal) human nature and (external) nature. If we follow reason's guidance we shall act freely, willing actions which it must be possible in principle for all to accomplish, laws which all must be able to follow. Kant's account suggests to many a strenuous form of moral athleticism; actions of moral worth are the product of a continuing internal struggle wherein agents wrestle with temptation. 'Do with repugnance what duty commands'[41] is one caricature of this style of morality.

Rousseau, writing before Kant, believed that this stern conception of duty expects too much of us. We are weaker creatures than Kant believes us to be, not least because our moral natures have been corrupted by the degenerate society which is the product of human history. We do not have the personal resources to consistently act well. Perhaps weakness of will, exhibited through our knowledge of what is right and our inability to achieve it, has become a social malaise. We recognize that social remedies are needed to cure what has become a social problem. This is the third ideal of positive liberty canvassed above. The state, making laws in accordance with the general will (of which more in Chapter 7) provides the collective resource we require. In a society where subjects endorse the rules of the sovereign – for Rousseau, a direct democracy – and accept that these should be backed by sanctions, citizens force themselves to be free by subjecting themselves to a common discipline. They give themselves additional (prudential) reasons to behave well, recognizing their (and others') susceptibility to go astray.

We can see this sort of reasoning at work in the case of laws which prohibit theft. Grant that I believe it is wrong to steal, right to respect the private property of others. But I also believe that I, along with many others would be severely tempted to steal if I were hard pressed and could escape with impunity. On these assumptions, I should have no objection to such a law, indeed may welcome it as improving the likelihood that I shall act well. Furthermore, I recognize, as a property holder, that my freedom is enhanced by the restrictions which such a law places on others. It makes them less likely to interfere with the use I may make of the property I own. My freedom is protected by laws which guard a domain where my own decisions and choices are decisive. Self-interested agents will look for a beneficial trade-off between the surrender of their own powers to take or use the property of others and the augmentation of their own powers of self-protection which the authority of the state can effect. Moral agents will see no loss. Of course they welcome the limitation of the powers of others who would inhibit their freedom but the surrender of their own powers to do wrong is something they equally endorse.

This story, of autonomous agents, willingly and rationally subjecting themselves to the coercive powers of the state, will be explored in Chapter 6, where we examine the grounds of political obligation. For the moment, the lesson to be taken is that laws which keep us and our fellow citizens on what we recognize to be the straight and narrow path of duty do not infringe our liberty.

As Berlin saw clearly, this is a dangerous argument, and the danger comes from two different quarters. First, there is the obvious threat that *others* may determine what our duty requires and then regiment us to perform it. This danger is avoided so long as we insist that the moral liberty which is achieved by state coercion be the product of political liberty, of democratic institutions. The second threat is that democratic majorities may get it wrong, proscribing under penalty of imprisonment and like measures of punishment activities which are innocent. Since the decisions of democratic bodies do not of themselves constitute verdicts on what is or is not morally acceptable, this is a permanent possibility. The pursuit of moral liberty may land us in political chains.

There are a number of complementary answers to this problem. The first is that we should buttress our specification of the institutions which promote political liberty with some condition that sets limits on the competence of the democratic decision procedures. Mill's harm principle sets out to do this, as do declarations of human rights which are embedded in the constitution of the state or which operate as supra-national conventions. The second, an explicit implication of Mill's principle, is a public recognition that the wrongs which may be prohibited consistently with liberty do not include wrongs which citizens may do to themselves alone – this is the issue of paternalism. Both of these questions will be taken up in what follows. The third issue is difficult and concerns the problem of toleration.

Toleration

If there can be such a thing as a liberal virtue, it is toleration. But, as one commentator has said 'it seems to be at once necessary and impossible'.[42] Toleration is necessary because folk who live together may find that there are deep differences between their moral beliefs which cannot be settled by argument from agreed premises. It is impossible because the circumstances of deep conflict which call for the exercise of toleration are all too often described in terms of the obtuseness and stubbornness of the conflicting parties. These differences, historically, have been of a kind that causes savage conflict. The point of disagreement may seem trivial to a neutral observer – is the bread and wine consumed at the Eucharist the real body and blood of Christ transubstantiated in the ritual or is it a representation? (I use this example because I heard it used *recently* by an extreme Protestant bigot to establish the metaphysical foundations of his duty to provoke and assault Roman Catholics, kicking them for preference, especially after soccer matches!) From disputes as arcane (to non-believers) as this, moral disagreements swiftly follow. Moral disagreements are *always* serious – I would say, by definition.

I want to approach the problem of toleration obliquely by

looking briefly at what I believe is a cognate problem – that of weakness of will. There are severe (and ancient) philosophical problems created by the phenomenon of weakness of will. How can people *know* what is the best thing to do and then do something else? The problem of toleration has a similar structure: How can people know what is the wrong thing for someone else to do and not stop it? Philosophers divide in respect of the problem of weakness of will. Some dissolve the difficulty by insisting that there are no such cases. If you *really* knew what was the right thing to do, you would do it. If you don't do it, you don't really know. Or you really know, but somehow your knowledge is not engaged in the decision you take. Your knowledge is overwhelmed by the power of your emotions, by your passionate commitments. Or there is some other story (e.g. you were drunk at the time) to explain why your knowledge of what is best didn't motivate you – and philosophers are imaginative in coming up with the sort of stories necessary to defend their theses.[43] Opponents insist that it is still possible, once we have discounted those cases where plausible stories may be told, that a moral agent may recognize the right thing to do – and then do something else.

Exactly the same structure of dispute can be unearthed with respect to toleration. Toleration is appropriate when we cannot expect to persuade someone with different views of the rights and wrongs of an issue. No matter how strong our beliefs or convictions, no matter how deep our feelings of certainty, no matter how articulate or eloquent our pleadings or how forceful our arguments, when we try to convince others we hit a brick wall. They are wrong – but we don't seem to be able to do anything about it. They're truly, madly, deeply, wrong but, as with the best of friends who fall in love with absolutely the wrong person, we can't get them to see their error. In which case why don't we just stop them doing wrong? The doctrine of toleration insists that there are cases where, for all our belief that others are acting wrongly, it would be wrong for us to stop them. But what, other than a belief that others are doing wrong, can *ever* be legitimate grounds for our stopping them?

Historically, doctrines of toleration developed as a response to the wars of religion in seventeenth-century Europe. It was discovered, the hard way, that whilst threats of death, torture, imprisonment and the rest may serve for a time to get people to behave in ways they would otherwise resist, no amount of coercion can command others' beliefs. The very model of a ludicrous public policy is that of 'forced conversion'; read Browning's poem 'Holy Cross Day', the most sardonic poem in English, for an account of the sentiments of Jews forced to attend an annual Christian sermon in Rome and watch a dozen of their company converted publicly to the true faith. (The Jews regularly surrendered up their thieves and vagabonds to this silly ritual, on Browning's account.)

We know that disputes of this order of seriousness generally have their origins in religion. Or religion and ethnicity. Or religion and sexuality. The modern form in which such problems arise is often cast as the problem of multicultural citizenship.[44] To my knowledge, neither individuals nor tribes fight about the permissibility of murder, though the religious doctrines to which they subscribe may permit or require the death of unbelievers.

Toleration, as I have described it, requires one not to interfere in conduct which one believes to be morally wrong. Why do we not leap to the conclusion, in cases where we do not think that we should interfere with the conduct of others, that we don't really believe it to be wrong? This thought, I believe, captures the liberal instinct. Let us look at some standard cases.

Think of a state with majority and minority religions, or more generally, one with religious divisions and where the power to legislate is in the hands of one religious community alone. Should the state tolerate those who do wrong in the minds of the legislators by breaking the dietary laws their religion prescribes? At least one dimension to this issue, which can go proxy for many other differences of religiously sanctioned morality, is whether the question is a truly moral one at all. Briefly, it may be argued that morality has a universal dimension which is belied by one who conceives its source to be an authoritative religious text. Of course, the believer will affirm the universal authority of the prescriptions – one can't expect such problems to be so swiftly settled – but the direction of the liberal argument can be easily grasped. The question of toleration does not arise, it is suggested, since the activities up for proscription are not truly wrong.

Consider similarly proscriptions on the travel or opportunities to earn a living of some ethnic group. Again the problem does not arise for one who believes that one does no wrong who sits at the front of buses or on park benches designated for others. Exactly the same issue arises with respect to areas of sexual conduct. Homosexuals, for example, will protest that it is an error (and worse) to regard permissive legislation as tolerance since they do no wrong.

In other areas of conduct, again, it may be mistaken to speak of tolerance, with the clear implication that the permitted behaviour is wrong. The point here may not be that one can confidently deny the immorality of the actions some would prescribe, but that the moral issues are not clear. If one can see two sides to a question, as may happen where one accepts that the moot behaviour is often wrong but may sometimes be justified, we may have instances of doubt inhibiting firm moral judgement. For many people, the rights and wrongs of abortion are clouded in just this fashion. If one does not believe firmly that such activities are wrong across the board, one's hesitancy may lead one to deny that toleration is at issue. This is especially true where the complexities of the circumstances afford a privileged perspective on the immediate circumstances to the agent who proposes to behave in the controversial manner. In judging that it is best to leave the decision on how to act up to the agents concerned, since they are in the best position to work out the implications of what they are doing, again one is claiming that tolerance is not an issue here.

Finally, and cases of this sort are akin to those where paternalism is an issue, there may be issues where the rights and wrongs of the matter just are a matter of personal decision. It is not a matter now of modesty, of leaving a decision to the person who can best decide the question. Rather the point is that the individual agent who is faced with the choice is the *only* person who can settle the matter. It is not easy to find examples which are not tainted by extraneous considerations (or marked by the tracks of some other philosophical agenda), but perhaps suicide and voluntary euthanasia are like that. Although in some cultures marriages are arranged, the liberal is likely to believe no wrong is done by the obstinate child who will not accept her parents' directions, since at bottom the right marriage partner is the one who is accepted or selected by the aspirant bride. If we distinguish, in the manner of Strawson, social morality and the individual ideal, we may be prepared to admit conflicting judgements with respect to conduct which may be endorsed and criticized from the perspective of different ideals. This may be an important site for identifying both the legitimacy of some degree of moral relativism and a correponding requirement of a measure of toleration.

Does this leave any cases of clear, generally acknowledged, wrong-doing which agents should be permitted to perpetrate? I am inclined to think, putting aside questions of moral duty to oneself and the issue of paternalism, that the only cases will be those where, as Mill insisted, proscription is too costly, where regimes which impose sanctions would be too intrusive. This is evidently true where the coercive regime is that of the state, less obviously so where the interference envisaged are social mechanisms of disapproval, disrespect or ostracism.

To conclude, we can see that modern nation-states exhibit striking differences of view concerning the acceptability or immorality of a range of practices. This is the reality of multiculturalism in all its dimensions. In the face of these differences and our knowledge of how easily they generate severe and historically long-lasting conflicts, modern democratic citizens should be modest in their claims to the sort of moral knowledge that may underpin the persecution of one community of persons by another. We should not be relativists about ethics of the stripe that insists that right and wrong generally is simply a function of the given practices of the communities of which different citizens find themselves members. This exacerbates rather than solves the problem of conflict wherever the parochial 'morality' makes claim to universal applicability. Far better that we be fallibilists when we recognize the fact of deep differences. Personal or societal humility in the face of a range of divergent prescriptions on how to live best is the strongest constraint on democratic majorities.

Free states and free citizens

Thus far, I have examined a number of different theories or analyses of the nature of freedom and discussed several different accounts of what gives freedom its value or explains its appeal. In the rest of this chapter, I shall draw these strands together in a complex account of the institutional framework which freedom requires. I shall organize this material around the insights of Rousseau. His account assembles the core materials of the theory I advocate, though we shall range beyond these sources in our exposition.

In the state of nature, Rousseau tells us, our freedom derives from our free will, our capacity to resist the desires which press us, together with our status as independent creatures, neither subject to the demands of others nor dependent on them to get what we want. We shall, as contractors, be satisfied with nothing less than that social state which best approximates to this natural condition. Natural freedom is lost, but the thought of it gives us a moral benchmark by which we can appraise (and, inevitably, on Rousseau's pessimistic account, criticize) the institutions of contemporary society. In society, a measure of freedom can be recovered along three dimensions: moral freedom we have already discussed, democratic freedom and civil freedom remain to be examined. I shall outline these in turn, departing from their source in Rousseau's work without scruple. We shall be systematizing many of the insights concerning freedom which have been unearthed in our previous discussions.

Democratic freedom

Since I shall have more to say about democracy later, I shall limit my discussion of it here. The essence of the case for democracy as a dimension of freedom is simple: democracy affords its citizens the opportunity to participate in making the decisions which, as laws, will govern their conduct. For Kant, autonomous action consists in living in accordance with the laws which one has determined for oneself as possible for each agent to follow. Democracy represents a rough political analogue of this model: freedom consists in living in accordance with laws one has created (alongside other voters) as applicable to all citizens, oneself included.

Berlin, as we have seen, argued that democracy is a very different ideal to liberty – majority decisions can threaten liberty, as J.S. Mill argued. It is a mistake to view this consideration, plausible though it may be, as decisive.[45]

The most obvious reason for rejecting it has the force of a *tu quoque* objection. Any system other than democracy will deny citizens the opportunity to engage in an activity that many regard as valuable. We know that many citizens are apathetic to the opportunity of voting, but in a mature democracy many others are keen to participate. They join political parties, paying an annual subscription where necessary, they go along to meetings of their local active group, they distribute leaflets and canvass support during elections. This may or may not be in pursuit of an ambition to hold office in a representative system. Either way, this is a respectable use of one's leisure time. Others may opt for a less onerous measure of political activity – voting at elections or referenda may suffice. Some may have no interest at all in political affairs, but for those who have, voting, minimally, and the life of a professional politician, maximally, represent opportunities best made available in a democratic system. The strictest negative theorist recognizes that laws which prevent the expression of political opinions are limitations on liberty, as are laws which forbid religious worship or group meetings. It is hard to see why one cannot draw the same conclusion in respect of constitutional arrangements which deny citizens the opportunity of acting in ways characteristic of the democratic participant. Just as soon as we focus on the kind of things politically motivated citizens wish to do, we see that Berlin's two questions find the same answer: political arrangements should permit the exercise of political power by citizens who desire to take an active part in the control of their state. They are free for two reasons: they engage in the activities which are decisive in respect of how they are governed, which opportunities are granted and secured by law.

It has often been pointed out that the analogy between self-control and the exercise of political power by participant voters is weak in a modern democracy. Rousseau accepted that the degree of political power exercised by participating citizens is in inverse proportion to the size of the participant community. Modern commentators have gleefully noted that this power may be effectively nil.[46] No single vote has been decisive in a British parliamentary election this century.

Citizens who vote in large-scale elections may be wiser than these observers. Even in the most attenuated representative systems some chance of a little power is available for those who pursue it – someone has to be President or Prime Minister, after all – but for most voters something other than a deluded ambition for power motivates their visit to the polling booth. Voting offers participant citizens the opportunity to endorse both the system for taking political decisions and the decisions which are the outcome of the operation of that system. If the democracy is representative in form, where enough other people wish to do so, they are free to change the representatives and the government which they compose. Equally, the opportunity to abstain or spoil a paper offers one the opportunity to protest the system and its works. In the same way, however much a rigmarole the application of the Categorical Imperative may be for Kant's moral agent, its exercise is an insistence that putative moral principles must be subjected to her own rational legitimation and cannot be the imposition of some external authority. In the political sphere, as in the moral, there is no shortage of claimants to this sort of authority. Democratic activity gives us the chance to assert that we are free of them. Democracy may be necessary to freedom, but it carries its own distinctive threats. Can these threats be disarmed?

Civil liberty

So it is important that we tackle directly the question that concerned John Stuart Mill so strongly – to the point where he published *On Liberty*: What are the limits that may be placed upon citizens who would interfere with the activities of their fellows, most perspicuously by their legislative activities, but most powerfully perhaps by the social pressures which lead to conformity? The account of liberty that I have given seems to place citizens at the mercy of majorities which operate with a limited or controversial conception of the public good and which are activist in its pursuit.

It is really important here to sort out the philosophical issues from the practical problem. So far as the philosophical issues are concerned, I am on the side of Rousseau. Citizens who value liberty and express this through their participation in democratic institutions which liberty requires will, in all consistency, be reluctant to interfere in the lives of their fellows, whether by law or less formal mechanisms. Their deep concern to establish institutions which empower everyone will make them cautious about introducing measures which constrain individual choice. Accepting the necessity of democratic institutions and their associated freedoms, valuing strongly the opportunities these afford for citizens to embody their various conceptions of the good life in constitutional and prescriptive laws, they will be hesitant to constrain their own pursuit of these values. What makes it necessary for them to countenance restrictions on their own law-making powers?

Nothing less than the thought that the values and sentiments which they endorse may be insufficient to accomplish the ends they seek. To the rational man, it is a miserable thought that others may defy the canons of rationality. Second-best rules may be called for which mimic the rules of reason in the ends they produce. So we ask claimants who cannot agree on the most reasonable rule of precedence to toss a coin – and produce some semblance of fairness. The political philosopher, likewise, has to accommodate embarassing facts which suggest that the highest standards of reflective conduct may not be endorsed by the community to which her arguments are addressed. Again this calls for an articulation of the second-best solution. Just as we are prepared to approve external constraints on our own decision-making, recognizing our vulnerability to temptation, so, too, must we be prepared to adopt institutions which guard against the worst of human folly. This is the place of the harm principle and other limitations on the societal weaknesses which democracies may reflect and amplify.

Mill's harm principle

In practice, liberty requires that law-making institutions, together with a society's informal but effective coercive powers, respect some limits of principle. The 'one very simple principle' which John Stuart Mill recommended reads as follows:

> that the sole end for which mankind are warranted, individually or collectively, in interfering with the liberty of action of any of

their number, is self-protection. That the only purpose for which power can be rightfully exercised over any member of a civilised community, against his will, is to prevent harm to others. His own good, either physical or moral, is not a sufficient warrant.[47]

An alternative principle requires institutions to respect the *rights* of their citizens. This block on institutional powers may be embedded in constitutions, as that of the United States, and the guardianship of this check on the executive and various legislative powers – from the President and Congress to mayors and town meetings – is vested in an independent judiciary with powers to review and strike down offending acts. I shall examine this proposal later.

Let us return to Mill's harm principle. We can see how it works; it expresses a *necessary* condition on the legitimacy of proposed interference, i.e. it details a test that proposals must satisfy. The burden of proof is thus placed on those who would limit our liberty; they must show that the putatively illegitimate conduct causes harm to others. It is a necessary but not sufficient condition on the justification of interference, Mill insists. He envisages plenty of cases where actions of a given type may cause harm to others, yet interference would be unwise. The costs of policing a general law against breaking promises, for example, would be excessive. Or perhaps the harmful conduct is of a type that promises incidental benefit. Business practices which make competitors bankrupt may be necessary elements of a system that is beneficial overall.

Mill's condition has been widely criticized from the moment of first publication. We shall examine some of the leading criticisms in due course. He made one indisputable error however, notably his claim that the principle is a 'very simple' one. Simple it is not. In the first place, we need a more careful analysis of harm than Mill himself provides. Recent literature supports two very different proposals. Judith Jarvis Thomson[48] defends a narrow conception of harm which identifies as core cases bodily and psychological impairment and physical disfigurement. Distress – feelings of pain and nausea, for example – is not harm, though it can cause harm, psychological harm, notably. On this account, Jim is not harmed if his car is stolen or the money under his mattress is burnt. By contrast, Joel Feinberg analyses harm in a much more capacious fashion.[49] Harm, as the term is employed in the harm principle, is a setback or invasion of a person's interest and the most characteristic interests are what he calls 'welfare interests', construed as 'the basic requisites of a man's well-being'.[50] There is perhaps no real dispute here; Feinberg's notion of harm is constructed with the defence of a harm principle in view, Thomson's is not. The implication is clear, though; if the harm principle is to operate as a *sharp* constraint on legitimate government interference, the concept of harm which is employed should permit disputes to be settled concerning whether action is harmless or not. Feinberg shows that this task is not easy. As ever, common sense needs sensitive articulation and careful defence. Let us assume this task of clarification can be accomplished – and move on.

Perhaps the most serious objection to the application of the principle to the purpose it is required to serve concerns the ubiquity of harm. Any act, it is observed, does or may cause harm to others.[51] This claim is either wrong or misguided. Since there are plenty of harmless actions (including, hopefully, my typing this sentence) the burden of the objection falls on the thought that any act *may* cause harm to others. If this were true, in the spirit of the objection, then the harm principle would fail to achieve its purpose of demarcating, on the one hand, a legitimate area of social interference and, on the other, a domain of personal decision beyond the legitimate reach of coercive agencies. All activities would be in principle liable to intervention and regulation.

What does the objector have in mind? Presumably, we are invited to take an example of an ostensibly harmless action and then show that circumstances may be described in which an action of that type causes indisputable harm. Thus, as a rule no harm is done by one's throwing a stone in a pond, but is easy to imagine cases where clear harm follows. The stone hits a diver who is just emerging from the water or it causes the water to rise to the critical level where the next flood will cause it to break its bank and flood the village or . . . The possibilities are endless. And so they are for any candidate harmless action. We are invited to conclude that actions of the type described are all possible objects of legislation. The argument, as put, embodies a serious type–token confusion.

(We talk about *types* in generalizations, thus 'The corncrake is a noisy creature, rarely seen nowadays though common last century' describes a type of bird. 'Theft goes rarely undiscovered' describes a type of activity. We speak of *tokens* when we speak of particulars, say e.g. 'The corncrake in the hay-field has raised three chicks' or 'The theft of my car was distressing'.) Actions are proscribed, by law or positive moralities which have coercive power, as types, not as tokens. Laws, and by implication, conditions which constrain their legitimacy such as the harm principle, address types of action rather than tokens, and so the issue to be considered by any court Sally has to face will be: Was her action of such a type as is proscribed by law? In the sort of cases described above, where harm *is* caused, the questions to be asked by the legislative and judicial institutions which review the details are, in the legislative context: Should we prohibit stone-throwing into ponds or should we rely on catch-all legislation covering negligence and putting others at risk? In the judicial context, it would be surprising if questions were raised concerning anything other than direct infliction of injury (perhaps the pond is a training area for divers) or, again, negligence. In all cases, questions about the agent's knowledge of the likely effects and her consequent intentions will be relevant.

So we shouldn't see the harm principle as the bluntest of blunt instruments. We should see it as operating, in the clearest case, as a constraint on the sort of action descriptions which can feature in legal or quasi-legal proscriptions. 'Assault and battery' is an obvious example of an action-type, tokens of which necessarily cause harm. 'Throwing stones into ponds' does not have this property. Obviously there are all kinds of action where the issue concerns the likely incidence or probability of token actions causing harm – too high, I assume, in the case of driving while drunk or at 50m.p.h. in a built-up area. Where probabilities or threshold effects are relevant, we encounter a grey area which no philosophical judgement can illuminate. Legislators and the sort of opinion-formers who guide the application of unofficial sanctions will have to debate and negotiate a trade-off between liberty and the prevention of some incidence of harm. The liberal, by instinct, counsels against panic measures. The timid press anxiety into legislative service. Both do right when they focus on the facts of the matter concerning harm and the risk of harm – and this is what the harm principle requires.[52]

One final objection to the harm principle hypothesizes the possibility of harmless actions in respect of which there can be no doubt that proscriptions and sanctions are appropriate. Gordon Graham discusses a series of examples which he believes show that the harm principle cannot work as the sole necessary condition.[53] My variation on his theme is the case of the Dirty Dentist – a familiar figure from the Sunday tabloids of my adolescence, devoured in those days as the most explicit media of sex education. The Dirty Dentist used to fondle the genitalia of patients whilst they were under general anaesthetic for a filling, there being no requirement that a nurse or assistant be in the room during the treatment. On recovery, we presume, they were all ignorant of the Dentist's assault. Were the patients harmed by their service to the dentist? Does the Peeping Tom harm the blithe and blissful objects of his smutty attentions? Graham thinks not – but is in no doubt that these activities should be prohibited. In which case we have to find grounds other than the harm principle for doing so. In which case, the principle is neither a necessary nor sufficient condition on the legitimacy of interference. Graham's solution is to advocate a principle of individual rights. When the dentist fondles his patients, he invades their rights – to bodily integrity or privacy. That is the substance of the case for making his conduct illegal, not the false claim that he harms them.

I see three ways forward here. First, one might substitute the Rights Condition for the harm principle as necessary to justify intervention. To be legitimate, legislation which interferes with citizens' agency must prevent them violating the rights of others. Second, one might supplement the harm principle, insisting that justifiable legislation *either* prevent harm to others *or* protect individuals' rights. (This is Graham's proposal.) Third, the harm principle may be defended – in which case some argument will need to be devised which establishes that harm is caused after all in the cases discussed. My preferred solution would be the last, but the argument will have to take a devious route. In brief, and to anticipate the conclusions of Chapter 4, I believe the ascription of rights requires that we describe the interests of individuals which rights claims typically protect. But since the violation of rights claims *ex*

hypothesi invades specifiable interests, and since the invasion or
setback of an interest constitutes harm, rights violations will generally be harmful – in the relaxed sense that actions of this type
will tend to cause harm. The hard task in cases like those of the
Dirty Dentist or Peeping Tom will be that of vindicating the right
which is violated. Most readers, I suspect, will believe that this can
be accomplished, but philosophers should not take for granted the
success of the enterprise. There is work to be done, but when it is
done I think two jobs will have been done at the same time. Not
only shall we have justified the right which underpins the legitimacy of the proposed interference, we shall have described clearly
and fully the harm such interference prevents.

Supplementary principles

If the theorist who accepts some version of the harm principle
cannot accept all cases of rights violation as species of harm, the
principle will need supplementation in the way we have seen. Are
there any other principles which have been found appropriate to
justify the range of governmental and unofficial interference?[54] If
there are, these will operate as just-about-sufficient conditions,
discounting the cost of legislation and enforcement. As described
they may or may not include the class of harmful actions, so they
may operate, if successfully defended, as a supplement to the harm
principle, working as conditions which are disjunctively necessary,
i.e. a full account of the necessary conditions for interference to be
legitimate will specify as proper cases that either harm is caused
or . . ., as the conditions are introduced. Three well-known candidates include moralism, an offence principle and paternalism.

Legal moralism

The legal moralist claims that interference is justified if it prevents immoral or wrongful acts. If this principle were acceptable,
we should note straight away that it would incorporate the harm
principle as I have explained it, since the harms which may be
legitimately prohibited are those types of harm which it would be
morally wrong to inflict on others. Clearly, in order to evaluate

such a principle as a supplement (or alternative) to the harm principle, we need to find a class of actions which are morally wrong yet do not involve harm or the risk of harm to others. It is notoriously hard to find any such class which can be demarcated with confidence.

Two sorts of case have been described. The first concerns actions the wrongfulness of which derives from self-harm or the agent's failure to comply with some duty that she holds to herself. I shall discuss this later under the heading of paternalism. The second sort has most often involved sexual behaviour, solitary or consensual, which is somehow not respectable. Unmarried or extra-marital sex, sex with contraceptives, homosexual relationships, sex with prostitutes, sado-masochism: the list of types of sexual behaviour which have been deemed immoral, and impermissible by implication, is as endless as the varieties of expressing human sexuality seem to be. If the behaviour is fully informed and consensual, I take it that it is either harmless or a type of harm to self. The thought that some sex is rational, all else irrational, strikes me as ludicrous, unless the rationality is strictly means–end and the end specified is such as the propagation of believers in the true faith or heirs to the throne – as good examples as any of rationality in the service of dangerous or cruel masters.

The only philosophical point at the bottom of all such suspicious prohibitions is the claim that communities are right to prohibit deviant (but, *ex hypothesi*, harmless) behaviour on the grounds that conformity to standard practice is either necessary for the survival of the community or integral to the very idea of community itself. Thank God (he says, letting slip his liberal credentials), both arguments can be strongly challenged.

The positive (actual) morality of any community comes all of a piece, Devlin tells us.[55] A 'seamless web', as his most prominent critic put it, though Devlin gently demurred. It is a structure of belief and practice which must remain intact if any society is to succeed in its collective goals. If particular moral beliefs are challenged or specific practices undermined, the community can respond by refuting the challenge or supporting the practice or, if the challenge is successful, it can disintegrate. The stakes are high. So high as to justify legislation which supports the practices of common morality. Principles governing the acceptability of sexual behaviour will be among the components of this web – in which case it will be otiose to ask what harm is or would be done by any particular practice. It is enough to know that it is deemed immoral.

Devlin's position was effectively refuted by H.L.A. Hart,[56] at least to my satisfaction. In the first place, he pointed out that Devlin's argument may be taken as an *a priori* claim that a society is constituted by its morality. If the morality of a society changes, so, *a fortiori*, does that society. We now have a different society. But that definitional claim is insufficient to ground the claim that a society may protect itself against *change* by the use of legal and social sanctions. The newborn society, constituted by its altered positive morality, may be an improvement on its predecessor. Unless Devlin's argument is underpinned by an (indefensible) claim that all change is for the worse, the demise of the old and the birth of the new may be cause for celebration rather than regret.

If, on the other hand, Devlin's claim is substantial rather than definitional, again it is open to challenge. At first inspection, it looks like an application rather than a refutation of the harm principle. It works as a high-level empirical claim, a generalization to the effect that the consequences of challenges to established moral practices are invariably harmful. If this is true, it is something the harm theorist can willingly take into account. Indeed it would comprise just the sort of information that must be taken into account when assessing the harmfulness of practices. So the next question is obvious. Do all changes in moral beliefs and practices cause harm to the point where immorality in general may be proscribed? No sooner is the question put than we can see how silly it is. Everyone is at liberty to select a firmly held, deeply entrenched moral belief which was integral to the operation of a specific society, yet which was clearly wrong (as well as damaging, both to individuals and the society as a whole). 'Some humans are natural slaves' is a good example. Hence the thesis, taken in full generality, falls. The specific proposals for change which were the occasion of Devlin's lecture – reform of the law concerning homosexuality and prostitution, as recommended by the Wolfenden Committee of 1957[57] – clearly require inspection in point of the respective merits of the status quo and the suggested reforms. And as Hart pointed out, we have to be willing to take evidence. We can't defend restrictions on homosexual practices by citing Justinian's belief that homosexuality is the cause of earthquakes. And when we review the evidence, it will not be relevant to quote opinion polls recounting the population's beliefs in respect of the immorality of the conduct to be permitted. The apt questions concern whether the practice which is up for assessment causes harm.

The practical problem is perennial – Devlin's views were published as a contribution to the debate provoked by the proposals of the Wolfenden Committee and the courts themselves throw up cases for decision with undiminished regularity. In 1986, the United States Supreme Court upheld the law of the state of Georgia which criminalized sodomy.[58] In a recent UK case, the House of Lords upheld the convictions for causing bodily harm of men engaged in consensual sadistic practices. But the Hart–Devlin debate had been, to my mind, a rare example of a philosophical question decisively settled. I should have known better. Devlin's thesis has re-emerged recently in more fashionable dress – that of the communitarian.

One strand of modern communitarianism has been the claim that the identity of the moral agent is constituted by social institutions of the community of which she is a member.[59] The contours of the good life are drawn by the specific pattern of proscriptions and prescriptions which are embedded in such institutional frameworks and the virtues and dispositions of character that are inculcated in citizens. A member cannot disengage from her community without a serious loss of self; she cannot step back from the principles which mark her community as an historically conditioned entity and appraise them from some other-worldly stance. For the most part, our citizen is stuck with what she believes to be right since the cost of independence of spirit is too great for humans to bear. It follows that each community will be optimally regulated by that set of rules and attitudes which members endorse as distinctive of their way of living well. Some of these rules – perhaps the most important to the ongoing life of the community thus constituted – will be embodied in legislation. Other rules, perhaps equally important but not judged suitable for legislative enactment, supposing that this carries with it the burdens of the criminal law (police, courts and prisons), will be enforced by unofficial communal instruments. The implication of this position (which, as Hart saw, elevates positive morality to the status of optimal critical morality) is that a society may give practical legislative effect to whatever rules of conduct identify its distinctiveness, not on the basis that this distinctiveness is worth preserving – from what stance could this be adjudicated? – but rather on the grounds that its members can endorse no other.

Far be it from me to deny that humans can think in this fashion about how their communities should be regulated. It is enough for the purposes of this argument to note one odd feature of the scenario. It supposes that citizens are so integrated[60] into the lives of their communities that they cannot but endorse the moral rules which define its collective (and their individual) identity. It therefore assumes an ethical homogeneity that is not to be found in modern nation-states. Patently, some citizens' identities are not defined by the moral rules underpinning the legislation which they are campaigning to reform. Telling people they must obey a law is one thing – the telling may carry authority. Telling people wherein their moral identity consists, against their explicit disavowal, is quite another. In some communities, we are voluntary recruits; in others, the family and the nation-state notably, we find ourselves members willy-nilly. But no community has the ethical authority to conscript us as moral team players in the face of our explicit dissent. Dissenters and bloody-minded protesters can get things wrong. The principles they advocate may be as evil or dotty as any. But if we believe so, such descriptions will serve; we don't need to locate their error in a mistaken sense of their moral identity which is witnessed in the mere fact that their principles differ from ours.

In 'Liberal Community', Dworkin parodies the communitarian challenge in his claim that those who subsume sexual behaviour as a collective interest of the political community must suppose 'that the political community also has a communal sex life . . . that the sexual activities of individual citizens somehow combine into a national sex life in the way in which the performances of individual musicians combine into an orchestral performance . . .'.[61] Maybe ridicule is as good a weapon as any against those who believe they have a legitimate interest in their neighbours' sex lives (as against being good old gossipy Nosey-Parkers). Still, there are difficult cases. I will mention one.

117

In the wake of a massacre of schoolchildren in Scotland, legislation was introduced against the possession of hand-guns in the UK. To many, the most impressive reason in favour of such legislation was that it marked a moral stand against an encroaching ethos of permissible private use of deadly weapons. Of course, that ethos is explicit in the defence of the culture of personal weapons in the USA and is exported in the films and TV programmes which display (and sometimes glorify) their casual use. What there is of such an ethos in the UK takes the form of an admiration for military exploits. Soldiers of the SAS protecting Queen and Country are a more recognizable model in Britain than the homesteader guarding the family ranch against rustlers and Red Indians. Politicians as well as private citizens were impatient of the pleas of members of private gun clubs that their hobby could be so regulated as to effectively limit the risk of sporting weapons being ill-used. Legislation which amounted to an absolute prohibition was claimed to be the only counter to an encroaching gun culture.

I confess I am disturbed by the thought that this amounts to legislation which is driven by moral sentiments quite independently of the question of whether the forms of hand-gun use to be banned are harmful. That much seemed to be explicit in the terms in which some of the debates were conducted. 'Cowboy morality must stop somewhere in the Atlantic.' 'The ideals of the pioneer and the frontiersman which seem entrenched in the American suburbs must be kept out.' This looks like morals legislation to me. The rhetoric reads as a defence of traditional community hostility to the use of personal firearms being shored up in the face of insidious threats. If so, the liberal who advocates the test of harm should not be sympathetic to it.

I find I am as susceptible to this rhetoric as most of my compatriots have been – but am equivocal as to the reasons for it. After all, the same exotic and alien morality is celebrated by the more colourful variety of Country and Western fans who wear cowboy uniforms, adopt curious nom-de-plumes (Hobo Harry, the Hombre from Huddersfield) and hold fast-draw competitions. Children can buy pistols and even imitation automatic weapons – to be filled with water. Everyone can see John Ford's Westerns on the television set. Few complain about these innocent pastimes as the incursion of an alien morality and demand prohibition. The difference seems to be that legislation to ban hand-guns has some connection with the distribution and use of dangerous weapons and some possible incidence of their harmful use. It cannot represent, *simpliciter*, a communal response to an alien ethos. But I leave readers to think through these issues for themselves.

Offence

If we were to judge straight off that one is harmed who is offended, offensive conduct could be considered for prohibition along the lines suggested by the harm principle. How harmful is the offending behaviour? Does it harm few, many or most people? Remembering that the harm principle is not proposed as a sufficent condition on legitimate interference, we should consider if the harm which is consequent upon the offence is offset by any countervailing benefit, or if the costs of interference would in any case be too high. If there is a difficulty in determining particular cases or in evaluating proposals for interference, the difficulty will be cognitive rather than philosophical. It may be that the evidence germane to these practical questions is hard to assess.

There is a philosophical problem here (for the proponent of a harm principle) only if one believes that the offensiveness of behaviour is a ground for restrictions independently of the harm that it may cause. To examine this we need to take examples of conduct which it is agreed is offensive and either harmless or harmful in some attenuated fashion that would not generally serve as a good reason for restricting liberty. Feinberg accepts that Louis B. Schwartz has found an example.[62] Consider a law whereby 'a rich homosexual may not not use a billboard on Times Square to promulgate to the general populace the techniques and pleasures of sodomy'. I cannot believe that the harm done by such a billboard is of a trivial kind, though the description of it may require a delicate and imaginative exercise. The nuisance of the distraction, the embarassment of the unavoidable encounter with feelings of shame and perhaps guilt, the shock of unanticipated self-exposure – all these on the way to work – may be reckoned harmful enough and assumed to be sufficiently universal to justify prohibition. The burden of proof of harm which is placed on those who would intervene is not onerous in such a case. When questions concerning the censorship of pornographic films, TV programmes, books or plays are raised, readers may recognize the relevance of voluntary subscription. Those questions are not raised here.

As Feinberg insists, we should be *reluctant* to admit offence as a defensible reason for interfering with the conduct of others, supplementary to the harm principle. And we should be careful of applying the harm principle indiscriminately for its prevention. I suggest that we think two ways on this issue. In the first place, offence is important to us. It is perhaps the most familiar way in which we are wronged. Many philosophers have developed the Kantian blunderbusses of respect for persons and recognition of others' autonomy – treat others as ends and not as means, merely – into sophisticated instruments of normative ethics. They capture core features of an individualistic ethics which is the legacy of Protestantism and the moral philosophy of the seventeenth and eighteenth centuries. And these ethical notions in turn capture a modern concern with the dignity of the individual, a dignity just about all moral agents educated in this tradition will assert freely. The arena in which these calls for respect are most readily made and most frequently affronted is that of commonplace personal interaction. Here, respect is a matter of courtesy and politeness; disrespect is easily recognized. The barman who retorts to the rude customer: 'What do you think I am – a f***ing vending machine?', perhaps breaks a rule of good business, but expresses clearly and directly a universal concern not to be treated as a means merely. Jack is, or demands to be, as good as his master nowadays and hierarchical honour codes have been flattened out. You're due courtesy even in the pawnbroker's shop, my father used to insist. So everyone, quite rightly, is sensitive to affront, bristles in the face of patronization, is quick to protect her dignity. So life becomes difficult where conceptions of what is and what is not respectable conduct change rapidly. Who will be offended by what in which circumstances in the way of bad language? Offence is easily given and readily taken. Rudeness is a moral wrong; it is not the sort of breach of etiquette committed by the ignoramus who picks up the wrong knife, though as the example of bad language shows, the boundary between the immoral and the infelicitous can be tricky and quickly shifting. But if we wish to live a comfortable life in a gracious society we had all better be connoisseurs of such distinctions. Of course, prevention of the sort of offence I have been discussing is not easily legislated for, and generally is better not, but this is a matter of practicalities. It is not because offence is a trivial or unimportant wrong.

On the other hand, offensiveness may serve important ethical and political purposes. In a moving defence of the rights of Salman Rushdie, when still under *fatwa* for the publication of *The Satanic Verses*, Jeremy Waldron insists that 'the great themes of religion matter too much to be closeted by the sensitivity of those who are to be counted as the pious'.[63] Who is a proper party to the debate as well as what counts as good manners may in themselves be points at issue. I'll quote Waldron at length; the issue merits his eloquence:

> The religions of the world make their claims, tell their stories, and consecrate their symbols, and all that goes out into the world too, as public property, as part of the cultural and psychological furniture which we cannot respectfully tiptoe around in our endeavour to make sense of our being. ... Things that seem sacred to some will in the hands of others be played with, joked about, taken seriously, taken lightly, sworn at, fantasized upon, juggled, dreamed about backward, sung about, and mixed up with all sorts of stuff. This is what happens in *The Satanic Verses*. ... Like all modern literature, it is a way of making sense of human experience.[64]

Three cheers for this. In a multicultural society, as in a multicultural world, offensiveness cannot be avoided. We are stuck between the rock of respect and appropriate courtesy and the hard place of polemical ridicule. We strive to protect our dignity as persons and then lampoon in literature and cartoons those whose values we challenge. We don't thereby violate our own ground-rules of debate. Where the ground-rules themselves are the question at issue, offence is ineliminable.

Paternalism again

This covers the second ideal of positive liberty canvassed earlier, embracing the idea that agents are liberated when the control of others is substituted for the self-control they cannot manage. Mill's harm principle explicitly excludes activities whereby individuals harm themselves from the range of acceptable social interference. He states that the agent's

> own good, either physical or moral, is not a sufficient warrant. He cannot rightfully be compelled to do or forbear because it will be better for him to do so, because it will make him happier, because in the opinion of others, to do so would be wise, or even right.[65]

Later in *On Liberty*, following Mill's introduction of a distinction between self- and other-regarding actions, cases in which the only harm that the agent causes is to himself are firmly placed in the category of the self-regarding, and the interference of others, whether by means of law or other coercive social agencies, is severely proscribed. This restriction is not universal. Uncontroversially, Mill insists that he is not speaking of children. More generally, those 'who are still in a state to require being taken care of by others, must be protected against their own actions as well as against external injury'. Notoriously, this disclaimer includes barbarians stuck in 'those backward states of society in which the race itself may be considered in its nonage'.[66] An example or two of appropriate paternalism towards uncivilized members of barbaric societies would help explain the point, but I am flummoxed. Just what practices of ignorant self-harm does he want to stop? Consensual *suttee* as practised in India is a possible candidate. Bear in mind, as some critics have not, that he is not anticipating the dubious claim of twentieth-century tyrants that freedom of speech, for example, limits the growth of gross national product.

To focus enquiry, let us list the leading characteristics of paternalistic interference and then give some examples. First, it will be coercive, exacting penalties in case of non-compliance. Hortatory messages of the sort put out by Ministers of Health (Take daily exercise!) may be paternalistic in spirit but they do not count for

the purposes of this discussion since they do not amount to com-
pulsion and control, to echo Mill. If governments could brainwash
their citizens into looking after themselves better, that would
count as paternalism, as does any policy which is intended to force
all citizens to ameliorate their condition. Fluoridization of the
water supply, as a strategy to improve *everyone's* (not just children's) teeth, would be an example. Second, the *main purpose* of the
interference must be to prevent citizens harming themselves. If the
intention of seat-belt legislation is to cut the costs of hospital
treatment following road accidents, it is not paternalistic. If the
desired effects of restrictions on smoking concern the comfort
and good health of non-smokers, again the interference is not
paternalistic.

Something like the law of double effect will be operating here,
since in cases of this sort, those who are made to wear their seat-
belts or limit their smoking reduce to some degree the likelihood
of harm to themselves. And mention of the law of double effect
should alert liberals to the possibility of hypocrisy. There are
whole armies of folk desperate that others improve themselves and
unconcerned that the objects of their sympathetic attention may
balk at their mission. If, in the pursuit of their goal they can sneak
their favoured proposals into the category of legitimate interference by the back-door citation of any small probability of harm to
others, they will leap on the evidence to whitewash the coercion
they believe to be warranted in any case.

Mill's instincts were sound; if the effects to be prevented can be
inhibited by some other means less intrusive on the citizen's freedom, if drivers, for example, could be got to pay a premium on their
insurance policies to cover the additional costs their choice of not
wearing a seat-belt might impose on others (and if this option
could be effectively enforced), one who goes down the route of
universal coercion is acting in a paternalistic fashion. All too
often, the intentions of would-be interferers is occult. Those who
would manipulate our conduct willy-nilly are not likely to restrain
their manipulation of the terms of the debate. Although paternalism is a characterization of the intentions or purposes of the inter-
ferer, those who oppose paternalism, as Mill did, have to identify it
solely in terms of the likely effects of proposed policies, and the
readiness of the proposers to consider alternatives. In any policy

debate which raises the spectre of paternalism, motives which are properly recognized as suspicious can rarely be challenged directly. Double-talk abounds, as well as double standards.

Here is a list of practices which have invited do-gooders to intervene on behalf of their benighted fellows: masturbation (doctors used to propose clitoridectomy for women self-abusers, and all manner of restraint for men), dangerous sports (boxing, notably, but never to my knowledge high-altitude mountaineering which until recently carried a one-in-nine chance of death per climber per expedition), gambling, smoking, drinking and drug-taking, eating ox-tail stew or T-bone steaks, driving cars without seat-belts, riding motorcycles without crash-helmets, suicide and consensually assisted euthanasia, incarceration of adults of unsound mind and prone to self-mutilation and injury. I have deliberately mixed up the daft, the controversial and the not-so-controversial, so as to prompt reflection amongst readers.

We know the *form* of the case that has to be made out for paternalistic interference because we find it readily justifiable in respect of children. When we lock the garden gate to prevent our children playing with the traffic, we suppose they are ignorant of the degree and likelihood of the danger. Or, if we have explained this carefully, we believe them prone to misjudgement in their evaluation of the likely costs and benefits. We insist that children attend school and force them to take nasty-tasting medicine. We prevent them harming themselves in the ways that their ignorance or poor judgement permits. As children mature, sensible parents allow them to take more decisions for themselves. Mistakes will be made, but one hopes that these will encourage the adolescent to develop the capacities necessary for prudence – a curiosity about the future effects on themselves of their conduct, the intelligence to investigate what these may be, sound judgement concerning the benefits of risky activities. These skills need to be cultivated through increasing the opportunities for their exercise. Then, hey presto, somewhere between 13 and 21 years of age, depending in most jurisdictions on the activity in question, adults emerge with the capacity to decide for themselves how best to pursue their own interests with whatever risk of harm to themselves.

At adulthood or thereabouts, there is a presumption that individual agents are in the best position to judge these matters – a

presumption we shall examine in due course. We suppose that
grown-ups are in possession of all information germane to their
decisions, but if this is arcane or technical, governments strive to
make it widely available, to the point, as with tobacco smoking,
of hitting folks over the head with it on every occasion of con-
sumption. 'Preappointed evidence' was Bentham's term for this
useful practice, approvingly cited by Mill.[67] We also suppose that
grown-ups can evaluate the benefits of a risky activity, can
achieve a reasonable measure of the worthwhileness for themselves of the sort of life they set about. Here there is less scope for
preappointed evidence; the attractions of high-altitude mountaineering are likely to be a mystery to non-participants, not least
to those who make some effort to comprehend them by reading
the grim accounts of the activity which the mountaineers themselves provide – five weeks of hell-on-earth, then one beautiful
sunset.

Is this presumption reasonable? With respect to the provision of
information concerning the degree and probability of harm, countries like the UK with compulsory education to the age of 16, sup-
plementing the advice of parents who for the most part wish their
children to be safe, have plenty of opportunities for putting over
appropriate messages. For the adult, preappointed evidence is ubiquitous as sports stars queue up for TV opportunities to convince
us of the benefits of walking to work, and government health
warnings are printed on billboards. Interestingly, Mill thought
this principle should apply, too, to the dangers of drugs and poi-
sons – as indeed it does, with appropriate doses and information
concerning contra-indications being supplied with prescribed
drugs. But 'Doctor Knows Best' is a safer policy for the majority of
us who are pharmacologically challenged. Mill thought that 'to
require in all cases the certificate of a medical practitioner would
make it sometimes impossible, always expensive, to obtain the article for legitimate uses'.[68] Most contemporary readers will regard
this as a prescription for a National Health Service, with readily
available services free or cheap at the point of delivery, rather than
a justification of self-prescription.

Matters are very different concerning the *value* of risky activities. Here, perforce, societies must leave most adults unprepared.
Again, the example of mountaineering is instructive. Schools and

families can give children a taste of the experience, but this will be diluted in homeopathic proportions; taking children on mountains is not like a trip to the ballet. Risk, at least for the schools and public authorities who regard their involvement as educational, must be excised as far as possible; no wonder the glories are obtuse to the many who cannot imagine what the free and self-directed pursuit may be like.

Further difficulties concern activities whose point is forever opaque to non-enthusiasts. At least in the case of mountaineering, society has cast the gloss of adventure over the game, and the culture of stoicism and self-knowledge promises a glimmer of imaginative identification, though aspirants will probably find the outcome disappointing. But think of train-spotting, beetle-collecting or playing dominoes![69] If one doesn't *do* these things, how can one appreciate their value? Mercifully, the question of paternalism does not arise here since the hobbies I have mentioned do not generally harm their practioners. But what, for example, do we innocents make of the life of the alcoholic or drug-taker? I read William Burroughs's *Junkie* [70] as an advertisement for the liberated existence of the heroin addict. There is no conventional vice which does not have, or may not find, its literary, or theatrical, or painterly celebrant of self-destruction. If the glory of seeing a steam-driven Britannia class locomotive, charging down the line, is utterly opaque to us, what chance do we have of imagining the transcendent effects of a shot of heroin?

There is a respectable answer to this question. At the point of experimental choice, there can be more or less commitment. A decision to try the heroin may be the cause of one's foregoing future acts of choice.[71] It is unlikely that the sight of *Britannia* herself or the exhilaration of winning a clever game of dominoes will prove addictive. I guess it wouldn't matter if heroin addiction were as harmless as the universal human addiction to fresh air. But, at least in the dismal circumstances in which this addiction is generally pursued, it is hard to think of addiction as a worthy lifestyle choice as opposed to the dreadful consequence of an ignorant or careless mistake. Hard, but not impossible – which alternative signals the difficulty of paternalist intervention. It is a just about universal feature of human society that its worst features (extreme poverty, homelessness, loneliness) have prompted personal strategies of self-oblivion which can be presented as perfectly rational in the awful circumstances.

It might be thought that paternalism, given the hostility to it which I have intimated, poses a particular difficulty to the account of liberty I have been developing. I argued, following Locke and Rousseau and, in modern times, Joseph Raz and Philip Pettit, that our liberty is not enhanced by the opportunity to do evil with impunity. In fact, concern for our moral liberty may lead us to endorse social constraints on our actions as the most effective means of self-discipline. From this point of view, one might judge that even laws which directly prevent harm to others, laws against theft, for example, have a paternalistic tinge if they are viewed as the outcome of citizens' desire that their resolve be bolstered in the face of temptation. This line of thought will positively encourage paternalistic interference, since it is predicated on a belief in its necessity.

I insist that the problem is not as severe as it appears. In the first place, this element of a theory of liberty must be placed alongside an insistence on a measure of political liberty as promoted by democratic institutions. Paternalistic interferences which are the product of rulers imposing their values on hapless citizens – as parents might regulate the conduct of their children – are not justifiable. The institutions of political decision-making must make it intelligible that citizens are imposing these limitations on themselves, however remote or indirect the mechanisms.

For some, the introduction of democracy onto the scene will make matters worse. Wasn't it the illiberal, tyrannical even, tendency of democratic egalitarianism to make everyone's lives their neighbours' business (and to put this prurient concern into social effect) that Mill noticed from de Tocqueville's writings on America which prompted him to write *On Liberty*?[72] Don't both democratic institutions and the democratic temper encourage intrusive paternalistic practices? I am prepared to admit that they might. The sensitive liberal ear *burns* daily at the rhetoric of elected politicians who are desperate to keep their fellows on the straight and narrow to their evident benefit.

To some, this seems to be how they interpret the pursuit of the public good that they were elected to serve. No sooner are local councillors elected (on platforms such as reducing unemployment or protection of the environment) than they enthusiastically set about censoring films, sitting on licensing committees and regulating the opening hours of clubs that young people attend. It never occurs to them that these matters may not be their proper business. Just this morning I heard a government (Home Office) minister on the radio announcing solemnly that a new system of on-line lotteries to be played in pubs represented a serious danger to the moral health of the nation. It *must* be investigated! The combination of alcohol and gambling is reprehensible and dangerous (everywhere, presumably, except the Royal Enclosure at Ascot). At no point in the discussion was the suggestion made that this sort of activity is outside the remit of government authority, that it represents an opportunity for pleasurable individual misbehaviour which should be immune to interference.

On the other hand, that democracies have developed in this intrusive fashion does not entail that they either must or should do so. Philosophical argument cannot of itself prevent the misuse of institutions – and even Mill's harm principle is just that: a *philosophical principle*. It is not a brick wall whereby households can be fenced off from their neighbours and all the coercive instruments of society at large. So we can insist, on the basis of a theory of liberty, that those who love liberty will not treat their fellow citizens as imbeciles whose lives are to be managed so as to prevent them harming themselves. In particular, having assured themselves that grown-ups have where possible all the information they need to make prudent choices, they will be cautious about restricting their fellows' engagement in risky activities since they will be humble about their own capacities to discern what good these activities serve. The democratic citizen who values liberty knows full well the difference between asking, of herself: Is this activity a temptation that I wish the state to assist me in controlling? and asking, in respect to others: Is this an activity that I wish to stop them pursuing? It is one lesson of Rousseau's doctrine of the general will, of which more later, that genuine democratic institutions require their participants to *think* along particular tracks. It is because he believes he addresses an audience who value liberty that he cannot accept that its members will violate each other's rights.

Finally, although we must acknowledge some space for paternalistic interference, we must insist that this does not give *carte blanche* to interfere to even the most straight-thinking, sound-valued *state*. Suppose I am correct to believe that I need the help of others if I am not to harm myself in ways I deplore but cannot avoid and I accept that self-discipline, on my part, requires social engagement. If one is alert to the facts of history concerning ambitious state projects of individual amelioration, projects ranging from Prohibition and temperance legislation to the War on Drugs (led in the UK at the moment by a *Drug Czar!*), one will recognize that the state is very good at creating criminals and not very good at changing their behaviour.

As we noticed before, we should worry about the effects of government interference, even where it is legitimated by the harm principle. First, it's likely to be inefficient, as claimed above; second, where it *is* efficient, we should consider the enervating effects of big government on the spirit and liveliness of the citizens.[73] Family, friends, self-help groups, churches even, represent better resources for the weak-willed than the agencies of the state. If the state has a role in enabling its citizens to conduct their lives in less self-harming ways, this duty may best be discharged, almost paradoxically, by state support of non-governmental agencies.

Conclusion

There have been times when philosophers radically circumscribed their task. In the middle years of the twentieth century, some claimed, modestly, that the analysis and articulation of concepts was the proper task of philosophers, the limit of legitimate philosophical ambition. In this period, amongst these philosophers, it is fair to say that political philosophy suffered grievously, although the clarity and precision of this work affords an example of best practice in point of style, if not philosophical methodology. Berlin's work on liberty represented a notable advance on the prevailing standards of philosophical correctness. He showed that an important ethical concept is susceptible of (at least) two, and possibly two hundred, different analyses. There is no one coherent way of thinking about liberty; there are at least two – and these amount, each of them, to rich traditions, each tradition dissolving into disparate components which challenge fellow contenders for the torch of 'the best way of thinking about the value of liberty'. As we have seen, Berlin has been criticized for the exclusiveness of his categories. Talk of 'negative' and 'positive' liberty occludes an underlying schema into which all mentions of liberty may be fitted. MacCallum's point may be taken as a legitimate demand on putative analysis, but Berlin's real purpose was to demonstrate the costly ethical commitments of one analysis against another – where each alternative satisfies the test of conceptual coherence.

If there are many ways of thinking clearly about liberty, as about democracy or justice, the important question concerns which way we are to select as most apt to characterize judgements about the importance of liberty as a political value. Which analysis, amongst the two (or twenty-two) available, best illuminates why so many people think liberty is worth striving for? The account I have been developing is complex – and these are its chief constituents. Basically, agents are free when they are not hindered in their pursuit of what they take to be the good life. Hindrances are to be construed widely. In a political, or more widely social context, they will include laws backed by sanctions as well as the coercive instruments of positive morality. But individuals can also claim to be unfree when governments in particular fail to empower them in sufficient measure to attain levels of accomplishment which are the necessary preconditions of a life which is authentically their own. In insisting that the object of liberty should be the pursuit of the good life, I mean to exclude from the value of liberty opportunities to do evil. I mean to include, not merely the wherewithal to pursue exalted ideals, but also the possibility of fashioning an autonomous track through the conflicting demands of various loyalties, interests and commitments. Political institutions can foster liberty on this capacious understanding in a range of ways. Democracy is necessary since for many a life of active political engagement is an important ingredient of the good, intrinsically a component of self-directed existence, as valuable in its fashion as the religious life or the life of artistic creation or appreciation. Democracy has instrumental importance since it enables the fastidious citizen to construct or embrace coercive measures which impose some discipline on her pursuit of worthwhile goals – where the imposition of such controls is a necessary supplement to her solitary strivings. Whether such constraints are necessary is a matter of personal moral strength, but even where they are not, coercion is still necessary to fashion a space for unhindered activity secure from the interventions of others.

A sound theory of liberty should recognize the Janus-face of the criminal law in particular. It can serve as a protection, demarcating with the force of sanctions the boundaries which freedom requires if the pursuit of the good life is to be safe within them. Equally, though, and just as obviously, such laws can limit liberty, as they do when the prospect of punishment makes forbidden pursuits too costly to contemplate. If such pursuits are innocent or necessary for a worthwhile life, the law is acting as a limitation on freedom.

We have claimed that democracy is a necessary condition of political freedom, but as the author of coercive laws it is also a threat. And perhaps de Tocqueville was right: democratic legislatures, in their representative form through the operation of the mandate, are prone to operate capriciously in the lives of citizens, legislating to solve social problems without a thought as to whether intervention in specific areas of conduct is their proper task. To deal with this problem of overbusy legislation, as well as to curtail a society's moral instincts for self-repression, limits have to be drawn to the competence of agencies with the capacity to curtail agents' freedom. The most familiar ways of doing this are through the applications of principles which may or may not be given constitutional entrenchment. Mill's harm principle is one such; a principle of protected rights is another. This may be thought an alternative to the harm principle or else as a supplement to it. Other candidate principles have been examined, including principles of legal moralism and offence. I have argued that these are not independent principles. Either they are defective or best taken as appeals to the relevance of specific types of harm. The most difficult cases for the harm principle concern paternalistic interference. Here the concern to prevent agent's harming themselves cuts across the value of autonomy which is the deepest justification of free institutions. Formally, there is something odd about the application of a principle of autonomy to justify coercion. It may be necessary where a measure of coercion establishes the social conditions necessary for an autonomous life to be engaged –

as with children. With adults the situation is altogether different. Governments and citizens individually should be modest in respect of both their ambitions and effectiveness concerning the likelihood of their interference promoting the good of their helpless and obdurate fellow citizens.

Chapter 4

Rights

Introduction

Nowadays the rhetoric of human rights seems to be just about universal. No tyrants, no autocracy, seem to be so benighted that they refuse, in public at least, to endorse the claims of human rights. In practice they may jail or torture political opponents, or refuse to educate women, but when applying for aid to the United Nations they will give solemn assurances that human rights are respected in their jurisdiction, respected at least as far as is practical under conditions of emergency, respected at least in point of intent: that when the current crisis has been alleviated, normal conditions will be swiftly resumed. 'Normal conditions', of course, will comprise the promotion and protection of a standard list of human rights. The 'standard list' is likely to be provided by the United Nations Universal Declaration of Human Rights or the European Convention for the Protection of Human Rights. If any political principles have been elevated to the pantheon of political correctness, to the point where denial of them taints the innocent philosophical sceptic, human rights have. This makes it all the more important that we examine their philosophical credentials.

Human rights have acquired a quite unique standing amongst political values, partly as a consequence of this official international recognition. Initially, they could be easily listed – rights to life, liberty and property. In the American Declaration of Independence, 'the Pursuit of Happiness' was included; The Rights of Man as declared by the French Revolutionary Assembly incorporated rights to liberty, property, security and resistance to oppression. In the United Nations Charter and the European Convention, the so-called social and economic rights have been included, rights to health, education, welfare provision and much else. The call for rights has overstepped even these capacious boundaries, to the point where readers will encounter demands that a previously unheard-of human right be recognized just about every time they open a newspaper. The infertile claim a human right to give birth and the fertile claim a human right to abortion. The practice of installing prepayment meters for water has been denounced in the UK as the violation of the human right to a mains water supply.

Such claims may be made to sound silly. Sometimes they are. Most often, they suggest that their claimants are deriving the legitimacy of the demands they make or the illegitimacy of the practices they denounce from more general principles of rights. Either way the language of rights has become ubiquitous.

In the comfortable West, at least, a cynical reason for this may be offered – a reason that I don't feel qualified to assess. Cold War warriors, it has been suggested, feared the obvious attractions of communist ideology to the poor and starving of this world, for much the same reason that nineteenth-century British politicians feared calls for the extension of the franchise: calls for the end of private property as we know it invite the poor to trespass and help themselves. An alternative ideology was necessary to combat this malign doctrine and the theory of human rights fitted the bill nicely. Citizens of the West, it is suggested, have come to believe the propaganda of their own governments. Criticisms which are expressed in terms of a denial or violation of human rights have acquired a distinct potency. For all these reasons, it is urgent that the political philosopher investigates closely the notion of human rights.

Analysis and definition

Preliminaries

The language of rights is lumbered with jargon – no bad thing if it serves a clear technical purpose. But the jargon has to be explained and clarified, and the task can be as nit-picking as any that philosophers have devised. Let us get down to it.

Our main focus will be on rights which are universal, universally claimed or universally ascribed, rights of the form that, if anyone has them, everyone does. These will be what the French declared to be the Rights of Man; often they have been described as natural rights. Hegel, for reasons I will return to later, called them abstract rights. The term 'human rights' is best, for two reasons: first, it connects with the language of the charters, declarations and conventions mentioned above which inscribe rights as a principle of international law. For better or worse, it is human rights to which these documents refer and so it is human rights that citizens claim against their governments. Second, the older term, natural rights, carries with it a distinct provenance. Natural rights, to simplify, were deemed natural because they were the product of natural law. What is natural law?[1] To many, it represented that law which God had prescribed as apt for creatures with natures like ours, those rules which God had determined that humans should follow if they are to fulfil the purposes He had laid down for them. If humans cannot be expected to fulfil their prescribed purposes unless they respect each others' claims of right, we have an argument that natural law sanctions natural rights. In a nut-shell, this is Locke's argument for natural rights.

It is a good argument, too – so long as one accepts the theological premises. We cannot imagine how humankind might be the trustees of God's purposes without God granting them the necessary wherewithal, the moral space and essential resources required for their accomplishment. If God's prescription of the moral space of rights is necessary for His subjects to fulfil His purposes, this severe injunction must bind not only persons who would wantonly interfere with each other's activity, but also the state, in particular, sovereigns, who were unaccustomed to finding normative limits to their exercise of absolute power.

However strong the argument, protagonists cannot expect it to find support from those who would deny, or remain agnostic, with respect to the theological premises. A secular counterpart is evidently needed. Locke himself suggests that one is available when he insists that reason may be employed to derive the necessity and content of a system of rights – and this track will be followed later. For the moment we should recognize that talk of natural rights carries the transcendental, non-naturalistic, imprint of talk of natural law. If the whiff of sanctity is unattractive to many, there is little value in trying to spread it. That is the further reason why it is best to speak of human rights.

Human rights are a species of moral rights; generally, they register moral claims and are to be vindicated by moral argument. As such they have been contrasted with *legal rights*, which are the product of some specific legal system. This contrast in provenance may conceal a good deal of overlap. The law may recognize moral rights, embodying in statutes standard liberal rights – to free speech, freedom of association or religion or whatever. This recognition may take the form of the explicit incorporation of an international charter into a municipal legal system or it may be effected as specific proscriptions outlaw e.g. theft or unpermitted use of personal property. But not all moral rights may be recognized in particular legal systems. The legal systems may be defective. There may also be good reason, in particular cases, why moral rights should not be made legally enforceable. The ancillary costs of legislation and enforcement, including the augmentation of police powers, for example, may be too costly to bear. Most often, one who claims a moral right will demand that this right become a legal right, enlisting the powers of the state for their protection or the delivery of some resource, or else requiring the state to constrain itself in the delivery of other goods if these services would involve the violation of rights. But this distinction is worth marking, not least since it sets up for discussion Bentham's dismissal of talk of natural rights as nonsense.[2] Legal rights, by contrast, are the creations of legal systems.

The straightforward distinction of legal and moral rights occludes a further distinction between positive rights and what we may call critical rights, echoing H.L.A. Hart's distinction between positive and critical morality.[3] On this account, positive rights will be rights that are recognized within some appropriate system of actual, operative, rules. Legal rights are evidently positive rights, but other systems of rules may recognize rights claims. Thus religious rights may be positive, as when worshippers have the right to be married in church or buried in a churchyard. Positive rights may be assigned within the rules of games. If an opponent leads out of turn in a game of bridge, declarer has rights to require one of a range of optional continuations of play. Most confusingly, one may also speak of moral rights as positive rights in circumstances where a recognized system of moral rules entitles one to make a legitimate claim. Thus parents may claim a positive moral right to obedience from their children and children a positive moral right of independence upon reaching maturity. Where all parties agree that this is part of the system of domestic regulation which binds them, that this is how, in fact, morality works here, positive moral rights are being described. One may, of course, accept that a parent's moral right to beat her child is positively established within a given community without endorsing that system of positive morality, just as one may identify a legal rule which one judges to be iniquitous.

By contrast, critical rights are the rights that *ought* to be recognized, whether, as a matter of fact, they are recognized or not. It would be odd to claim a critical legal right. Why not state simply that the law ought to recognize such and such a right where, in fact, it does not? But there is logical space for such a locution. There is a special point for insisting on its application in the case of morality, since a system of positive morality may be criticized in respect of rights on two fronts: first, it may recognize rights which can find no critical endorsement. We can use again the example mentioned above. Parents may insist, wrongly, the critic protests, that they have the right to beat their children. The parents may be correct so far as the positive morality of their community is concerned. Third parties may judge that they do no wrong, perhaps that they should be praised even for not sparing the lash, not spoiling the child. The critic, on the other hand, judges that there is no such critical moral right, that the practice of corporal punishment does not satisfy whatever tests critical reflection imposes – and, obviously, the critic may claim that the exercise of such a positive moral right violates a right not to be physically assaulted.

Second, critical reflection may support the case for rights which positive morality does not recognize. Where positive morality may grant parents a veto over the prospective marriage partners of their children, critics may demand that adult children have the critical moral right to decide these things for themselves, independently of parental permission. Of course, just as legal rights may coincide with moral rights, so may positive moral rights coincide with the rights demanded by a critical morality. In such cases, one acknowledges that the positive system of moral rights is in no need of repair.

One may think that this distinction – of positive and critical moral rights – is a distinction with a rationale but no purpose. Later in this chapter, we shall see that much hinges on the question of whether rights have some distinctive moral force. At that point, I shall insist that the distinction which I have just drawn is vital for a clear construal and successful answer to the question.

Hohfeld's classification

Wesley Hohfeld's analysis of rights is an exemplary study in jurisprudence. Hohfeld's prime concern, as the title of his book, *Fundamental Legal Conceptions as Applied in Judicial Reasoning*, reminds us, was the understanding of fundamental legal concepts.[4] His analysis of rights was focused on legal rights, but it has proved useful to students of rights more generally. Basically, he claimed that the notion of a legal right was ambiguous, having four distinct senses. He himself believed the ambiguity was so endemic and productive of confusion that we should cease to speak of legal rights altogether. It is fair to say that his disambiguation was so successful, the lessons of his careful analysis so widely learnt, that this proposal has proved unnecessary.

Liberty rights or privileges

When we say 'P has a right to x', we may mean no more than 'P has no duty not to x'. A right of this sort was termed a privilege by Hohfeld; others have termed it a bare liberty or a liberty right. The most important feature of such rights is that they are compatible with others acting in ways that prevent the bearer of rights from x-ing. The most famous example of a liberty right is that of Thomas Hobbes's right of nature, defined as 'the Liberty each man hath, to use his own power, as he will himselfe, for the preservation of his own nature'.[5] Hobbes's point, in insisting that persons may use even one another's bodies, is that if one's life is at stake, all is permitted. It is rational to use others as a human shield, perhaps, when the bullets begin to fly. But if, for Hobbes, I do no wrong when I use your body in this way, you, equally, do no wrong when you resist (or duck). No one else has a duty to permit you to exercise the right. Suppose, as Locke believed, one has the right to labour on land that is unowned and thereby to bring it under ownership. This right, too, is a liberty right. Everyone has this right. If you reach the vacant land before I do, and work upon it productively, the land is yours, notwithstanding my efforts to claim it.

Claim rights

Claim rights are undoubtedly the most important rights in political theory. On this understanding, one who asserts a claim right to x, claims that some other party has a duty to let him x or a duty to provide x. Thus 'P has right to x' entails that some Q (a specific agent, a government or, indeed, everyone) has the duty not to interfere with P's x-ing or a duty to provide x, where x is some good or service. Already we have introduced some complexity into the analysis, and this is worth teasing out.

Rights, we are often told, imply duties. Often, this is the barely concealed threat of the politician who wishes to instruct people that if they do not act responsibly and toe the line, rights will be withdrawn. For others, such a statement may be a gentle reminder that those who claim the moral stature of bearers of rights also have the stature of holders of responsibilities. In both cases, the appearance of logic is doing swift service for what are, at bottom, substantial theses which require careful argument and considered application in the circumstances of their employment. It is at least open to argument that one may have rights but no duties. In essence, this is how Hobbes characterized the position of the sovereign *vis-à-vis* the citizens – the sovereign has rights against the citizens but no duties to them. The citizens have duties to the sovereign, but no rights, other than the residual right of nature, which they can claim against the sovereign who threatens their lives. This is as clear a characterization of absolute sovereign power as any. The thesis, Hobbes's thesis, that a rational agent would endorse this asymmetrical pattern of rights and duties, cannot be repudiated by any logical thesis to the effect that rights entail duties on the part of the rights holder.

In the case of claim rights, a clear logical thesis is available. Claim rights are, logically, correlative to duties. This correlativity thesis is what distinguishes claim rights from liberty rights. In the case where P's right to x entails a duty on the part of Q not to interfere with P's x-ing, we have a right of the classical liberal form, a right of non-interference. Thus one who claims a right of free speech claims that the state (and, no doubt, other citizens severally) have a duty not to prevent her making her opinions known to other citizens. They may not have a duty to listen, but they do have a duty not to shut her up. Rights of this sort have been termed negative rights and rights of action.[6]

By contrast, claim rights of provision (positive rights, rights of recipience) engage a different dimension of correlativity. This is the case where P's claim right to x imposes a duty of service on some Q. P's right that Q fulfil a contract is of this sort. Amongst human rights, such rights as those to education, decent working conditions and health-care impose a duty of service provision on the appropriate governmental (or international) agencies.

The correlativity of rights and duties in the case of claim rights should not be taken as a thesis asserting the analyticity of the corresponding claims concerning rights and duties. In insisting that P's claim right to x imposes a duty on some Q, we suggest (and most certainly do not preclude) a justicationary thesis to the effect that Q's duty may be derived from P's right, that P's right is the ground of Q's duty.[7] Exactly how the derivation may be accomplished may be a complex issue. P's right may give rise to a range of duties distributed amongst different agencies.[8] My right to life imposes a duty on other persons not to kill me and perhaps a duty of care whenever others (in a manner not too costly to themselves) can prevent third parties killing me or, in Good Samaritan cases, give me necessary first-aid. This right may also impose a duty on the state to protect me against killers.

This cluster of distinctions (rights of non-interference vs rights of provision, rights of action vs rights of recipience, negative rights vs positive rights) has been the source of continued argument concerning human rights, not least since it has been related to the distinction of classical liberal rights from the social and economic rights promulgated in the 1948 UN Charter, and I shall return to it later. For the moment let us continue the task of charting the terminology appropriate for claim rights.

The next distinction to be uncovered is a point of jurisprudence, as signalled by the Latin vocabulary – the distinction between rights *in personam* and rights *in rem*. Rights *in personam* entail correlative duties on the part of assigned individuals. The classical example is that of the right of the creditor to the debtor's service. If you promised to pay me £100, I have the right, *in personam*, to claim the £100 from you. Rights *in rem* are rights claimable against anyone or any institution. My right to wander through the streets of Glasgow is a right I can claim against anyone who tells me to clear off, individuals or officials, a right against the world. Where human rights are concerned, rights of non-interference are generally rights *in rem* – rights claimable against anyone who may contemplate interference. Human rights *in personam* are hard to find, but there may be examples. The rights of children against their parents, to fostering care, may be an example. Certainly the duties of parents are not the same as the duties of citizens, although tax-payers may have a duty to foot bills for the costs of child-care where parents prove incapable of fulfilling their duties.

A last distinction has been usefully explored in recent years by Jeremy Waldron – that between *special* rights and *general* rights.[9] Special rights arise out of some contingent deed or transaction; the standard example, again, would be the rights arising out of a promise or contract. It is (just) imaginable that there could be a world without promises. In which case, in this peculiar world, there would be no promisee's rights. If victims have a right to compensation from those who violate their rights, this right, too, would be a special right. It is contingent on the occasion of negligence or crime. General rights, by contrast, are not the product of contingencies. A person's right to life, violated by his murder, holds independently of anything that he may have done or suffered. It follows that general rights are universal. A right is general which 'all men have if they are capable of choice: they have it qua men and not only if they are members of some society or stand in some special relation to each other'.[10] An equally useful way of drawing this distinction is to equate special rights with *conditional* rights and general rights with *unconditional* rights. In fact, this second way of putting things strikes me as superior. It allows us to say that everyone has the right that promises to them be kept, subject to the condition that a promise has been made. Everyone has the right to compensation, subject to the condition that they have been injured.

These distinctions offer us a useful apparatus for characterizing philosophical disputes. But they are not sledgehammers designed to effect knock-down arguments, capable of silencing opponents by their sure-handed employment. Take the distinction of rights of non-interference and rights of provision. Some have insisted that genuine human rights are general rights holding *in rem*. This is unproblematic if one is characterizing the traditional liberal freedoms – the rights to life, free speech, association etc. . . . All persons may have them, claiming them against all others who may interfere. It is held, by contrast, that rights of provision, positive rights, in particular the social and economic rights recognized by the United Nations Charter, immediately give rise to problems. With rights of non-interference, everyone has a correlative duty not to interfere. With rights of provision, someone must have a duty to make available the goods and services claimed of right. But who, exactly?[11]

The wrong way to settle this issue is to insist that since genuine human rights are rights *in rem*, held against everyone, and since it is impossible to hold *everyone* responsible for the provision of the necessary goods, in the same way that everyone has a responsibility not to kill others, rights to the provision of goods and services, such as the economic and social rights, cannot be genuine human rights at all. A proponent of economic and social rights may simply challenge the premiss that genuine economic rights are rights *in rem*. Clearly a lot of work has to be done in specifying exactly who or which agency has the duty to provide the goods demanded. In the case of the right to education, for example, duties may be assigned to parents, to tax-payers, to schoolteachers, to local authorities and the state, or to international, intergovernmental agencies. Everything depends on what the right to education is thought to entail in the particular circumstances.

It may look as though the lack of specificity here, in respect of the agent or agency against which the right is claimed, itself marks a striking contrast between rights of non-interference and rights of provision. But this would be a mistake. Take a standard negative right, what looks at first sight to be incontrovertibly a right of non-interference – the right to life, in pristine colours, construed as the right not to be killed, a right claimed against all others. In any realistic circumstances, one who claims such a right will not be satisfied with proscriptions that make it clear that one who violates such a right does wrong. She will require protections more solid than this. She will require, of her government, that such acts are declared illegal. Further, she will require that the institutions of government (in this case, primarily the police), take whatever actions are necessarary to protect her from potential violations. Against explicit threats to herself or to those of her sex, race, ethnic or religious community, special protection may be required. Against a background of general risk, she may demand that the agencies of the state undertake whatever preventive measures may best protect her and all others. Whatever the social background or perceived incidence of danger, citizens may demand institutions to back up the legal proscriptions designed to protect rights. They will insist upon courts of law to judge guilt and penal institutions to inflict whatever punishments the courts deem appropriate. Just as soon as one begins to specify the form of institution required to achieve protection, to guarantee as far as possible the moral space required to pursue whatever activities one claims to be legitimate as of right, one is committed to the provision of resources to finance the protective activities. Characteristically, rights of non-interference are claimable both *in rem*, against all and sundry who would agress against the individual, and *in personam*, where specific individuals or agencies have duties of protection, prevention or care. We saw above the range of persons and agencies who may be assigned the duty of providing education for the young. Much the same list of agencies may be enlisted as guardians of the security of young people.

A similar reply can be made to those who urge that it is a condition of the existence of human rights that it be practically possible to fulfil the duties to respect them. This is easy, it is claimed for rights of non-interference. These call on agents not to interfere, not to stop others wandering the streets, using their private property, worshipping their gods. There is an infinite number of actions I can be called upon *not* to do. Logically, I can comply with an infinite number of such claims against me. This is not so with respect to duties of provision, since these require resources for their fulfilment – and the resources at anyone's disposal may be limited. This is as true of states as it is of individuals.

This is a striking difference between rights of non-interference and rights of provision. Controversy arises just as soon as this distinction is deemed to coincide exactly with that between the classical liberal rights and social and economic rights, and the social and economic rights are downgraded, judged improper because they are impracticable. As we have seen, rights of non-interference can be very onerous in respect of the costs placed on agencies deemed apt for their protection. As soon as the prevention of crime is judged a proper strategy for those charged with the protection of citizen's rights – and this looks sensible to me – where does crime prevention stop? Many have pointed out that, since the Devil finds work for idle hands, a strategy of full employment is a constructive way for a society to protect the negative rights of its members. We know that most violent crime is inflicted by the desperately poor upon those as poor as themselves. Some believe that more generous welfare provision will reduce the incidence of this sort of rights violation. They may well be right. This is a straightforwardly empirical matter. But again, if as a matter of fact, they *are* right, the resources required for the effective protection of citizens against assault and robbery may need to be massive.

The most reasonable conclusion to draw is not that it is improper to ascribe rights in circumstances where provision or protection is costly, but that such protection and provision should be effected in a systematic, institutional fashion, and the costs of systematic provision should be widely borne. Of course, *I* should not be responsible for the entire costs of your child's health-care, but then I alone should not be responsible for the costs of protecting your child (and every other child) from assault. All rights, negative or positive, liberal or socio-economic, require institutional support and the costs of such support should be distributed amongst members of the community which is responsible for making provision. Assigning responsibility, and issuing the appropriate tax bills, may be a controversial political exercise but the difficulty of the task should not lead us to devalue the rights which require us to engage it.

The analytic apparatus I have been introducing promises simplicity and clarity in the way we think about claim rights. It does not promise simplicity and clarity in respect of working out what thinly described rights (e.g. the right to physical security) demand of whom in what circumstances or of devising policy proposals for giving them effect.

Powers

The third element of Hohfeld's analysis of legal rights concerns rights as powers. The classic example of such a power is the right to bequeath property. The species of power in question is the power to alter assignments of rights and duties. This may seem a peripheral sense of legal right and its application in the field of human rights may seem even more limited. There are striking examples, though, of human rights or elements of human rights which look very much like powers as Hohfeld describes them.

One element of the right to private property is the right to acquire or take into possession goods that are unowned. There is a very great puzzle here that much exercised John Locke. Think of unowned goods as common stock, unowned land as a common resource. Suppose everyone has a liberty right to use what they can get hold of or work upon. On what grounds may anyone be able to take goods or land from this common stock, claim it legitimately as his or her private possession and disbar all others from the use of it? This is not a problem we shall take up here – but notice the form of the right claimed by the first occupant or labourer who takes the good into private property. It is presumably the right to alter the rights and duties of all others who may hitherto have had the opportunity to use the resource. If the argument works as follows: Through my useful labour on this unowned land, I acquire the right to exclude all others from its use, I am claiming a right in the sense of a power to alter the rights of others. Hitherto, they had a liberty right of acquisition or occasional use, maybe. Now they have no such right. Indeed my act of appropriation has created for them the duty not to use the land or travel across it without permission.

Another right which looks very like a Hohfeldian power is the democratic right of political participation, construed as the right to take part in political decision-making by casting a vote, either directly for a policy option as in a referendum, or indirectly, for a representative who will have further decision-making powers. It is not easy to see this as a claim right, analysable as negative or positive, a right of non-interference or provision (though voting mechanisms need to be organized and made available as a common service and interference with the citizen's access to this service needs to be prohibited).[12] Perhaps it is best seen as a Hohfeldian power, to institute or alter, along with other voters, the legal rights and duties of fellow citizens.

Immunities

Hohfeld's final category of rights, immunities, is perhaps the least important or least noticed. An immunity, technically, is the obverse of a power. P has an immunity with respect to x if no Q has the right, in the sense of a power, to alter P's legal standing with respect to x. An immunity is frequently an important element of rights more loosely construed. As Waldron points out, rights which are entrenched as the subject of constitutional guarantees, protected by a Bill of Rights, say, involve an element of immunity: 'not only do I have no duty not to do x or not only do others have a duty to let me do x but also no one – not even the legislature – has a power to alter that situation.'[13]

A different example is found in the idea of 'due process'. Law courts, evidently, have powers to alter the rights of those found guilty. Many of the rights which come under the heading of rights to a fair trial in accordance with the due processes of law, can be best understood as immunities, as protections against arbitrariness or excess in the use of those powers. Thus one aspect of the right of silence is best understood as an immunity against the power of juries to draw the inference of guilt or self-serving concealment against defendants who refuse to testify at their trial.

Generic rights and specific rights

Hohfeld's analysis was a virtuoso enterprise. Its success, in forcing us to think through the logical implications of rights claims, throws up a further problem. Declarations and charters, as well as common usage, list rights in very general terms: life, property, worship, association, health-care, education, to list a few. We know that matters are much more complicated than this. We know that the central terms, 'life', 'property', etc. are serving almost as slogans for a complex constellation of Hohfeldian privileges, claims, powers and immunities, in any concrete employment. If we ask, in respect of the positive assignment of rights in any specific legal system, what, say, the right of private property amounts to, we may be given volumes of legal textbooks, detailing case and statute law – all with the proviso that things will have changed since publication: check the latest Law Reports. This is the state of affairs with respect to positive law. Add to it the complexities of unenforceable positive morality concerning private property. This would lengthen the library shelves were it to be codified – which, of course, it could not be. When should we say 'Please . . .' and 'Thank you' and when not?

As philosophers, it looks as though we are faced with two alternatives: Is there in some sense a generic right to be defended or opposed – in this case the right to private property – or do we need to justify, severally, each of a number of specific rights (which may have the character of liberty rights, claim rights, powers or immunities) which somehow together amount to the right in question, the right of ownership?

Clearly arguments at both levels may be engaged. Waldron, for example distinguishes ideals of collective, common and private property[14] and argues that, at this level of abstraction, the different property systems may be compared under an evaluative schema. This is plausible, or at least recognizable: one philosopher may point to the advantages in point of utility of a system of private property; another may defend a system of common property as necessary for the promotion of freedom. They both agree that it is the property system, thus abstractly conceived, that calls for defence.

But the opposite view is equally plausible. One may believe that the system of private (or common) property can only be justified piecemeal, in a bottom-up fashion. Suppose one believes that the right to private property is a congeries of discrete rules concerning possession, exclusive use, management, receipt of income, capital value, security and transmission, etc. . . .[15] One may require that each of these be vindicated separately. One may endorse rights of bequest – but these may conflict with rights of inheritance. One may insist upon rights of income from property and dispute that these give rise to the liability of payment of tax. What looks to be the core right – exclusive use of what one owns – may be limited or rejected on occasion of national emergency, or because a local authority requires the land for a bypass route or the construction of necessary housing. Individual rights may have to co-exist with incompatible national or local rights according to some established system of adjudication. A tidy solution would find a line of justification for the generic right which could be employed to examine the credentials of the separate elements of that right as these are examined. An untidy solution would find one argumentative strategy being employed in defence of the generic right and then different approaches being adopted for whatever specific rights are deemed to comprise it. Thus one may find oneself justifying the generic right to private property as necessary for freedom and yet recognizing that rights of inheritance (as against, perhaps, rights of bequest) cannot be justified in this way. Maybe utilitarian arguments are the only ones which can find a purchase here.

Individual and group rights

There can be no doubt that the traditional rhetoric of natural and human rights focused directly on the rights of individual human agents. Rights are held by individuals against each other and against supra-individual agencies, most particularly the state. Although Hegel claimed that notions of individual rights originate in the concepts of Roman Law, and Richard Tuck, a modern historian, traces their origins to the early Middle Ages,[16] the notion of equal, universal rights first blossomed in the seventeenth century: for some a product of the individualism explicit in Protestant theology (each person having her own access to God and His revelation in sacred writings, unmediated by priests and saints), for others the ideology apt to emergent capitalism, for still others, a political response to the development of the nation-state – and all of these stories have some claim to truth.

Central to all these accounts is the idea of the *person* as the proper subject of rights, where *person* denotes the minimal moral status to which modern individuals do (or should) aspire. *Person* thus becomes a technical term of moral metaphysics, designating the individual human being as the maker of moral claims, the bearer of fundamental rights. To see oneself as a person is to make claims of right and, an important corollary for most rights theorists, to recognize the equivalent claims of others. Hegel characterizes this conception of morality in his commandment of right: 'be a person and respect others as persons.'[17] For Hegel (not frequently, and for good reason, thought to be one of the classical advocates of human rights), it is a distinctive feature of the modern world that individuals see themselves as discrete and different, atomistic loci of personal moral claims of right, a status asserted against others and recognized when asserted by others. You may well ask: What is the default position? How could persons *not* identify themselves in this elementary and obvious fashion? Hegel's answer is that this reflective perspective on the moral self is an historical achievement. Time was, man's first response to the question: What or who am I? put as an enquiry into one's moral identity, would be answered by spelling out one's membership of a family, tribe or wider community – an ancient Greek polis, perhaps.

We don't need to concern ourselves with this historical debate.

It may be that Hegel is wrong to view the claims of personality as historically emergent and parochial. Maybe individual human beings always, as a matter of fact, saw themselves as discrete human atoms. Hegel himself emphasizes that this is at best a partial and incomplete conception of the moral self. Nonetheless, as a description of the associated metaphysics of the human rights tradition, this account of the person is spot on. It enables us to see very clearly the foundation of rights claims in a social ontology which emphasizes the moral potency of discrete individuals, since rights claims serve to establish the moral boundaries of distinct persons. Moral rights serve as 'hyper-planes in moral space' for Robert Nozick,[18] partitioning the moral universe into a collection of individual rights bearers. The language of rights, paradigmatically, expresses the distinctive moral vocabulary of the metaphysical perspective of discrete persons. Both Hegel, in his discussion of 'abstract rights' ('abstract' because all that persons have to say for themselves *qua* persons is that they are essentially different from each other – there are no ends or goods distinctive of the sense each has of himself as a person) and Nozick, in modern times, in his discussion of rights as side-constraints (of which, more later) capture the heart of rights talk.

But to say that they capture the heart of rights talk is not to endorse that talk or the metaphysical doctrines it encapsulates, nor is it to claim that this individualistic perspective gives us the whole story about rights. It clearly does not. It explains the force, and for some, the priority of negative rights. It explains the sense in which rights violations are seen as boundary-crossings, but not the sense in which they may be failures of provision. But this is water under the bridge. Our central issue here concerns the typical subjects or bearers of rights, and, according to the account just sketched, these will be individual human beings. There is an intimate connection between a metaphysics of social singularity, social atomism, if you like, and claims of right which demarcate the boundaries of that singularity.

This has been noticed by critics of human rights as well as their advocates. Within the socialist tradition in particular, there has been a marked hostility to human rights talk predicated on this implicit individualism. With respect to Marx himself, this hostility principally derived from the thought that this metaphysics of the person cut no deeper than economic man, the isolated consumer, producer or party to economic contracts, more particularly, the bourgeois capitalist entrepreneur. So the rights of man are in truth the rights of capital; the morality of rights is the appropriate ideology of capitalist production.[19] But Marx's point is wider than this and has been taken up by many who would repudiate the typically Marxist critique. The more general claim is that the metaphysics of the person, which stands as the foundation of doctrines of human rights, is fundamentally mistaken. This charge comes in a variety of forms. At its most radical it is the thesis that the person, as thus technically construed, is a fiction. There is no such thing as the isolated, atomic, bounded and discrete human agent. We are all of us, through birth and history, members of various communities – families, tribes, nations: whatever living associations frame our identities. This is the central theme of modern communitarianism.[20]

It is obviously true, if we think of the person-as-bearer-of-rights as a solitary individual, a Robinson Crusoe, or as a person bereft of all affective ties to other human beings, recognizing no allegiances or claims of membership, that there are few or none such. The 'unencumbered self' *is* a fiction.[21] But to speak of the person as discrete and bounded should not be taken to express the whole truth concerning the social ontology of individual human beings or their derivative moral or political standing.

The metaphysical debates of liberals and communitarians concerning the proper ontological locus of rights and duties cannot be reviewed here. So let me state my own view without argument and with an invitation to readers to pursue matters further: of course we are, severally, discrete human beings. The further thought that we are *persons* confers moral potency to this, now almost universal, perspective amongst self-conscious agents. As *individuals* we have interests so strong that they require us to impose duties on others. The right to life, taken as an assertion against others that they shall not murder us, is a clear example of this way of thinking. So is the right to health-care, where this is not claimed on the basis of e.g. one's role as family breadwinner, but on the basis of one's own interest in continued living. The right to freedom of occupation, taken as a denial that others may allocate to us tasks which match *their* conception of our abilities, is another. The nearest we get to an argument here is the thought that such claims as these would be unintelligible were we not to identify them as the demands of individual human beings. But this is not to insist that all human rights claims have this character. The obvious counterexamples are the political rights: standardly the right to vote, but otherwise the various rights which are required by the ideal of participation in the political life of the community – rights to the free expression of opinions, of free access to information, to the free association of like-minded individuals to review, and if necessary amend, their political commitments and to publically agitate on behalf of these – to hold public meetings or otherwise demonstrate their policy proposals. None of these rights make sense as the precondition of individual projects. Each of them presupposes a basic recognition of citizenship: the thought that, alongside others, one has an active part to play in the political life of the community. Political rights, for the most part, make sense against a background of communal participation in the decision-making processes of the community. The citizen takes part *qua* citizen, in a manner that would be unintelligible if allegiance to the decision-making powers of the community were not understood. It is as citizen, not as person, that one claims political rights.

This idea – that individuals first cite their association with others, then demand as rights whatever this effective association demands, has application over a wide range of characteristically human activities. Not only do we think of individuals having rights as members of groups, we think of groups of people having rights themselves. Talk of families having rights, or clubs, or churches, or firms, or still wider communities being rights bearers, is not metaphorical, nor does it reduce to a concatenation of individuals' rights. The relation between the rights of a community and the rights of individual members may be complex and distinctive. A crofting township has exclusive rights of land use. Only members may graze cattle on the common land. Individual crofters have inclusive rights; each may graze up to five cattle, let us say, without infringing the grazing rights of other crofters.[22] Often the articles of association of groups will make provision for individual rights to be assigned upon dissolution of the group. Club members may have individual rights to a share of receipts, should jointly held property be sold, for example. Individual members of families will be assigned rights to a portion of the family assets should the family dissolve in divorce. It would be a mistake to deduce that the assignment of rights which follows dissolution reveals the basic pattern of rights holding when the association is operative. A structure of inclusive rights is not shown to be exclusive after all simply because exclusive rights are granted when the association is wound up. Following divorce I may expect to claim half the value of family assets. It does not follow from this that I, presently married, own exclusively half the family car.

Group rights are tricky to analyse because groups have radically different normative structures. Still, one interesting thought may be hazarded – that the assertion of group rights always attests the existence of the group as a unit of moral agency, having something of the boundedness and singularity claimed for individual persons. One way of making sense of the notion of an artificial or corporate person is to mark the distinctiveness of the hypothesized group in terms of the legitimacy of rights claims. Families have rights that may be asserted against other families or other institutions. As a parent, I recalled being mildly worried by my children's reports that they had been invited by their class teacher to recite some 'news'. Principle (I insist!), rather than bad conscience or potential embarrassment, caused me to worry that family privacy rights may well be invaded by this practice. Nations, likewise, advertise themselves as units of moral agency when they claim rights of territorial sovereignty against invaders. It would be a mistake to think that politicians who denounce territorial aggression are speaking up as the agents of those individuals whose private holdings are under threat. Does it make sense to speak of the rights of the human race? I can think of no actual cases where it does. Could it possibly make sense? Only, I think, in circumstances where it is recognizable that the interests of the species as a group need to be asserted against outsiders – Martians, say, to use an image from outdated science fiction. It is not suprising that when such talk is used to legitimate the eating of meat or animal experimentation that critics denounce it as 'speciesism', since that is exactly the presupposition: the human species is a distinct grouping with proper interests to defend and promote against the competing claims of other groups.

Mention of group rights gives rise to a special difficulty which should be noted before we move on. I have not so far explained how group rights (or, indeed, any rights) may be defended, having sought to explain only how they may be understood. Recent literature on group rights, motivated in part by efforts to come to philosophical terms with the practical problems of multicultural coexistence, has revealed a distinctive form of conflict between rights claims.[23] This is the conflict between rights claimed by some specific group, generally to live lives in accordance with their distinctive religious beliefs, and rights which members of that group may claim as individuals against that group. The conflict is especially hard where the individual rights equate to or are derived from universal rights such as freedom of conscience. One example that Kymlicka discusses concerns the right of Amish parents to withdraw their children from school before the age of 16, thus isolating them from the attractions of the outside world and better securing their allegiance to the traditions of their community. This practice severely reduces the opportunities for Amish children to determine for themselves whether they wish to continue to subscribe to the faith and lifestyle of their community, since it reduces their ability to canvass alternatives. It poses, for the liberal, the general question of whether individual rights should be assigned priority over group rights, and readers may find many other, less starkly described, cases which raise similar issues. When freedom of worship licenses freedom to indoctrinate the young, freedom of the individual conscience may be effectively compromised. Conflicts of individual rights are endemic. Suppose they can be resolved piecemeal by investigating the relative stringencies of the rights in conflict or the relative importance of the interests that the right claims protect or promote. So long as we accept that group rights may not be decomposed into a set of individual rights (and the existence of conflicts of the sort decribed may itself count as a reason for supposing that they may not), the question at issue may be put as the question of whether group rights are systematically less stringent than individual rights. In advance of broaching more general questions concerning the justification of rights claims, I can think of no reason why they might be – which suggests that we turn immediately to the hard problem of justification.

The justification of rights

Having distinguished, in Hohfeldian manner, the variety of rights
and having broached other questions concerning the analysis of
rights claims, we can move forward to discuss how rights claims
are to be justified. We can make a useful beginning by looking at
the classical doctrines of John Locke.

Lockean themes: modes of ownership

As we saw briefly above, Locke offers a most straightforward argument for natural rights. Mankind, he tells us, is God's creation. He
made us and He owns us. Our appointed task is to serve His purposes and our life of service requires that we all find equal protection in our independent pursuit of His design for us. Since we
cannot act as trustees of His purposes unless our lives, health,
liberty and possessions are respected, we have a natural right to
these goods, subject to our respecting equivalent claims that other
trustees of his purposes make upon us. A natural right is a right
asserted in accordance with natural law, that is God's law, prescribed to us as His creation.[24] Hence we can claim against others
that (negatively) they do not interfere with our life in God's service
and (positively) as parents or, in extremis, fellow creatures, that
they provide us with the wherewithal of properly human life.

This is a lovely argument. Grant the premises and the conclusion swiftly follows: each may claim and all must respect the rights
deemed necessary for the achievement of values everyone should
endorse. What is more, this line of argument is fertile; it enables us
to work through in detail and state limits on the generic rights
Locke describes. It enables us to flesh out the right to property and
to detail the political rights appropriate to the right of equal liberty. These turn out to include rights of punishment and rebellion,
in case these further rights are necessary for the protection of
individual rights. Sadly, the argument has no more strength than
its premises bestow, and however much one approves of Locke's
conclusions (or looks forward to developing the argument
further in directions Locke never dreamed of) one cannot expect
all of those to whom claims of right are directed to accept the

theological foundations. Well and good if these premisses find acceptance. But if they don't, and one can expect that for many they won't, other arguments will need to be advanced.

Locke himself believed that the natural law which vindicated natural rights was discernible by reason. It is a matter of scholarly debate how far reason, as Locke construes it, can operate independently of one's acceptance of religious doctrine. If reason is a matter of exploring the implications of truths revealed in scripture, evidently it is not a guide to natural law or morality which non-believers can be expected to trust.

We can put this dispute concerning the interpretation of Locke's doctrines to one side, since some have found in his writings premisses they believe all can accept, premisses which might serve to ground human rights. When, in Chapter V of the *Second Treatise*, Locke tackles the hard problem of the right to private property, he insists that 'every Man has a *Property* in his own *Person*. This no Body has any Right to but himself. The *Labour* of his Body and the *Work* of his Hands, we may say, are properly his.'[25] Call this doctrine the Thesis of Self-Ownership.

The self-ownership thesis has powerful friends and creates strange allies. It vindicates Robert Nozick's claim that the taxation of income for redistributive purposes is 'forced labour',[26] and it serves to ground the charge of exploitation of labour under capitalism pressed by G.A. Cohen.[27] The thought that we naturally own ourselves is of the first importance in understanding historical debates concerning the legitimacy of slavery and the frequently associated thesis that legitimate hierarchical social and political relations must have consensual foundations. Some argued that, owning ourselves, we may sell ourselves or otherwise consent to slavery or political subjection. Others claimed that the property we have in ourselves is inalienable – slavery and subjection are thereby unjustifiable. Others argue that, since the self cannot be alienated in the fashion of private property, the self cannot intelligibly be owned – by others or by ourselves.

It is clear that there are vital issues canvassed in these disputes – but I shan't engage them in any depth. I see the vindication of human rights in terms of self-ownership as a kind of philosophical shadow-boxing whereby metaphor, allusion and analogy take the place of argument. Let me explain. Rights of ownership are generally exclusionary (but not always so – the possibility of *inclusive* rights of ownership should be kept in mind by the sceptic). A standard element of the generic right to private property is the right to exclusive occupation and use. What one owns one may employ for one's private use. Already we have a picture of the owner acting within a space of private possession, which space is determined and bounded by specific rights to assignable property. The picture can be elaborated; if the possession is land, the boundaries of my rights are drawn at my fences. You may not cross without my permission otherwise you violate my rights.

The thesis of self-ownership states that persons stand in a relationship of ownership to themselves. Since we take them to own themselves, there are things which others may not do to them without violating their rights as self-owners. We can trace out a rough symmetry between the rights of self-owners and the rights of owners proper. Just as you have a duty not to destroy, damage, use or invade my property, so you have duties not to kill, injure, enslave or otherwise aggress against me. A thesis of self-ownership is perfectly acceptable if it collects together agreed rights and then operates as a sort of shorthand for them. To say that rape offends a principle of self-ownership will go proxy for an argument to the effect that persons have a right to physical integrity (along with other rights in the self-ownership list) and that rape is a violation of this right, i.e. one right amongst the collection. On this account, one might distinguish rights of self-ownership from rights of collective pursuit, rights to engage in activities alongside others, taking this latter category to include political rights and rights of non-political association. No one can object to a vocabulary which usefully synthesizes a range of operational concepts.

If we think of rights of self-ownership in this way, believing the concept finds useful philosophical employment, who can gainsay it? Unfortunately, though, it may be paraded as a justificatory claim – that persons have such and such rights *in virtue* of being owners of themselves, that claims of right may be *derived* from a person's status as self-owner. This is clearly Locke's strategy in the argument cited above. Suppose one were to make such a claim. Straight away one would face the demand that the right of self-ownership itself be justified. I don't want to insist that this is impossible, illogical or inconsistent since I don't know how this might be shown. I do insist, however, that this effort would be misdirected. Murder, rape, assault, theft, damage and trespass: each of these should be determined as wrong quite independently of any theory of self-ownership. Rights to life, bodily integrity, and property do not need us to defend an antecedent right of self-ownership.

An open-minded, reflective individual of the sort that is attracted to philosophical speculation may well be stumped by the question: Why is it wrong to murder or rape or steal? I think it is unlikely that anyone such could find an answer that is both convincing and recognizably deeper than the intuitions which prompt their recognition of the moral seriousness of questions such as these. This is blunt assertion. I may be wrong. No doubt questions will multiply. Of one thing I am sure: no one should advance the concept of self-ownership as somehow foundational. And this not because novel doctrines can't turn out to be true or illuminating. Rather, doctrines of ownership are *too* familiar. They carry the baggage of ancient debates concerning property rights – and such doctrines as these have been put in question. It is a counsel of despair to urge that one first settle philosophical questions concerning ownership and then move on to derive a full account of human rights from the conclusions reached.

As suggested above, the idea of self-ownership has shown itself to be particularly attractive to liberals in the context of debates about slavery. For if the self-ownership theory is recognized as a self-evident truth, it challenges straight off the claim that one person may be the property of another, that is, a slave. But this challenge may be met. Some might disagree with the claim that the right to liberty is inalienable, imagining circumstances in which one might literally trade risky or impecunious freedom for wellfattened slavery. If the alternative is death (certainly) or great shame (perhaps), slavery might look an attractive option. These questions are deep and ancient (and modern) philosophers have explored them.[28] At the heart of these discussions is the attempt to characterize a minimal moral status attributable to all (or just about all) human beings – the moral status, as mentioned above, of the person. I claim that the thesis of self-ownership cannot explicate this status. At best, it can summarize the results of such a conceptual exploration. Is there a better alternative to the Lockean theme of self-ownership? Many will find this in the concept of autonomy.

Autonomy again

We encountered the concept of autonomy when discussing the value of freedom. For many philosophers, discussions of freedom and rights cover the same conceptual terrain. It seems to matter little whether we think of private property, for example, as the object of a human right or as one of the classical freedoms. It would be hard to disentangle discussions of the right to practice one's religion from discussions of freedom of worship. Rights may be described in terms of freedom – the right to free speech is an obvious example. The relation may be even deeper than that evinced by coincidence or connectedness of usage: in a famous paper, H.L.A. Hart argued for the thesis that, 'if there are any moral rights at all, it follows that there is at least one natural right, the equal right of all men to be free'.[29] Those who advocate negative claim rights, rights to non-interference, evidently value freedom of action within the space created by the proscription. Positive claim rights, demanding the provision of some good or service, may articulate the requirements of positive freedom. Generally, those who value freedom may express their claims in terms of rights, insisting as a matter of human rights that the valued opportunities be provided or protected. This suggests, albeit at the cost of some strain in ordinary usage, that the languages of rights and freedom are intertranslatable, that liberal values may be expressed as rights or freedoms, that the liberal is given a choice of moral idiom.

Furthermore, one may believe that this conceptual luxury has analytic foundations in the concept of autonomy. We have already noticed how, for some, the value of freedom is founded in the ideal of autonomy and we have given this thesis qualified endorsement. Suppose that one is operating with a simplified model of autonomy characterized as reflective choice.[30] We can now tie the analysis of both rights and freedom to autonomy. An agent's freedom is his capacity to select a way of life that suits him and act in accordance with this choice. In similar fashion, one has a right in case he is empowered to make a protected choice.

The relation between freedom and rights is a philosophical minefield and the relation of each to grounding considerations of autonomy cautions us to step very carefully. If one employs a simple (negative) conception of personal freedom and restricts rights to negative rights of individual action, one can see straight away that the appropriate sphere of freedom is demarcated by the ascription of rights which impose duties of non-interference on governments and other agencies. At its most basic, the value of autonomy grounds rights claims which impose duties which thereby protect freedom. Freedom is violated when agents transgress the duties required of them in virtue of the legitimate rights of autonomous agents. Would that philosophy were so simple! We have already seen the value of freedom is too complex to permit such swift analysis. We should not be surprised if the same conclusion is forced by our investigation of rights.

Let us advance the thesis that human rights are justified on the grounds that they promote autonomy. One bad argument for this thesis is that it follows directly from a central feature of rights – that rights bearers are essentially in a position of choice with respect to the fulfilment of the duties imposed by the rights they claim. To have a right is to have a choice – which is to express the agent's autonomy. Thus if I have an exclusive right of access to my property, it's up to me whether I grant you permission to walk around it. The element of choice that figures in all rights claims consists in the rights bearer's power of waiving the duties which his possession of the right imposes.[31]

The central claim of this thesis may be disputed. Some rights may be inalienable, their bearers may not be able to waive them. The right to be free has been thought by some to have this status, as mentioned above; one cannot legitimately give oneself up to slavery. The right to life has been thought inalienable, to the point where suicide is proscribed. The alienability of these rights is controversial, but the issues cannot be settled by conceptual *fiat*, by an insistence that no right can be inalienable since rights holders always, by definition, have a power of waiver. A different kind of case, but one making a similar point, concerns those who have the right to vote in jurisdictions where submitting a ballot paper is compulsory. They may or may not have the freedom to vote – analysts differ on this issue – but voters who do what the law requires of them are acting in accordance with a valuable right. Some may think the right would be more valuable were citizens to be offered the associated right to abstain, but that it is less valuable (if indeed it is less valuable) should not lead us to discount it as a right.

There is a different strand of argument connecting autonomy and rights. The sense of 'autonomy' which is employed is an informal development of the skeletal Kantian account given in terms of a capacity to formulate universally applicable moral laws and act in accordance with them or the right not to be treated as a means, merely. As a recent theorist puts it:

> Recognizing autonomy as a right requires us to respect the dignity of the person: to treat others not as playthings or objects or resources that we may use for our own purposes but as individuals who are capable, at least potentially, of forming plans, entering into relationships, pursuing projects, and living in accordance with an ideal of a worthwhile life.[32]

Dagger describes autonomy as the capacity to lead a self-governed life. 'Every other right either derives from it or is in some sense a manifestation of our human right to autonomy.'[33] This echoes associated themes familiar in the work of other celebrated modern liberals: rights reflect the fact of our separate existences, the fact that there are distinct individuals, each with his own life *to lead* (Nozick); they require us to take seriously the distinction between persons (Rawls); persons equally have a right of moral independence (Dworkin). Such rhetoric is frequently heard in discussions of utilitarianism, which is held, through its principle of aggregation, to violate our recognition of the discreteness of moral persons – and we shall return to this issue later. But whether directly, in celebration of autonomy, or indirectly, by way of the refutation of utilitarianism, such arguments highlight the conceptual linkage between the notion of the person as a separate and self-governing agent and the normative language of rights.

Take Dagger's claim at its most ambitious. Is the value of autonomy strong enough or clear enough for us to be confident that it can deliver a full derivation of human rights? There are certainly human rights which seem to manifest the value of autonomy. In the case of the right to life, if we construe this as requiring others not to kill us, it is easy, too easy perhaps, to see why killing us would violate our autonomy. An autonomous life is a life after all. No life, no autonomy – just as the most effective way to stop me breathing is to kill me stone dead. Suppose we think of the right to life as a positive claim right. Again, I won't be autonomous (or much else, apart from a corpse) if you deny me the life-saving medicine. If there is an oddity here, and I think there is, it lies in the thought that what is wrong with killing a person is the denial of their autonomy. Take someone who is not autonomous. Whatever capacities underly autonomy, rationality say, or the ability to abstract from and appraise, then control, her desires: if these are absent through some psychological condition, the wrong of killing her cannot be a function of the denial of her autonomy. Whatever horrible example we have in mind – the baby, the severely handicapped adult or the demented old person – theory has got out of hand if we deny them the right to life which is accorded to other (more real?) persons. And most readers will recognize an *ad hoc* solution in the claim that to kill them would be wrong, but for reasons other than that they have a right to life which we claim for ourselves – as though to kill us would be to double the wrong which is inflicted on such poor souls, or be wrong for more reasons.

Think, to make a different point, of my right to physical integrity which would be violated were you to punch me on the nose as you passed me in the street. You hit me and pass on. I clear myself up and make my way home. I can think of lots of reasons why you have done me wrong. Your violence has cost me – some pain and a dry-cleaner's bill to take the blood off my suit. Have you diminished my capacity for self-governance? Have you altered my plan of life? You may or may not have done. If you reduce me to a timid, housebound wreck, you surely have. But I may not be thus affected. I may regard a mugger's assault as yet another cost to be borne by those unfortunates like myself who, all things considered, choose to work in the inner city. In such a case, I may well deem that my rights have been violated yet regard my autonomy as intact. I may resolve not to alter my route to work. Don't let these people win, I say, sensibly or otherwise, whistling in the wind.

There are clearly wrongs done to individuals which may impair or eliminate their autonomy which are not wrongs only, or primarily so, on just these grounds. And there are violations of rights which may, but may not, violate their autonomy. My hunch is this: if we construe respect for rights as respecting autonomy and then think of the violation of autonomy on Kantian grounds, as treating folks not as ends but as means merely, of course my rights are violated when you treat me as a punchbag. But then (and this is also a thought many Kantians endorse) this is the mark of all wrong-doing.[34] This conclusion strikes me as too strong (as does the lesser claim associated with Nozick and Dworkin that all political morality lies within the domain of persons' rights).

At bottom, my worry is that the value of autonomy is being asked to do too much work when it is employed as the foundational value of *all* ascriptions of human rights. If one uses a thin (Kantian) conception of autonomy, the line of derivation from the claim that persons are ends-in-themselves to the justification of human rights is likely to be too attenuated to be convincing. If one uses a thick conception of autonomy – and we have seen how Dagger amplifies the core Kantian insights – the autonomous life becomes, quite generally, the life well led, a life distinguished by plans, projects, relationships and ideals. If we demand: Which plans, projects etc. . . . count as expressive of autonomy? we can expect both a formal and a substantive answer. The formal answer may restrict plans and projects to those that are compatible with others' pursuit of their plans and projects; my autonomy should not be purchased at the cost of the autonomy of others. This strikes me as overly restrictive. Why should Jane not interfere with Jill's pursuit of the relationship of her choosing if they've both selected Jack as the best father for their children? The substantive answer to the question will require an inspection of candidate projects and ideals to see if they pass muster. What tests do we have available? I'm sure there are plenty. One question to be asked concerns the harmfulness of the canvassed project or ideal. Remember, as we noticed in Chapter 3, it isn't a good feature of a career of child abuse that it is autonomously pursued. Racial supremacy is another rotten conception of the good life, but if it is mine own, can I call in the value of autonomy to support me in its pursuit? Surely not.

None of this is meant to demonstrate that human rights cannot be justified in terms of the autonomy of the agent who wishes her deliberations and activities to be protected. When agents reflect on their successes and failures, it is important in many cases that the endeavours they have pursued be identifiably their *own*. Nothing is more saddening than the guilt or shame felt by the child who has failed to live up to her parents' excessive expectations. The erosion of self-respect, the developing sense of personal inadequacy in the face of others' improper expectations or unrealistic standards is genuinely tragic because the flaw is unreal, though the personal consequences may be devastating. We argued before that a parent's imposition of life goals on a child represents a severe breach of that child's autonomy where the child internalizes the parental ambitions at a crucial point in her development. This familiar aetiology of personal desperation tells us much about the real value of autonomy.

The thought that moral agents are self-governing, that they have their own lives to lead, their own ideals to formulate and pursue, should not be represented as a bloodless ontological truth reflected in the metaphysics of morality. Or at least it should not be represented thus for the purposes of deriving some specification of human rights. The ideal of personal autonomy that is violated by the sad stories I have sketched serves perfectly well for the delineation of some human rights. It is a beautiful but sensitive plant, concealed as effectively by heavyweight philosophical apparatus as it is destroyed by strong alien intrusion. It is vulnerable to well-meaning family aspirations, peer pressure, mechanisms of social conformity, as well as the designs of states (or their representative politicians) to generate a well-structured labour force. All of these (and many other) agencies of coercion stand between the vulnerable person and her achievement of a decent and satisfying life. Autonomy, thus described, demands a manifesto of human rights, but it would be a mistake to understand all human rights as having their grounding in individual autonomy.

Are there any human rights which cannot be derived from the value of autonomy, or not from the value of autonomy alone? I think it is counterintuitive, as I have argued, to claim that the right to life which is violated by murder or the right to physical integrity which is violated by assault derive from some story about how these actions violate autonomy. I think it is just as misleading to claim that the political rights derive from autonomy alone. Of course the autonomous agent will wish to have powers of participation in democratic forums, but the exercise of citizens' powers in activities such as voting, speaking up and marching with others is a social performance more than a personal project. To anticipate the argument of Chapter 7, it is we, the people, who so act, in concert with each other. Democracy may be represented as a stage on which solitary actors strut their stuff in a public display of private aspirations, but this is an impoverished representation of a most likely deluded activity. Politics, like church-going, is one of those activities that does not locate the sense that it is worthwhile in individual evaluations of the projects that make sense of them.

Rights and interests

Persons have interests. Some are weighty, some are trivial. Some are idiosyncratic, some are just about universal. These categories evidently intersect. Some interests are so important and so widespread that they give rise to claims against others that these interests be served. The resultant claims may be against others, that they not kill, hurt or steal from us, or against governments that they provide protective services. For Mill, a right is a valid claim on society for protection. 'To have a right, then, is, I conceive, to have something which society ought to defend me in the possession of.'[35] Mill's example was that of security, 'to everyone's feelings the most vital of all interests'.[36] And this reminds us, though this was not Mill's intention, that crucial rights may be either or both, negative and positive, depending on the terms in which they are spelled out. On this account, to have a right is to have a justifiable claim against others that some interest be protected or promoted. What rights, then, do we have? All will depend on the interests that are cited as demanding protection and promotion. In some cases, as Mill's example of security suggests, these will be universal. In which case, they may well be deemed human rights. In other cases, they will be particular or conditional. The rights distinctive of members of a club are examples.

Talk of interests is irremediably vague. Small wonder that dispute about rights is endemic and that new claims of right proliferate daily. A novel example, which I suspect I am bringing to the attention of readers for the first time, is the right of adults born through a process of artificial insemination to be granted knowledge of the identity of the sperm donor. Clearly the first step claimants to such a right must take if they are to have it recognized, is to convince others of the importance of the interest they have in acquiring such knowledge. The phenomenon of 'rights inflation', well described by L.W. Sumner,[37] witnesses the variety of interests that individuals attest as grounds for the claims they make on others. Rights collide and compete as differing interests struggle for prominence in policy debates. The interest a natural parent takes in bringing up her child may conflict with the child's interest in having a healthy, supportive upbringing – and courts may be asked to adjudicate what emerges as a collision of rights in terms of laws or principles which establish a hierarchy or ranking between them. 'The rights of the child should be decisive', some will say.

Problems of two kinds are foregrounded by the conceptual association of rights and interests: philosophical problems concerning whether interests are subjective or objective,[38] and moral problems concerning the importance or weight of the declared interest and its implications for the duties which the claimed right imposes on others. Problems of the first kind, I put to one side (which is not to derogate their importance). Problems of the second kind seem endless and intractable. But that should be taken as an incentive for effort rather than a counsel of despair. Claims of right are not self-validating. It is an important feature of the view that takes rights claims as expressions of interests which warrant promotion and protection that it tells us where to look when disputes are to be settled: examine the interests which ground the claims.

Interests, we should note, may be individual interests or group interests. This distinction may seem misguided. Whether interests are taken as subjective or objective, aren't we always thinking, at bottom, of the interests of individuals? Who or what else could take or have an interest? There is evidently some connection between the interests of individuals and the interests of groups. It would be astonishing if one were to attest a group interest which bore no relation to any identifiable interest of the members of the group. It is hard to think of a project being in the interests of a some firm without it being in the interests of the shareholders or of a policy being in the interest of some nation without it being in the interests of citizens. It is generally supposed that a firm's interests will be identical with those of a majority of shareholders. The national interest may be similarly decomposed into the interests of most citizens. On this view, if you wish to determine the group interest, consult or otherwise seek evidence concerning the interests of the members. Ask them, or otherwise find out, what their interests consist in. How else could one determine the interests of groups?

This direct approach is philosophically tainted. The common sense which underlies it is infected with a species of individualism which incorporates a distinctive and controversial philosophical view of the relationship of individuals to the groups of which they are members. The central feature of this view is that groups are identified as instrumental to the achievement of antecedent individual interests. Group interests, on this account, amount to a concatenation of individual interests. The decision procedures of such groups will be designed to give effect to these individual interests.

This view is doubtless true of many groups – but not of all, or indeed most, once groups have become stable. A useful distinction here is that between natural and artificial groups (or associations). Artificial groups enlist members on the basis of a declared prospectus. Standardly, membership will be voluntary, as will be continued subscription. The purpose of membership will be to pursue an individual interest which is more effectively achieved when individuals act in concert. As soon as the convener, secretary and treasurer are in place, a division of labour can increase efficiency and effectiveness in the use of resources to the common end. One can expect such groups to come into existence as soon as common interests are identified and to disband when the object of interest is secured. The evident mistake is to suppose that all groups are of this kind.

Natural groups are those groups of which agents find themselves as members, willy-nilly. Families and clans are obvious examples. The nation-state is a controversial contender for natural status. Aristotle thought that the state in the form of the Greek *polis* was

167

natural – man is *zoon politikon*, a creature of the *polis*, because the *polis* is the minimum-sized unit of human self-sufficiency.[39] Hobbes, by contrast, believed the state to be an artificial group (or person) – the creation of individuals with a congruent set of purposes through their individual pursuit of the preservation of their lives and 'commodious living'.[40] This distinction of natural and artificial groups is too complex for us to pursue here, but one implication is noteworthy in respect of the interests group members attest. Artificial groups may be identified in terms of the antecedent interests which membership promotes. In the case of natural groups, some members' interests may be consequent upon the fact of their group membership. It is because they are members of such and such a group that they form certain interests; their interest in the well-being of the group itself will be the most conspicuous example.

This pair of distinctions, between natural and artificial groups, and interests formed antecedently to or consequent upon membership, conceals a good deal of overlap. Humans notoriously form groups for specific purposes, sometimes explicitly self-interested but often not so, and then find the group which has been created develops a life of its own. Parents form or join a parents association to promote the better education of their children, then find that the habit of association generates social activities which have a pleasure of their own independently of the original purposes of association. Some folks seem born clubbers, keen to join, organize and serve groups in which they enlist. Groucho Marx, keen to avoid any club which would have him as a member, seems very much the exception. Group membership forms as well as serves individual interests, even in the case of those whose original interest is self-interest. Hegel describes this process as the mediation of the particular through the universal. It is distinctive of Civil Society, the social sphere in which family members seek their particular welfare in the world of work.[41] I suspect that only those groups formed to serve very narrow and temporary interests can escape this dynamic. But the implication is clear. Groups can form individuals' interests just as effectively as the interests of individuals lead them to form groups. Where this happens, we can speak intelligibly of a group interest. And where groups express a distinctive group interest, we should expect them to claim that these interests be protected and perhaps promoted as of right. The dynamic of transformation between individual interest and group interest can make it very difficult to establish whether the rights which are claimed in consequence are group rights or individual rights. Imagine a religious congregation which wishes to build a place of worship amidst a community of non-believers. Suppose planning permission is denied on grounds of bigotry. 'We tolerate the Muslims here, but let them not try to build a mosque!', I once heard said by a benighted Presbyterian. When the congregation appeals, citing their right to worship together in an appropriate building, is this a group right or a collection of individual rights that is being asserted? Only subscription to a mistaken view concerning individuals' interests would lead one to conclude that there couldn't be a group right at stake.

Rights and utility

Interests, as we have seen, may be widespread and important. Rights claims, whether established in international conventions or municipal legislation, are the favoured method of protecting and promoting them. How can interests, as the objects of rights, work to justify institutional provision? The simplest answer, though not the only one, is to register the interests which rights serve in a consequentialist, broadly utilitarian, calculation. Persons have interests as individuals or in virtue of their membership of groups. Consult these interests, expressed in terms of the best value theory, and enquire whether their fulfilment through institutional provision maximizes utility. If it does, one has established a moral right, construed as a claim against the institution designers that recognition of the particular interests be accorded by the most effective institutional structures. Generally, the most effective structures will be the legal processes of individual nation-states. Sometimes international legal structures, as in the recently established International Criminal Court, may be judged the best way of protecting human rights on a worldwide basis by prosecuting those responsible for genocide, crimes against humanity and war crimes.[42] Some specific provisions, derivable from more general rights may find informal protection within positive morality.

To see how this project might work, take the example I mentioned earlier of a novel rights claim – the right of adults born following artificial insemination to be informed of the identity of the donor. Those who claim such a right will declare an interest in knowing the identity of their natural father. They will cite their ignorance as a deprivation and source of suffering. They will anticipate the possible pleasure of future acquaintance. Those who oppose such a right will argue that the benefits to recipients of AID (parent(s) and perhaps child, too) will be reduced as donors are frightened off by the prospect of future telephone calls from developed embryos for whose creation they have some measure of responsibility. And one could go on, recording the good and bad news for the different persons likely to be affected by a policy of recording details to which putative rights bearers claim access. If, after registering the effects of such institutional innovation on all parties who have an interest in such affairs, it is judged that disclosure is more beneficial overall than secrecy, then a case has been made for a moral right. Public recognition of this right requires that the institutions which most effectively secure disclosure be put in place. Or not, as the case may be. It should be noted that this process of calculation requires that everyone's interests be taken into account. This includes those who claim e.g. that their right to AID would be compromised or their right to privacy would be violated by a process of disclosure. These rights, too, are decomposed into the registration of the interests their rights protect.

The variety of consequentialism which justifies the assignment of rights is evidently indirect.[43] Once rights are established, actions are wrong if they involve violations of claims of right or permissible if they are within the sphere of a legitimate rights claim. If it is granted, on grounds of general utility, say, that persons have a right to the exclusive use of private property, it is permissible for folk to use their own property but impermissible for others to do so without the owner's permission. This derivation of rights and the implied verdicts in the case of particular actions is no stronger than the variety of consequentialism which underpins it. I shall put to one side here general criticisms of the utilitarian project and shall address directly a few central objections to the utilitarian defence of rights.

First, let us tackle a number of slogans. Rights, as we have seen, are claims made by individuals or groups. In the simplest, albeit misleading, case, they amount to claims that the individuals' (or groups') moral boundaries be respected. Historically they are linked to a burgeoning individualism. So rights presuppose 'the distinction of persons . . . the separateness of life and experience' (Rawls),[44] 'this root idea, namely, that there are different individuals with separate lives' (Nozick).[45] The implication of this position for Nozick is that rights are 'side-constraints' on the pursuit of goals.

These claims have assumed an enormous importance in discussions of utilitarianism and rights since many of those who have taken them to be obviously true have also believed (as Rawls and Nozick believe) that they are incompatible with utilitarianism in so far as it incorporates aggregative and maximizing elements. Aggregation and maximization may reveal the best policy to be one which trades off the interests of some persons to achieve maximal well-being overall. One does not need to be a card-carrying utilitarian to recognize the weakness of arguments as sketchy as these. One of the distinctive features of utilitarianism is its insistence that everyone's interests be counted, and counted equally, in the aggregation. 'Everybody to count for one, nobody for more than one', was Mill's statement of the Benthamite orthodoxy.[46] Just one of the reasons why the classical utilitarians were deemed philosophical *radicals* was their insistence that the interests of *all* be computed in a judgement of the common good. No one's distinctive or separate interest, however idiosyncratic, should be ignored. This thought is bolstered by the obvious truth that the goods to be reckoned in any calculation are goods to individuals. Whether they be computed in terms of happiness, pleasure net pain, desire-satisfaction or elements of an objective list, individuals are the only possible beneficiaries. The thought that groups might have interests antecedently to the interests of individuals comprising the groups does not challenge this conclusion. Wherever the interests come from, the utility achieved by satisfying them will accrue to individuals severally. If the separateness of persons is recognized in the calculation of utility, and if the calculations of utility support the recognition of individual rights, what reason have we for concluding that the utilitarian project fails to recognize the fact that different individuals have their separate lives to lead? For this conclusion to be justified there must be some other respect in which the separateness of persons is not recognized.

Before we investigate this further claim, let us look at another slogan – one deriving from Ronald Dworkin who argues, famously, that rights are trumps; in particular, rights claims trump competing judgements of utility. In Dworkin's words, 'Rights are best understood as trumps over some background justification for political decisions that states a goal for the community as a whole'.[47] The 'background justification' that Dworkin has in mind is utilitarianism. The metaphor of trumps, for those ignorant of the rules of whist, implies that no matter how grand the advantage of a policy in point of utility, if, in a specific case, implementation of that policy violates rights, it is unjustifiable. No matter how grand one's card in the other three suits (the ace of spades, perhaps) if clubs are trumps, the two of clubs wins the trick.

As with the other slogans, there is an argument behind it – and as with them, I shall ignore the details. It is important to see what this argument cannot establish. It cannot show that it is somehow analytic or conceptually integral to rights claims that they countervail arguments from utility. The utilitarian case for rights is cogent, though it may fail if the background theory is found unacceptable. It can't fall at the first hurdle on the grounds that it proposes to evaluate rights whose credentials are somehow immune to utilitarian inspection, that it is improper, conceptually speaking, to bring rights to the bar of utility.

There is a further implication of Dworkin's claim that rights trump utility that needs to be pinned down. Recall – if clubs are trumps, the two of clubs beats the ace of spades. This suggests that the meanest right, if granted, defeats arguments from utility that purport to justify its violation in the particular case. However much disutility may accrue, the right should be respected. Now the utilitarian can agree with this, so long as the right is in place and justified by good utilitarian reasons. The detailed specification of the right will make clear the scope of rights claims. Suppose we all agree, utilitarians and non-utilitarians alike, that a right to private property should be recognized. We can expect the detail of any such right to incorporate specific exclusions. The state will claim the right (eminent domain) to requisition farmland for the construction of airports during an emergency, or a civic authority may have powers of compulsory purchase to build a city bypass. All zoning or planning regulations articulate, through limitations, the contours of specific rights. Once the cluster of rules deemed optimum have been set out and accepted, there will be no provision for arbitrary executive breach of them, as Rawls pointed out in 'Two Concepts of Rules'. At no trumps, the lead of the ace of spades will win the trick against the play of the two of clubs, but if the rules of the game establish a trump suit, and if clubs are trumps, not so. All depends on the precise rules of the game. One cannot insist that the rules of whist are distinctively non-utilitarian, because they make provision for a trump suit.

In a similar vein, it has been suggested by David Lyons that the utilitarian cannot capture the distinctive moral force of rights claims.[48] Call the moral theory which does capture the moral force of rights claims T. I see no reason to exclude the possibility that application of the principle of utility might not yield exactly the same set of institutional arrangements as T. This is clearly a contingent matter, since which institution finds utilitarian favour depends on the facts of the matter. So suppose both T and utilitarian reasoning support a given structure of rights. In this case the thought that the utilitarian cannot capture the moral force of rights boils down to the hypothesis that utilitarianism licenses a discretion on the part of officials to break the rules if they judge that this will produce utility. I see no reason why the utilitarian should accept this. Whatever discretion officials may exercise will be laid down *within* the system of rules – and, *ex hypothesi*, these are the same for both theories.

Some are not content with the contingency at the heart of utilitarian theories. Which institutions we endorse evidently depends on how the facts pan out. The utilitarian cannot deny this element of contingency. To settle the issue we should need to confront the utilitarian position with an alternative, as with T above, which derives rights in all their specificity from different foundations, and we should need to inspect the factual credentials of utilitarian proposals. This latter is a massive task, but we should not expect theory T to find straightforward *a priori* grounding and direct application. On my understanding of rights, T would have to bear on the interests that rights protect. This is an analytic feature of rights claims and it severely limits the range of alternative derivations.

Often a different point is being made by those who deem rights to be trumps or possessed of some distinctive moral force which belies their grounding in utility. Suppose, as before, that both utilitarianism and theory T yield exactly the same set of rules granting rights. The claim may be that rights as trumps have such moral force as to warrant respect even in the face of catastrophe. Respect rights though the heavens fall. Respect rights no matter what amount of human interests are sacrificed thereby.[49] If rights are protective of human interests, such claims look preposterous. If rights are trumps in the sense of being absolute, we are better off without them. But I leave the reader to judge.

The no-theory theory

Before we close our discussion of rights, I want to mention one further theory. Let me begin with a story from Arthur Danto:

> In the afterwash of 1968, I found myself a member of a group charged with working out the disciplinary procedures for acts against my university. It was an exemplary group from the perspective of representation so urgent at the time: administrators, tenured and non-tenured faculty, graduate and undergraduate students, men and women, whites and blacks. We all wondered, nevertheless, what right we had to do what was asked of us, and a good bit of time went into expressing our insecurities. Finally, a man from the law-school said, with the tried patience of someone required to explain what should be as plain as day, and in a tone of voice I can still hear: 'This is the way it is with rights. You want'em, so you say you got'em, and if nobody says you don't then you do.' In the end he was right. We worked a code out which nobody liked, but in debating it the community acknowledged the rights. Jefferson did not say that it was self-evident that there were human rights and which they were: he said we *hold* this for self-evident. He chose this locution mainly, I think, because he was more certain we have them than he was of any argument alleged to entail them, or of any premises from

which their existence was to follow. This is the way it is with rights. We *declare* we have them, and see if they are recognized.[50]

From one point of view, this no-theory theory is a counsel of despair. Suppose we are impressed by claims of human rights and yet, being philosophically scrupulous, we despair of establishing a foundation for them which we find convincing. We can see sense in various foundationalist projects: for some rights claims, in some circumstances, autonomy serves as the value which rights promote; for other rights, in different circumstances, utility promises convincing grounds; for still other rights, whose force we acknowledge, we may find ourselves stumped – no justification seems to serve. Where we accept justificatory claims we may still be hesitant to propose that we have to hand a convincing theory which can be deployed across the board. At this point, the thought that rights claim are an ethical bedrock, resistant to further exploration may look attractive. We can accord them the status of first principles, perhaps clouding the waters further by speaking of them as intuitions.

This would be to misread the point of Danto's homily, since it fails to recognize a distinctive feature of the logical grammar of rights – that they are generally asserted as claims on others. If others acknowledge the force of claims of right (perhaps, as is likely, they make similar claims, themselves, against others) that is all that is necessary for the rights to be established. All parties are involved in a practice of making, acknowledging and respecting rights claims.

If this is true, if rights are claimed, acknowledged and respected amongst a community, no further argument is needed to establish their provenance. The obvious objection to this strategy is that the right in question, on any occasion of its assertion, may be denied. So it looks as though rights exist at the whim of tyrants or bloody-minded opponents. Just one determined nay-sayer on Danto's committee would have been sufficient to block progress.

The defender of the no-theory theory need not be disheartened at this point. The obvious resources will be history and sociology. Nobody, any more, I claim confidently, accepts the arguments in favour of slavery advanced in the seventeenth century. The various documents attesting human rights are established as the norms of international and municipal political correctness. Folks just do make claims of individual and group rights nowadays, expecting, often correctly, that they will meet with sufficiently widespread acceptance. And so rights have emerged alongside the increasing embarrassment of their public detractors, composing a central ingredient of acceptable political rhetoric. Even the most benighted political conservative has lost the folk-memory or myth of a society with the sort of organic civic unity that precludes claims of right. Heirs of the Reformation, of the anti-slavery debates, of the struggles for the achievement of the rights of man and the citizen, we are all of us bloody-minded enough to keep cognizance of our rights.

The no-theory theory may look depressingly like a no-argument theory, impotent in the face of persistent dispute. If one can't get the dissenter to acknowledge the fact of her claiming the rights she repudiates, how is advance possible? This is the point at which a battery of other arguments kick in. We can try, *ad hominem*, the Lockean strategy, the Kantian strategy, the Millian strategy: whatever argumentative path will take the dissenter from her premises to our conclusion. Pluralism may be the enemy of philosophical tidiness but it is a friend to the project of finding agreement.

Chapter 5

Distributive justice

In this chapter we shall address the problem of distributive justice, the vexed issue of how wealth and income, goods and services should be distributed or allocated amongst the population of a state. There are many candidate principles that may be applied, some of which I discuss explicitly in what follows, but before we advance any further, I should bring to your attention a restriction which I have placed on this investigation which you may well judge to be arbitrary. For many, the problem of social justice amounts in practice to the social question of how a society should cope with poverty, assuming that the poor are always with us, that even in the richest nations pockets of seemingly uneradicable poverty exist alongside extremes of wealth. This was noticed by the earliest philosophers to observe the social mechanics of developing capitalism. Hegel, to take one example, tells us that 'civil society affords a spectacle of extravagance and misery as well as of the physical and ethical corruption common to both'.[1]

But if the co-existence of great wealth and deep poverty is a problem within states, it is a much greater problem between states or between the peoples of different states. In the face of these dismal facts, one important philosophical question is this: are these different problems – one of social justice, say, the other of global or international justice – or are we confronted by the same problem arising in different contexts? Relatedly, are the philosophical principles which one might employ to judge the justice of these different manifestations of radical inequality the same in each case or are different principles needed to address them and to prescribe redistribution where that is deemed necessary? It is fair to say that the problems of international distributive justice are in their academic infancy, though already one can identify utilitarian, Kantian and contractualist approaches.[2] With great reluctance, I shall put these questions to one side, trusting, perhaps naïvely, that one will have made a start to the consideration of them if one has deliberated carefully about social justice within states.

I shall begin the discussion by investigating one of the latest entries to the field of competing theories, the entitlement theory of Robert Nozick. I begin here, anachronistically, because I believe Nozick's account is the simplest and most straightforward account of social justice; if not the best-founded, it most readily captures our untutored intuitions concerning who can validly claim the right to what property. As we shall see, these intuitions will need to be corrected.

Entitlement

With luck, you will own the book you are presently reading. Let me assume so. How do you vindicate your claims of ownership if these are challenged? 'Is that your copy?', someone may ask. If you are careful and well-organized, the issue of proper ownership will likely be settled as soon as you produce a receipt. This may not fully allay the enquirer's worries. She may be investigating your earnings and wonder how you acquired the wherewithal for this expensive purchase. So you bring out your pay-slips and bank statement and show that the item was purchased within your publicly declared means. What more can you be expected to do? The challenge was made and met. You have shown that you are entitled to the copy you possess. You have demonstrated that it is your private property.

Nozick's theory of entitlement

Concealed in this episode is a theory of entitlement, associated in recent times with Robert Nozick. On Nozick's account, a distribution of holdings is just if it meets three conditions:

(1) *Justice in Acquisition*: 'A person who acquires a holding in accordance with the principle of justice in acquisition is entitled to that holding.'
(2) *Justice in Transfer*: 'A person who acquires a holding in accordance with the principle of justice in transfer, from someone else entitled to the holding, is entitled to the holding.'
(3) *Rectification of Injustice*: 'No one is entitled to a holding except by (repeated) applications of (1) and (2).'[3]

The principles of just acquisition concern the 'legitimate first moves'. Acquisition, here, means first or original acquisition of goods which are owned either by nobody, or else inclusively, by everyone in common. The principles of just transfer concern 'the legitimate means of moving from one distribution to another'; standard examples would include sale or gift. Principles of rectification operate when holdings are illegitimate in respect of acquisition or transfer. They would require, for example, that stolen goods be returned to the legitimate owner. If we apply the bones of this entitlement theory to the episode described above, where your possession of this book was challenged, you vindicate your possession by application of the principles of justice in transfer when you give evidence of purchase. Had the book turned out to be stolen or kept following a loan, restitution to the owner would be prescribed by application of justice in rectification. As Nozick points out, 'the entitlement theory of justice in distribution is *historical*; whether a distribution is just depends upon how it came about'.[4]

Nozick's entitlement theory serves as a mighty critical instrument. All manner of theories of distribution are rejected as they are revealed to be inconsistent with it, as we shall see later. The oddity of his presentation is that, having given a general outline of the form of the entitlement theory, he should do so little to give it substance by way of a detailed specification and defence of the three principles. 'I shall not attempt that task here',[5] he tells us, and to my knowledge he has never returned to it. What he does have to say concerning the first principle, for example, is a repudiation of Locke's attempt to vindicate original acquisition. Nonetheless, if there is a default position concerning the justice of any particular distribution of private property, Nozick has evidently given us the structure of it. Any theory of distributive justice must, when fully articulated and consistently applied, give rise to a specification of who owns what property which can be adjudicated by reference to the legitimacy of the transactions which produced the given distribution. Whether these transactions amount to the private agreements on which Nozick concentrates, i.e. gifts, bequests, sales etc. or government transfers, which Nozick deems illegitimate, e.g. social security grants or payments, state pensions or whatever, *some* story must be available to be recited when holdings are challenged. If a system of private property is held to be unjust, this must entail that some members of a community are not entitled, *vis-à-vis* the range of *permissible* stories which may be told, to the goods that they claim.[6] Justice will be done when the goods are reallocated in accordance with an appropriate scheme of rectification.

The glamour of Nozick's proposal derived from its link to common-sense intuitions governing who owns what, as exemplified by my story concerning your book, together with its promise to undercut reams of published debate on the subject of justice. All readers will be familiar with the thought that a just distribution is an equal distribution. Some may have moved on to the thought that we can improve on equality if the worst off in a society with an unequal distribution are better off than they would be under conditions of equality. Others will insist that a just distribution will be responsive to claims of need; others, still, may require that desert and merit be recognized. Philosophically tainted contributors to the debate will argue that no distribution can be just which does not maximize utility.

Nozick himself was well aware of the power of his entitlement theory to counter theories developed from intuitions or theoretical stances of the kind rehearsed above. He contrasts his *historical* conception of justice with *current time-slice* principles which employ a structural principle to determine whether a distribution is just. A current time-slice principle will ask not: How has this distribution come about? but: Does this distribution achieve a specific goal or *end-state*, does it exemplify a specific *pattern*? Any theory of the sort that begins: 'from each according to his _____ and concludes: 'to each according to his____', is a patterned theory, as is equality of wealth and income.

An unusual example of a patterned principle is the one Hume deemed hopeless, if well-meaning: 'to each according to his moral virtue.' Nozick's point is that such a principle commits us to an inspection of the current distribution of goods to individuals to see whether or not it accords with this principle. If it does – the more virtue a person displays, the more goods they hold in comparison to others of lesser virtue – the distribution is just, *regardless of how that distribution came about*. If we find persons of lesser virtue holding more goods than the more virtuous, the distribution is unjust, again *regardless of the provenance of that distribution*. Nozick now goes on to reveal what he takes to be a systematic weakness in principles of this form.

He proposes a thought-experiment. Take your favoured pattern of just distribution (D1) – not wealth proportionate to virtue, but, say (more familiar, if equally implausible) strict equality of wealth – and suppose it is exemplified. Now, Wilt Chamberlain signs for a basketball team that will pay him twenty-five cents for each fan admitted to home games and so collects $250,000 by the end of the season from the million fans who have willingly turned up to watch him. (Multiply the total by twenty or more to make it realistic in terms of current prices and earnings.) Is he entitled to these earnings? Clearly, the resulting distribution (D2) is unjust as measured by the principle of equality. Each fan has $25 less and Wilt has $250,000 more. Yet 'each of these persons *chose* to give twenty-five cents of their money to Chamberlain. They could have spent it on going to the movies, or on candy bars, or on copies of *Dissent* magazine, or of *Monthly Review*.'[7] The implication of patterned theories of justice is that, since this society has moved from a just to an unjust pattern of holdings, this position needs to be rectified:

most easily by confiscating Chamberlain's earnings and restoring them to the willing punters. Nozick's conclusion looks devastating: 'The general point illustrated by the Wilt Chamberlain example ... is that no end-state principle or distributional patterned principle of justice can be continuously realized without continuous interference with people's lives.'[8] Liberty upsets patterns.

This conclusion should not be judged to be as iconoclastic as Nozick would have it. Those who value liberty may be disturbed at the prospect of 'continuous interference with people's lives'. But if they reflect that the form taken by interference is likely to be taxation and that, for most folks, 'continuous' means every time they receive a pay-slip or purchase a meal, they may judge that they do not experience this continuous interference as a significant loss of liberty. The value of keeping one's pre-tax earnings may not be negligible, the payment of income or sales taxes may be a burden, but most folks get used to it. Perhaps they notice that it is those who earn much the most who gripe the most – and who are most likely to emigrate to some tax-haven. For many people, the pain of paying their tax bills is as irritating as the pain of traffic lights switching to red whenever they are in a hurry, of pedestrians appearing on a zebra crossing just as they are about to drive across it. They see tax cuts as a notable gain rather than an insignificant reduction of an unjustified impost. As we discovered when thinking about liberty, not every restriction or impediment or interference weighs significantly on the scales.

Of course, those who are sanguine about taxation, seeing it, alongside death, as the fate of all mortals, may be underestimating the moral iniquity of their predicament. They may be the sort of victims of a prevailing ideology that a quick dose of smart philosophy may cure. They may read and think, and recognize Nozick as a philosophical faith-healer. 'Taxation of earnings from labor is on a par with forced labor', Nozick tells us.[9] I doubt it. What's more, I think it would be seriously impertinent to ask those who *have* undertaken forced labour – in the Gulag, in Nazi factories, in the Cultural Revolution in China, in the fields of Cambodia – whether they agree.

It's fair to combat rhetoric with rhetoric. But if an argument reads as truly sinister in the light of one's antecedent political commitments, the philosopher should cough discreetly and get down to the business of exposing its weaknesses. One should put the rhetoric to one side and concentrate on the detail of the arguments. There are good arguments against Nozick's position and they should be carefully rehearsed.

The best way to start is to take up the entitlement theory. Its first element is the theory of just acquisition. Acquirers are first holders, first occupants. What was the status of, say, land before it was first taken into possession? There are two answers to this question, each of which makes first occupancy a puzzle. The first answer is that the land belonged to no one. Anyone could legitimately walk across it or pick mushrooms from it. The first acquirer then has a singular moral power. Suppose, as Locke thought, property is acquired by mixing one's labour, by working on the unowned land. We now have the possibility that agents may, by their diligent pursuit of their own interest, create obligations for all others which hitherto did not exist. A right of ownership having been acquired by proper means, everyone else is now under a duty to respect the owner's exclusive possession.[10] What can be the source of such a radical moral power?

The same question arises even more pointedly when the normative background is not a state of no-ownership, but rather one of co-ownership. Locke believed that God had granted the world to mankind in common. Everyone, originally, had *inclusive* property rights to the earth, its fruits and its beasts: 'this being supposed, it seems to some a very great difficulty, how anyone should ever come to have a *Property* in any thing'.[11] It does indeed, not least since those who have acquired an obligation in place of a previous inclusive liberty right have demonstrably *lost* a moral right they could legitimately claim hitherto. Locke throws a battery of arguments at the reader to justify a right of original acquisition. Famously, that property which one has in one's own person is somehow annexed to the portion of the world with which one has mixed one's labour. Rights of self-ownership are fuelled into the possessions one has created. The metaphors are normatively impotent as many commentators have seen, including, ironically, Nozick who asks: 'why isn't mixing what I own with what I don't own a way of losing what I own rather than a way of gaining what I don't?'.[12] If I add value to the land, why do I gain the land rather than just the added value? Locke's argument can be read as a claim of desert. The digger with dirty hands has earned the right to make exclusive claims. Maybe, but what can justify the losses that everyone else undertakes? They have done nothing to deserve these. Locke's condition, that there be 'enough, and as good left in common for others', counters this objection, but if the 'others' are to include all future possible claimants (and why not?) that condition can never be met. Distinctively consequentialist arguments are suggested by Locke, too. Had there been no private property (strictly, had the consent of all the co-owners been required to legitimize acquisition), mankind would have starved, notwithstanding the original plenty. Further, private property is a condition for industriousness from which everyone benefits. These arguments are promising, but we shall keep them up our sleeve, since if they do justify original acquisition they may also serve to justify redistribution and the taxation of Wilt Chamberlain.

The most obvious objection to the employment of arguments concerning original acquisition to justify present holdings is the obvious fact that, even if there were arguments strong enough to justify the would-be property owners simultaneously benefiting themselves and dumping the costs of their acquisition on others, it would be quite impossible to track down episodes of original acquisition with respect to most of the goods of this earth. Provenance has vanished. Original acquisition is shrouded behind the same mists that conceal the Original Contract. If the entitlement argument is to be taken seriously in the way Nozick suggests, acquisition refers to literally first occupancy, first ownership, first title to land and the fruits of it. And no one has a clue about such ancestral claims.

Suppose we ignore the possibility of claims of justice originating in acquisition. Why can't we just draw a blank over disputes that take us back beyond, say, 1750, assuming the legitimacy of ownership claims at that point and legitimating the present in terms of legitimate transfers, supposing these are properly recorded after that date? To simplify massively, suppose further we are concerned solely with transactions classified as wages, gifts, sales and bequests. We must not suppose that transactions of each of these kinds represent legitimate transfers so long as parties to them are fully informed and the executions are voluntary and properly registered. Take gift, for example. This may look simple, but there are alternative and incompatible rules in the field. One says: all transfers by gift are legitimate. Another says: transfers by gift up to the value of £x are legitimate; gifts above that value are legitimate only if y per cent of the value of the goods is paid by recipients to the government. Exactly the same structure of alternatives can be articulated in respect of wages, sales and bequests. How is one to decide which transfer principles are best? One can say: all subventions from gifts are confiscations, all reallocations of sales receipts are theft, all reapportionment of bequests is grave-robbing, as one can say that all taxation of earnings from labour is on a par with forced labour – but saying these things doesn't make it so.

The Scots, in a recent constitutional settlement, voted both to institute a devolved Parliament in Edinburgh and to give that Parliament tax-raising powers in addition to those assumed by Westminster. Does this mean that the Scots are (illegitimately?) forcing themselves to labour for the benefit of those amongst them who receive the public services which the taxation funds? Of course, the fact that a majority of those voting in a referendum supports a policy of granting their representatives the power to tax does not settle the philosophical issue. If all taxation violates rights, and if rights are side-constraints on government action, then no taxation is justified. But not even Nozick believes this. Taxation for the purposes of the nightwatchman, to guard the city walls (defence expenditure), to keep safe the city streets and protect citizens in their private homes (law and order), is justified – and provision for tax collection must be made.

It follows that one cannot simply wave the flags of the separateness of persons and the importance of autonomous lives to those who have only one life to lead and watch the proponents of compulsory taxation give up the fight. The substantive issues concern the *boundaries* of legitimate compulsory taxation and one cannot expect these to be derived *a priori* from foundational moral principles.

The specification of rules of transfer for any given society will be the work of centuries of careful adjustment to the circumstances of production, distribution and exchange, to the demands of existent patterns of domesticity and family life, and to the

details of specific constitutions governing hierarchies of local and
national political institutions. We can expect these arrangements
to be vindicated by a range of values. We can expect the detailed
rights concerning transfer to cut across one another. Rights of
bequest and rights of inheritance qualify each other. We can
expect the general utility of specific arrangements to recommend
their institution as rights. What else could vindicate a state's right
of compulsory purchase as required for the provision of a public
good? We are likely to find a distinct value in private property –
which leads us to notice another real weakness in Nozick's
argument.[13]

His core intuitions concern the separateness of persons and the
value to each of them of their leading an autonomous life. Respect
for persons on the Kantian model requires us to treat persons as
ends, not as means merely, to echo the *Groundwork*.[14] This is a
vague demand, but assume it can be put to work in central cases. It
evidently proscribes slavery, rape and other non-consensual ways
of using other persons and their bodies to one's own advantage.
Kant was quite clear that this principle does not govern the way
that we treat the earth, the fruits of the earth and the beasts of the
field. These do not possess that rational will which is a necessary
and sufficient condition for treating agents as autonomous
beings.[15] Your autonomy is violated if I take one of your kidneys
without your consent, but what rule do I violate if I saw a branch
off a tree or quarry rocks from a mountain? The tree and the hill-
side have to be attached to someone as property before any harm or
injury is done, and then it is the owner who is wronged, not the
tree or the mountain. So we need to understand property as a mode
of attachment, a relation between persons and things. And we
need to justify the claims that persons make who stand in such a
relation.

One interesting theory in the field is that of Hegel. His argument in defence of private property is that private property is
necessary for persons to be free.[16] The story is complex, but the
core idea is that personal freedom – which is but one dimension of
freedom for Hegel – is achieved when the will of agents is
embodied in the objects they individually possess. Property
enables the will to be projected in a fashion which permits it to
be intelligible to the owner and to others – and intelligibility,

self-understanding in a sphere of public meaning, is a condition of freedom. When we look at our friends' bookshelves, we may be interested in the books, but just as likely we are interested in our friends in a way that supposes they themselves understand how their choices may be read by those who recognize the titles. Freedom entails interpretation – which licenses subterfuge. We all know what's going on when the novelist portrays the parvenu buying a whole library at auction.

I caricature Hegel's arguments with scandalous brevity, but consider the upshot. If we understand private property as an expression of freedom, and if personal freedom is a distinctive and universal value, oughtn't everyone to have some? It is a matter of difficult textual exegesis to determine whether Hegel accepted this conclusion. In *The Philosophy of Right*, at §49, he denies that his account of private property has any distributional implications, though in an appended note he is reported as saying that everyone should have some property and, at §§240–5, he suggests that poverty is a moral affront, depriving citizens of their personal integrity. Whatever the nuances of his published views, he ought to have stated firmly that the lack of all property is a personal disaster in a society which recognizes private property as central to freedom.

Exactly the same charge may be made against Nozick. Whatever grounds are advanced as foundations for a right to private property are likely to have some implications concerning the distribution of it. The greater the importance private property assumes, the more necessary it is that some canons of distribution be acknowledged.

In Nozick's case, we must guess what the groundings of a value of private property might be. Presumably property is necessary if individuals are to live their lives as separate autonomous agents. This makes sense; without property in a propertied society individuals are driven from pillar to post. One doesn't need to endorse all the details of the Hegelian story to understand this. In which case, it is necessary to work out how much private property, and of what kind, is necessary for an autonomous life. Ignore the difficulties of this task for the moment. My conclusion is formal. If *stuff*, things, bits and pieces of physical matter, cannot be treated as means merely, by anybody, this can only be because they are the private property of someone else, because in treating things in this way we are failing to respect some person's property rights. Whatever account we give – of how using things can be damaging people – it will stress the value to people of the things they claim to own. If ownership is of some such value, some measure of private property should be accorded to everyone. What measure? Who knows? But whatever the measure that emerges from a philosophical investigation of the value of property, it will be applied in a *patterned* theory of justice. If private property is a condition of a free and truly autonomous life, we should work to make everyone autonomous. We should make sure they all have enough property to live a life of value. The pattern that freedom necessitates may indeed require that freedom (in the specific respect, say, of being in command of all of one's earnings) be compromised – and compromised continually in the fashion of regular taxation – but I can think of no defence of private property that does not yield this consequence. To be blunt: if private property is *that* important, everybody had better have some and enough of it.

F.A. Hayek

This lesson is worth reiterating against another theory (or nontheory) of social justice – that of F.A. Hayek. Hayek's published work is a distinctive amalgam of studies in economics, politics and public administration. In an age when political philosophy was proclaimed to have died the death, a seminal work such as *The Constitution of Liberty* (1960) had the appearance of an academic dinosaur lumbering around fields now devoted to the cultivation of other interests. Then, spectacularly, Hayek lived long enough to see his work taken up by powerful and determined politicians, notably Keith Joseph and Margaret Thatcher in the United Kingdom in the 1970s and 1980s, as a new orthodoxy to which 'there is no alternative'. Dying in 1992, he lived long enough, too, to see some of the misery and social disintegration caused by his disciples.[17]

Hayek is a sceptic concerning the value of social or distributive justice. The term 'social justice' is 'empty and meaningless', a 'hollow incantation'; he perceives that the 'Emperor has no clothes', that the ideal of social justice is a mirage.[18] One element of his scepticism derives from an argument that should carry no weight. Justice, he insists, is a negative value expressed by conformity to a system of rules that have the logical form of Nozick's side-constraints: 'Do not. . . .' Injustice is witnessed only when one individual intentionally and illegitimately coerces another.[19]

Suppose a pattern of ownership emerges from voluntary inter-personal transactions of the sort imagined in Nozick's Wilt Chamberlain example. This new array of holdings cannot be deemed unjust because it was intended by no one; it is the unintended (though perhaps anticipated – by clever Wilt) outcome of thousands of independently taken decisions. Wilt is lucky that his skills elicit such a response. My mother's skill at dominoes, though equally distinctive, has earned her little. Expand this example so that all sorts of free market transactions are included. The pattern of holdings that results, willy-nilly, from thousands and thousands of market transactions cannot be deemed unjust because no one intended their realization, however well-off the winners and however poor the losers. Michael sells his council house, purchased for £5,000 in Lewisham in 1984 for £300,000 and retires to Spain; Judy finds that she cannot keep up the payments on hers and is forced into repossession. John starts a business and fails, losing his house in the process. Bridget offers the same services, five years on, and finds an eager market. She's rich. This is the diet of awful warnings and splendid examples that feed our gossip and fill the commercial pages of local newspapers. Good news – bad news. No one was coerced or fiddled. The outcomes are not unjust however uneven the pattern of wealth and income and however discrepant it may be with persons' skills, efforts or qualities of character.

We can see the logic of this conclusion, but should reject it nonetheless since its premise is tendentious. If we were operating with a concept of justice so clear and uncontentious that the derivative concept of social justice were an evident solecism, Hayek's argument would be decisive. But we aren't. As things stand, it's as though one were to argue that since promises are transactions between persons and treaties are supposed to be promises effected between states, no treaties are binding since states cannot, by definition, make promises. We don't disallow the concepts of social justice and international treaties. We go back to the drawing-board and articulate our concepts in a way that permits further discussion.

One notion behind Hayek's dismissal of social justice is the thought that the targets of moral judgements can only be individual persons and their activities. It's bad luck but not unfair if one is born with cerebral palsy or a severe learning disability. It is not a condition of injustice that some (most) persons are mobile and others not, that some (most) can learn to read and write and earn their own living and others not. In the absence of a God who has intentionally portioned these goods unequally, states of affairs such as these are not subject to moral judgement. They are the product of misfortune. This point must be conceded. So far as the origin of these states of affairs are concerned, they are not unjust.

So far as the maintenance of these states are concerned, they well may be. It's bad luck that Jim was born with palsy, but this should not be thought to settle the issue of justice with respect to his continued immobility or with respect to his inability to cope with the physical demands of a normal schooling. If practical remedies exist, and nowadays they do, then the question of whether social provision should be made for them in the name of justice is open (and will be considered later). Is the same true in respect of the outcome of market transactions? I don't see why not. If markets collapse and whole industries go under, large numbers of people may be unemployed and unable to find gainful work through no fault of their own. Their resultant poverty is not the product of injustice, but their continuance in a state where they do not have the resources to fend for themselves may well present a moral issue to the society in which such structural unemployment has occurred and it is natural to use the language of justice to frame the demands of the poor for assistance. Social justice, the sort of justice that requires the redistribution of goods within a society, does not have to be understood as the remedy for intended injustice, as though injustice has to be demonstrated before the demand for justice has any purchase. The examples I have been using suggest that the fact of dire need will serve.

Hayek denies this, believing that the concept of need is tainted by the normativity of the variety of conceptions of human nature that are employed to specify its content, but now, of course, the argument has moved on (and we shall review this objection to arguments from needs later). He does not deny that all persons should be guaranteed a minimum level of subsistence represented as a minimum level of income but insists that this is not a matter of justice. Often it will be a socially prudent safeguard against the possibility of serious social unrest.[20] At other times it may be a socially organized charitable response to the embarrassingly in-your-face challenge of widespread indigence. In point of fact, responses to desperate poverty or conspicuous health needs may be of these kinds and may be justified in these ways, but the contingent availability of other reasons for redistributing wealth and income does not disallow the claims of justice.

The crucial weakness of Hayek's denial of social justice is exactly the same as Nozick's. He must assume the legitimacy of some starting point from which a pattern of market-based holdings can emerge. In Nozick's case we postulated some quasi-Kantian doctrine of rights deriving from persons' autonomy as the candidate justification most consonant with his moral outlook, and then insisted that any such doctrine must issue in at least a minimally patterned theory of justice in holdings: that everyone should possess sufficient property and receive sufficient income to live an autonomous life. Hayek shows no inclination to follow such an abstract route. By contrast, but to the same effect, he supposes along with David Hume that the institutions of property, the rules and practices which dictate who owns what in a modern capitalist society have evolved as an efficient solution to the problems of the allocation of goods. He supposes that the rules governing property acquisition and exchange must have a functional utility, otherwise they would have been jettisoned hitherto.

This is a perfectly cogent line of argument. Indeed we noticed this brand of conservative utilitarianism earlier. But it is important to realize that it yields only a default position. If justice amounts to the assumption of utility in the rules of the market, then those rules are open to amendment and change in the name of justice if utility can be better served by amending them. On this account, social justice is not distinct from utility, but as a derivative principle it should not be thought to be idle. It may well provide the sort of bulwark against widespread social experimentation that Hayek insists upon, but equally it may license the challenge that social justice is violated by extreme disparities of wealth and income or the fact of debilitating need. *Whatever* principle is employed to defend the distribution of income and wealth prior to the sequence of market transactions must be available for judgement on the outcome. That the outcome was not anticipated, that the consequences were not intended, that the resultant pattern was not designed: none of these claims (and we can grant their truth) are to the point if the upshot is inconsistent with the principles of justice employed to vindicate the initial set of holdings.

I said earlier that this discussion of Hayek would amount to crude surgery. Followers of Hayek will no doubt call it butchery. So be it. It certainly does no justice to Hayek's positive defence of the free market as against regimes of central planning (but one can deny that the only way of recognizing demands of social justice is by establishing the bureaucracy of the pre-1989 Soviet-style planned economy or through the acceptance of institutions which irrevocably lead in that or other totalitarian directions) and it does not address Hayek's philosophical criticisms of specific conceptions of social justice. It does not discuss his conception of the rule of law (except to insist that the law of property must be justified in accordance with principles that find application in the moral judgement of states of affairs that issue from the observance of such laws) and it does not examine his anguished discussion of constitutional law-making (fuelled by a distrust of the common people who are at once citizens of a democracy and members of trades unions). What I claim (to a readership whom, I suppose, can easily identify my hostility to Hayek's views) is that social justice is not a value that can be dumped in the rubbish bin of philosophical fairy-stories or pseudo-concepts as a consequence of Hayek's assaults, but must be carefully articulated and investigated.

Private property

My conclusion is that, in considering the problem of justice in the distribution of goods, the first step must always be the articulation of a theory of property. We need to know what principles can be advanced to legitimate a system of holdings. Thus far we have been assuming that what is at stake is private property. This is because, in following Nozick's treatment of justice, we have been concerned with the allocation of property to individuals, with individual claim rights to property. But as we noticed in Chapter 4, there may be group rights as well as individual rights, and we are perfectly familiar with groups or collectives, as well as individuals, claiming exclusive property rights. There may be family property, university property, church property, company property, village, city, county or regional property, the property of the state and, indeed, of international associations. These may give rise to inclusive property rights, in virtue of which group members claim access, or they may not. A crofter may put his cow to graze the common land of the township, but a citizen cannot wander over state property at will. In addition, there are arguments of principle concerning which sort of ownership is most apt for which type of good. Are the means of production, distribution and exchange best owned by individuals or groups? If groups, which groups – those who work on or with the means of production, or the state?

Definitions at this point are hazardous. We can imagine someone arguing that all property is private – private, that is, to the agency which claims exclusive rights over the domain, private though the agency is a collective, private in the sense that the collective agency asserts rights against other agencies or individuals who are not members of it. Contrariwise, one may claim that all ownership is group ownership, since every domain will be regulated by rules of use and access which are ultimately legislated for by the state. The sovereign, insists Hobbes, has 'the whole power of prescribing the Rules, whereby every man may know what Goods he may enjoy and what Actions he may doe, without being molested by any of his fellow Subjects: and this is it men call *Propriety*'.[21]

Two hundred years of argument concerning private versus public ownership, capitalism versus socialism or communism, can be organized around stipulated definitions of private versus public property which are deployed in debates over justice. My focus in this chapter will be on private ownership in the utterly conventional sense of ownership by individual persons or families. I confess that this decision may seem to beg questions and to pre-empt contributions from collectivist traditions which emphasize group membership or interpersonal solidarity as an integral element in the identity of all persons. It may be that in the course of this enquiry we ignore our species being, the fact of our humanity, as we must take Marx to mean,[22] or perhaps we fail to recognize fundamental features of our relatedness to others (our equality or our fraternity or solidarity as compromised by class antagonism) in virtue of our standing in respect of the way production of commodities is organized in the societies we inhabit. Oh well – we can't fight all our battles on the same terrain. At bottom, I shall assume, all of us live and die as discrete individual persons: a poor, meagre truth, but irrefutable. As individuals we require the goods of this earth to feed, shelter and otherwise sustain us. And so we must, as individuals, make claims against others for sufficient access to the bare necessities. We all of us require that the earth sustain us. Clean air, nourishing food, unpolluted water, clothing, whatever materials are necessary for warmth and shelter: such goods are all earthly, all are the product of our natural environment, and each of us would (or should) claim access to them in circumstances where they are denied or unavailable. At the point where the food and the fingers meet the mouth of the starving child, no one can deny her access. The object of property is centrally physical, a portion of the natural world.[23]

There may be a range of schemes which aim to deliver the necessary goods to the individuals who require them. At the extremes we have respectively, private ownership and collective, but inclusive, ownership. In the middle, there are a myriad of combinations of each and we can expect political parties to fight amongst themselves for the optimal division. My intuition is this: in circumstances where the goods of the earth can be so apportioned that no one may die (or be subject to extreme discomfort whilst others prosper) as a result of an ill division, any distribution of these goods which has these dreadful consequences is unjust.

In conclusion, I deem the debate between private and public property to be peripheral to the issue of personal rights to the means of subsistence. This debate concerns the means of production and exchange rather than the rights which govern allocation. Issues concerning which is the optimum system for organizing production, which is the most efficient means of distribution, are secondary to questions of who requires which goods in order to live – and live commodiously, as Hobbes would put it. At bottom, individuals, who live and may perish, are the subjects of moral claims. To suggest that philosophical problems concerning production and exchange are secondary is not to say such problems are insignificant, or to hint that the socialist agenda is to be cast aside following the triumph of the free market. That would be silly. After all it may emerge that a collective (socialist) system of ownership, production and exchange is required in order that persons be free as well as fit for a decent life. But these are questions we shall have to put aside for the moment. The first thing that we should address is the bottom line my argument has put into the foreground of discussion: what are our human needs?

Human needs

Suppose we have in place a property system governed by rules of entitlement and transfer concerning income and wealth. We can expect, following Hume, that all sorts of curious principles will find a place, given the contingencies of history, as mankind in our locality have responded to opportunities for finding mutual advantage and perspicuous general utility.[24] This will give us an inventory of who owns which goods. The rules of this game, explicit in the law, will likely be formulated in terms of rights of the different varieties charted in Chapter 4. A theory of justice will approach the detail of any given property system, whatever the story of its origins, as a standard, a test that the system must pass if it is to be judged legitimate and granted moral approval. Many such tests have been proposed, and we can consider only a few here. Arguably the most familiar, and probably the most contentious amongst philosophers, is the test of need. Does the property system that we are appraising meet distinctive human needs? So much social policy is predicated on the satisfaction of needs that one must suppose that a correct employment of the term is often sufficient to decide arguments concerning just distribution. In practice, and as with arguments concerning liberty and human rights, once contending parties come to agree that such and such a policy meets an evident need, policy disputes are concluded. But philosophical debates often begin at the point where political disagreements are settled. The very prominence of the concept of needs, its obvious appeal as an element in the rhetoric of politicians and interest-groups as well as the claims of individuals, requires that the philosopher subject it to the closest investigation.

The first task which evaluation of needs as a principle of justice imposes is that of understanding the concept of need. The second task is that of describing the application of this concept: what are the needs familiarly adduced? If these tasks can be accomplished, a third is immediately suggested: is justice in part or in whole a matter of meeting citizens' needs?

The requirement that we articulate carefully the concept of needs derives from an obvious challenge. Remember the standard objection to Mill's harm principle: since any activity may be deemed harmful, the principle has no cutting edge to be employed in the distinction of legitimate and illegitimate interference. If the concept of needs were as vague or inchoate as this objection supposes the concept of harm to be, it would be equally impotent in the determination of which elements of a property system could be deemed just or unjust. The danger here is that the concept cannot be fixed with sufficient precision to distinguish clearly claims of need from claims which derive from wants, desires, preferences, likings, whims or fancies. Hegel, for example, described the economic system as a system of needs, where needs amount to consumer demands and these are recognized to have become increasingly sophisticated and refined.[25] The terminology does no harm to Hegel's argument, but given his recognition of the mechanisms by which needs, thus construed, multiply in modern society (as, for example, people struggle to keep up with the Joneses), justice can hardly be a matter of meeting needs if these needs include purchasing a car at least as powerful as that of one's neighbours.

Fortunately the technical apparatus of analytic philosophy enables us to sharpen the distinction which Hegel deliberately occludes – that between needs on the one hand and wants, desires, preferences, whims and fancies on the other. Take desires: the following argument form is taken to show that desires are psychological states:

(1) William desires to meet Elton John.
(2) Elton John is Reg Dwight.
(3) Therefore, William desires to meet Reg Dwight.

The inference is fallacious, moving from true premises to a false conclusion. Since, in the case where William has never heard of Reg Dwight he evidently does not desire to meet Reg Dwight, the construction 'x desires y' is in technical parlance *intensional*.

Contrast:

(4) William met Elton John.
(5) Elton John is Reg Dwight.
(6) Therefore, William met Reg Dwight.

Here the conclusion is evidently true and the argument form valid. The sentence form, 'x met y', is *extensional*, permitting the substitution of terms denoting the same object, whilst preserving the truth-value of the sentence.

Now, compare (1) – (3) with:

(7) William needs water.
(8) Water is H_2O.
(9) Therefore, William needs H_2O.

Here, as with (4) – (6), the conclusion goes through. William does need H_2O whether he realizes this or not. What does this argument show?[26]

First, let me mention a caveat to the terms in which this argument is generally presented. Standardly, needs are contrasted with wants, not, as I have presented matters, with desires. This is because I feel that if the crux of the argument depends on a technicality, we had better get it absolutely right. I think there is a use of 'want' (noun) and 'want' (verb) which exhibits the same extensional character as 'needs'. 'War on Want' names a charity which is not directed to the satisfaction of appetitive states of mind. 'You want a haircut', can be prescriptive or descriptive; if the former, it is not false because you disavow it. The ambiguity over 'want' (extensional) and 'want' (intensional) feeds many a rhetorical flourish in the battle between teenagers and their parents. As correctives of the work of other philosophers go, this is a minor cavil. I console myself against the charge that this is mere linguistic pedantry with the thought that if you make the complaint you understand the drift of the arguments I qualify.

We may conclude that needs are not a particularly strong or pressing form of desire, at one end of a continuum of psychological states, with fancies, say, at the other. To say that one needs something is not to ascribe a psychological state to him at all. One is tempted to say, except that the terms are slippery, that needs are objective, desires subjective. That one desires something is a fact about one's state of mind. That one needs something does not depend (always) on one's mental state, more likely on the state of one's health. Thus doctors can tell you what you need (by way of medicine), but they are not authoritative on what you desire. To shift the target of opprobrium, you may desire Viagara, but the doctors will not prescribe it on demand unless they judge you need it.

If these arguments have force, we have countered the charge that needs are indistinguishable from desires at the point where arguments from justice get a purchase. There is still plenty of work to be done. In particular, we need to argue why needs give rise to claims in a way that desires evidently do not. But this task is not compromised by the thought that needs are a species of desires. We need to look at the world, at the condition of humanity and its particular specimens, to judge whether needs are met or ignored. This is not a matter of whether or not desires are satisfied. The poor child needs the medicine though he doesn't want to take it. That this thought makes sense establishes the conceptual distinction we desire.

A second challenge to the conceptual integrity of claims of need arises from the thought that all needs are instrumental. If x needs y, we can always ask: what for? If so, the value of answering the need is parasitic on the value of the purpose or goal which is furthered by meeting the need. If so, meeting needs has no value independently of achieving the specified goals. If so, we can dispense with talk of the value of meeting needs and concentrate on the achievement of valuable goals.[27]

There can be no doubt that many judgements truly attesting specific needs are instrumental in the manner suggested. 'I need change for the parking meter. Do you have two 50p pieces for a pound?', one may be asked in the street. If someone says she needs two 50p pieces, I guess it is always appropriate (if not tactful or diplomatic) to ask: What for? Such a request always carries the implication of ellipsis which the question 'What for?' addresses directly. In another range of cases such a question would seem plain silly. The doctor says this casualty needs morphine, the social worker says these parents need a holiday, the aid worker says this village needs a well. In such cases we expect any intelligent person to be able to read off from the use of the word 'need', exactly what exigency is being addressed. We can dub needs absolute in cases where their citation does not leave open the question of what purpose will be served by meeting the need.

This shouldn't be taken as claiming that there is no answer in cases of absolute need when the question: What for? is inappropriately put. There will be an answer and the precise mode in which need is met may give it. The morphine will kill the extreme pain; the holiday will relieve the parents from the stress of looking after the handicapped child; the well will spare the village women a round trip of ten miles per day. David Wiggins argues that these answers or something like them are explicit or prefigured in the statement of need. There is no question of an ellipsis in such judgements. 'One does not have to supply what is already there.'[28]

If the sceptic presses hard, asking: What is already there? a schematic answer is at hand, which the questioner, had he truly understood this concept of need, could have worked out for himself. It is a judgement that if the need is not met the agent will be harmed in some serious fashion, she will suffer, some crucial interest will be set back, some minimal level of human flourishing will not be attained. The full story has not been told, but what is explicit in any judgement of absolute need of this sort is that some such story is tellable. The complete analysis of a judgement of absolute need now runs as follows:

I need [absolutely] to have x
   if and only if
I need [instrumentally] to have x if I am to avoid being harmed
   if and only if
It is necessary, things being what they actually are, that if I avoid being harmed then I have x. [29]

Now we can see why a principle of need is in the same boat as a harm principle. Its employment requires some conception of the good life for human beings which a condition of need or harm directly frustrates. But this is not a weakness of the concept in advance of such a conception being elaborated. It is only a weakness if we have good reason to believe that such an account could not be given or, if it could be given, the conception of harm were too broad to serve the purposes of articulating a theory of justice, if, for example, one thought a person harmed were they to fail to get whatever they desire. But one has no reason to believe either of these things absent a strong argument for them.

Having distinguished instrumental and absolute needs, we have opened up a conceptual space which permits other questions to be asked. Needs vary in their *gravity* and their *urgency*. Fred's need for a heart bypass operation is more grave than Sylvia's need to have her broken leg splinted and plastered, but Fred's need can wait, being less urgent. A need may be judged *basic* if a person cannot go unharmed unless it is met, given fundamental and unalterable facts about the world and the typical human constitution.[30]

There are good reasons for believing that the concept of needs and their satisfaction does not exhaust the concept of human well-being[31] or human flourishing. We can perfectly well imagine a community of scholars trading off some years of their lives in order to refurbish a library. We can understand the scientist who is so ambitious to advance knowledge that he performs a risky experiment on himself. Parents may buy a computer or hi-fi for a handicapped child rather than a wheelchair if they judge that that is what he most wants. Nonetheless, in the particular context of justice, where what is at issue is the distribution within a society of generally transferable goods and services, it is proposed that the principal, i.e. governmental, agencies of distribution should pay direct attention to the issue of how far basic needs are met. Here, what has been called the Principle of Precedence – that the needs of a population take priority over their preferences or anyone else's – finds its home.[32] No distribution can be just if it fails to meet the basic needs of citizens, if some minimum standards are not met in respect of the provision of goods and services.

Basic needs do not represent a fundamental value. The case for attending to them rests on whatever value attaches to the human well-being, human flourishing or distinctive human agency for which their satisfaction is deemed a necessary condition. These deeper values may be entrenched in utilitarian, perfectionist or Kantian normative ethics. Indeed, it is hard to think of any system of ethics, which, when applied to the responsibilities of government for meeting the requirements of justice, does not demand the satisfaction of human needs.

The concept of human needs has been cleared of the charge of being ill-formed. But is it operational? It rests on a deeper foundation, in an account of human good; it makes a charge on governments in the name of justice. But can the charge be made good in respect of specific policies? Between the concept of need as an element of justice and the specific policies required if needs are to be met is the open ground wherein the determination of needs must be fixed. What needs must be recognized and catered for? Lurking in the background here are the linked threats of relativism and needs-inflation.

Talk of basic human needs suggests that we might draw up a list of goods which anyone needs if they are to flourish as humans or achieve some minimum standard of well-being. First, they need the wherewithal of survival; second they need to be able to command whatever resources are necessary if they are to live freely under their own direction, under some realistic plan of their own devising or in some social role that they endorse. The very poor, driven from pillar to post in the effort to achieve the shortest-term goals of immediate nourishment and shelter, do not live well during the period they survive. Yet we all know that in different societies folk are well-used to different levels of life expectancy or infant mortality, more or less vulnerable to endemic disease. Even in the comfortable West, indicators of longevity and good health reveal marked differences between social classes. There are even significant differences between those at different levels in the hierarchy in the British service. Do all of these differences mark differences in the degree to which basic needs are met? We can accept that a condition of homelessness is a drastic limitation on the freedom of those who suffer it, that those who are 'born to fail' have their life choices severely curtailed, but how much in the way of resources does one need to command before one is judged to live a life of minimum freedom? The answer to this question, too, will seem to differ massively between different societies. Freedom, for citizens of the UK, may require sufficient educational accomplishment for them to approach the job market with confidence that they will not be forced to accept what they regard as the most demeaning and exploitative employment. This thought, hence this need, may make little sense to members of traditional, agricultural, societies for whom work is a means of self-sufficient family survival rather than the exploration of a range of individual capacities.

If the baseline of human need is dictated by the objective conditions of the minimum standard of living of human beings who live contentedly in a manner as commodious as their neighbours, it is likely to be fixed at a level which is completely unacceptable to the worst off in better-off societies – as well as to observers of their plight. If it is a necessary condition of sociability that one be able to discuss the marriage prospects of a TV soap-opera character with one's neighbours, one had better have a television. Less controversially, if citizens in Western democracies need to have some access to the news media if they are to act as well-informed participators in a democratic decision-making process (and if denial of this political standing is agreed to be deeply demeaning and disrespectful) they had better be able to purchase TVs, radios and newspapers or have access to libraries.

The drift of arguments like these is easy to follow. If we are not careful we shall be forced into a position of accepting that people in Glasgow need television sets, whereas tribesmen in New Guinea do not need antibiotics. We would not be worried if opinion surveys revealed that these very different people do and do not desire such things, but we should be worried by arguments which yield such a pattern of obviously relative needs.

The argument thus far should not be thought to imply that philosophers have avoided the embarassingly empirical task of describing basic needs.[33] David Braybrooke lists the following as candidate matters of need, distinguishing a first part concerned with physical functioning and a second part that concerns functioning as a social being:

Part 1 includes:

1 The need to have a life-supporting relation to the environment.
2 The need for food and water.
3 The need to excrete.
4 The need for exercise.
5 The need for periodic rest, including sleep.
6 The need (beyond what is covered under the preceding needs) for whatever is indispensable to preserving the body intact in important respects.

Part 2 continues:

7 The need for companionship.
8 The need for education.
9 The need for social acceptance and recognition.
10 The need for sexual activity.
11 The need to be free from harassment, including not being continually frightened.
12 The need for recreation.

This list, from a philosopher, is heroic. Braybrooke does not pretend that the list should be regarded as complete. To do so, we should have to claim that there is nothing more that we have to learn about what is necessary for human beings to live well. There is enough precision in the list for it to be clear why provision to meet the needs specified will have to be different from society to society. Take the need for education. As has been indicated already, the nature of the skills which need to be inculcated and the level of proficiency required will vary depending upon the demands of the society in which adults are required to take their place.

Relativities of this sort look to be a real problem if the context of justice is international and if the question of resource allocation is posed across frontiers. Is it self-indulgent for Western nations to spend so much money on secondary and higher education whilst the basic health needs of those who live in hovels in Calcutta go unmet? Questions of this sort cannot be avoided.[34] It would be a real mistake, though, to conclude that the philosophical and practical difficulties of detailing standards of international justice mean that the concept of needs has no place in addressing them. The opposite, in fact, is true: it is because the appeal of universal need satisfaction is so strong that these questions exhibit such difficulty and urgency.

One feature of the debate about international justice which gives it the appearance of intractability is the absence of any agency to adjudicate in the case of conflict. Within a democratic state, there will be a forum for expressing and resolving conflicts concerning provision for needs – the political process. We can observe (we don't need to imagine) individuals making claims of need whenever resource allocations concerning health, education and social security payments are publicly discussed. What is controversial in many policy proposals is not the philosophical question of whether the appeal to need is a claim of justice, but the quasi-philosophical question of whether, say, publicly funded nursery education meets a real need or, if one agrees that it does, what is the measure of gravity or urgency involved, what comparitive judgements should be reviewed. We observe endemic dispute here and it is evident that the disputes often have their origin in conflicting assessment of needs. None of this should lead us to believe that the concept of need is unfitted to constitute a standard of just provision since the relativities involved disable impartial assessment. We can tinker with the list, we can debate the modalities of assessment as we work out what the service of a specific need warrants by way of provision, and finally, we can leave fine-grain decision-making in respect of policy proposals to the political process.

Does this establish that provision for needs is a requirement of justice? This last question links a Humean conception of justice as the principles which govern the allocation of resources within a society to a normative ethics which determines which principles are appropriate. Needs, on this account, have an intermediate status. At bottom will be competing accounts of the good, what it is for human lives to go well. Any such account will yield a set of necessary conditions which amount to statements of need. The task of working out all of the details is immense, but since it is a matter of working out what justice requires, the task is unavoidable.

To review our progress so far: we must suppose that a well-ordered society has in place a set of rules which settle conflicts amongst competing claimants to goods. The details of these rules will likely fill shelves of texts in a law library. I think we can fairly suppose in advance of detailed criticism that these rules promote utility, perhaps in the detail of their operation, but most likely through their general function of serving expectations and set-tling disputes. Hume believed that such an existent system amounted to a system of justice, but we have seen that unless the distribution of resources meets the needs of those subject to it, this verdict is premature. Consideration of needs at this point will require transfers from those whose property exceeds what they need towards those who are needy.

There are many different ways in which such transfers may be effected. Those with goods in excess of their needs may recognize a duty of care or exhibit their benevolent nature by charitable dona-tions. The resulting transfers will be unsystematic and haphazard but it is perfectly possible to imagine needs being met in this fash-ion in a very small society. And even in very large (and rich) mod-ern societies it is likely that a substantial proportion of personal needs will be met in this way, not least within families. We are all used to reading that some charity has funded equipment in hos-pitals, that parents and neighbours have supported the local school, that volunteers are providing soup kitchens for the indi-gent. More important, however, are transfers which are organized by the state. Generally these will involve taxation of earnings or sales, less often wealth; governments exact their imposts in ways that are minimally perspicuous. But confiscation and re-distribution of capital assets may be effected to the same purpose, though the history of such efforts in the twentieth century has been conspicuously inglorious. Whereas individual benefactors respond to the needs of fellow citizens by ostentatious public bene-factions, modern democratic governments meet needs by stealth, believing, often truly, that there are fewer voting gainers than losers.

Despite their objective condition, people do not like to be iden-tified as needy, as worthy recipients of the charity or the ultim-ately coercive redistribution of their fellow citizens' assets, unless these are ill-gotten gains. Nozick's claim that taxation is forced labour, the philosophical shadow of a cocktail-bar grudge, may as likely prompt guilt and shame on the part of recipients as resent-ment amongst the providers. The effective operation of the welfare state in Britain needs welfare rights officials to prod people into making their legitimate claims. And still, take-up levels are well below the computations of statisticians employed to determine the maximum possible costs of the exercise in redistribution. Talk of 'the needy' carries echoes of Lady Bountiful. Those who identify and respond to unmet needs may find that their rhetoric meets the resistance of the poor objects of their attention. Perhaps it is better to speak of rights rather than duties and to ground the rights of the needy in the language of equality. For many the language of equality carries a dignity which is threatened by talk of needs.

Equality of what?

It is a familiar thought that justice in distribution is at least in part, or in some respects, a matter of equality. It may be that one who advances such a claim has some specific egalitarian system in mind as constituting the heart of justice, most simply perhaps the condition that a system of just property distribution requires that everyone get equal shares. If property were a homogenous good, like a cake, then everyone should get an equal slice. But equality may be more vaguely construed. It may amount to the requirement that the principles of justice will not be acceptable unless they grant equal consideration in some sense to all who are subject to them. Otherwise, and one does not need to be a contractarian to see the force of this objection, those who are not granted equal consideration have strong prima facie grounds for complaint.

Amartya Sen has argued that:

'a characteristic of virtually all the approaches to the ethics of social arrangements that have stood the test of time is to want equality of *something* – something that has an important place in the particular theory. Not only do income egalitarians ... demand equal incomes, and welfare egalitarians ask for equal welfare levels, but also classical utilitarians insist on equal weights on the utilities of all, and pure libertarians demand equality with respect to an entire class of rights and liberties. They are all 'egalitarians' in some essential way ... [35]

This is a helpful way of putting matters, not least since it opens up the right questions. Instead of debating the pros and cons of egalitarianism versus anti-egalitarianism, we can consider in sequence the forms of equality that have been deemed constitutive of justice. We can ask, in the words of Sen's famous paper, 'Equality of What?'.[36] Once the different accounts have been clarified, we can return to the issue of whether principles of equality meet, or are properly considered as supplementary to, considerations arising from needs.

The most straightforward answer to Sen's question is equality of goods or resources. Rawls's account of justice incorporates a version of this. I quote it now in its most general form: 'All social values – liberty and opportunity, income and wealth and the bases of self-respect – are to be distributed equally unless an unequal distribution of any, or all, of these values is to everyone's advantage.'[37]

Rawls's Difference Principle, specifying that social and economic inequalities are to be arranged so that they are reasonably expected to be to everyone's advantage, is 'strongly egalitarian in the sense that unless there is a distribution that makes [everyone] better off . . . an equal distribution is to be preferred'.[38] The goods to be distributed in accordance with the principle are the social primary goods – things that every rational man is presumed to want, being all-purpose means whatever one's plan of life and susceptible to social distribution. Income and wealth are the primary goods Rawls has in mind at this point. Equality and inequality (and hence justice in distribution) concern the allocation of economic resources.

This is a natural suggestion, since economic goods are just the sort of goods that government *can* distribute through effecting transfers. The modality in which equality is sought – income and wealth – is peculiarly apt for the purposes of governments which recognize the demands of justice. If the difference principle were acceptable, its policy implications would be clear. Progressive taxation, particularly of incomes, together with a negative income tax, is an obvious means of effecting redistribution towards equality. The point at which redistribution would be limited would be that at which transfers from rich to poor reduced the goods available to the poor. This would be the case if, for example, taxation were a sufficient disincentive to productive activity that entrepreneurs ceased or restricted their production or relocated their economic activity (and their capacity to provide work) to another tax jurisdiction.

The weakness of this proposal lies in its insensitivity to claims which arise on the basis of need. We can easily imagine a society where wealth and income is divided equally. We can imagine all members of such a society moving towards a condition of inequality if those who are worst off in the new dispensation are better off than they were under equality. But justice so construed ignores marked differences in the personal characteristics of members of this society. As Sen points out,

> these are important for assessing inequality. For example, equal incomes can still leave much inequality in our ability to do what we would value doing. A disabled person cannot function in the way an able-bodied person can, even if both have exactly the same income.[39]

Of course this criticism would have no purchase if we had no concern for inequalities in 'our ability to do what we would value doing', or if, as in the particular case of the person with special needs, we did not think that justice was at least, in part, a matter of meeting these needs. But we should notice that ideals of equality in the distribution of economic goods would be a real puzzle unless we thought that some underlying principles motivated our concern with such inequality. We accept that individuals are unequal in respect of their height, weight and beauty without identifying an injustice. Why should differences in income or size of house cause us to register concern? We must think that such inequalities violate some principle of equal respect or fail to recognize equal claims on the product of social co-operation. In which case, we shall have to work out whether these underlying principles demand an inequality of resources as the just response to claims of need.

Equality of goods may be thought of as equality of input. The objection concerning special needs may be read as drawing attention to inequalities of output – the goods which are allocated do not serve uniformly to produce equal levels of well-being, given the very great disparity in the conditions in which individuals find themselves. Perhaps we should concentrate on output, on the well-being of those in the circumstances of justice. This suggests that we pursue equal utility, directing our attention to the happiness or desire-satisfaction of those in receipt of goods. At this point, as we have already noticed, the utilitarian will press a claim.

Utilitarian arguments are no more cogent than the facts permit. Diminishing marginal utility suggests that movements away from equality which have both winners and losers benefit the utility-gainers by a lesser amount than the disutility suffered by the losers. But this supposes that both winners and losers are equally efficient transformers of the good to be distributed. In cases of special needs, physical or mental disability, there may be a threshold of resource provision below which allocations do little good. If Harry's problem is mobility, nothing less than an electric wheelchair will enable him to get to the shops. Travel vouchers or discounted fares will not assist him, supposing that even if he could sell these concessions he would not have enough money to purchase the wheelchair. Sally, by contrast would get enormous pleasure from a sports car. It is all too easy to imagine social circumstances in which total utility is increased by allocating the sports car to Sally at the cost of inefficient allocations to Harry and many others like him. In such circumstances, as Sen points out,

> The cripple would then be doubly worse off: both since he gets less utility from the same level of income, and since he will also get *less* income. Utilitarianism must lead to this thanks to its single-minded concern with maximising the utility sum.[40]

This example is important because it reinforces the lesson drawn from considering goods or resources as the metric of equality. Human diversity makes a difference. One might have thought that justice, being a central province of government, must always be a matter of rough justice, that successful policies must abstract from the specificities of differences in the condition and circumstances of individuals. On the contrary, the specific circumstances in which groups of people find themselves may evince the sort of special need which it is precisely the task of government policies directed towards the promotion of justice to redress.

In the example just discussed, the crucial feature is the manner in which the cripple and the speedster (Sen's term is 'pleasure-wizard') are able to transform the input of goods into the output of utility, where utility denotes some positive mental state of the persons affected. Such facts are well-known. Young children are notably efficient transformers of toys into utility. One doesn't (or didn't) need to spend much to make them happy. Diversities in respect of the contribution of goods to individual happiness work in another fashion to undermine varieties of utilitarianism which count happiness or desire-satisfaction as the good to be maximized. Societies as we encounter them are deeply riven by inequalities deriving from group membership. Societies apportion goods in line with ethnic, religious, sex and gender role, caste and class differences which, contingently, have established a social hierarchy. Objectively, the circumstances of the unfortunates at the bottom of a particular pile may be dire, but subjectively, they may be cheerful enough with their lot. Perhaps they believe one well-known story:

> The rich man in his castle,
> The poor man at his gate,
> God made them, high or lowly
> And ordered their estate.[41]

Many of the lowly have sung along with their superiors, sensibly coming to terms with inequalities they can do little about in a stoic fashion which leaves them as happy as anyone in the castle. They may be poorly housed, ill-fed, suffer from poor health and come to an early death, but in point of utility their lives may go no worse.[42] Despite their lack of gripes and grumbles, one may fairly describe their condition as unjust if basic needs go unmet.

The lesson of Sen's review of equality as a metric of goods on the one hand and utility on the other is that we should focus on equality of something else. His positive recommendation is that we concentrate on equality with respect to persons' capabilities to achieve functionings, what he calls, in 'Equality of What?', 'basic capability equality'. A human functioning is a state of a person or an activity, something a person may do. So good health is a functioning as is the taking of exercise. Functionings such as these are arguably necessary for human flourishing, yet we can understand someone who risks or foregoes them in the service of some other ideal. I risk my health in order to make the scientific discovery, I stop taking exercise until I have finished writing the book. Given these possibilities we can see how what is valuable is the capability to maintain my health or take regular exercise should I choose to do so.

Capabilities are distinct from the primary goods that serve them in so far as equality of primary goods will not ensure equality in respect of capability. They are distinct from utilities in that social conditions may produce equality of happiness and yet some of the happy people may be severely restricted in respect of important functionings. Of course there are lots of human functionings that are of little or no theoretical interest. To adapt an example of Sen's, if the Blanco washing powder company goes bust, I cannot use the product any more nor am I free to select it from the range of equally good alternatives.[43] Technically, my functioning is impaired, my capability reduced. Other functionings, by contrast, are vital, and these will be the functionings identified less technically as human needs.

If we are concerned primarily with policies which promote equality with respect to persons' capability to function in ways necessary for them to have a decent life in the society they inhabit, we shall have given ourselves a hard task in respect of identifying specific policy objectives. This will require a delicate mixture of philosophy, economics and sociology which cannot, in principle, be reduced to a democratic practice of counting preferences, since needs are in part objective and, as we have seen, preferences can be seriously and systematically distorted. Next we shall need to engage the political task of organizing a society in such a way as to effect the transfers necessary to meet the needs that have been identified. The social democratic societies of Western Europe have all given lip-service to this ideal of equality in respect of meeting needs, but the attainment of it is beginning to have the air of an intractable practical problem. When sociologists (or, more likely social workers) point out the level of unmet needs in a variety of different policy contexts, e.g. health, education, housing, provision for the elderly, and urge a greater measure of redistribution of resources, politicians, increasingly of *all* mainstream parties, respond that meeting these needs first requires further economic growth, that the strategic political priority must be the effectively painless process of raising more resources, achieving a greater social fund of income and profit which can be taxed without creating disincentive effects.

This may have the appearance of a strategic problem particular to the political representatives who take policy decisions in fear of upsetting the comfortable majority, but there is reason to think the practical difficulties have deeper origins. The claims of justice as I have been developing them require that basic human needs impose duties of service on the part of those who possess the resources to meet them. Whilst there is plenty of evidence that citizens of the comfortable West are severely discomfited by the obtrusive, conspicuous needs of, say, fellow citizens who are reduced to living in cardboard boxes, queueing at soup kitchens or begging in the street, the task of serving these needs is bestowed on politicians who guarantee that social amelioration will not be too costly. This may be a realistic recognition of a severe tension within the practical reason of citizens, a tension between their acceptance of claims of need on the one hand and their belief, on the other hand, that needs can only be met by an economic system that is powered by the strong incentives of self-interest that are integral to capitalism.[44]

The argument has been skimpy, but assume we have established as a minimum requirement of justice, that citizens' basic needs, their capability to achieve a minimum set of vital functionings, be met in equal measure. Suppose, too, that there is agreement on the nature of these needs and the policies that serve them. Suppose further that the needs are generously identified. People not only live, but have the opportunity to live commodiously. Is that enough equality? Should we care, if all have the opportunity to live decently, that some have the capability to live much better lives than others in respect of their having available more resources, more income and wealth?

If one were speaking here of a political ideal which might be recommended as a personal project, the pursuit of equality beyond that of meeting needs would be ludicrously utopian. There is enough work for a lifetime in pursuing the more modest aim, even in the more generous of liberal democracies. But does justice require a greater equality than this? Should we be concerned about or morally indifferent to inequalities of income and wealth if the worst off cannot be described as needy?

It is clear that inequality can be an instrumental evil. Rousseau insisted that 'the social state is advantageous to men only when all have something and none too much'.[45] How much is too much? We must suppose it is represented by such a degree of inequality as will enable the better off to suborn the ideal of equal political power, by purchasing the allegiance of others. Nowadays one might identify such harmful inequalities in the workings of a property system which enables power seekers to buy newspapers or television stations which they use unashamedly to advance their own political causes. Deeper, and more insidious, is the way in which inequalities of wealth are transformed into social differences and fossilized by processes of social stratification whenever the laws of property permit inequalities to be transmitted from one generation to another. No human characteristic is more faithfully transmitted from one generation to the next than earning power. The laws of inheritance are more effective than the laws of evolution in transmitting the holding of wealth to successor generations.

We can imagine a society in which there is no inherited wealth. Members are permitted to acquire as much as they can by way of effort and the use of their talents. But on death, all assets are pooled into a social fund and redistributed equally to all members of society. My guess is that such a measure of involuntary potlach would dissolve the rigid class formations which disfigure even the most settled social democracies. This is not meant as a practical proposal, nor even as a recommendation concerning the principles of justice. Rather, if this exercise in utopian guesswork is plausible, it should cause us measure the degree to which inequalities in wealth holdings freeze into other inequalities. They inhibit widespread social mobility by limiting expectations. Systems of education serve to reproduce rather than reduce class divisions. Arrogance and social blindness, deference or strategic impertinence occupy the moral space which should be inhabited by respect and mutual recognition. Our experience of societies which exhibit inequalities of wealth and income teaches us that inequality does great psychological damage. This is the lesson successively, of

Rousseau, Hegel and Marx: social stratifications, of rich and poor, masters and slaves, capitalists and workers, universally distort the self-perceptions of all those located within them.

If differences of income and wealth were merely a matter of individuals having access to a lesser or wider basket of commodities – so that you buy a poster, I buy a print and John Paul Getty buys a Botticelli – I suspect little harm is done. Clichés may express truisms: no one seriously believes that money buys happiness. Although all of us would welcome being better off, those with seats in the front stalls of the opera are unlikely to be enjoying themselves much more than the scruffs in the third circle. Given an adequate social baseline, inequalities in primary goods take on an obvious ethical significance only at the point where they are transformed into inequalities of something else, of political power, social prestige or opportunities for advancement. Unfortunately, societies have managed to organize themselves in such a way that inequalities in primary goods are transformed and magnified into more damaging inequalities. This is the great lesson of Rousseau's *Discourse on the Origins of Inequality*.

I can't think of an argument to establish this conclusion beyond an appeal to the facts of history and sociology and I can't present my idiosyncratic versions of these here. We are left with one clear philosophical question: Assume no one is needy and that there are no social mechanisms in place which might transform inequalities in the holdings of primary goods into other more entrenched or iniquitous inequalities, is equality of primary goods in any sense a requirement of justice? I have suggested that inequality might do little harm, but the absence of harm does not preclude injustice. We might laugh at the gross flaunting of wealth in popular magazines devoted to the adulation of celebrity and even be grateful that the photographers are not queuing up outside our doors. Still, the gross disparities of wealth which are paraded before us daily may still attest a measure of injustice. To investigate this question, I shall focus on the work of John Rawls.

John Rawls's theory of justice

First, a diversion on Rawls's work and its place in this study. It is nearly thirty years since Rawls published *A Theory of Justice*. It has been the subject of intense investigation, stimulating full-length critical studies and papers galore. I remember the sense of momentous academic achievement which accompanied its publication and the excitement of buying the heavy, black-covered, hardback edition in 1972. And I remember the pleasure of reading it from cover to cover. It advances a distinctive thesis, but, like all great works of philosophy, it is a treasure-house. And the treasures have been augmented by a succession of later papers and the publication of *Political Liberalism* in 1993.[46] I doubt there is any topic to be broached in this introduction which could not have been tackled by way of a discussion of Rawls. Against this background of Rawls's eminence, it may seem odd that, so far, he has been a minor character in this book. I shall try to make amends, but it is as well to note in advance that I shall be able to discuss only a small portion of his work. Even this task is complicated because Rawls's thinking is distinctively systematic. One can't fillet out arguments whilst paying no heed to the overall structure of the theory. The reader is commended to study all of it.

Justice as fairness

The scope of Rawls's theory of justice is almost Platonic. For Rawls, justice is not distributive justice, the narrow matter of who is entitled to what in the way of property. It is the virtue of a well-ordered state and comprises all aspects of its ethical well-being.[47] States are natural associations. For the most part, individuals just find themselves in one as members, and find that the mode of governance of the state has a major influence on their prospects for a decent life. The basic structure of a society (Rawls's term for the major social institutions) assigns rights and duties to citizens, as well as specifying how the advantages that accrue from social co-operation should be allocated

A theory of justice is required for familiar Humean reasons. Persons are supposed to inhabit a world of moderate scarcity, such a degree of scarcity as ensures conflicting claims on the pool of resources. If there were abundance, justice would be unnecessary; if there were a desperate shortage, schemes of social co-operation would break down. The theory of justice will consist of principles which regulate the competing claims. What is distinctive about Rawls's theory of justice is the form of argument employed to derive it. This is a hypothetical contract argument.

The classical social contract arguments, as used by Hobbes, Locke, Rousseau and Kant were used for several different purposes: to justify the claims to authority of the state, to determine the limits of the state's claims to authority and to vindicate rebellion where those limits are overstepped, to determine the principles which must be respected by the institutions of the state if its constitution is to be legitimate and the content of legislation valid. These are questions we shall be examining in the next chapter. The social contract argument had two forms: first, actual contracts, covenants or universal consent were described or conjectured as the basis for real obligations. Obviously, such arguments are only as good as their premisses. If no actual contracts can be reported or if modern citizens could not be supposed to be party to them, no obligations follow.

The hypothetical contract argument is an animal of a different stripe. As Dworkin famously observes, 'a hypothetical contract is not simply a pale form of an actual contract; it is not a contract at all'.[48] Whereas an actual contract argument cites a specific occasion or a particular activity as the basis of an obligation: 'You signed on the dotted line, so you are obliged to pay me the money', in a hypothetical contract argument, there is no contract to which one may appeal. An argument is employed which sets matters up *as if* those who are required to accept its conclusion were party to a contract or agreement. It is a matter of great controversy whether or not the classical authors I mentioned above are using actual or hypothetical contract arguments or both, mixing them together in a promiscuous and confusing fashion.

In its classical form a hypothetical contract argument works as follows: Everyone wants certain goods, notably self-preservation, (and/or pursues certain values e.g. liberty). In a state of nature, i.e. in circumstances where there is no government, these goods are threatened (and/or these values thwarted). The state, and only the state, will protect these goods (and/or promote these values). Therefore, those who seek these goods and pursue these values (generally, everyone) have good reason to accept the authority of the state. We can portray this conclusion as a contract, an agreement. It is *as though* everyone has agreed to accept a sovereign authority. They haven't, of course, as a matter of fact. Contract theory is thus a deliver-the-goods theory. It asks people to deduce the properties of just such an institution as is necessary to promote the good, by asking them to consider what life would be like without it – in a state of nature – and how this condition could be remedied.

Why invoke the non-existent contract? Why represent people as behaving in a way in which they have not, in fact, behaved? Plainly this is an argumentative device, a strategem of practical reason, but what use does this device serve, what point does it signify? In the classical theorists, the argument form serves to remind us that we are modelling the deliberations of everyone in pursuit of a conclusion that we can represent everyone as accepting. We model 'agreement' in the minimal sense of congruence of reasoning – everyone has the same (however specified) goals and everyone can see the means necessary to achieve them. We *portray* this congruence as 'agreement' in the sense of concert, everyone acting together, assuming the same obligations. There is a second sense in which the contract model is apt. The problems that we identify in the state of nature are problems that we create for each other. In seeking to protect our lives, we threaten or pre-emptively strike at everyone else, each regarding the others as competitors or foes. In order to gain the security which the behaviour of all of us tends to undermine, we have to give up something, generally the right to govern ourselves or the right to punish those who violate our rights. We give in order to get; we trade off our independence for our security. This may be represented as a contract with each other or as a contract with a government. The contract device calls attention to this familiar strategy for procuring mutual advantage. The terms of our contract state that you are to get the money as soon as I get the coal. Of course it would be better for you to get the money without delivering the coal, as it would be better for me to get the coal without paying the money, but since these alternatives are not available, we contract with each other, giving in order to get.

Rawls's social contract theory differs from that of his celebrated predecessors in that his prime concern is not to spell out the conditions under which a government should be judged to be legitimate, although he does have something to say about these questions.[49] His major interest is to spell out the rights and duties of citizens and the just allocation of the benefits and burdens of citizenship. But the same question that we put to the classical theorists can be put to Rawls. No doubt if we *had* contracted with each other or with the government to assume a given set of rights and duties and to apportion goods and services in accordance with specific principles we *would be* obliged to respect the terms of our agreement. But we haven't; so if we are so obliged, it isn't because we have accepted the terms of the agreement as parties to a contract. So what is the point of casting the argument in the form of a hypothetical contract?

In the most simple terms the answer is that Rawls conceives of justice as fairness. The principles of justice should be recognized as fair impositions on all those subject to them. But what does fairness demand? It looks as if we have substituted one difficult and contentious term – fairness – for another – justice. Philosophically anyway, we were in the dark about the demands of justice. We shall not feel illuminated by the announcement that justice is fairness. We need to see how fairness is construed in detail. That's the next task. But already we should have some intimation of why a social contract argument is an apt instrument for displaying the reasoning of citizens who ponder questions of justice. A model contract is fair to all parties. Each treats the other as an independent equal who may accept or reject the proposed terms depending upon whether his interests and values are served.

In thinking about justice, as arguably in thinking about morality generally, we give ourselves the task of establishing principles which command universal assent and we do this by taking into account the reasons anyone might have for accepting or rejecting the principles. This requirement has been thought by many to be a logical implication of the fact that a judgement is a moral principle. Others have supposed that universalizability is a strategy for establishing the plausibility of moral principles. If we wish others to accept the principles we propose, we had better first step into their shoes and investigate if they are likely to accept them in the light of interests we can presume them to have. Rawls insists on the universality of the principles of justice.[50] One way of presenting this condition is to represent the principles as the outcome of a contract, an agreement amongst *all* parties.

This last is a very weak motivation for adopting a contractarian argument, but, as we shall see, it is important in understanding one strand of Rawls's presentation. A more important conception of the role of fairness in the argument rests on a distinctive view of how we should think about the problem of justice. We are to think of the principles of justice as determining the allocation of benefits and burdens which accrue from the system through which individuals co-operate. The system must be structured by principles which everyone can recognize as procuring their advantage; everyone will identify the fruits of their co-operation and make a claim on them. The strategic way of deriving principles which give effect to universal advantage is to adopt a deliberative stance which is impartial between the claims of all who contribute to the co-operative scheme. From the point of view of any individual who is seeking rules to govern a co-operative scheme to remedy the circumstances of justice, egoistic reasoning might suggest that such a person goes for whatever scheme promotes his best advantage, but a little thought would convince him that the promotion of his best advantage is hardly likely to commend the scheme to those others whose co-operation is required. People will demand a system which is fair in the further sense of being the product of unbiased or impartial reasoning; 'it should be impossible to tailor principles to the circumstances of one's own case'.[51] We need a process of reasoning which embodies this impartiality. Furthermore, we should recognize that impartiality between the claims of all those who are party to the necessary co-operative scheme entails that each should be thought of as advancing claims of equal weight on the product of social co-operation. As Rawls insists, 'the purpose of these conditions [of impartiality] is to represent equality between human beings as moral persons, as creatures having a conception of their good and a sense of justice'.[52] If the principles of justice commend a scheme of strict equality in the distribution of benefits and burdens, no one can complain that their claims have been ignored or devalued.

So far we have no details of the procedures of the social contract account, but already we can see why Rawls's methodology is captured by his term 'reflective equilibrium'. We recognize the necessity for having some principles of justice, but prior to the elaboration of these principles we recognize that they must conform to deep-seated intuitions. In this case the crucial intuitions cluster around the idea of fairness. We derive principles that are binding on all parties because the interest of each party has been given equal weight in a process of deliberation that is strictly impartial between their conflicting claims. Rawls's distinctive contribution is to elaborate a hypothetical social contract argument that does justice to these intuitions. He believes that only a social contract argument could succeed. Intuitionism, whereby independent principles are endorsed as separately compelling, cannot serve the purpose because we are unable to judge which principle should take priority in the case of conflict. And further, such a collection of principles, in the absence of a theory that binds them together, would have no resources for deciding cases that strike us as novel, as inappropriate for the application of the principles with which we are already familiar. Utilitarian reasoning fails because it is judged to compromise the equality of moral persons as separately the locus of moral claims. It may so fail where the optimal system of co-operation in point of utility requires that the well-being of some be sacrificed to achieve maximum utility for all, considered as an aggregation of sources of recorded or expected utility. Uniquely, the social contract method can yield an ordered and projectible set of principles which is fair in respect of its recognition of the claims of all parties subject to them.

But this abstract characterization of Rawls's enterprise needs to be fleshed out before we can judge its cogency. We need to describe the impartialist stance – then we shall see more clearly why the hypothetical social contract is an apt device for practical reasoning about the subject of justice.

The Original Position

There are two distinctive features of Rawls's hypothetical social contract. In deliberating about justice, we place ourselves in what Rawls calls the Original Position. The first feature of this hypothetical stance is that we suppose ourselves to be located behind a veil of ignorance characterized by a specific combination of knowledge and ignorance. We are supposed to know:

(1) The thin theory of the good. This is a list of what Rawls describes as primary social goods, all-purpose means for achieving a rational long-term plan of life. The thought is that *whatever* one's plan of life turns out to be, rights and liberties, opportunities and powers, income and wealth, and the social bases of self-respect, will be needed to accomplish it. Goods are included on this list only if their distribution can be regulated by the basic structure of society, the main social institutions. The basic structure will define the liberties and powers of subjects and determine the allocation of income and wealth. Other lists of all-purpose goods may seem more compendious – Hobbes's list of natural and instrumental powers is a good example.[53] In the case of items which one may be tempted to add to Rawls's list we may find that they are specifications of goods which already appear there. Knowledge, one may think, is such an asset, but Rawls believes that the skills and capacities which are the product of education are included as opportunities or powers. Important personal assets such as beauty and charm ('Forme' and 'Affability' on Hobbes's list) are not in the gift of government or its agencies. So these natural primary goods will not feature on the list. Health is a moot example; the onset of disease may be thought of as a brute contingency, but the odds against suffering disease can be increased by public health policies and resources can be shifted around to provide health-care.[54] The list of social primary goods, or further specification of it, is open-ended. But however it is specified, we can suppose that people want more rather than less of these goods.

(2) The laws of the social sciences. We must suppose, further, that subjects in the Original Position have a sufficient knowledge of the facts of social life to work out the policy implications of the principles they select. 'They understand political affairs and the principles of economic theory; they know the basis of social organization and the laws of human psychology.'[55] But this knowledge, as we shall see, is quite general. It is as though

they had available the resources of a good social science library with all proper names erased.

By contrast, we must suppose that, behind the veil of ignorance, we are ignorant of:

(3) Our place in society, our position in respect of class or social status, our actual or prospective income and wealth, the natural assets at our disposal – our strength, intelligence or particular psychology – as well as the generation we belong to. One could add (and others have found these supplementations of Rawls to be a valuable resource in pursuit of social justice) ignorance of one's sex and sexual orientation, race or ethnic grouping.

(4) Further, we are not to know specific details of the society we inhabit, 'its economic or political situation, or the level of civilization and culture it has been able to achieve'.[56]

(5) Finally, and most controversially, we do not know our *thick* conception of the good. Rawls believes, and as we have seen in Chapter 3, this is almost definitive of the liberal position, that individual persons will differ radically in respect of their conception of the good life, of the details of the plan of life we can presume them to have adopted. Some persons will pursue the life of the aesthete, others a life of cheerful vulgarity, hunting, shooting and fishing. Some will be hedonists, counting the score of their pleasures, others, ascetics, valuing simplicity or their triumphs over temptation. Some will be devoted to their families and friends, others, not quite misanthropes, will seek a life of limited interpersonal relationships. Some will be atheists or agnostics, seeking to live their life in accordance with whatever meaning they find or construct from their natural conditions of existence. Others may pursue a life of religious devotion, and the varieties of religious expression encourage a particularly noxious tendency towards fissiparity and conflict. As I mentioned before, we can suppose that there are at least as many widely held conceptions of the good life as there are monthly magazines on the shelves of the average newspaper shop – multipled by the possibilities of permutation by conjunction. We come across (in literature, if not too often in life)

parsons who love to hunt and swill the claret as well as ascetic atheists with a fastidious taste in modern jazz.

All of these conceptions of the good life are swept behind the veil of ignorance. We know enough about our fellows behind the veil of ignorance to understand the magnificent variety of thick conceptions of the good that will be revealed when the veil is parted, but we are to presume ourselves ignorant of the contours of our own plan of life for the purposes of deliberating about justice.

The motivation behind this hypothetical combination of knowledge and ignorance is the elimination of partiality and bias. How can I be accused of serving my own distinctive conception of the good life if I don't know what it will turn out to be? How can I be accused of disvaluing the way of life you judge to be best if I don't know the plan of life you have selected? The device of hypothetical ignorance has evident resonances with the way we think about justice. One way of judging the impact of some proposal or the justice of some policy is to place oneself in the shoes of some other party who is affected by it and then ask would the subsequent distribution of benefits and burdens be acceptable if you didn't know which position was the one you occupy. Suppose the dispute concerned the allocation of housework. Harry doesn't want to do any of the work in the kitchen. Sally points out that they both work outside the home from 9.00a.m. to 5.00p.m. She already does the washing and the cleaning. If Harry's proposal, that he do nothing other than earn his wages, were accepted, there would be two parties, one doing all the housework, the other doing none. Asking Harry to hypothesize that he doesn't know which bundle of chores he might be assigned is a nice way of bringing home to him the unacceptability of either party's being asked to shoulder all the burdens. If his most advantageous option is crystal clear, so is that of the other party. If he would hate to have all the chores to do, he can understand Sally's complaint and should review the distribution of tasks.

Some have claimed that Rawls's theory of the veil of ignorance in the original position expresses a strong view of the role of the state as neutral between competing conceptions of the good life, that this is a clear implication of the doctrine of the priority of the right over the good, which Rawls explicitly claims to be a central feature of his conception of justice.[57] I will have something to say about these issues later, but for the moment I want to stress that the primary intuition to be cashed out by the requirement of the hypothetical veil of ignorance is impartiality, not neutrality. When it comes to articulating, as is necessary, the theory of the primary goods, Rawls conclusions are *not* neutral, as one important critic has pointed out.[58] The basic structures of society should not be neutral in respect of their recognition of the value of the primary goods and their task of promoting them. Although Rawls believes that detailing the contents of the list of primary goods amounts to a weak premiss in the overall argument (he clearly did not anticipate the level of criticism directed towards this aspect of his theory), the list itself does not present an anodyne prescription for the activities of the state. In respect of both inclusions within the list and exclusions from it, the list is controversial. What holds the list together is the idea of the primary goods as all-purpose means to whatever thick conception of the good parties may have developed as rational for themselves to pursue. What governs exclusions from the list is the thought that the principles of justice must be the product of a process of deliberation with such a measure of impartiality that it is accessible to all parties. Whether or not Rawls achieves fairness in the process of deliberating about justice is an open question. There can be no doubt that he wishes fairness to constrain these deliberations.

The original position details the hypothetical circumstances in which we must place ourselves to address the question of justice. How do we deliberate once we have broached this thought-experiment? At this point we meet the second distinctive feature of Rawls's social contract approach. Rawls believes we should reason as egoists seeking to maximize our protections and advance our holdings of primary goods, helping ourselves to the technical resources of rational choice theory in order to derive the principles of justice. Let me stress at this point, having introduced the term 'egoist', that Rawls is most definitely *not* proposing that we adopt any variety of egoism. The kind of egoism that is put to work behind the veil of ignorance is a thesis about the motivation of the parties who inhabit that hypothetical condition: the primary goods constitute the ends that they value for themselves and the principles of justice represent the best means to advance them.

Now Thomas Hobbes did hold this kind of egoistic view in respect of the motivation of all persons generally. On his account, human beings are predominantly motivated by a conception of what is in their own best interest, and he argued that the rule of justice, narrowly construed as the principle 'that men performe their covenants made', i.e. keep their promises, could be derived by anyone who pondered how best to achieve their long-term goal of commodious living. Hobbes was speaking of *us*, of how, granted his theory of human nature, people like us should deliberate about how to behave. Rawls is not describing our behaviour or the behaviour of people like us. We are not egoists. Most particularly we are not egoists because we have a sense of justice and wish to govern our transactions with each other in accordance with principles we judge to be fair. Self-interest in the original position, behind the veil of ignorance, is not self-interest beyond it. Self-interest behind the veil of ignorance is not a strategy of self-interest at all, because the parties in the original position have foresworn any of the knowledge that would enable them to advance the interests distinctive to themselves. In the original position, subjects do not know who they are or what they want except as specified by the conditions of the veil of ignorance. What Rawls has attempted to capture by his device of the social contract, the veil of ignorance and the postulate of rational choice is a method of impartial deliberation on the question of everyone's best advantage. Let us see how this deliberation works out.

The principles of justice

In order to see how the argument works, let us first state the principles, then outline the argument for them. First, let us state the general conception of justice:

> All social primary goods – liberty and opportunity, income and wealth, and the bases of self-respect – are to be distributed equally unless an unequal distribution of any or all of these goods is to the advantage of the least favored.

The famous two principles of justice are deemed to be a special case of this:

First Principle. Each person is to have an equal right to the most extensive total system of equal basic liberties compatible with a similar system of liberty for all.

Second Principle. Social and economic inequalities are to be arranged so that they are both:

(a) to the greatest benefit of the least advantaged, consistent with the just savings principle, and

(b) attached to offices and positions open to all under conditions of fair equality of opportunity.[59]

Before we proceed, a few clarificatory notes are in order. The First Principle, the equal liberty principle, has lexical priority in the special conception. This forbids trade-offs which sacrifice equal liberty to some gain in respect of the other primary goods. The second element of the Second Principle, equality of opportunity, likewise has lexical priority over the first element, the difference principle. The special conception of justice, with its division of two principles and the associated priority rules, comes into play when a certain level of prosperity has been reached. Sacrifices of liberty to promote wealth are only justified when the wealth creation is necessary in order to raise a society to an economic level where liberty can be enjoyed.[60] In *Political Liberalism*, this standard is sketchily described in terms of citizens' needs being satisfied – needs expressing requirements which have to be met if citizens are to 'maintain their role and status, or achieve their essential aims'[61]. We shall concentrate on the special conception, being convinced that liberty, rather than being an exotic and corrupting Western implantation that a disciplined emergent society can ill afford, is a precondition of the creation of sufficient wealth to meet citizens' most basic needs. Further, we shall concentrate in what follows on the Second Principle, barely mentioning the liberty principle and its priority.[62]

First though, to capture a central feature of Rawls's reasoning, let us look at the argument for the general conception and, *a fortiori*, for the difference principle. This proposes an equal division of the primary goods unless an unequal distribution is to the advantage of the least well off. Why should anyone placed behind the veil of ignorance in the original position choose first, equality, next, if it represents an improvement, inequality? Remember, behind the veil of ignorance, contractors do not know their position in society etc. In these circumstances, Rawls believes, contractors would adopt a safety-first outlook. They would inspect an array of alternative distributions and select those principles which guarantee the best worst outcome. They would adopt a *maximin* strategy.

Suppose there are just two classes of people, A and B, and suppose candidate distributions are as follows, the numbers recording units of primary goods:

	A	B
(1)	50	50
(2)	30	150

Rawls thinks his contractors would select outcome (1). Departures from equality, above and below the level of 50 units, register the possibility of gains or losses. If the worst outcomes are ranked in order of which is best, the strategy of maximin requires the choice of (1), 50 units being better than 30. Contrast (1) however with a third possibility

(3)	55	65

Since more primary goods are better than less, Rawls believes contractors who are seeking to advance their holdings will select (3) in comparison to either (1) or, since (2) has already been judged inferior to (1), *a fortiori*, (2). Technically, outcome (3) is 'weakly Pareto superior' to (1). Everyone is better off so it is a change for the better. Whether they turn out to be in the better-off class or the worst-off class, they will register an improvement over the distribution in (1). The difference principle, reflecting maximin reasoning, ranks (3) higher than (1) and (1) higher than (2).

Under conditions of uncertainty, it is controversial which principle of practical reasoning one should adopt in order to rank alternatives. There are plenty of cases which suggest that *maximin*, going for the best worst alternative, is counterintuitive. Do we climb the mountain or do we stay at home and go out in the afternoon to see a film. Climbing the mountain, one of us may slip and be killed. We may be killed walking to the cinema, but there's less chance of it. Climbing is not very dangerous, but it's dangerous enough for us always to prefer an alternative way of spending our free time, so long as we reason in *maximin* fashion. Were we *maximiners* we would never venture onto a steep slope. There is always something safer we could be doing.

What is the alternative to maximin? It is time to bring the reasoning in favour of (2) out of the woodwork. As (2) suggests, it is maximum average utility. Between classes A and B, supposing members of these classes are equal in numbers, one might suppose that some people, those who like a gamble, would compute average expected utility at 90 units – and go for it. They may find themselves in the class who receive 30 units, and worse off than they would be under *maximin*, but they may be better off than they would be under either equality or the difference principle. If we do the sums we find that average utility under (2) will amount to 90 units (30 plus 150 = 180; the sum divided by 2, = 90 units of utility). Computing in the same fashion, the average utility of (1) is 50; the average utility of (3) is 60 units of the primary goods. Since the utility of (2) is greater than the utility of either (1) or (3) why not go for it? The objection to Rawls can be phrased more strongly as: what reasons are there for not taking the approach of average utility, gambling on the chance of being one of the better off, gaining 150 units, and risking the prospect of losing – receiving 30 rather than 50 under equality or 55 under the difference principle?

Rawls's answer is that we wouldn't dare.[63] We only have one life to lead and the basic structure of the society in which we live is crucial to our well-being, and just as importantly, to that of our children. We would be wrong to risk the possibility of receiving 30 units when we can guarantee the receipt of 50 units or better. The utilitarian, as ever, has a cogent reply. In the comparison of (1) and (2), if (2) is represented as an outcome that the proponent of maximum average utilitarianism would endorse, either like is not being compared with like or the situation is underdescribed. It looks as though like is not being compared with like since the utilitarian will be concerned to envisage outcomes primarily in terms of the distribution of utilities, rather than primary goods. As we saw in

Chapter 2, the utilitarian has reason to believe that the sorts of allocation that maximize utility will be those that tend towards equality. With departures from equality, the gainers gain less than is lost by the losers, so average utility is diminished. If this is right, the utilitarian can properly ask for more details of how the unequal distribution of primary goods is supposed to maximize utility. If it is claimed that the facts of the matter are contingent, that things *might* work out this way, the utilitarian can agree, but insist that, as a matter of fact, they don't so work out – and Rawls's contractors, well aware of the laws of the social world, will be aware that they don't.

Let us put this issue to one side and concentrate on the question of whether we should select (1) the condition of equality, or go for (3) a situation of inequality in which everyone is better off. The answer looks obvious. How could it be rational to be the dog in the manger, refusing to move to a better position on the grounds that others are doing better still? Rawls insists that it couldn't. Envy is irrational. This might be so, but if inequality is known to be a general cause of envy, human nature being what it is, isn't this a reason not to move towards inequality?[64] One might point to the debilitating effects of social hierarchy and a stratified society, as we have had occasion to mention, but Rawls has a good reply at this point. As the second element of the second principle emphasizes, he insists that there be fair equality of opportunity, that everyone has the possibility of moving into the positions which offer the prospect of the highest income and wealth. We should also notice a corollary. The most mysterious of the primary goods, which is also mentioned as the most important, is self-respect or self-esteem, since without self-respect, 'all desire and activity becomes empty and vain and we sink into apathy and cynicism. Therefore the parties in the original position would wish to avoid at almost any cost the social conditions that undermine self-respect'.[65]

It is hard to place this primary good into the framework of the two principles; Rawls seems to think that it is served by the liberty principle as this is worked up into constitutional arrangements that guarantee equal political status. We could add that it should disallow inequalities of income and wealth of such a type and from such sources as corrupt the sense of the worst off that, notwithstanding their lesser holdings are greater than they would possess under equality, they are treated as, or come to see themselves as, being of lesser moral or social standing than others. Hegel noticed that the condition of the unemployed can be utterly demeaning. We have learned that this lack of self-respect may persist even though the unemployed are in receipt of a minimum social income. If such lesser standing is a consequence of a specific aetiology of inequality, it should be factored into the index of primary goods which defines the condition of the worst off. They may well judge that despite their greater holdings of income and wealth, they are overall worse off than they would be under conditions of equality of income and wealth. Clearly *everything* depends upon the wider social ramifications of such differences.

Now we can return to our original question. If basic needs are met, and if as we have just insisted, inequalities of wealth and income are not magnified into the sort of social differences that inhibit equality of opportunity and undermine self-respect, should we not accept the inequalities that are licensed by the difference principle? I think we should.

Before we leave the discussion of Rawls and the topic of social justice, there are a few issues to be tidied up. At the heart of Rawls's conception of a just society is a conception of how we should think about the problem of distribution. We begin with a Humean conception of 'a society as a co-operative venture for mutual advantage',[66] developed as a response to the circumstances of justice which demand that conflicts of interest be resolved. I take it that this leads us to endorse, as a first step, a system of property rules that govern entitlements, enabling us to judge who owns what. We noticed when discussing Nozick's account that some system of adjudicating property claims is necessary (although we noticed, too, the absence of any specification of what the appropriate rules might be). I assume that in any *stable* society a conservative principle applies which supposes that the rules in place can be vindicated on grounds of their utility. (I don't suppose that either Nozick or Rawls would accept this judgement, but let us proceed. Both of them, I take it, suppose that we reflect upon the problem of justice against a background of rules having *de facto* authority in the jurisdictions which they examine.)

It is only against some such background – of established rules and (moderately) successful practice – that we can identify society as a co-operative venture for mutual advantage. How else? We now have a fresh problem which Hume did not have to consider because he thought the problem of justice was settled. Granted that the institutions in place, with their constituent rules, secure mutual advantage or general utility, are they just? This question has point only if we accept that there is a standpoint for asking questions of justice which departs from the standard of utility. Rawls insists that there must be. There is the question: Is the distribution of benefits and burdens *fair* ? His answer is that it may be, but if it is, this is a coincidence, a matter of contingency, because the fairness of the system is to be adjudicated by principles other than utility.

Fairness requires that we review the benefits of social co-operation from the perspective of each of those who are affected by the scheme in place. Perhaps, as Thomas Scanlon, one of Rawls's most constructive critics has insisted, we can ask this question directly: Can the rules governing the allocation of benefits and burdens be reasonably rejected by any of those subject to the distributive scheme which is purportively required by principles of justice?[67] If anyone could reasonably reject such a scheme, its requirements would not meet the standards of universalizability proposed by Kant and accepted by Rawls.[68] Although this is a good question to ask, given Rawls's general endorsement of Scanlon's variety of contractualism in *Political Liberalism* and his advertisement of his argument as a species of Kantian constructivism, we have no clear answer. Rawls's canonical method is indirect, employing the original position and its veil of ignorance, because these argumentative strategems embody the intuitions concerning impartiality that fairness requires.

So the argumentative apparatus of *A Theory of Justice* directs us to appraise the institutions of any stable society from the point of view of one who requires that the principles be fair, as well as, or despite, the rules in place serving general utility. The Rawlsian prospectus, as I have described it, is utterly abstract. It is time to put some flesh on these bones. Suppose we accept that a free market economy, based on private property, has demonstrated its credentials in point of overall utility. (It hasn't; other sub-optimal systems, e.g. central government planning, have demonstrated their inefficiency – but then utilitarianism has no *a priori* conclusions to defeat opposing intuitions.[69]) What Rawls has in mind as a system of political and economic organization which satisfies his principles of justice is the liberal democratic welfare state.[70] Democracy and liberty are guaranteed by the liberty principle, welfarism by the modified equality guaranteed by the difference principle. Putting liberty to one side in the context of evaluating distributive justice, we can see that the implementation of justice, as required by the difference principle, requires a system of transfers to be imposed upon the system of entitlements that are in place. Smith owns such and such, given the rules, but . . . Jones earns such and such, but . . . In each case holdings are reviewed in the light of the difference principle and transfers to or from Smith and Jones will be effected by such means as the taxation of income, sales, inheritance or wealth.

At this point, an obvious objection kicks in. We have a historically determined property system subject to continuous modification by application of the difference principle. We have institutions which guarantee equality of opportunity in respect of access to those offices and positions which yield the greater income and wealth in systems where differentials in income and wealth are judged to improve the position of the worst off, the details presumably fixed by the operation of a market in labour. What place is there in this system for the application of a principle of desert?[71]

Desert

We can think of a wide range of circumstances in which different allocations of income and wealth might be justified on the grounds of unequal desert. Smith works harder than Jones, or equally hard for a longer time, or with the same effort but with more skill, or with as much effort, for as long, and with as much skill, but at a dirtier job. In each of these cases, Smith produces more goods, and untutored intuitions or popular sentiment might have it that Smith earns a greater reward, deserving the premium his efforts or skill attracts. Regardless of whether his increased productivity has benefited the worst off, say through the trickle-down effects of his economic success, he deserves his unequal receipts. This is not a case of claims of desert conflicting with claims of justice, since it will be argued that the reward of desert is an established principle of justice. So much the worse for a theory of justice that does not respect such claims.

Rawls distrusts such arguments – and he is quite right to do so; which is not to say that they have no philosophical weight. He accepts that persons are born with very different natural endowments. It may be that not only are individuals born with different skills and talents, but that they are unequally blessed in the ability to exploit them. Two mountaineers may be equally strong and agile, but one of them may lack the nerve to tackle the more dangerous routes, or the intelligence to approach them with an appropriate degree of safety, or the staying-power to proceed in the face of difficulties. Who is to say which of these qualities is *not* the product of a natural lottery? If the wonderfully talented jazz-player has a self-destructive streak it makes as little sense to praise him for the first as blame him for the second. This argument does not assume some sort of genetic determinism which establishes that all personal qualities are the product of natural inheritance. Rather it registers, in more modest fashion, our inability to measure the respective contributions of natural endowment and freely directed effort towards any specific accomplishment. Thus, Smith works harder or longer than Jones – but it may be that he was born stronger. Grant also that the effects of the natural lottery may be magnified by favourable personal circumstances – a supportive family, a solid education, strategically-placed friends – and we can see that the problem of isolating a distinctively personal contribution as the proper subject of merit or desert becomes even harder. Of all the moral principles constitutive in their way to the idea of justice, conceptions of desert are the most puzzling.[72]

From the standpoint of the original position, desert has no place. When we deliberate with that quality of impartiality that embodies fairness, we shall see society as a co-operative endeavour and adopt the difference principle as 'an agreement to regard the distribution of natural talents as a common asset and to share in the benefits of this distribution whatever it turns out to be'.[73] On the other hand, once we examine the institutions necessary to implement the principles of justice, we can expect to find elements of the economic system mimicking those residues of desert which linger in the thought that reward is due to effort or skill, since these are the sort of individual qualities that are sought out in the labour market under conditions of fair equality of opportunity. Efficiency of the kind from which everyone benefits will often see to it that effort and skill are rewarded (though this cannot be guaranteed; skills fall out of demand and effort may be misplaced).[74]

Such considerations cannot be expected to satisfy those who insist that desert is a principle independent of incentive effects and market operations. Everyone dines well at Rawls's feast, but, it will be insisted, some have no right to be there. In particular, the spoiler of many a draft welfare scheme, the wastrel, idler, shirker or benefits scrounger, should have no seat at the table. This ignoble character precisely does not co-operate in the scheme for mutual advantage and is not a worthy recipient of any of its fruits. Far from being a member of the worst off class and due whatever amelioration unequal rewards to others may generate, he is due nothing.

If everyone were born with at least the capacity to develop some marketable skills, if they were educated to expect work and be trained to apply their skills in the labour market, if the market could supply jobs to meet their demand to work, if, in short, we could distinguish the idle from the unemployable and otherwise contingently unemployed, this argument would have a great deal of force. Until these distinctions can be confidently made, it is a distraction.

The detail of Rawls's arguments for the two principles of justice has been subjected to massive technical criticism which I shall leave readers to pursue for themselves. I hope I have elaborated its greatest strength – its insistence that the fashioning of principles of justice (which should include responsiveness to need) requires us to adopt a deliberative stance that ensures fairness in the specific sense of impartiality as we review competing claims on the limited pool of resources. If the aim of the exercise is to produce principles that all could accept as fairly governing the terms under which they co-operate with each other, it is vital that such principles do not favour or sacrifice the interests of any particular group of individuals, since, if they were so biased, they would not command the support of all those whose behaviour they are designed to regulate. Once one grants the necessity of such a deliberative stance it is hard to see how any principle other than the modified equality of the diffference principle could find acceptance.

The communitarian challenge

Before we leave the topic of distributive justice, we should examine (too briefly) a set of claims, widely advanced in response to Rawls's work, to the effect that the deliberative stance of fairness, as I have explained it, is just not possible for creatures like us. This challenge has been made by a number of thinkers who have been grouped together as communitarians. Amongst contemporary philosophers, the most prominent communitarians include Alasdair MacIntyre, Charles Taylor, Michael Sandel and Michael Walzer. One has to be careful in thinking of these philosophers as members of a distinctive school or group, since the differences between them are often as great as their similarities.[75] I shall broach just a portion of their work in concentrating on their criticism of Rawls's (and other liberal theories) of justice.

I have claimed that the distinctively valuable contribution of Rawls's theory of justice is his attempt to articulate an appropriate stance from which to deliberate the problem of justice. We take up the Original Position, locating ourselves behind the veil of ignorance and seeking to advance our holdings of primary goods. In so doing, we abstract ourselves in thought from the societies we inhabit and the concrete relationships in which we stand to other people. We deem ourselves ignorant of those goods which endow our lives with the particular meanings we ascribe to them, the thick theories of the good to which we subscribe. Communitarians object that we cannot conduct this exercise of intellectual abstraction, or, if we could, such abstraction could not yield principles of justice which would command our allegiance once we have departed the Original Position and relocated ourselves in our given, historically conditioned communities.

Now readers may have registered any number of doubts concerning the course of Rawls's argument. I have tried to explain the point of Rawls's exercise in abstraction, his withdrawal behind the veil of ignorance into the original position, in terms of a pretheoretical commitment to fairness, but critics may charge that this manoeuvre is unnecessary or unsuccessful. They may ask why individuals who do not live behind a veil of ignorance should regard themselves as committed to principles they would adopt were they, hypothetically, to find themselves so located. Rawls, operating in the social contract tradition, has advocated something like a thought-experiment in order to advance our thinking about justice. The first element of the communitarian challenge is the striking claim, not that the thought-experiment is otiose or fruitless, but that we cannot genuinely conduct it.

Construction of the Rawlsian hypothetical contract requires that we think of ourselves as discrete individuals capable of dissociating from the ethical ties that bind us to others in our communities. We must be able to do this if we are to examine whether such ties are just. I think it appropriate as a poor man to doff my cap as the rich man enters the gate of his castle. Someone may challenge my habitual deference and cause me to think hard about my hitherto unexamined place in the established hierarchy. For a Rawlsian, the form of rationality distinctive of philosophizing about justice requires such exercises in detachment. Once I accept the demand that familiar obligations and allegiances be subject to rational examination, I should seek to distance myself in thought from the fact of my allegiance in order to conduct my investigation. If, as a matter of fact, I can't achieve the independence of thought necessary to attain such detachment, if I am so absorbed by the practices of my community that I cannot put them to question, then I can't deliberate about justice. Rawls's Original Position represents an ethical stance external to the obligations up for inspection which guarantees that my reflections will be conducted in an impartial spirit.

For the communitarian, such detachment and dissociation are impossible. I am constituted by a deep network of ends and purposes, furnished, willy-nilly, by the established social structures of the society in which I was raised. The interpersonal commitments which these ends and purposes embody comprise my identity as the person I am. It would not be *me* who retreated behind the veil of ignorance, but some shadowy simulacrum. How could it be *me*, if *I* am required to shed, in thought, constitutive ideals which contribute essentially to the identification of who *I am*, ideals which

Rawls has allocated to the theoretically inert realm of the 'thick conception of the good'. Take Holy Willie, the subject of Burns's eponymous poem, 'Holy Willie's Prayer'. The reader may suppose that Willie cannot, without becoming someone else, entirely detach himself from his Calvinist principles, and specifically, his sense that he is one of the Elect. Since he speaks to himself (though he is sure that his God is listening), we should judge him to be disabled by self-deception rather than common-or-garden hypocrisy.

Read the poem. You might think that Holy Willie has got things wrong somewhere – agreeing with Burns and most of his readers on this. He is clearly unable to confront seriously the question of whether the rigorous standards which he uses to judge the conduct of others, apply equally to himself. The syndrome is familiar. If this is a true description of Willie's state of mind, I think he is constitutionally unable to deliberate about moral questions.

I can't tackle here the range and sophistication of communitarian arguments against liberalism. Their prime focus, in any case, is Rawls's philosophical methodology rather than his specific contribution to discussions of distributive justice. But we know enough about the communitarian position to understand that the heart of it is a claim about the limits of our reasoning powers, about how far we can dissociate ourselves in thought from the values that frame our concrete social identities. There are some questions that we cannot ask – or, if we can ask them, that we cannot take seriously because we cannot achieve the detachment necessary to see the questions as open. We are, as a matter of fact, constrained in respect of the ethical questions we are able to tackle. A favoured example of this sort of constraint in operation concerns a good parent's inability to contemplate seriously whether she has an obligation to promote a child's welfare. Love will blind her to a review of the pro's and con's.

This may or may not be true. If it is true, it will be true because that is how human beings characteristically think about these matters. I cannot see how questions of distributive justice might become practically otiose in a similar fashion. Once folks learn how to question the conventional allocation of benefits and burdens, Pandora's box is open. It might be hard to attain the impartiality required by Rawls's invocation of the Original

Position. It might be even harder to stick with the principles of justice furnished by this ethical stance once the thought-experiment is concluded. Some may be unable to achieve the required detachment, some may fail to carry through the principles derived by their intellectual efforts, but I cannot see how any philosophical arguments could be expected to demonstrate that the attempt to reflect on principles of justice is overambitious.

Chapter 6

Political obligation

The problems

Alfred Russell Whitehead is said to have said that all philosophy is a series of footnotes to Plato and Aristotle. It is a good saying and wouldn't be such a memorable falsehood if it did not contain a strong element of truth. It is a falsehood because, in the tradition of Western philosophy the Pre-Socratic philosophers deserve a mention. But just as obvious, there are more philosophical problems than were dreamt of by Plato and Aristotle in their philosophies (but perhaps not many more) and, equally, the repertory of arguments pro and con, the range of responses to these problems, has been enlarged well beyond the category of footnotes. But one can easily mistake the show for the substance in respect of touted philosophical advances. Another way of making Whitehead's point would be to say that Plato and Aristotle 'set the agenda' and this would be more true as well as more trendy, but still a falsehood. However, there is one philosophical problem which has not advanced far beyond the elaboration of Plato's arguments and the development of challenges to it: the problem of political obligation.

In the *Crito*, Socrates is invited to collude with the plans of Crito and other friends and admirers who sympathize with his predicament by escaping gaol and the imminent (self)infliction of the sentence of death. He will be quite safe, he is assured, in Thessaly. If he accedes to Crito's scheme (the gaoler is beholden to him and informers can be bought off) Socrates will evidently be failing to fulfil the duties of a citizen of Athens. Should he or shouldn't he take up Crito's invitation? Should he do what the city requires of him? Or should he attempt to escape? Plato represents Socrates speaking in the voice of the Laws and Constitution of Athens and this voice argues convincingly in favour of his accepting the decreed punishment. The major themes of Socrates are first that he has consented to obey the laws and so to flee would be to break the covenants and undertakings he freely made; second, that he has received evident benefits from the city, that he ought to be grateful for these benefits, and that since by fleeing the city he would be doing it harm, this would be an ill return for the benefits received. These two arguments, the consent argument and the argument from received benefits have dominated the literature ever since, though they have taken many different forms, as we shall see.

First though, we should try to become clear about the precise nature of the problem of political obligation. We do best to think of our political obligations as obligations owed by us as citizens to the state. It is tempting to elucidate this concept by first outlining the general nature of an obligation and then explaining how specifically political obligations are to be construed. Such a course would require us to distinguish obligations from duties, and perhaps duties from reasons for action of a distinctively moral sort. The enterprise would be tricky and maybe interesting, but I am reluctant to engage in it for two reasons: in the first place, I doubt whether the exercise could be successfully concluded without excessive semantic legislation. Such distinctions could no doubt be forced. The language could be cleared up by careful stipulation which builds on distinctions made in the way we generally speak. I have no ambitions in this direction and, since judgement on whether such an exercise is valuable or pointless would have to wait upon its outcome, I shall do no more here than register my doubts. In the second place, our chief interest is in the specific issue of political obligation, and it may well be the case that whatever distinctions can be traced between, say, obligations and duties taken generally, do not apply in the specific context of political obligation. In fact, I think this is the case. It makes no difference whether we speak of the political obligations incumbent on citizens or of the duties of citizens or, to my ear, of the moral reasons citizens should recognize as governing their conduct with respect to the political institutions of the state. The last of these locutions is a mouthful, so I shall try to avoid it. The first has all the virtues and vices of familiarity. I prefer the second.

My reason is informal and pragmatic. The concepts of legal obligation and political obligation are closely linked and the closeness of the linkage invites a narrowness of focus I wish to avoid. We speak of legal obligation when we wish to identify the demands legitimately made of subjects within a particular legal system. The model here is that of the (generally justified)[1] coercive law, proscribing or prescribing conduct on penalty of sanctions for non-compliance. Speaking substantively, our legal obligations comprise our obligations to obey the law. There may be one big legal obligation – to obey the law – or as many obligations as there are prescriptive or proscriptive laws. We are apt to think that political obligations march in step with legal obligations, and this is a natural assumption since legislation is a political process, effected or authorized by the sovereign. So we are apt to think that political obligation equates to the obligation to obey the law. If so, we are in error.

I think we have a political obligation wherever good moral reasons dictate the terms of our relationship with the political institutions of the state. If there are good moral reasons why we should obey the laws promulgated by the state, then we have a political obligation to obey the law. If there are good moral reasons why we should follow a call to arms made by the state, then we have a political obligation to volunteer. If there are are good moral reasons why we should participate in processes which elect representatives or enact laws through plebiscites, then we have a political obligation to do these things. Since I recognize that this list of standard political obligations is wider than is sanctioned by the customary association of political and legal obligation, and since I don't want to beg the conceptual questions canvassed above, I think it most felicitous in point of style to speak of the duties of the citizen. There is nothing odd about the thought that citizens may have duties to volunteer some service to the state or vote in elections in circumstances where such conduct is *not* required of them on pain of sanction.

So the problem of political obligation is not on my account the narrow question of whether citizens have an obligation to obey the law. That problem can perfectly well be pursued within a wider agenda that includes other duties that may be imputed to the citizen. It may well take centre stage because characteristically the duty to obey the law is a duty that is *exacted* against the citizen and so one might expect arguments in favour of it to be the strongest available. But it is not the only duty that is in question, and, as we shall see, the question of whether we have such a duty may be most clearly answered in a context which brings into view other duties which citizens may recognize. That said, for the moment we shall retain the traditional focus on the duty to obey the law in order to frame more clearly other introductory questions.

The first such question concerns the ambition of the arguments that purport to establish this duty. How universal is the scope of application of the argument? Are these arguments designed to show that if any citizen should recognize such a duty then so should all?[2] Or may the arguments be custom-built, bespoke to the demands of citizens, severally? The classical liberal dialectic can be envisaged as a series of claims made by the state against citizens who independently review the cogency of these claims. The state advances its claims by way of arguments directed to all citizens. But each modern citizen assumes the right to examine these arguments independently. We imagine the state rehearsing its arguments because no modern state can expect its claims to be vindicated solely on the basis of its pre-established authority.[3]

The state hopes that its arguments will be of universal validity, convincing everyone. But of course it may not succeed. The arguments it employs may be failures, convincing no one, or they may be partially successful, convincing some but not all of those to whom they are addressed. I shall suggest that this is likely, and so shall represent the state as advancing a series of arguments that successively widen the net over those it seeks to convince of its legitimate authority. The following outcomes are possible: (a) no argument convinces any citizen; (b) at least one argument convinces some citizens; (c) all citizens are convinced by at least one argument; but they are different arguments for different citizens; (d) there is at least one argument that convinces all citizens that they have a duty to obey the law. Outcome (d) is best for the state, but it may turn out that the state need not be so ambitious. If, as the dialectic proceeds, it transpires that there are no citizens who can reject every one of the arguments the state advances (outcome (c)), then its objective – of laying a legitimate claim to the obedience of all citizens – has been achieved. Third best, from the point of view of the state, would be the acceptance by most citizens of some of the arguments it puts forward.

The next question concerns the content of the state's requirements, a second dimension to its ambitions. The state, as we have surmised, will lay claim to the obedience of all of its citizens, for one reason or another. But does the state's claim on the obedience of its citizens require that they obey *all* of its laws? I think not. Again, this is too ambitious. First, we should recognize that the laws in place are likely to be a ramshackle collection. They are likely to be cluttered with dead wood. Alert students of the law of modern states will recognize plenty of laws in desuetude, relics of forms of life long gone, governing, perhaps, the rules of the road according priority to horses over pedestrians or vice versa. The invocation of such rules, as in the case of *Shaw* v. *Director of Public Prosecutions*,[4] whereby the Star Chamber offence of 'conspiracy to corrupt public morals' was resurrected to convict poor Shaw, is widely deemed unjust. Second, some laws seem designed to be broken so long as law-breaking remains within acceptable limits. I confess to having broken the licensing laws as a juvenile drinking below the age of state consent, as an adult serving drinks after closing time, and as a parent buying alcohol for my under-age children. (If you are not sympathetic to this example, think of *your* violation, as driver or willing accessory, of the Road Traffic Acts.) We are all, all of us car-drivers, law-breakers on a regular basis. So we shouldn't be too po-faced (unless we have chosen to be politicians!) about the content of the requirement to obey the law.

To be effective *at all*, laws need to be precise in contexts which defy calculation and invite contravention. Citizens, unless they are paradoxically pernickety, know this too well, and are willing to accept, say, parking fines, as a tax rather than accept the imputation of moral wrong-doing which they would generally attach to law-breaking. They invoke parameters, of good luck or good judgement, where the law asserts specific constraints. Are such 'criminals' self-deceiving or do they draw fine but valid distinctions concerning the import of the criminal law? The argumentative terrain is unfamiliar to philosophers, but certain obvious truths deserve to be recited. Unless one accepts that all illegal behaviour is morally wrong – which is the question too often up for begging – one will be hard put to explain the wrongness of well-judged, unimpugned and harmless, law-breaking. The most sensible conclusion to reach, in the face of the philosopher who insists that we should emulate the rare but precious driver who never, or hardly ever, exceeds 70m.p.h. on a motorway, is that the state requires, not so much absolute literal obedience to its declared laws, as a disposition to law-abidingness.

This whole issue is cluttered by the evident overlap of laws and moral requirements. Where the dictates of law repeat and thereby endorse the requirements of morality, the scope for unashamed law-breaking will be severely constrained. Where the conduct is conventionally regulated – there must be *some* limit on the speed of cars, *some* limit on the age of permissible drinking of alcohol: what should it be? – one may expect social tolerance and personal insouciance. The most a sensible state will require, in respect of the private judgements, if not public statements by its representatives, is that citizens are disposed to take seriously its regulations, disposed within parameters of realistic laxity, to obey its laws. This is not quite the view, as told me by a local policeman, that Sicilians regard the traffic laws as possibly useful advice.

Finally, one should realize that laxity, on the part of the state, and low standards, on the part of the citizens, are one thing, conscientious disobedience quite another. This issue is too complex to take on board in its fine detail here. But we are required, as a final qualification to the thesis that the duties of the citizen require her to obey *all* of the laws, to acknowledge that normally obedient citizens may find, as a matter of idiosyncratic but not thereby mistaken moral beliefs, that they cannot, in good conscience, obey the law. They may judge that the proper duty of the citizen in such cases is to disobey the law. In these (possibly tragic) circumstances, the state must accept the possibility that well-meaning citizens may get things right or wrong, without impugning the overall authority of the state. Indeed, such citizens may endorse this authority, in a peculiarly self-denying but recognizable fashion, if they invite prosecution as the inevitable, but publicity-acquiring, cost of disobedience.[5] They may view their disobedience as the most appropriate, because most effective, way of discharging their citizenly duty to participate in the enactment of just laws. Civil disobedience in appropriate circumstances may well be one of the duties of the good citizen.

The last formal point I shall raise concerns the stringency of the duties of the citizen. We should consider, in the first place, whether the duties are conditional or unconditional. Hobbes believed that the duties of the citizen were unconditional in the precise sense that their successful ascription did not require the fulfilment of any duty on the part of the sovereign. He used both formal and substantive arguments to make this point. Formally, the contract which is the normative basis of the citizens' duties is a contract made amongst the citizens themselves, 'a Covenant of every man with every man'. The sovereign is not a party to the contract: 'That he which is made Soveraigne maketh no Covenant with his subjects beforehand, is manifest.'[6] Since for Hobbes, duties can only arise by the voluntary concession of a liberty, and since the sovereign concedes nothing, the sovereign has no duties to the citizens which might operate as conditions on the citizens' fulfilment of their duties in turn. If this argument works by applying Hobbes's analytical apparatus to the facts of the matter (a Covenant was made amongst the people, the sovereign did not in fact take part, etc. . . .), it is worthless, since there are no facts to support it. The strength of the argument relies upon its standing as a reconstruction of how rational agents would behave were there, hypothetically, no government. Against the background of such a thought-experiment, Hobbes conjectures that rational agents would not endorse a limited sovereign, since, if the sovereign's competence were limited, his performance would be subject to adjudication. If the possibility of such adjudication were to be institutionalized, this would require an institution superior to the sovereign to make a judgement of whether the sovereign had complied with his duties – and that institution would be the true sovereign. If, on the other hand, adjudication of whether or not the sovereign had met the conditions which constrain his exercise of sovereign power were not institutionalized, each citizen would retain exactly that power of private judgement which creates the problems of the state of nature in the first place, problems which the institution of the sovereign is designed to resolve. For Hobbes, there are these alternatives: either an absolute, unconditional sovereign and its corrollary, a citizen body with unconditional duties, or a degeneration of political life back into the state of nature, the condition of anarchy.[7] Life under even the worst, most self-serving, sovereign could not be as bad as reversion to the state of nature.

Hobbes's rigorous and daunting conclusion is disputed by John Locke, whose arguments, again, I brutally condense. Hobbesian man, famously, is motivated primarily by self-interest. He seeks to preserve his life and to enjoy commodious living. Lockean man is motivated by these goods, too, but in addition, he respects the tenets of natural law: 'Reason, which is that Law, teaches all Mankind, who will but consult it, that being all equal and independent, no one ought to harm another in his Life, Health, Liberty or Possessions.'[8] Such duties comprise a set of natural (negative) rights – 'side-constraints' in Nozick's useful terminology. Rational citizens recognize that such rights need to be enforced by punishment, but realize that effective punishment requires a state. Hence they would endorse a state which served the specific purposes of protecting the rights everyone claims. It follows that they would have no duty to obey a state whose demands exceed, and powers reach beyond, what is necessary to carry out this specific function and a right to rebel against a state which actively threatened the rights it was instituted to protect. The conclusion of this line of argument is that the duties of the citizen are conditional on the state's fulfilment of its assigned duties.

Should we deem the authority of the state to be absolute or limited, the duties of the citizen, unconditional or conditional on the satisfactory exercise of the powers assigned to the state? Should we follow Hobbes or Locke?[9] Technical weaknesses undermine Hobbes's position, since rational individuals could not be understood to give up their right of self-preservation and must retain a power of judging how far the state threatens rather than secures their life prospects. But aside from this, at the heart of Hobbes's defence of absolutism is an empirical claim that the worst of governments is better than the state of nature. This supposes first, what many will dispute, that Hobbes is correct in describing life in the state of nature as so awful – 'solitary, poore, nasty, brutish, and short'.[10] But granting him this; it certainly does not follow that any sovereign is better. He was quite wrong to suppose that the self-interest of sovereigns would invariably counsel them to promote the well-being of their people, 'in whose vigor consisteth their own strength and glory'.[11] To be fair to Hobbes, the sovereign he envisaged was more like a jolly Restoration monarch than a Pol Pot or Hitler, his main concern being to let his subjects get back to dancing round the maypole whilst he sorted out the fractious clerics who disturbed the peace. But this won't do for the twentieth or twenty-first centuries. No state is so poor – think of Haiti – that a Papa or Baby Doc can't enrich himself at the expense of his tyrannized people and salt away the proceeds in some secure Swiss Bank prior to a hasty departure and secure retirement. Tyranny may even undermine the rationality of those who inflict it, dictators becoming madder than most of their citizens and striking out at them in a deadly uninhibited fashion. In the matter of the rationality of absolute sovereigns, history rather than Hobbes's cod psychology is decisive.

This judgement supposed, what Hobbes thought most efficacious, that the absolute sovereign would be a single figure, a monarch or her modern equivalent, the dictator with a gang of henchmen. Arguably, the position is different if the absolute sovereign is the people, as in a direct democracy, or complex, articulated, representative institutions governed by the rule of law. In such cases, more attention has to be paid to the meanings of 'absolute' and 'limited' sovereignty and it may well turn out that absolute authority and unconditional duty are not correlative terms. For the moment we should draw the more modest conclusion that citizens' duties are conditional on the proper exercise of sovereign power, however that is characterized.

Anarchism and communitarianism

Before we proceed to examine the cogency of the arguments advanced by the state we should notice two dissenting voices to the enterprise as I have characterized it. The first such voice – that of the anarchist – insists that we are attempting the impossible. Since the state is an evil, the effort to justify it is wasted ink, rhetoric designed to dignify a solecism. The second voice also emphasizes the futility of the exercise, but on radically different grounds. The communitarian (I can think of no better soubriquet) disputes a crucial presupposition of the exercise – that we have the philosophical resources or intellectual capacity to conduct the enquiry. We are assuming that the citizen is able to detach herself from the force of social duties which bind her and investigate, as it were from the outside, the credentials of the claims of the state. In this respect we help ourselves to a distinctively liberal assumption – that the claims of the state are susceptible to review on the part of citizens.

In a passage we have noticed before, Kant expressed this assumption nicely in the first Preface to *The Critique of Pure Reason*:

> Our age is the genuine age of criticism, to which everything must submit. Religion through its holiness and legislation through its majesty commonly seek to exempt themselves from it. But in this way they excite a just suspicion against themselves, and cannot lay claim to that unfeigned respect that reason grants only to that which has been able to withstand its free and public examination.[12]

The communitarian, as I distinguish that position, challenges this distinctively liberal claim that the authority of the state can be subjected to the requirements of rational legitimation. Both of these positions – the anarchist and the communitarian – are worthy of lengthy examination. We shall have to treat them briskly.

First, then, anarchism. It is impossible to portray the depth and richness of anarchist writings on the small canvas available here.[13] But we can state the central elements of the anarchist case. The characterization I shall offer will be a composite picture, the elements drawn from a range of classical and modern theorists. I hope it will serve to draw readers to the great anarchist texts, not least because anarchism is surely the most attractive of the great political '-isms' through the generosity of its various conceptions of human nature and its optimism concerning the possibility of human goodness. This point is worth stressing right at the start of any treatment of anarchism, because the conventional associations of the term 'anarchy' and its cognates are so disreputable. Speak of the anarchist and thoughts drift towards Victorian images, Conrad's *Secret Agent*, and stories of Peter the Painter and the Siege of Sidney Street, pictures of black-coated, top-hatted foreigners ready to lob a smoking bomb in the direction of some royal carriage.

One belief is distinctive of all versions of anarchism: the state is an evil too great to be tolerable. 'All coercion is an evil', thought John Stuart Mill but on his account it may evidently be the lesser of two evils, notably when it is threatened or inflicted by the state in order to prevent some folk harming others. The anarchist would demur, believing either that the cure (laws, police, criminal courts and gaols) is worse than the disease (immorality or law-breaking) or, more radically, that the touted cure may be the cause of the illness. We shan't attempt here to define the state – it's hard to define anything that has a history – but Max Weber's account will serve: the state is whichever institution successfully claims 'a monopoly of the legitimate use of physical force within a given territory'.[14] The anarchist will latch on to the element of this epithet which employs the idea of physical force and claim that the institutional use of physical force against persons is always wrong, because physical force is generally unnecessary to prevent wrong-doing.

This claim may strike you as incredible. You may look around (or more likely read the newspapers) and observe (or read about) thieves and murderers galore. This may justly be deemed the Hobbesian perspective on current affairs. We may correctly judge ourselves to be vulnerable to these criminals, or, perhaps exaggerating our vulnerability, may nonetheless demand a quality of protection that we cannot provide for ourselves. Isn't it reasonable, not to *call* our neighbour a knave – that might result in our being sued for defamation – but to assume that he may be one and in light of this possibility, however remote, insure ourselves against the eventuality? Isn't the endorsement of a state with effective coercive mechanisms the best form of insurance? The anarchist insists not.

Once the state is at work, commanding people to do this, punishing them for doing that, the mechanisms of threat and enforcement will undermine the moral consciousness of citizens. The capacities that individuals have to decide what morality requires of them will shrink and petrify, for want of active engagement. Citizens ask: What does the law require? What penalties might contravention incur? What is the risk of suffering them? Is the game worth the candle? True moral agents, by contrast, consider only whether proposed lines of conduct are morally right, wrong or permissible and invest effort in the employment of the reflective capacities that can give them an answer. Citizens of the state have no more moral authenticity than a ventriloquist's doll; they mouth the rules that the state legislates. It is unsurprising therefore that the moral dwarfs who are the product of the densely coercive activities of the state, activities which reach into the home, practices of education and maybe religion, too, will act wickedly if they identify an opportunity to advance their own interests by harming others with impunity. Under the regime of a coercive state it is reasonable to assume your neighbour is a knave, but this assumption holds only under the conditions of moral ineptitude that the state induces.

This is the gist of Rousseau's criticism of Hobbes and other theorists of the state of nature: 'in speaking of the savage, they described a social man.'[15] So far as the interpretation of Hobbes goes, Rousseau is mistaken; Hobbes only ever attempted to describe the psychology of social man, himself and his contemporaries. The state of nature was a hypothetical construction, a portrayal of how man as we experience him would behave were there no sovereign power. It was never intended to portray prepolitical social relations, as Rousseau attempts to do. But Rousseau is right in his substantive point that descriptions of human nature that proceed from data concerning mankind's psychology and behaviour in conditions governed by the state should not purport to be universal if there is any possibility that humans might think and act differently were they not to live under the shadow cast by the state's employment of physical force. This is the opportunity that the anarchist exploits and it yields a rich literature.

Has the coercive apparatus of the state suffused our decision-making to the point where we either unthinkingly endorse the state's commands or surreptitiously contravene them for reasons of self-interest? Our inclination is to deny the charge – after all, it is directed against us and neither alternative is admirable. It is we, we docile, unreflective citizens of whatever state, who are alleged to be the moral incompetents the anarchist describes. And so the anarchist expects massive resistance to her most fundamental claim. Who will admit that their reasoning and decision-making is corrupt? The issue would be a stand-off, with the anarchist position perhaps weakened by its whiff of knowing unimpugnability (who knows what folks would be like if . . . ?) if there were no empirical evidence available to decide the issue. But fortunately there is, and it does not make comfortable reading.

In the early 1970s, Stanley Milgram conducted a series of experiments which exposed people's willingness to obey authority. His (unknowing) experimental subjects accepted the invitation to take part in trials which required them to inflict pain on ostensible subjects (mercifully, good actors) who answered questions wrongly. The experimental scenario was designed to emphasize the authority of those who conducted the experiment – it stank of *science*, which is to say the experiments took place in a university and the instructors wore white coats. The lessons were salutary – to the point that Milgram's work should be Lesson One in any course designed to educate children in how to be a good citizen. Willingly, although often reluctantly and against their evidently better judgement in many cases, far too many subjects did what they were told and inflicted what they believed to be great pain upon the actors. The lesson is humbling – who knows what you or I would have done had we been recruited as experimental subjects? We hope, pray and trust that we would have been amongst the very small minority who resisted the imperatives communicated by the authoritative scenario. But we cannot deny the claim that we would likely be dupes who would collude with the requests made of us in the name of scientific advance.[16]

If we are likely to behave like this because we believe that the pursuit of knowledge requires our collaboration and obedience, how realistic is the thought that we would be heroically independent when the state calls upon us to follow the rules? Might not the habits of deferential compliance revealed in Milgram's experimental subjects be a consequence of our induction into rigmaroles of obedience sanctioned and supervised by the state? Whatever its origin, our tendency to obey authority runs deep and it undercuts our ability to review our conduct in light of the thought that it might be misplaced. It might never occur to us that what we are doing is wrong, and even if it does occur to us, we might have lost the capacity to deliberate in an independent fashion about how we ought to behave. As Mill instructs us in *On Liberty*,[17] this capacity is threatened by authority and needs liberty to flourish. Anarchy is the extremity of liberty, as the anarchist emphasizes.

Most discussions of anarchy focus on the possibility of resolving conflict and achieving the rewards of co-operation without the state apparatus of rules and sanctions. And as one might expect, the discussions are inconclusive since at bottom the issues are empirical, the facts are contested and conclusive experiments impossible. Models of successful anarchy are available[18] and examples of efficient yet anarchical practice should be familiar to most readers. My own favourite example is the unregulated Boyd Orr car-park in the University of Glasgow which daily accommodates a greater density of vehicles than any planner pushing a white-line machine would dare prescribe – and rarely are exits blocked. But the sceptic asks, cogently, whether such examples, as well as the case-histories beloved of anarchists, of ungoverned communities managing better than their closely regulated neighbours,[19] can be persuasively generalized without significant losses of welfare. What would be the anarchist equivalent of the National Health Service or, for that matter, the armed forces, if citizens were to move towards anarchy in one country? One does not need to be a Hobbesian (or even take a quasi-Hobbesian approach, emphasizing the priority rather than the ubiquity of self-interest) to worry about one's vulnerability. The conscientious can get things wrong, the pure-in-heart can pursue evil ends, and the incorruptible can resolutely send their compatriots to the gallows or the guillotine.

It is easy to reconstruct debates which are irresolvable, and this I suspect is one of them. I think it is a great and cheering lesson that the anarchist will not be silenced, not least since her survival attests the extension of human kindness and generosity into the emotionally arid fields of political speculation. But I do not expect many readers to enlist under the black flag of anarchism and confess, with just a little measure of shame, that I do not do so myself. I don't trust you enough to dispense with the forces of law and order, and suspect, without being self-deceiving, that most of you would not trust me enough either. And sadly, I cannot assure myself that your distrust would not be justified. The Achilles heel of anarchism is that little bit of self-doubt that generates suspicion which prompts caution and quickly ramifies into demands for the kind of security which only the state can provide.

Before we leave the topic of anarchism we should note a distinctive modern variant – that of philosophical anarchism. This takes two forms. The first is primarily a sceptical position induced by the perceived failure of all arguments in favour of the authority of the state and citizens' consequent duties to support it. Since we shall be reviewing a range of standard arguments in what follows, we should reserve judgement on this conclusion. The second brand of philosophical anarchism, elegantly stated in modern times by Robert Paul Wolff, argues that acceptance of the authority of the state is inconsistent with the highest duty of mankind, the duty to act autonomously. To accept the authority of the state is to accept the moral weight of the fact that the state makes demands on our conduct, quite independently of our judgement of the rightness or wrongness of what the state requires us to do. (This moral weight need not be decisive or overriding.) Yet, 'for the autonomous man, there is no such thing, strictly speaking, as a *command*'.[20] Autonomy requires that each moral agent deliberate independently on how they should behave. Authority requires that those subject to it give up their autonomous moral judgement over the domain that authority governs. The value of autonomy deems this submission to be irrational. This is a striking thesis – but having stated it in brisk terms, I am content to leave it on the table, since discussion of it would take us too far afield. Further consideration of it requires these things: careful elaboration of the concept of authority and the investigation of the standing and claims of specifically political authority; further articulation of the concept of autonomy and a clear view of the strength of the duty to act autonomously; and lastly an explicit judgement of how far the autonomy of the agent is compromised by his submission to the authority of the state or his acceptance of political obligation. All of these matters are controversial, with very deep ramifications in moral philosophy.[21]

Reluctantly, let us put anarchism to one side and consider the other claim that there is no philosophical problem of political obligation. The communitarian[22] does not advance his argument on the ground that nothing can justify an institution as evil as the state, rather he claims that the state is immune to the demand for rational legitimation. I think, endorsing the judgement of Kant that we cited above, that this conclusion should sound incredible to the modern ear. 'This is the genuine age of criticism.' So let us try to make it sound persuasive. Let us advance the most plausible case.

We can begin with an analogy. Consider family life – or family life that is going well – or, best – family life that is going as well as its most fervent apologists tell us it can go: not *The Simpsons*, more *Little House On The Prairie*; not *King Lear*, more *The Darling Buds of May*. Mother and father love each other, care for their children and look after ageing parents. Where family matters are concerned they think about things, not as individuals pursuing their own discrete agendas, but as a couple, an organic unity speaking in the first-person as 'We'. They recognize their evident duties, of fidelity to each other, of loving care to their children and honour to their parents, and fulfil them gladly. These duties don't pose any evident ethical problem. Ask them why they do things in this way and they are puzzled. 'Because we are a family', they say. 'What other reason could there be?' A similar question could be put to the children. 'Why do you believe you have a duty to obey your parents?' And we expect these respectful children to be equally stumped.

Then they twig that philosophical questions are being asked: 'What are the reasons why you accept these duties? Just why do you think it would be wrong to reject them or fail to fulfil them?' The questioner should realize that she is unlikely to elicit answers that reveal foundations in the sense of deeper principles from which the duties concerned can be derived. What is being probed is the sense of identity of the family members. Seeing themselves as parents or children amounts to recognizing the duties incumbent on them in these roles. Some say duties of this kind constitute the identity of their bearers – in which case we should not be surprised at the inarticulacy of those who are questioned or their puzzled repetition of obvious facts like 'But I am their parent', 'But I am their child'.

This conception of duties as constitutive of social roles which persons generally find themselves occupying, which they haven't chosen to inhabit, receives its most systematic and articulate philosophical expression in Hegel's account of 'Ethical Life' (*Sittlichkeit)* in *The Philosophy of Right.* In a rational state, individuals will find themselves related to other family members in a specific kind of domestic structure, working alongside others in an economy which organizes their relationships with fellow producers and consumers, subject to the rule of law and the disciplines of regulatory bodies, and living in a political world with a constitution that promotes their freedom and is a focus for their patriotic sentiments. These nested relationships comprise an ethical home, complete with a full moral address. The model citizen will just find that, being describable as John Smith, son of Arthur and Margaret, husband of Annie and father of Katy and Helen, colleague of Jones and client of Microsoft, member of the Association of University Lecturers, inspected regularly by the Quality in Teaching Agency (QUIT), member of the Freedom for Old Labour Democracy Party (FOLD), and citizen of the UK, he has duties galore!

Duties of these sorts, some that John selected, some that he was born with and some that have just grown, emerge out of every citizen's life-story. We have before us the example of the duties of family life – a soft-hearted version of Hegel's account. I think it makes good sense to accept that one who regards himself as a family member, on the model thus described, may not be able to question the duties ascribed to him, although he can of course decide not to comply, to do what he believes to be wrong.

Arguments of this form gain their plausibility from the reader's approval of the social arrangements which arc being described. It is important that Hegel believes he is describing the uniquely rational form of family life, that which best permits humans to express distinctive elements of their nature. The rules of ethical life do not operate as constraints, they liberate persons who would otherwise be unable to develop, as in family life, their capacities for long-term commitment to other persons. Marriage thus is not a ball and chain but an opportunity for persons to grow out of the bonds of atomized self-concern.[23] If the social arrangements which are described were thought to be inhibiting, as they are for women under Hegel's description of their proper social role, then those who suffer under them could perfectly well challenge the specification of their duties. They may not, in fact, do so. They may be self-deceiving or, more likely, victims of false consciousness, embracing an ideology which limits rather than promotes their personal growth.

Hegel believes that he has explained the rationality of the institutions which constitute the modern state. He has traced their history and can explain how they meet the aspirations which mankind has learned to articulate as they have thrown over the institutions which crippled them. The different dimensions of social life, domestic, economic, legal and political, fit together in a fashion he described as dialectical but which we can see as coherent, making it possible to be all these kinds of person at once, to fulfil the duties of one's various stations without generating social conflict or personal fragmentation. It was also important to him that citizens could recognize the rationality of their condition, although commentators vary wildly in their assessment of how seriously Hegel took this requirement. Endorsement must be given but the reflections from which it issues do not permit the possibility of challenge. But, there again, why should anyone want to challenge institutions which, in their broad framework at least, cannot be improved? At the end of history, 'what is rational is actual; and what is actual is rational'.[24]

It follows that there cannot be a problem of political obligation any more than there can be a problem of terraced housing. Once we understand the nature of the modern state, interpreting its distinctive institutions as serving necessary functions given the desires and values humanity has developed through its history, once we acknowledge the state's contribution to our freedom, we find that in describing it, we recognize its legitimacy. Rational legitimation is, as it were, built into the structure of the moral world we inhabit.

There is another, more philosophically parochial, less method-ologically explicit, way of making these points which owes some-thing to Wittgenstein. Some claim that our understanding and endorsement of central elements of our political life is likewise built into the language we use to talk about them. Such language is suffused with normativity, with a recognition of the requirements made on us by the institutions we use such language to describe. If we know what it means to talk about the state, authority, govern-ment and the law, if we can play this particular set of language games, we can see that asking, 'Why can't I break the law?' is like asking 'Why can't I move a rook along a diagonal?' whilst playing chess. Thus T. MacPherson insists that:

'Why should I obey the government?' is an absurd question. We have not understood what it *means* to be a member of political society if we suppose that political obligation is something that we might not have had and that therefore needs to be *justified*.[25]

In similar fashion, Hannah Pitkin argues that:

The same line of reasoning [as that adopted to dispose of the question 'Why should I keep a promise?'] can be applied to the question 'why does even a legitimate government, a valid law, a genuine authority ever obligate me to obey?' As with promises, and as our new doctrine about political obligation suggests, we may say that this is what 'legitimate government', 'valid law', 'genuine authority' *mean*. It is part of the concept, the meaning of 'authority' that those subject to it are required to obey, that it has a right to command. It is part of the concept, the meaning of 'law', that those to whom it is applicable are obligated to obey it. As with promises, so with authority, government, and law: there is a *prima facie* obligation involved in each, and normally you must perform it.[26]

To be rude, we can recognize the Wittgensteinian tenor of the argument when we hear the *sound* of the italics. These arguments derive their plausibility from conceptual connections which are evident enough: once we modify the nouns with the adjectives 'legitimate', 'valid' and 'genuine', 'prima facie' even, there is very little room to manoeuvre. (But there is some: couldn't a legitimate government or genuine authority get things wrong and make an unjust law, a law that one is not obligated to obey?) Obligation falls out of the legitimacy, if, as is plausible, we understand a legitimate government as generally having the power to impose obligations. But notice, in the Pitkin quotation in particular, how the adjectives slip out of the argument. As soon as we see that we can properly speak of lousy governments as well as legitimate ones, of unjust laws as well as valid ones, of spurious authorities as well as genuine ones (the last with only the slightest whiff of solecism), we can see how these arguments trade on the assumption that is explicit in Hegel, viz. that the institutions to which these terms are applied have already passed the test of rational legitimation. If we do not make this assumption, then we shall find that we do *not* judge that 'it is part of the concept, the meaning of "law" that those to whom it is applicable are obligated to obey it'.

The implication of Kant's quotation is that we are never so engulfed or encumbered by an institution that we cannot step back from it, detach ourself from its embrace and adopt a perspective from which we can examine its credentials, asking whether this is the best way to live. Whether or not we can do so is, I believe, an empirical question. With respect to any given institution, some may be able to do so, others not. Some, in philosophical mood, may attempt to justify, for example, the requirement that they care for their children and find that there is no answer that they can come up with that is as certain as the conviction that this is just the right thing to do. Nonetheless, although the search for foundations or an accommodating reflective equilibrium may turn out to be fruitless, it is important that we see the necessity of making an attempt. There is no duty so sharp and clear, so inherently indisputable, that we don't find, or find reports of, people who just don't see it. However confident we might be in our own case that we see things right, we are likely to find, dialectically, that we need something in the way of an argument to support our views in order to shift the moral perspective of those who get these things wrong. We tend to believe that what is beyond the pale of decency is beyond the reach of argument. But to ask, rhetorically, 'Do I need to be able to demonstrate the wrongness of sexual relations with infants?' is to give up on the task of educating the moral sensibilities of those who, as a matter of fact, do not recognize their wrong-doing. It is also to give up on the task of defending one's certainties against the challenge of wilful objectors, and also, probably least important, to fail to acknowledge the possibility of conscientious error on one's own part.

The ethical perspective of those I have dubbed 'communitarians'[27] is blinkered in this fashion. There are two things that are odd about this position: in the first place it has been used by conservatives to challenge the impertinent, inherently questioning stance of modern liberal individualism. But as Kant (and Hegel) recognized, this sceptical perspective on the claims of authority is distinctive of the contemporary mind-set.[28] Now there are postmodernist philosophers who repudiate the enterprise of rational legitimation as a defunct because discredited element of the 'Enlightenment Project'. The task should be banished along with the associated acceptance of science and belief in human progress. But it is difficult for the conservative to ally himself with this style of argument, since the obstinate questioning attitude that Kant celebrated is part of our intellectual inheritance. It should by now be sanctified as a well-entrenched and unrenounceable element of our traditional beliefs. Its corollary sin, intellectual forelock tugging in the face of monarch, priest or professor, is as disreputable as pre-Copernican cosmology. Bluntly, the conservative cannot shout at those who raise questions about the legitimacy of institutions that it is impossible for these questions to be intelligibly put. 'Who are you to challenge the state or the family?' carries no rhetorical weight because it is likely to get a sensible positive response, namely, 'I am one who has been brought up in a society with a philosophical and political tradition of raising such questions and attempting to find an answer'.

When applied to the question of political obligation, the second oddity of this approach is that its proponents write as though the anarchist had never lived, had never written, could not even be a figment of a lively philosophical imagination. Imagine Godwin, Proudhon, Bakunin or Kropotkin reading the texts I quoted above. They would roar with laughter and then rage louder in their pamphlets. They would invent new words to describe the political institutions they detested (or put the old ones in inverted commas) and invite their opponents to describe the grammar of their fresh coinage. Reluctantly, I abandoned serious investigation of the anarchists' claims by reciting the sort of 'common-sensical' wisdom about the rationality of trusting ourselves and others at which any anarchist worth their salt would scoff. *Mea culpa.* But in a spirit of half-hearted apology, I insist that the anarchist position cannot be defeated by reading him a few lessons in how treacherous fellow travellers like me (not to say, zealots for the state) actually speak. Between the two extreme positions, of rejecting the state and all its works on the one hand, and wondering what all the philosophical fuss is about on the other, I think there are good questions to be asked. So let us proceed.

Consent and contract

In the *Discourse on the Origin of Inequality*, Rousseau asks himself what could have been the origin of the state, how could such a social condition have originated? A good question, one might think, given the formidable coercive powers of the state. But the context in which Rousseau poses the question – a conjectural history of the human race, adducing no 'facts' and speculation running riot – might lead one to believe that the question is silly. Who knows when politics was invented, which was the first state and why people accepted it, if they did? Who cares? Rousseau's history of the world in thirty pages is not intended as a crib for the historically challenged. It is a document written with a strong ethical purpose – to establish a benchmark description of human nature which enables us to chart the measure of human degradation, as revealed, in particular, by the development of structures of inequality.

When Rousseau reaches the point where he supposes political institutions must have developed, he makes two striking claims. First, he argues that to be accepted as legitimate, all those subject to the authority of the constituted sovereign must have consented to its institution. Arguing in a fashion that he will later reproduce in the opening chapters of *The Social Contract*, he concludes that legitimate authority could not have originated in exercises of force, since no rational person would accept that might is right, that the exercise of arbitrary power carries its own legitimizing credentials. Prudence might dictate compliance, but grudging, enforced compliance does not amount to a recognition of authority. Nor should the legitimate exercise of sovereign power be thought to derive from any natural properties of those who claim it. The only natural relationships which confer authority occur within the family and Rousseau summarizes a whole tradition refuting the application of this model to political life when he says that 'instead of saying that civil society is derived from paternal authority, we ought to say rather that the latter derives its principal force from the former'.[29] A process of argument from elimination leads him to endorse the 'common opinion' that regards 'the establishment of the political body as a real contract between the people and the chiefs chosen by them'.[30] Second, since the contract was evidently between unequal parties, establishing political inequalities on top of structures of economic inequality, entrenching and exacerbating what are already conditions of injustice, the 'real contract' must have been a fraud.

What is interesting here is Rousseau's appropriation of what he takes to be common opinion. 'We're all contract theorists nowadays', he seems to be saying. We should look carefully at this tradition of argument and tease out the complexities.

Contract arguments trade on the more fundamental notion of consent. If you and I contract (or covenant – that is the term Hobbes uses) we are voluntary parties to an agreement we have set up to bind us. I want the coal and you want the business. We agree that you will deliver it and I shall pay the bill. The transaction is consensual and both of us are bound by it. This model represents the primitive beginnings of dense and finely articulated structures of morality and, most importantly, law, whereby conditions and qualifications galore are written up and spread over library shelves. At the heart of such institutions is the thought that things that are otherwise painful, your loss of the coal, my loss of the money in payment, are transformed into states of affairs which are, on balance, preferable to the *status quo ante* the transaction. Consent (suitably qualified – we suppose it to be uncoerced, fully informed, rationally judged and generally not in pursuit of an immoral objective) is the miracle ingredient which transforms what would otherwise be a violation of rights into a legitimate performance. Consent marks a crucial difference between legitimate sexual intercourse and rape, between my proper use of your car and theft, between slavery and hired labour, just as it marks the beginnings of ethical debate in these areas about what can be counted as proper, legitimizing agreement.

The state has its laws, its police, courts and prisons. It certainly looks nasty and in dire need of legitimization. Here, too, consent is the miracle ingredient. If it can be shown that citizens consent to it, that's that – the task of legitimization has been accomplished. I can't see any challenge to this argument.

I can see plenty of challenges to its application. The anarchist may say that the act of submission to a political sovereign is so harmful as to be irrational, just as Rousseau, following Locke and arguing against Grotius, insisted that voluntary slavery is inherently irrational. Suppose the anarchist is right. The conclusion we are invited to draw strikes at a crucial premiss in the statement of a contract argument, suggesting that, whatever persons say or do, if submission is irrational then their actions do not amount to rational, fully informed agreement. Such arguments do not attack the conditional judgement: if citizens consent to obey, they have an obligation to do so. They attack the assertion of a minor premiss to the effect that citizens do so consent. In the same way, the radical feminist who claims that marital intercourse is rape, is challenging the view that marriage vows or any permission subsequent to them can be taken to express rational consent.

So far as the form of the argument goes, consent arguments are unimpugnable: if x consents to y then x is obliged to accept y. X does so consent. Therefore x is obliged to accept y. Consent arguments are good arguments, which is why they are so familiar. In political philosophy, contract arguments are a generalization of them, preparatory to a conclusion that all parties consent to the established dispensation of power. Having claimed that consent arguments are good arguments, and having explained their general force and attractiveness, their status as 'common opinion' in Rousseau's terms, I want to insist that all the crucial issues concern their usefulness since it is an open question whether or not they may be successfully applied. We should think of the dialectic as working in this fashion: we all agree that consent entails obligation. The state then attempts to impute consent on the part of its citizens, recognizing that obligation will follow. Citizens then examine the imputation, hence testing whether they are indeed subject to the obligation which the state asserts. The state is resourceful. It advances a range of different claims in support of its imputation of consent. Let us look at these in sequence.

Original contracts

Rousseau's argument in the *Discourse on the Origin of Inequality* cites an historical (but fraudulent) contract between the people and the chiefs as the origin of government. Other models are available. In *Leviathan*, Hobbes describes the citizens covenanting with each other to accept the rule of whoever the majority of them authorize in a future election.[31] Locke concurs. Free men unanimously agree to form a civil society, community, government or body politic,[32] which then entrusts power to whatever form of government they see fit. Suppose each of these authors is relating the facts of the matter as they see or conjecture them to have been.[33] Would such a contract support an obligation to obey the authorized sovereign? Evidently it would. Is this argument useful? Everything depends on whether or not there ever was such a contract.

When Locke was writing. many clearly believed that such a contract was in place, at least in the version where the sovereign contracts with the people. Following the flight of King James VII of Scotland and II of England in 1688, Parliament resolved that 'having endeavoured to subvert the Constitution of the Kingdom, by breaking the original contract between King and people . . .' he had *de facto* abdicated. Locating the original contract and specifying its content was a cottage industry amongst the students of the 'Ancient Constitution'. The quest was hopeless. Nonetheless it is a familiar aspect of modern political practice that new constitutions or striking constitutional innovations are put to the people in a referendum so that the ensuing settlement can be recognized as legitimate. De Gaulle's Fifth Republic was instituted by referendum in 1958 and modified, again following a referendum, in 1962. Following the downfall of the Communist regimes, referendums proposing draft constitutions were held throughout Eastern Europe. Britain's membership of the EEC was endorsed by a referendum in 1975 and a devolved parliament in Scotland was established following a referendum in 1998.

Such modern constitutional settlements differ in detail from the sketchy accounts found in the classics. The condition of unanimity at the first stage (again supposing these texts are offering descriptions) is not met. But they are sufficiently like the historical contracts for similar conclusions to be drawn. If the state, as it addresses its citizens in the appeal for obedience can point to something akin to an original contractual settlement, it has made a good start. Of course, there will be many qualifications, and some of these will emerge later when we ask how far the citizen's participation in democratic politics can be taken as consent. But for the moment we can accept that those who participate in the institution of government have the responsibility of contractors to accept the legitimacy of institutions they have endorsed. The consent argument can properly be applied in such circumstances to those who may fairly be described as contractors.

That said, it should be equally obvious that there are many regimes wherein such considerations do not apply. There may have been no constitutional settlement put up for popular approval, or there may have been one, but many present citizens have not been party to it. So far as it is the *contract* (or referendum) which is adduced as the occasion of consent, those who were not party to it cannot be held to be obliged to accept the outcome. The state must come up with other arguments if it is to establish that non-contractors have obligations.

Express consent

To consent expressly is to put one's name on the dotted line or otherwise publicly avow that one accepts some state of affairs. Married couples standardly consent twice over, first in reciting their vows, next in signing a register. Does anything work like that in the political realm? Some take explicit vows of allegiance – these may well be office-holders in the state, whose commitment to the specific duties of their office is assumed within an avowal of wide scope. And some countries go in for this sort of thing more than others, reciting 'I pledge allegiance . . .' and so on, at the drop of a hat. Naturalization ceremonies constitute a public affirm-ation; in the UK, respecting traditions of modesty and reticence, aspirant citizens merely sign the appropriate form.

There can be no doubt that those who actively affirm citizenship in this fashion (supposing their actions to be rational, fully informed, uncoerced etc. . . .) have accepted an obligation, have undertaken the duties of the citizen. It is worth noting however that exactly what duties they have undertaken may be moot. The only time I have been called upon to give advice on the strength of my profession as a philosopher was when a student who had arrived at the final stage of the naturalization process – signing the papers – asked me if he could do so in good conscience. His prob-lem was that the declaration he was invited to make required him to recognize the authority of 'Her Majesty Queen Elizabeth II and all the descendants begat therein' (I quote from memory). He was troubled because he couldn't accept the principle of monarchy, not even the impotent, symbolic, soap-opera variety. Believing my dis-ingenuousness to be sanctioned by the faint sniff of a philo-sophical problem lurking hereabouts, I told him not to worry. He could sign up in good faith since accepting a monarchical prin-ciple is not a duty of citizenship. Good British citizens can and do campaign for the abolition of the monarchy.

The moral of this story, and it applies to original contract argu-ments too, is that it is not obvious or uncontroversial what the duties of the citizen include, even when these may fairly be judged to be the upshot of express consent, for it is not clear what even those who expressly consent, actually consent *to*. This is worth stating because the state is greedy when it tracks down its citizens' obligations and is likely to assume that, if the citizen can fairly be deemed to accept any duty, she must accept the lot, capaciously and optimistically specified. Even those who accept the duties entailed by their express consent, should take a cautious, if not quite sceptical approach to detailed specifications. The state drafts the terms of the agreement and is a master of the small print, not to say the unspoken implications and the traditional understandings.

All that said again, the limitations on the applicability of this argument are obvious. I haven't expressed any such consent, nor have many of my fellow citizens. Nor should we be expected to

265

welcome the open solicitation of such consent. Oaths of allegiance, unless they are the procedures of states which solicit the enthusiasm of the new recruit, are suspect, a familiar stratagem of tough states which invite martyrdom or self-imposed exile as the optimum way of dealing with inconvenient but conscientious dissenters. The state has widened its net and trawled in more obliging citizens. But the net evidently needs to be widened further. It looks to adduce tacit consent.

Tacit consent

To begin with, we need a clear example of tacit consent. What we are looking for is an example of behaviour which non-controversially assumes an obligation which does not derive from a contract or an explicit act of consent, behaviour which nonetheless may be said to express consent. Suppose I see, unexpectedly, a group of my students in a bar and join them at their invitation. I am lucky, and as soon as I sit down, one of them announces that it is her round and she buys us all drinks. The rounds continue and I take a drink each time one is offered. When my turn comes around, I say 'Thank you very much for your kindness. I've enjoyed your company. I have to be off' and leave. Have I done wrong? Of course I have. I've broken the rules. What rules?

The demand that the rules be specified, were anyone to make it in these circumstances, would be impertinent. My behaviour is not acceptable. I cannot say that there aren't any rules, nor that the rules aren't clear. The rules which govern our behaviour in circumstances of the sort that I have described are not explicit in the sense of being written down in the definitive field guide to social conformity. There are no explicit prescriptions that I know of which should govern one's response. It's just that I know, or, stretching the point that innocence demands of incredulity, should know, that I have undertaken an obligation to reciprocate my students' generosity. I have tacitly consented to the practice whereby the company buys a round of drinks in turn.

In the modern literature on political obligation the philosopher who brought tacit consent to the forefront of discussion was John Locke. Locke asks exactly the right question. Granted that one who consents to government acquires an obligation to obey, and granted *a fortiori* that tacit consent is consent,

> the difficulty is, what ought to be look'd upon as a *tacit Consent*, and how far it binds, *i.e.* how far anyone shall be looked on to have consented and thereby submitted to any government, where he has made no Expression of it at all.[34]

Scholars of Locke have distinguished two strands in his answer to this question. First, tacit consent is witnessed in the enjoyment or possession of land which is under the dominion of the government. In the background is the supposition that all property within a territory is susceptible to the law of the land for only thus could citizens enjoy their property in security. Hence the convention that underlies the attribution of consent is that property holders submit to the government that regulates property to their advantage. This convention we must take it is as well understood as the rule of boozers' etiquette which requires that rounds of drinks be purchased in turn. If Locke is right, the state can present its bill to those who enjoy property, even to those who are 'barely travelling freely on the Highway' and demand of them obedience as the proper duty of the citizen (or transient alien).

The second line of argument is derived as a qualification of this first. Since 'The Obligation that anyone is under, by Virtue of such Enjoyment, to submit to the Government, begins and ends with the Enjoyment',[35] one who sells up and leaves can quit the obligation. There is a particular opportunity for explicit dissent, so one may suppose that those who do not take it tacitly consent. Thus the state may extend its reach even further, attributing consent and the duties entailed by it to those who choose to stay and, presumably, continue to enjoy the benefits of secure possession.

Are these arguments persuasive? In considering the first, we should recognize that everything depends upon the existence of the convention that Locke describes. Clearly, if there is such a convention in place and if everyone understands and accepts it, then we may fairly judge that those to whom it applies have the consequent obligation. If there is a rule or convention of the Common Room that those who take a cup of coffee pay 50p into the kitty, then those who enjoy the provision are obliged to pay. In similar fashion, we need to investigate whether there is such a rule binding those who accept the benefits of the state. If there is, Locke's judgement is correct, but if there isn't any such convention, or if its existence is a matter of genuine dispute, then the state is not entitled to claim obedience.

This point may seem obvious – indeed it is obvious – but it is worth making since it alerts us to an equivocation in the argumentative strategy employed by the state. As represented by Locke, it looks as though the state is arguing two points at once, claiming both that if there is such a convention then obligations follow, and further, that there is in fact such a convention and citizens should recognize in consequence their proper duties. Of course, it is perfectly open to the state to advance both of these claims. The first thesis is conceptual and, I think, should be readily accepted. The second thesis, by contrast, states a matter of fact concerning the existence of a norm or moral rule and this is contentious. As we have seen, there are anarchists in the field, and they will deny it. We shall return to this question later when we consider the implications for political obligation of the fact that citizens are in receipt of benefits. It may be that one can argue for a different conclusion: that those who accept the benefits of the state ought to accept the duties of citizenship, even if, as a matter of fact, they do not. They ought to recognize such a convention, even if as things stand there is no such convention to presently bind them.

A second oddity about this argument deserves notice and it was brought to prominence by Hume.[36] Suppose there is a rule in a particular society that those who receive benefits from the state incur the duties of the citizen. There are many reasons why such a rule may carry conviction. Some may claim that each citizen finds such a rule to be in their best interest, others may say, in utilitarian fashion, that observance of such a rule maximizes the well-being of citizens, and there are plenty more arguments in the offing. But once such a rule is recognized as bearing on citizens' obligations, why should one take the further step of claiming that the acceptance of benefits witnesses consent, albeit tacit? If the rule is in place, and if a citizen does accept the benefits, does not that, on its own, establish the fact of the citizens' obligations without one's having to establish the further or entailed fact of their tacit consent?

If we return to the example of boozer's etiquette, we see that a crucial feature of it was that the person who incurred the obligation freely accepted the drinks in full knowledge of the rule of reciprocity which operates in pubs. He need not have accepted the drinks or he could have accepted a drink after having given an explanation that he would be unable to reciprocate. These precautions would have discharged any obligation on him to pay for a round. It is the fact that these choices are, and are known to be, open to him that makes it reasonable to speak of consent of the tacit variety. It is not obvious that such conditions operate in the case of the state, which standardly does not present us with the option of not taking up the goods and remaining a free agent. Many of the benefits touted, good maternity care, the cod liver oil and the orange juice, free educational provision, are dumped at the door of the unwitting recipient. Many of the rounds of drinks will have been bought before the child becomes an adult and is expected to pay.

Nonetheless, there is something to this argument. If someone feels that they have accepted benefits from the state believing that this brings with it an obligation to obey, they may fairly judge themselves to have consented to the regime. Some who accept this argument may make every effort to dissociate themselves from the benefits, detaching themselves physically from the state which provides them. They may exile themselves to the wilds of Montana or Idaho, living a life which is self-sufficient apart from periodic trips to the local rifle store. This is Militia Man, the bane of all theories of political obligation. Whatever grounds may be cited in favour of his consent he will disavow sincerely – which is not to say that all other arguments that can be adduced in favour of his having the duties of the citizen must fail.

This example requires us to examine the second mark of tacit consent, viz. the lack of explicit dissent. Again, as with the example of the pub, one can think of circumstances wherein the lack of explicit dissent can fairly be taken to witness assent. If the woman in charge of the meeting asks us if we have any objections to register against her proposal and we remain silent, our silence, we should think, testifies explicitly to our consent for all that it is tacit. This is a useful convention which expedites the business of committees, though it opens the door to a lot of hypocrisy and self-deception when a subsequent account of one's conduct is called for. We know when politicians ominously write in their diaries, 'I remained silent' that something is up. The space created for disingenuous strategies alerts us to the fact of an unwritten convention in the background. Can such a convention be attested in the case of the citizen's duties?

Again it might be. A citizen may feel compromised by her unwillingness to dissent when an opportunity for dissent was available and judge that her silence has implicated her in the policies in which she acquiesced. This is a duty of citizens which often goes unnoticed, but passive citizenship as well as active participation can require that one has a duty to take some responsibility for the actions of the government. As with the acceptance of benefits, the fact of the citizen's not expressly dissenting can serve to attest consent and ground consequent obligations.

But remember: both of these arguments, authoritative when rehearsed by citizens, can be spoken in the voice of the government and in this context, they may carry little conviction. They will carry *no* conviction where dissent is costly to the citizen, exposing them to risks of harm. The state that pursues dissenters efficiently cannot cite the lack of dissent in support of its legitimacy. Locke had in mind, as an occasion of express dissent, the citizen's opportunity, 'by Donation, Sale or otherwise, [to] quit the said Possession', to leave the country, perhaps along with other dissenters, founding a new society in empty lands.[37] The state may echo this judgement, telling us that our continuing presence marks our tacit consent. Such a claim deserves Hume's mocking response:

> Can we seriously say that a poor peasant or artisan has a free choice to leave his country, when he knows no foreign language or manners, and lives, from day to day, by the small wages which he acquires? We may as well assert that a man, by remaining in a vessel, freely consents to the dominion of the master; though he was carried on board while asleep, and must leap into the ocean and perish, the moment he leaves her.[38]

Hume's strictures are just, but there is a rider to the dialectic which he did not acknowledge. There have been plenty of cases where citizens have possessed the resources to emigrate and have identified a state which would welcome them, a state they, too, would welcome as infinitely better than the one they want to quit, and yet they have not been permitted to emigrate, or else the process of emigration has been made hazardous, overcostly or humiliating. One thinks of the predicament of Jews in the former Soviet Union. This episode makes it clear that states which frustrate their citizens' wishes to emigrate cannot attribute to such citizens a tacit consent deriving from their continuing residence. Nor can it use such an argument in the case of citizens who do not wish to leave. That these conclusions are obvious shows that the argument for tacit consent from the lack of explicit dissent need not be as crude as it is in Locke's statement, nor quite as vulnerable as Hume's counterexample suggests.

Arguments from tacit consent, in these familiar forms, do apply to some. The state has widened its net yet again and caught some more citizens in it. But there will still remain plenty of citizens who can, in good faith, reject its imputation. So the state seeks out further arguments.

Quasi-consent

In *Democracy and Disobedience*, Peter Singer discusses the specific question of whether citizens of a democratic state have particular reasons to accept the duties of the citizen as determined by majority rule. Thus far, we have spoken of the state and ignored the nature of its constitution. We could have been discussing any old state. The only question in hand was whether the citizens actually consented through the mechanisms of original contract, express or tacit consent. Singer introduces the notion of quasi-consent to explain the distinctive form of not-quite-consent which is implicit in the behaviour of voters. Their behaviour, he believes, mimics consent. They act *as if* they consent and the same normative conclusions may be drawn from their behaviour as are drawn in the case of actual consent.[39] If we describe the action of voting, taking the polling card and handing it over to the polling officer, receiving a voting slip and crossing the box in a private booth then placing the voting paper in a ballot box for counting, nothing amounts to express consent. It would be easy to require valid papers to include a signature affirming that the voter consents to abide by the outcome of the ballot. To my knowledge, such a statement is never demanded as a condition of participation. So if voting attests consent, it is not express consent.

Singer tries to distinguish tacit consent from quasi-consent, claiming that the attribution of tacit consent, as explained by Locke (or some of his prominent interpreters), supposes that citizens actually give it – if not expressly, then 'as saying in their heart' that they consent, as acknowledging at the moment that they act in the manner from which consent can be inferred that they do so willingly.[40] The phenomenon of quasi-consent, by contrast, attests the implications of voting behaviour, specifically that citizens should accept that their participation in the voting process requires them to abide by the majority result, whether or not they realize that this is what they have committed themselves to. I don't see the difference. If one had flown in from Mars and had been entertained by a group of hospitable students, if one was truly ignorant of the ruling conventions of pub visiting, tacit consent could fairly be repudiated. The only points at issue are: (i) is there a rule in place governing everyone's behaviour; (ii) did the Martian or the guest know the rule; and (iii) in case they didn't, ought they to have done so? Should the Martian or the lucky teacher have done their homework before they entered the pub? Generally, ignorance, as displayed by a 'No' answer to (ii), will excuse, though the excuse stretches the point if the answer to (iii) is deemed to be 'Yes'. If we conclude that the beneficiary did, or ought to have, understood the ethical implications of his behaviour we will judge that he has the same duties as one who expressly consents.

But this is to prejudge the issue. I endorse Singer's terminology of quasi-consent, not because it has a normative structure different from that of tacit consent – it doesn't – but because it signals a distinctive argument which finds application in the specific context of voters's behaviour. The quasi-consent the voter attests is attributable on the basis of a convention which is unique to the context of democratic decisions. I would have no dispute with the philosopher who insists that participation in democratic decision procedures is a third mark of tacit consent. But it is worth insisting that this mark is distinctive. It is not a case of benefits accepted or dissent foregone.

The argument for the conclusion that the voter has consented to abide by the decision taken by the majority elaborates our understanding of the voting process. It articulates what the voters believe (or ought to be able to work out) that they are doing. Think of any occasion of voting: for or against a strike by the workers who are being ballotted, for a representative to serve in a parliament or a local council, for or against a policy proposal put to a referendum. In every case it is supposed that the majority decision is binding on all those who take part. This is an assumption that can be challenged. I have spoken, for example, to some who voted in a strike ballot and did not accept that they were obliged to accept the outcome. They thought that, if striking would violate a personal obligation of service to the university authorities, they should do everything in their power to prevent others from striking, which efforts included voting against a strike, whilst not accepting the outcome should (as happened) the majority decision go against them. Such are the frustrations of the picket-line at a university.

In the next chapter I shall have more to say about democracy. For the moment, all I can say, of what is repeatable, against the voter who repudiates the majority decision, is that they do not understand the point of the exercise in which they were engaged. In a reputable democracy, no one has to vote pro or con a particular policy. Anyone can abstain, or, where filling in a voting paper is compulsory, spoil their vote. Perhaps this is an innocent construction of the reality of voting in all regimes in the modern world. Perhaps those who wish a plague on both their houses will be found out and persecuted. All one can do, given the many ways things can go wrong, the many resources of the manipulators of any decision procedure, is to insist that whatever reasons there may be for deciding issues by democratic processes should commend themselves to participators. Where these reasons are acknowledged, those who take part in democratic procedures should abide by the outcome.

This may not be obvious. Certainly, as we have seen, there is no rule book which states the convention and those who have the right to vote do not have to pass a test establishing that they understand the ethical implications of voting. There is no way of making a case for the thesis that voters consent to abide by the result of the ballot other than by insisting, lamely, that 'there is a conceptual connection between voting and consenting'.[41] The conceptual connection can be articulated by explaining the point of the voting process. It is not a method of canvassing opinion, a poll designed to establish which policy or representative is most favoured, which information may be taken into account when a decision is taken. It is, itself, a way of taking a decision. Once the votes are counted, the decision is made. There is no logical space for further decision-making of the sort that might provide an opportunity for demurral between the act of voting and the announcement of a decision.

We shall see in the next chapter that there are many reasons for taking decisions in a democratic fashion. We have here encountered one that is of the utmost importance – that democratic decisions bind those who participate in the making of them to an acceptance of the result. Where the result is the establishment of a government, voters have assumed the duties of citizenship as these will be defined by the state. Although I cannot think of any objections to this argument – yet again the state has found a good one – it should not be thought that it entitles any specific regime to claim universal allegiance. The real world is a messy place and there are many qualifications that need to be registered.[42] Most obviously, since the argument establishes that those who participate as voters take on the duties of citizenship, this entails that one clear way of repudiating the obligations is not to participate. If you don't want to be bound by a decision to strike, don't take part in the ballot.

This limits the scope of the state's appeal since we can be sure that some – Militia Men again – will refuse to enter the polling booth, or entering it, spoil their paper or, indeed, strip off in protest as Jerry Rubin advised voters to do in the 1968 Presidential Election in the United States.[43] But the story gets messier still. If we are thinking of elections to a representative assembly, the assembly may have structural flaws which limit the legitimacy of its decisions. It may represent an entrenched majority, directing its policies towards the violation of minority rights. It may contravene an explicit mandate, either failing to introduce policies announced in the manifesto of the winning party or introducing policies unannounced at the time of its election. Considerations such as these reveal that the consent adduced by voting does not amount to the issue of a blank cheque. The consent will, in practice, be qualified by further understandings of what it is rational for the citizen to accept. Some qualifications, e.g. the requirement of respect for minority rights, may lead to the withdrawal of all authority with respect to the state's decisions. Others, concerning the detail of the mandate, may lead citizens to challenge the validity of specific laws. Thus some in the UK who were led to protest the Tory Poll Tax legislation of 1988 by refusing to pay the locally raised charge, were willingly to continue paying income tax.

Having advanced the argument adducing quasi-consent on the part of voters, the state will find that it has gathered in more support for its claim to allegiance, that more citizens will recognize that the duties of the citizen are incumbent on them or that there are further grounds for them to acknowledge duties which they already accept. If it is lucky, the state will find that all citizens have in fact consented to the duties it imposes. If it is scrupulous, it will make every effort to ensure that citizens are willing to do so. It should not anticipate this measure of success, since the anarchist, for one, has deep reasons for resisting its charms, and as the persistence of bloody-minded Militia Man shows, some will do anything to resist the imputation of consent. If folk don't actually consent, whether in an original contract or constitutional settlement, expressly, tacitly or in the manner of voters, their consent cannot be used to ground their duties.

This result will not satisfy the state, which is ambitious. It will seek to find other grounds for imputing duties to its recalcitrant citizens, other reasons for bolstering the allegiance of those who do consent.[44] Perhaps it will seek to establish that those who don't consent ought to do so and claim in consequence their hypothetical consent or their partnership in an hypothetical contract. We shall examine these arguments next.

Hypothetical consent and hypothetical contract

Dworkin tells us, in a famous quotation, that 'A hypothetical contract is not simply a pale form of an actual contract; it is no contract at all'.[45] This tells us that there is some work to be done in establishing the credentials of arguments that rely on hypothetical consent or contract. They cannot rely on the normative implications of actions of consent or contract. Their force must derive from elsewhere.

Hypothetical consent works like this: hospital patients are generally asked to consent to surgical procedures being carried out on them. Otherwise, the invasion of their bodies would be an assault. Yet some patients, notably those who are comatose, cannot give consent. In such circumstances, it behoves the surgeon to ask a hypothetical question: would the patient consent were he conscious, rational and fully informed of the nature and likely success of the proposed operation? Surgeons' temperaments dispose them to intervene, to save life or cure illness or advance medical science, so it is important to see that the answer to the hypothetical question may be 'No'. The way to answer the hypothetical question is to gather the sort of information that friends and family can provide so that the surgeon has as good an idea as is possible of how the patient would decide. This may be easy – the patient may have clear religious beliefs which proscribe surgical procedures of the sort envisaged. Or perhaps the patient has told his family that he does not wish any more expensive, painful interventions which have little chance of success. Or perhaps he has told people that he would grasp at any straw to have a longer life of even meagre quality. Using this sort of information, the surgeon takes the decision she believes the patient would have reached, substituting her judgement for his. It is useful to speak of hypothetical consent here because it signals that the decision is being taken from the point of view of the patient, mustering the sort of information that would have been relevant to his decision, were he in a position to make it. The surgeon, considering what would be best overall, may well have reached a different decision, taking into account values such as the advance of medical knowledge or techniques which may mean little to the patient.

Hypothetical consent, thus construed, looks as though it has little part to play in working out whether citizens have duties to the state. Why should one seek to establish it if there exist mechanisms for finding out whether or not citizens actually consent? What kind of information about citizens' preferences could be a substitute for that elicited by asking them? The only sort of presumption that could motivate the investigation of hypothetical consent is that of widespread irrationality. One must assume that citizens, like the patient, but for different reasons, are incapable of judging rationally whether or not they have the obligations with which they are charged by the state. This assumption we should take to be false. Who would openly acknowledge that it holds for themselves? Just because we understand so clearly the circumstances which call for the investigation and imputation of hypothetical consent, we should be very reluctant to use this strategy in seeking to derive citizens' duties.

Hypothetical contract is a close cousin of hypothetical consent. As an argument form, it suffers from not having available a simple example or model which illustrates the domain of its possible application outside the context of philosophical dispute. Perhaps some sorts of historical judgement require arguments which hypothesize a contract. One way of deciding whether or not the Treaty of Versailles was a good thing, or whether those who imposed it should be criticized for the harshness of their impositions on Germany in 1919 is to ask whether we would have proposed or accepted its terms. But the fit with hypothetical consent is imperfect in an important fashion. In the case of the patient, it is *his* reasoning we are attempting to reconstruct. In the case of the Treaty, it is our own judgement that we are seeking to apply in the circumstances of decision-making available to the original parties.

We can best judge the applicability of an hypothetical contract by trying to deploy it in the present case. Again we should adopt the perspective of the ambitious state. We are supposing that it has failed to establish consent where its attribution matters most, in the case, that is, of the recalcitrant citizen. If we haven't established that he does consent, can we show him that he ought to? Can we get him to accept that he ought to agree to the state's imposition of the duties of citizenship although he hasn't in fact done so? Can we claim that other things he believes require him to accept the conclusion he disavows?

We can take it for granted that accepting the duties of citizenship is costly. The state exacts its impositions. It threatens its citizens with penalties for non-compliance. As we saw when discussing the challenge of the anarchist, these powers are unattractive to anyone in their reach. The hypothetical contract argument attempts to show that a rational citizen should accept these powers as legitimate as the price of achieving goods that he values more. The decisive move is made when the citizen recognizes that he faces a social problem, not a personal dilemma, when he realizes that an acceptable solution embraces others besides himself. The simplest way to outline this model of reasoning is to bowdlerize Hobbes, the master of this line of argument.

First, imagine that we are living without the state, in the state of nature. We seek to advance our own interests, placing a premium on the preservation of our lives. Yet we find ourselves systematically thwarted. We find, each of us as individuals, that our pursuit of power, both to satisfy our desires and to protect ourselves from others who seek to use our powers for their own ends, is continually frustrated by the power-seeking activities of others. In the state of nature, nothing constrains this pursuit of power. Since as things stand, no one is getting what they want, the circumstances of human interaction need to be changed. Since the unimpeded pursuit of our own interests undermines its own achievement, the rules of the game need to be revised.

There are four possibilities: the first, the status quo wherein we each of us struggle for power, is hopeless. The second possibility is that I have all the power, but no one else will accept that. The third option is that someone else has all the power, but that won't suit me. The final possibility is that no one has power over anybody else. We can achieve this outcome by all of us renouncing the private pursuit of power, by handing over our powers to some third party who will establish the conditions of peace. We conclude that it is rational for agents who wish to preserve their lives under conditions of commodious living to accept a sovereign power to rule over them. The result of our several deliberations is that each of us judges that if we do not have a sovereign we should institute one; if we do have a sovereign we should keep it, recognizing its authority.

You will have plenty of reservations about this story. But look at the outcome. We have portrayed an exercise of practical reason undertaken by each party to the conflict as giving rise to a mutually acceptable solution. It is not that everyone has agreed with each other in the way of shaking hands or signing a treaty. The agreement that has been modelled is agreement in the minimal sense of congruence in the reasoning undertaken and the conclusion reached. We each reach the same conclusion, since we all reason in the same fashion from the same premises. Matters stand *as if* we had made a contract. It might be objected that this is a poor sort of contract. After all, if we are all asked to write down the answer to the following sum: $2 + 2 = ?$, and we all write down 4, what is gained by representing the agreed answer as the outcome of a contract? It is as though we had agreed, but what are the implications of this? We should certainly *not* conclude that $2 + 2 = 4$ on the basis of a hypothetical contract.

This objection forgets a central feature of the story. Unlike the mathematical case, as each person reviewed the possible outcomes, they were forced to consider the responses of others and restructure their priorities in line with their judgements of what outcome others could reasonably be expected to accept. Each person conducted the moral arithmetic separately, but each person found themselves having to take into account the anticipated responses of others. The first preference of each, that he or she has all the power, could not survive the obvious thought that this would not be acceptable to others. So each 'contractor' trimmed their aspirations, seeking only solutions that would be mutually agreeable. A hypothetical contract works as a device for modelling the practical reason of individual agents seeking an answer to a common problem where it is a condition of the acceptability of a solution that everyone agrees to it because agreement is the only way forward.

I find this model of reasoning explicit in Hobbes, implicit in Locke, and both implicit (in *The Discourse on the Origins of Inequality*) and explicit (in *The Social Contract*) in Rousseau – but I shan't defend these attributions here. It remains to be seen how far it amounts to a cogent argument in favour of sovereign authority and the citizens' duty to accept it. One implication of the use of this argument form should be made explicit. I mentioned earlier that there was something objectionable about the application of a hypothetical consent argument to settle the question of political obligation. It seemed to presuppose that citizens cannot work out for themselves whether they have the obligations of citizens, that they are treated as irrational when arguments were imputed to them which they would likely reject. The hypothetical contract argument does not carry this implication. On the other hand it must accommodate the inconvenient fact that persons may be ignorant of the values and preferences of other persons, or that they may discount these in their reasonings, and thereby may be unable, in so far as they fail to take these things into account, of reaching a solution to problems which they throw up for themselves. The hypothetical contract model articulates an ideal process of reasoning. Moral ignorance or short-sightedness, if not straightforward irrationality, makes application of the model necessary in circumstances where we cannot expect those to whom it applies to respect either its premises or its conclusions.

In particular, it represents a democratic sovereign as a fair compromise between conflicting claims to power. We can test this thought by seeing how such an argument applies to Militia Man. Note that although he has withdrawn to the wilds of Montana or wherever, he hasn't succeeded in inoculating himself from the contagion of other members of his society. He still makes claims against them, notably that they keep off his land, and reinforces these by threatening to use his automatic rifle. He makes a claim even in this restricted domain, so it is important to work out how it might be adjudicated when it comes into conflict with the claims of others. If he is wise, he will not rely on physical force or weaponry. An alliance of rival claimants will get him sooner or later, as Hobbes foresaw. He can't insist that he isn't a threat. His neighbours will worry that he may take pot-shots at straying cattle or children. Whatever his antecedent principles about big government and the like, he should realize that he has to make an accommodation, which amounts to accepting a procedure for the arbitration of conflicting claims. He has to do this because otherwise everything he holds dear is threatened. The state puts itself forward to recalcitrants such as Militia Man as adjudicator of disputes and enforcer of valid claims. Hobbes would accept any third party as long as it can settle disputes effectively. Just in case Militia Man distrusts the state, it can offer him a place in the making of rules and the settling of claims as a participant in democratic decision procedures. He would do well to accept the offer, but if he doesn't its terms may fairly be imposed upon him anyway.[46]

In explaining the notion of hypothetical consent, I have done little more than elaborate an argument form and illustrate its use in sketchy fashion. Despite its ancient provenance, of all the classical arguments underpinning political obligation it is the most underdeveloped in the kind of detail it requires. It looks to be vulnerable at two specific points: the first concerns its Hobbesian antecedents. It assumes an ambitious theory of human nature, a universalist psychology. Hobbes's own version, stressing self-interest, is unattractive, but these can fairly be seen as weak, rather than strong premises. We may be concerned with many other goods than self-interest, but if our lives are at stake one interest is indubitably threatened, an interest that cannot be compromised without all other interests being sacrificed too. The Militia Man may say, 'Give me liberty or give me death', but this is better understood as an appeal against colonial tyranny rather than the modern bureaucratic state's practice of sending out income tax forms. It is odd that one who willingly pays purchase tax in order to buy a rifle should genuinely think martyrdom a rational alternative to the payment of other taxes. Stronger versions of the grounding premiss offer greater hostages to fortune, but may succeed in deflecting objections. Locke identifies life, liberty and property as the goods which we require a state to protect. Rousseau would have us recognize as legitimate a state that protects our life and property under conditions of maximal liberty and equality, assuming that were we not vulnerable in respect of these goods there would be no point in a political association.

Since these premisses amount to empirical claims at least in so far as they attest universal desires and values, they are clearly vulnerable. Nonetheless it is hard to find spokesmen for opposing positions. I can imagine religious opinions to the effect that these things do not really matter. In the order of things, they count for little against the purity of the soul and the promise of salvation. Such views generally preface an argument for theocracy rather than a religiously motivated propagation of anarchy. Still, I guess it is a distinctive position. We have seen cult members dying on television rather than accept state regulation of their weaponry.

This should alert us to the second vulnerable aspect of the hypothetical consent argument. It requires us to accept that the goods
that we value cannot be protected or promoted without the state; it
requires a denial of the anarchist claim that the state as we have
encountered it, or as any political utopia is likely to develop, will
ultimately threaten the things we most value. This, too, is at bottom
an empirical claim, so I shall leave adjudication of it to the reader.

The benefits of good government

The arguments from consent or contract that we have been examining have claimed either that we do or have contracted or consented to the duties of citizenship or, in the case of hypothetical
contract, that we ought to accept the duties of citizenship. In the
case of actual consent, it is strictly speaking irrelevant why we
consent. That we express marriage vows binds us to our partners.
Why we do so is immaterial to the reality of our obligations – and
the same must be true of the duties of citizenship. Nonetheless, we
can expect a state which wishes to elicit our consent to give us
grounds for doing so, and the obvious way for it to proceed is for it
to provide us with benefits. As we have seen, there may well be
circumstances in which our willing receipt of benefits is an index
of tacit consent, although the supply of benefits is not, of itself, a
reason for imputing it. Arguments which employ the notion of
hypothetical consent also rely on the state delivering the goods.
The strategy which underlies the argument is an exploration of the
claim that the costs of obedience are the price a rational agent will
pay to receive the benefits of others' compliance. In plausible versions of each of these arguments we reach the conclusion that we
ought to accept the duties of citizenship through attesting consent
as a result of an examination of the benefits we shall attain. This
makes good sense. Why should anyone consent to the imposition of
duties unless they expect to benefit? Why should anyone contract
with others to limit their liberty unless their interests are
advanced or their values promoted by so doing?

It is worth stopping at this point, though, to reconsider the force
of Hume's question. Why seek out or presume consent when the
benefits of government are apparent? Doesn't the fact of universal

advantage itself constitute good reason for us to accept the duties of citizenship without taking the unnecessary circuit of attesting consent? It might, as we shall see, but if in fact consent is elicited or contracts undertaken that is an important fact which the state can be expected to emphasize. In the case of hypothetical contract, there is no contract to be attested. As I have emphasized before, consent arguments are perfectly acceptable. We can expect those who have consented to recognize their force. But some will not consent. They will not expressly consent or be party to anything that resembles a contract. As soon as they suspect that tacit consent may be presumed, they will act differently or explicitly repudiate the imputation. They will not vote or otherwise participate in democratic decision procedures. And they will challenge the applicability of premises employed to derive hypothetical contracts.

Does the state have further arguments at its disposal? Yes it does. Both of the further arguments we shall consider proceed directly from the supposition that the state benefits its citizens, in the manner Hume thought sensible. In what follows, I shall assume that Hume was right on the matter of fact. If he wasn't, the arguments that follow have no purchase. This qualification is of more than academic importance, however, to the state that wishes to claim our allegiance and the citizen who wishes to appraise its claims. It requires that the state which presses our obligations to it should demonstrate how the citizens' advantage is served. It places a burden of proof on the state which accords with the instincts of liberalism.

The principle of fairness

This argument states that considerations of fairness require those in receipt of benefits from the state to reciprocate by accepting the appropriate burdens, by accepting the duties of citizenship. In modern times it was first sketched by H.L.A. Hart:

> When a number of persons conduct any joint enterprise according to rules and thus restrict their liberty, those who have submitted to these restrictions when required have the right to

a similar submission from those who have benefitted from their submission.

The argument was further developed by Rawls in his 1964 paper, 'Legal Obligation and the Duty of Fair Play'. It was mauled by Nozick in *Anarchy, State and Utopia*. It was reported, expanded, defended and ultimately dismissed by Simmons in *Moral Principles and Political Obligations* and it has been revivified, developed and endorsed by Klosko in *The Principle of Fairness and Political Obligation*.[47] Hart is clear that this account of the grounding of political obligation should be sharply distinguished from those that derive obligation from consent or promises. If the argument works, it has the same power as the argument from hypothetical consent (of which it may be presented as an elaboration) to attribute obligations to those who expressly disavow consent. That said, there is a very real difficulty in distinguishing cases where the argument applies from obvious cases of tacit consent. To see this, consider Robert Nozick's well-known objection:

> Suppose some of the people in your neighbourhood (there are 364 other adults) have found a public address system and decide to institute a system of public entertainment. They post a list of names, one for each day, yours among them. On his assigned day (one can easily switch days) a person is to run the public address system, play records over it, give news bulletins, tell amusing stories he has heard, and so on. After 138 days on which each person has done his part, your day arrives. Are you obligated to take your turn? You *have* benefited from it, occasionally opening the window to listen, enjoying some music or chuckling at someone's funny story. The other people *have* put themselves out. But must you answer the call when it is your turn to do so? As it stands, surely not. Though you benefit from the arrangement, you may know all along that 364 days of entertainment supplied by others will not be worth giving up *one* day. You would rather not have any of it and not give up a day than have it all and spend one of your days at it.

It is hard to reject Nozick's conclusion in respect of this particular example, not least since we are naturally wary of others' foisting gifts on us and then expecting us to reciprocate in some fashion. How would the story need to be amplified in order for us to agree that an obligation had been created? The most obvious ways would be to describe the reluctant payer agreeing to set up such a scheme, or voting for (or against) its institution in a neighbourhood poll, or else failing to dissent when an invitation to do so had been extended. But then the argument would attest some sort of consent. Perhaps one could fill out the story so that the dissenter gets great pleasure from listening, looks forward to transmissions and then seeks to avoid doing her stint in the way fare dodgers get on buses and avoid payment. Now she looks tightfisted with her time in the way folk who leave a pub without paying their round are tight-fisted with their wallet. We can elaborate the story to show that she is a poor neighbour, ungenerous and miserly, but unlike the non-payer in the pub, I don't think we can accuse her of being unfair to the point of failing an obligation unless we can articulate some convention that she understands and violates.

Of course, those who defend the principle of fairness will insist that the principle itself is the operative convention. But this can't be right. Nozick's counterexample illustrates the need for much more specificity. My instinct is that the more specificity is provided to make intelligible the particular case, the more evident it will be that we are charting understandings which are familiar to those engaged in the co-operative ventures. And the more explicit such understandings become, the more clearly we shall find that we are witnessing good old-fashioned tacit consent.

That is a hunch which would need to be verified in the discussion of particular cases. But we can save ourselves the work by examining directly the use of this argument to establish that citizens have duties. An interesting wrinkle on Hart's argument is that if citizens have such duties (he is thinking primarily of the obligation to obey the law) then these duties are owed, not to the sovereign, but to other citizens. So we can consider how well Hart's principle applies.

I think it is odd to consider the conduct of life in a state as a joint enterprise that citizens undertake. Rather like Nozick's hapless listener, or Hume's shipbound traveller, we just find ourselves here (and probably stuck here, too). Nonetheless, we may find that living here has its benefits. The state is a great provider of services. It recruits armies to protect us from alien aggression, police forces and other instruments of law and order to protect us from criminals, health services to keep us alive and well, education services to enable us to make a living. The state may be what it claims – the servant of the people. Some of these services we find provided willy-nilly. Some of these we may endorse in a half-hearted fashion – this is how the police force views our view of them – but some of them we may actively pursue. We may queue up for social service benefits or rush into hospitals for treatment. We may require the state to build more motorways or make better provision to collect our rubbish. Some of these services we may detest, believing that they compromise both our safety and our principles. Many feel this way about the 'nuclear umbrella'. God help us if it rains!

Suppose we do seek out what the state has on offer, we do identify specific benefits and demand them, we do request protection or assistance from the state. Are we being unfair to fellow citizens if we do not accept the concomitant burdens of citizenship? I think we might be. Certainly it is possible to describe examples which present the appearance of unfairness in the sense of folks who benefit mightily being unwilling to accept a reasonable burden. In the 1970s in Britain, there was a well-publicized case of a very wealthy family, polo players and friends of royalty, owners of great estates in the Highlands of Scotland as well as a chain of butchers, who had paid no taxation on the profits of their businesses for most of the century. (My mother-in-law, on reading this story, turned from a Conservative to a Trotskyite overnight.)

Such people aren't paying their way. Who knows what songs the sirens of self-deception sing to them as they sign the income tax forms their clever accountants prepare? Governments approve and encourage the sentiments of disapproval, but sadly, most often, when the villains are no great gainers, being 'welfare scroungers' or the like. It is cases like these which lend most plausibility to Hart's insight, where the principle of fairness is employed to identify cheats – those who aren't playing by the rules of the game, though if they are rich enough, they will be abiding by the rule of law.

Hart's principle is very abstract, too abstract, I suggest, for universal application without examining the details of the circumstances in which it is employed. When it is articulated in circumstances wherein it finds plausible employment, it amounts to the claim that it is unfair if, for example, people aren't paying for goods they enjoy, if their enjoyment is secured by the payments of others on whose willingness, or mute acceptance, or inability to escape payment, they freeload or free-ride. As a justification of one's legal obligation not to steal, for example, the argument is unnecessary. Theft, as many other crimes, violates moral rights which the state affirms and reinforces. The thief is first and foremost a thief. We don't need to find him guilty of free-riding in our anxiety to specify a moral wrong as a justification of legal punishment.

Nozick's cheeky counterexample serves a useful purpose. In forcing us to examine the circumstances in which benefits are extended and enjoyed, it requires us to examine what we ask of the state, and how it is to be paid for. Hart's argument is, at bottom, sound. We shouldn't both insist on the provision of benefits and then make every effort to avoid paying for them when this inevitably puts the burden of payment on others. The principle of fairness requires that we shouldn't cheat, that we shouldn't dump the costs of services we embrace on others. I think we all understand this. I think no one believes that the services of government are costless, manna from a bureaucratic heaven. In which case, we need to explore the understandings, to find the conventions concealed within our acceptance or pursuit of the goods government provides. If we are honest we should recognize the burdens our acceptances entail. But if we are clear-sighted, we shall deny that these burdens come in a package that cannot be dismembered, as though if we buy one we buy all.

This is what governments are prone to tell us. We don't need to believe them. They say: if we want the protection of the local constabulary, we have to pay for the nuclear weapons. And we know that they have ways of making you pay. What they cannot do, wherever benefits are touted but rejected, is insist that fairness grounds the demand for payment.

Hart's principle of fairness is silly if it purports to justify those restraints on my liberty which would prevent me harming others, as though it would be quite wrong for me to assault them or steal from them only in so far as I require the state to protect me against the predations of others. Such behaviour would be wrong even if

287

one made no such claims and announced that one regarded himself as in a Hobbesian state of nature with everyone else. Think again of Militia Man. This is the sort of independence he is likely to assert. It would be a futile exercise to try to track down the state services he accepts. We are likely to find ourselves trying to pin him down to accepting the Department of Defence and the nuclear umbrella. He is likely to take us seriously and buy more ammunition. Those who think this argument has strength, as I do, should draw in their horns. If folks solicit benefits, they should recognize that these have a cost and they should accept that the cost is civility, a willingness to otherwise pay their way.

I say this is a good argument. This doesn't mean that it applies to everyone or that anyone to whom it does apply should accept all the burdens the state is eager to impose. It suggests a caution: don't seek out the the goodies that the state dangles before you without exploring the small print. In a sense this advice is otiose: there is no small print governing our transactions with the state. Unless the understandings are written up explicitly and published in print large enough for even, or to be literal, especially, the blind to read, we are not committed to them, and should not find ourselves presumed to accept them. The state should welcome Hart's argument; it captures a wider segment of the population than heretofore could be enlisted as dutiful citizens. But obviously there will be some who announce that they will take all that is offered so long as this does not entail any obligations on their own part. They are oblivious to considerations of fairness since they pronounce themselves willing to do without the touted benefits. Perhaps, being Militia Men, they are well armed.

Gratitude and good government

I can think of one last argument the state may advance – and perhaps the last should have been first, since this argument was outlined by Socrates in Plato's *Crito*. This argument claims that citizens ought to be grateful for what they have received from the state, and, further, the gratitude should be signalled by the citizens' acceptance of their duties. Again, the first step in the argument is a claim that the citizen has received benefits, so to proceed we must assume that this is true. Clearly, if the citizens do not receive benefits from the state, there is nothing for them to be grateful for. The next step in the argument is the claim that citizens ought to feel grateful to the state. The final step is the claim that acceptance of the duties of citizenship is the appropriate expression of gratitude. We can see the distinctness of steps two and three in the details of a recent immigration case, reported in the newspapers, which captures this structure nicely.

An army officer's life was saved by one of his Gurkha soldiers. Properly, he felt grateful and expressed his gratitude by promising to educate the soldier's son in Britain. As these things go, the son was refused the necessary immigration credentials, so the former officer (a wealthy man) said he would leave the country, too. I think (but am not sure) that the story had a happy ending. In the first place, the officer was right to feel grateful. In the second place he chose to express his gratitude by taking on an obligation to the father, and to the boy, to see to his education. Having taken on board this obligation, the officer judged correctly that he was morally required to fulfil it. One can think of other ways in which the officer could have expressed his gratitude, ways which did not place him under an obligation – indeed, this is a nice example of how acts of gratitude can be as generous as the services that give rise to them.

It is important that steps two and three in the argument are distinguished. They can easily become conflated when we speak of 'debts of gratitude' as though the government pursues payment of these debts when it holds us to our obligations. Rousseau stated that 'gratitude is a duty to be paid, but not a right to be exacted': not exacted, that is by parents against children or by the state against its citizens.[48] Since many of the duties of the citizen are enforceable, Rousseau thought they could not be derived from gratitude. As we shall see, this is a mistake. For the moment, though, we should register the philosophical oddity of speaking of *debts* of gratitude, of announcing feelings of gratitude in the language of 'I owe you one'. The payment of debts can be insisted on as an obligation of the debtor, whereas however appropriate or felicitous gratitude might be, it can't be the proper object of a demand or claim, the issue of a special right.[49]

It is perfectly clear, on the other hand, that we can insist that persons *ought* to be grateful, taking gratitude to be a distinctive feeling or attitude appropriate in one who has received a benefit. We teach our children that gifts cannot be claimed as rights and that they ought to feel appropriately grateful. We train them to feel grateful by making them act out the rituals of gratitude, minimally saying, 'Thank you', and undertaking the chore of writing conventional 'Thank you' letters following birthdays and Christmas. We trust that in these ways we teach them what to feel as well as how to behave. We teach good habits as a way of inculcating good dispositions of character.

These commonplaces are worth bringing to mind because they effectively refute one line of argument against the claim that political obligations may derive from gratitude. The bad argument goes as follows:

> If political obligation is an obligation of gratitude, and if an obligation of gratitude is an obligation to feel certain things, there can be no political obligations (on these grounds, at least) since we cannot make sense of obligations or duties to feel certain things in a certain way. Feelings cannot be the objects of obligations. In any case, political obligations are obligations to act, not to feel, to act obediently, for example, rather than to feel obedient.[50]

This argument runs together the different steps in the argument that I have been at pains to distinguish, but at the heart of it is a claim that should be disputed to the effect that we cannot be required to have specific feelings since feelings aren't the sort of things we can be expected to control by way of trying to have or inhibit.[51] This is a blunder of a crudely Kantian sort. Feelings can be taught and learned, modified, sharpened or quietened by effort on the part of the sufferer and her educators – and this includes feelings of gratitude. Indeed, if feelings were not, in some measure, in the control of those who exhibit them, it would be odd to criticize folk for the lack of them. In the case of ingratitude this is particularly obvious. I accept that it is odd to speak of obligations to feel gratitude but that is not the claim that I am trying to establish. Rather I seek to show that one can claim that people *ought* to feel gratitude without committing a philosophical blunder.

The next claim that needs to be defended is that it is philosophically acceptable to say of citizens that they ought to feel grateful for the goods and services they receive from government. I don't want to claim that any such judgement is true – who knows which government is being discussed? – just that the proposition makes sense. This claim needs defence because there are objections in the field. The first objection begins with the plausible thought that feelings of gratitude are only appropriate as a response to benefits which have been conferred with a suitable motive. If you give me a fast motorbike in the hope that I will soon come a cropper, I will feel no gratitude as soon as I learn of your devious plan. To generalize, the identification of goodwill in the provision of the benefit is required before gratitude is appropriate.

In the case of gratitude for the services of the state, we must therefore be able to impute motives to the state. But 'the attribution of motives to a government may be impossible or incoherent'.[52] The only possible reply is that we do it all the time. And we are equally cavalier in our imputation of motives to other institutions. This firm cares (or doesn't care) for its staff, this university takes seriously (or ignores) its task of teaching students, this hospital is helpful to (or hates) patients' visitors. One could reply that this talk is metaphorical, but this would not be a statement of the obvious. Rather, I suspect, it would indicate a strong and controversial philosophical position, most likely some variety of methodological individualism. We can shelve these discussions and move on, supposing that when, for example, it is claimed that 'This government really cares for old age pensioners' the claim may be true or false but is not incoherent.

Let us accept that motives can be fairly attributed to the state. A further difficulty is encountered. In attributing, minimally, motives of goodwill to the state, we are thinking of the state as Lady Bountiful (or more likely Big Brother), viewing its disposing of goods and services in the manner of gifts. On the contrary, the state is our servant; it has nothing but duties to fulfil. And we should not be grateful when it complies with its duties to its citizens. We should not be grateful to the policeman who rescues us from the football fans who are just about to beat us up; he is doing his job.

This, too, is an error, but it is understandable. We should resent the posture of the statesman who speaks as though he is spending his own money. Nonetheless, the ancient analogy with the family can be usefully employed here. Parents have duties to their children willy-nilly, as children nowadays are prone to remind them. 'I didn't ask to be born!' you might have heard. This does not disqualify the thought that children should be grateful for what they have received of right. The duties of the parent can be fulfilled with love and grace, but even a grudging concession to a legitimate demand can merit gratitude. After all, as we know too well, some parents can't manage even this.

Isn't the same true of governments? Don't we recognize the difference between an ethos of genuine service and a time-serving reluctance to respect claimants? And shouldn't we be grateful even to heartless bureaucrats who are efficient and conscientious in the delivery of goods they are appointed to distribute? I can imagine – indeed have heard – arguments pro and con, but I don't believe that the logical space for such disputes is the product of fallacious reasoning. I don't see, in principle, why one who does their duty should not merit our gratitude.

The final objection to the idea that one may be grateful to the state for the goods and services it provides draws attention to the constitution of the state. It asks, in the first place: to whom or to what should one be grateful? Some, abhorring the possibility that an exotic metaphysic may be imputed to them, insist that the citizen who has grounds for gratitude should be grateful to her fellow citizens.[53] This strikes me as an evasion. One should not be grateful to all of one's fellow citizens severally. Some, as we have seen, have resolutely avoided paying their share towards the provision of services of which they have been massive beneficiaries. Others, perforce, have been recipients only, being too poor to make any payment towards social provision. Shame on the first, damn shame for the second – but in either case, feelings of gratitude would be misplaced. So if we should be grateful to our fellow citizens, we have to think of them collectively, which on my reading amounts to our being grateful to the state.

There is something creepy about sentiments of gratitude being directed towards the modern state, but part of this may be due to a reluctance to see the state as 'other'. Aren't we all democrats nowadays? We shall have more to say about democracy in the final chapter, but for the moment we should recognize that one element in democratic thinking is the claim that we all have equal political standing. Regarding the state as other and in some measure alien to us, seems to presuppose a hierarchical relationship between state and citizen which does not sit well with the democratic ideal. The instinct which grounds the suspicion that there is something undemocratic about institutions to which one may direct gratitude expresses a truth which is hard to weigh.

The only form of state in which gratitude seems to be inappropriate would be a direct democracy which takes all decisions by plebiscite, a simple Rousseauian model wherein all are equally citizens and subjects. In this model, citizens should be viewed as providing goods and services for themselves. Like members of a winning football team, they should feel pride rather than gratitude for their success in self-provision. But even in these circumstances, gratitude might not be entirely out of place. Citizens may think of their democracy as a unity which serves all its members. Players in winning teams may feel grateful to the team and their fellow members for granting them the opportunity of success, as well as pride for the part they have played in achieving it. In any event the modern representative forms of democracy do not work like this. The structures of decision-making and the bureaucracies created to put policies into effect are sufficiently alien to citizens that gratitude may be appropriate when they perform their assigned functions conscientiously and well.

I conclude that one who feels grateful for the provision of state services has not committed a philosophical error, though in particular circumstances gratitude may be misplaced, may indeed be witness to the citizen's capture by a successful ideology. If this is right, we can now move on to the final question: what does gratitude require of the citizen who properly feels it? Here, there are two routes we can take. The first is indirect, arguing that one who fails to comply with the duties of citizenship harms the state. The focus is not so much on the requirement of gratitude but on the evil of ingratitude. As Hobbes saw, ingratitude is often imprudent; the fourth law of nature thus requires that 'a man which receiveth benefit from another of meer Grace, Endeavour that he which giveth it, have no reasonable cause to repent him of his good will'.[54]

But as many have taught us, as well as being imprudent, it is also a great vice to harm a benefactor.

Is this what we are doing when we fail in our political obligations? We certainly may be. The state is harmed directly if we evade payment of taxes, commit treason or encourage others to break the law. But not all law-breaking is like this. It is surely a matter of fact whether the state is harmed when citizens break the licensing laws or drive beyond the speed limits, and often such acts will be harmless. I don't see any argument that could take us to the conclusion that all law-breaking amounts to ingratitude since it harms the state or one's fellow citizens.

The direct way of arguing will serve us just as well. All that gratitude to the state could require is that citizens do their duty by it. It is entirely disingenuous to suggest that we might willingly take the benefits the state provides, send a 'Thank you' letter, then dodge the demands of the state, refusing to take compliance as an obligation. But on the other side, as I stated before, we should not be too po-faced about these duties, identifying them as an all-or-nothing requirement that citizens obey all the laws all the time. The good society and the sensible state can afford to be relaxed about the incidence and severity of law-breaking. Individuals should not be worried that their standing as good citizens is impugned by an episode of after-hours drinking or opportunistic speeding on an empty motorway. The duties of citizenship under good government should not generally weigh in as an onerous burden or tight constriction, though on occasions, for example, a call for military service, the demands may be severe.

Finally, it may be suggested that it is odd to think of compliance as a grateful response, since the state exacts compliance, most of the citizens' duties being enforceable, demanded under threat of penalty. But demanding isn't getting. However forceful the demands of the state, the liberal insists that they have no legitimacy until they are endorsed by the citizen. It is in the process of inspecting the demands of the state that the citizen should take account of the fact, if it is a fact, that he has benefited in a fashion for which he should be grateful.

Before we leave this question, there is one qualification that ought to be made. Gratitude is the appropriate response to good government, not merely government that provides us with the goods and services we value. Suppose a state has two classes of citizens, those who receive benefits and those who are excluded from benefits. Should those in the lucky class feel grateful and endorse the political obligations which are thereby incumbent on them? My inclination is to conclude that they should not. To use the analogy of the family (which gives me particular pleasure, given the derision it has met with from modern contributors to this debate who dismiss swiftly the lessons Plato derives from it): Should the Ugly Sisters feel grateful to their parents for the benefits they have been granted (and thereby accept an obligation to follow their parents' wishes or obey their commands) if they know that their good fortune has been achieved at Cinderella's expense? Nothing has been spent on poor Cinders, and the only reason the Ugly Sisters have time to paint their faces and primp their hair is because Cinders is busy doing the chores. Probably the Ugly Sisters feel grateful, but ought they to?

For all that the duties of parents have their foundations in love and other sloppy sentiments, they can be partly specified as duties incumbent on them in virtue of a role, a role or position of moral responsibility in which they stand to all of their children equally. Something has gone wrong in a family where there is a grossly inequitable division of labours and favours. Whereas parents can't be commanded to love all their children equally or in the same fashion, all the children should recognize that something has gone drastically wrong if it is always one of them who has to sweep the hearth. The Ugly Sisters should be ashamed of themselves, and this shame should qualify their gratitude. They should feel unworthy of the favouritism they enjoy.

I shall take it that this example finds a consensus of approval, having found that in pantomimes, we all 'Boo' in the same places. I claim something similar should be working with respect to our attitudes to the state. If some (in a democracy, it will generally be a majority) receive benefits which others do not enjoy, or receive benefits in conspicuously and comparatively generous measure, they should regard the benefits as a poisoned chalice, morally tainted by the inequity of its distribution. They should regard themselves as morally compromised, shamed in a fashion the Ugly Sisters ought to recognize. This is an intuition; I can't think of any arguments that might support it beyond the thought that gratitude is not appropriate for benefits with an unjust or immoral provenance.

Conclusion

We have examined a variety of arguments that purport to give grounds for citizens accepting the duties of the citizen, construing these widely. With the exception of the hypothetical contract argument which needs much careful expansion and defence, all of these arguments are conditional on the citizen *doing* something – swearing allegiance, being party to a constitutional settlement, behaving in such a way that one may fairly conclude that he accepts a convention which entails obligations, including perspicuously conventions which ground the practice of voting in democracies or conventions or moral rules associated with the acceptance of benefits, concerning fairness or gratitude.

These are all useful arguments, so long as they are not advanced in the expectation that they must be accepted by everyone, so long as they are not taken to be universal in scope. This looks to be a weakness from the point of view of the state that advances them. It seeks to capture all citizens in its net, but if citizens don't do the things from which their obligations may be deduced to follow, they can't be captured. It looks as though it is possible that there will always be citizens who can properly repudiate the duties imputed to them by the state.

The conclusion we may be tempted to draw is that dubbed 'philosophical anarchism', which openly accepts the limitations of the arguments cited. The 'philosophical' anarchists, as against the real variety, are content to cite the philosophical deficits in the arguments of the ambitious state. They are a gentlemanly lot, not too bothered by the thought, which the real anarchist will detest, that prudence for the most part dictates compliance with the state's demands. They will be disposed, not so much to protest or wave the black flag in insurrection, but to say, 'Excuse me, your arguments aren't quite as good as you believe them to be'. This conclusion may well be false. A hypothetical contract has some prospect of success (and some utilitarians believe that they can establish the rules which govern the duties of the citizen).

A wise state will see the philosophical anarchist, and even Militia Man, as a challenge. It will seek to seduce them rather than trample them underfoot, by providing benefits they cannot resist and making clear how far their receipt invokes conventions or moral principles which require the acceptance of obligations in consequence. As the arguments in favour of political obligation have been reviewed, I have characterized the stance of the state as adverse, as seeking to 'capture' the allegiance of the citizen, as being able to announce 'Aha! That's you dealt with' to the citizen who would naturally be a reluctant recruit. It's easy to amplify Hume's example of the shipbound traveller and identify the state as the Press Gang.

This would be a mistake. We do better to think of the state as seducer and the clever citizen as raising the stakes, requesting more and more blandishments, insisting that the goods be delivered. The conservative will hate this talk, recognizing the introduction of a customer or client mentality into the sacred domain of allegiance. But then the conservative is always out of date, defending the intuitions of the last-but-one epoch against advances which are already securely in place. The state which is eager to claim that its citizens have obligations to it does best if it works out how to serve them well. It may well find that there is no philosophical deficit, that Militia Man is fleeing his own good. More fool him.

It is vital that we see clearly the moral stance taken by the state towards its citizens, so the details of the constitution matter when we investigate the obligations of the citizen. We have seen how a democratic constitution can give rise to its own specific reasons for adducing such obligations in the case of the quasi-consent described by Singer. The fact that such an argument is available is a mighty reason for endorsing democracy. But there are other reasons, too, for us to commend this family of methods of decision-making (as well as objections). It is to the examination of these arguments that we now turn.

Chapter 7

Democracy

Introduction

Thus far we have examined normative theories, notably utilitarianism, in their application to political questions, we have investigated central political ideals, liberty, rights and justice, and we have tackled the problem of political obligation. Much of this discussion has been conducted in a manner that supposed that there were two central characters: the state and the citizen. The question of the proper constitution of the state has arisen in a variety of contexts: political liberty requires that citizens be able to take part in the decision-making processes of the state, the right of citizens to participate is a crucial human right and, in Rawls's theory of justice, is a vital element of the liberty principle. The form taken by government may well make a difference to the issue of whether citizens have good moral reasons to obey the state, since if they participate in democratic procedures, this may witness a measure of consent to the outcome. It is fair to say that the background to many of the arguments we have pursued has invoked a subscription to democratic principles. These principles, which apply directly to the mechanisms of taking political decisions, need a more careful and explicit investigation. In discussing democracy, we shall be gathering together some of the leading themes of previous chapters.

So far as the rhetoric of decision-making goes, it may seem that democracy is the only game in town. As with human rights, the rhetoric is so powerful that there are few tyrants so benighted that they will deny the ideal of democratic institutions. It may be that the society they govern is not yet ready or mature enough for democracy. It may be that democracy exists in a peculiarly apt local version, like the democratic centralism of the former Soviet Union, which located democracy within the mechanisms of one-party rule. But few would follow Plato and denounce democracy as an inefficient and corrupt mechanism for taking political decisions. In the face of a value so ubiquitous, not to say politically correct, the philosopher wakes up and starts to ask the questions begged by the overwhelmingly positive connotations of the term. We need to begin afresh and examine the questions raised by universal subscription to this mode of decision-making, to this universal constitutional ideal.

Thomas Hobbes, as is well known, upset everybody. Republicans accepted his conclusion that the citizens' reason to obey a sovereign lay in their judgement (portrayed as a covenant or agreement) that a sovereign was conducive to their best interests. Thus the authority of the sovereign derives from the citizens' agreement with each other to recognize a sovereign and their subsequent selection or endorsement of him or her as their representative. Republicans, however, did not like his considered judgement that they would do best to select one person, a monarch, to perform the tasks of sovereignty. Monarchists, by contrast, applauded his view of monarchy as the most efficient form of sovereignty, but hated the thought that the monarch's sovereign authority derives from the will of the people.

Hobbes believed that three types of sovereign were possible: monarchy, that is, government by one person; democracy, that is, government by an assembly of all subjects; lastly, aristocracy, an assembly of some nominated part of the commonwealth. His preference for monarchy was dictated by his low opinion of the capacity of assemblies, whether of all or the few, to deliver the goods to the citizens. But Hobbes's view of the efficiency of monarchs can be challenged and forms of assembly can be constructed with a view to their better procurement of the goods of sovereignty – personal safety and commodious living. If one accepts Hobbes's methodology and premises it is but a short step to the endorsement of some form of democracy, as James Mill saw. Slyly noting that the typical English gentleman ('a favourable specimen of civilization, of knowledge, of humanity, of all the qualities, in short, that make human nature estimable') acts as a tyrant when he emigrates to the West Indies and becomes a slave-owner, he rejects Hobbes's claim that the shepherd will not feed off his flock, finding his own interests best served by the 'riches, strength and reputation of his Subjects'. What is required is an assembly which the subjects tightly control, that is, a representative democracy.[1]

John Locke, too, disputed Hobbes cheerful acceptance of monarchy (and by extension, indissoluble assemblies), noting that

> there is danger still, that they will think themselves to have a distinct interest, from the rest of their Community; and so will be apt to increase their own Riches and Power, by taking, what they think fit, from the people.[2]

Locke is a proto-democrat, accepting that men (and nowadays, we insist, women) who are born free and equal will demand a sovereign power which will reliably put their own will into effect through legislation and the application of executive and federative (roughly, foreign policy) powers. This requires a representative assembly, though the principles of representation are not worked out in detail.

Rousseau, writing seventy years after Locke, had worked out from scratch the constitutional implications of the thought, not quite common wisdom at the time, that men are born free and equal. For Rousseau the only legitimate sovereign was a direct democracy, each citizen being a law-making member of the sovereign as well as being subject to its laws. We shall begin our discussion of democracy by presenting Rousseau's contribution to democratic theory. This contribution is so seminal that one might fairly conclude that much of contemporary democratic theory is a series of footnotes to Rousseau. 'Much' but not 'all' since, as we have seen, utilitarian thought has made a distinctive contribution to our thinking about democracy.

Rousseau: freedom, equality and the general will

Rousseau accepts that we have a natural care for ourselves (*amour de soi*) as well as a natural feeling of compassion (*pitié*) for the suffering of others. We have also come to acquire, in the course of the dreadful history of our species, a concern for private property. In addition though, we attach a particular value to our own independence. Or rather we would value independence if we had not been corrupted by the social institutions we have created. Rousseau can describe this natural independence because the traces of it still remain in his own obdurate, genuinely and acknowledgedly anti-social personality. We could see it, if, as in the thought experiment he conducts in *Emile*, we were to insulate a child from all the influences of society and educate him in a fashion that develops rather than smothers his natural capacities. We could see it, too, if we were to observe the origins of our species as solitary but healthy and well-satisfied hunter-gatherers, as he conjectures in the *Discourse on the Origins of Inequality*. Rousseau's visions of natural man are tantalizing, but hopeless starting points for an argument.

We do better if we simply state the conclusions licensed by his speculations and see how these work as premises in the argument that follows. We may well be sympathetic to them, recognizing how they incorporate insights familiar from the liberal tradition in which he is working. Since for the most part they represent conclusions we have already drawn in previous chapters, we can take them as familiar and plausible premises for the argument to follow.

Independence has two related dimensions – liberty and equality. If we are independent of each other, we are free in the sense that we do not depend on the assistance or goodwill of others in order to satisfy our desires. Dependency is also a condition of inequality. In fact, Rousseau believes everyone becomes dependent under conditions of inequality: 'each became in some degree a slave even in becoming the master of other men: if rich, they stood in need of the services of others; if poor, of their assistance.'[3] For Rousseau, these are natural values. It follows that those who value survival, and could not live well unless their liberty and equality were not protected, would not accept the state unless it were necessary to promote these goods. The state, Rousseau believes, is required when life, property, liberty and equality are threatened. This is entirely a formal condition. If, as a matter of fact these goods are secure, there is no need for the state.[4]

Suppose then that a state is necessary; what form should it take for those concerned with the protection and promotion of these goods? In the first place, it should protect life and (some measure of) property, but it should seek these goals in a way that respects (perhaps maximizes, perhaps renders optimally coherent) principles of liberty and equality. The natural versions of these values are lost in the recesses of history, and, more importantly for those who think history beside the point, are inconsistent with the necessity of the state. The optimal state will institutionalize some analogues of natural liberty and equality; it will command our allegiance if it can reproduce in its constitution and ongoing life social conditions which are faithful to these values.

Before we look at the details, let me reproduce the essentials of the constitution of the republic of the *Social Contract* so that we can better understand 'the principles of political right' (the subtitle of the book) in the light of their institutional embodiment. Citizens are active members of the sovereign. The state is composed of subjects. All citizens are equally subjects, obliged to obey laws they enact collectively by majority decision in an assembly, so 'the sovereign' designates the active, law-making power of the republic, 'the state' designates its rulebound character, these terms being different descriptions of the same institution.[5] The republic is a direct democracy since rational agents would not delegate their law-making powers to a representative.

In what ways does an institution of this form respect the liberty of the citizens? In the first place, moral liberty is secured. Moral liberty has two elements: it amounts to free will, which Rousseau tells us in the *Discourse on the Origins of Inequality* is the distinctive ability of humans, as against animals, to resist the beckonings of desire, to reject temptation. 'Nature lays her commands on every animal, and the brute obeys her voice. Man receives the same

impulsion, but at the same time knows himself at liberty to acquiesce or resist.'[7] Modern man, as Rousseau describes him, is
enslaved to all manner of factitious and unnatural desires. He evidently does not have the resources of individual free agency which
would enable him to control them – otherwise there would be no
need of the state. The state, enacting laws with penalties attached,
is an indirect mechanism for enabling citizens to keep to the
straight and narrow path of virtue, a means of social self-control.
Free agency in the modern world is a social achievement.

The second aspect to moral liberty concerns the source of the
laws which procure freedom. They cannot be the imposition of a
wise and paternal authority. The laws which guide and coerce us
along the paths of virtue, forcing us to be free,[7] are laws of our own
making: 'man acquires in the civil state, moral liberty, which alone
makes him master of himself; for the mere impulse of appetite is
slavery, while obedience to a law which we prescribe to ourselves is
liberty.'[8]

The second dimension of liberty which is promoted in the republic of the *Social Contract* is civil liberty. Rousseau faces a difficulty
here, which he well recognizes.[9] Citizens yield all their rights to
the sovereign, which has absolute unlimited authority. Civil liberty is the space for private activity and the enjoyment of possessions which is both limited and protected by the law. The law which
prevents me from stealing your goods equally protects me from
your thieving. But how can a measure of civil liberty be preserved
against the authority of a sovereign to whom all rights have been
ceded? Rousseau argues that his citizens value liberty. Would
those who love liberty abrogate it to no useful purpose? We must
suppose the same values which dictate the form of the constitution
to motivate those who act as citizen legislators. Rousseau believed
that he had deflected the threat of what was later diagnosed as the
threat of majority tyranny. We shall take up this problem later.

The final dimension of liberty I shall dub political liberty, echoing my usage in Chapter 3. It is the liberty of the self-legislator,
adduced above as moral liberty, but now taking an explicitly political form as the right of citizens to vote in assemblies which
determine the law. Berlin, as we saw, was very suspicious of the
claim that this truly amounts to liberty – democracy or self-
government is one value, liberty another, and these may conflict

when civil (negative) liberties are infringed by democratic decisions. We may limit liberties if a majority so decides or con-strain majority decisions if this is necessary to protect liberty, but we should not claim that we are maximizing or effecting trade-offs in respect of one value. A plurality of values are at stake here. But Rousseau is clear that one who participates in assemblies which make the law is not subject to alien impositions, which subjection is a clear infringement of liberty. Rousseau is surely right – and it is worth recalling the obvious but neglected point that those who possess such legislative powers have the opportunity to take part in (are not hindered in their pursuit of) an activity which they independently value – as clear a manifestation of Berlin's negative liberty as any.

Natural liberty, the liberty of the independent soul who fashions a life for herself in conditions which do not require any interaction with others, is lost. In its place, individuals have acquired a strengthening of their moral liberty and a protected sphere of civil liberty through the exercise of political liberty which the opportunity for democratic participation yields. But the second natural value which is concomitant with independence is equality. In what way is that preserved under the constitution of the democratic republic?

Equality, too, has three dimensions for Rousseau. First, let us look at political equality. The citizen who has political liberty, the power of participation, insists that this be *equal* political power. 'Men become everyone equal by convention and legal right.'[10] Each has one vote to contribute in the decision-making process. Since political power is equal, no one is dependent on the power of others, nor do they have others dependent on themselves. Equality of political power and political liberty reinforce each other. No one is enslaved by inequities of political power, neither seeking to enslave others nor being vulnerable to the ambitions of others for political mastery.

A second kind of equality is necessary for democracy to work well – rough equality of material possessions. In the *Discourse on Inequality*, Rousseau had demonstrated the corrupting effect of divisions of rich and poor. Such divisions corrode liberty through the effects of patterns of dependence within the economy. Inevit-ably, an unequal distribution of wealth will transform itself into an unequal distribution of political power. In the *Social Contract* he insists that democracy cannot work with extremes of wealth and poverty. It requires, not an exact equality of riches, but a distribution of them such that 'no citizen shall ever be wealthy enough to buy another, and none poor enough to be forced to sell himself'. 'Allow neither rich men nor beggars', he observes in the footnote to this passage.[11] As we have seen, there are many arguments favouring distributions of wealth which tend towards equality. This is a fresh one, and one that is easily overlooked. If political equality is an important value, Rousseau is surely right that some measure of material equality is a necessary condition of it. We should recognize that the sort of private wealth that permits effective campaign contributions or active campaigning through the private ownership of influential media is undemocratic through its subversion of the ideal of equal political power.

The final kind of equality which Rousseau's democracy serves is equality before the law. Rousseau has in mind Harrington's ideal of a 'government of laws, not of men', believing that law is properly general in form, its prescriptions detailing types of action and being directed to all members of a community. No one is above the law, but just as important, no one may be subjected to attainder, picked out as an individual fit for punishment, her offence being that of being designated an offender. If Rousseau's point seems strange, that is because the battle has been won for his cause. The value at stake is more likely nowadays to be described as one element in a specification of due process of law. The phenomenon he detested, arbitrary arrest and punishment, is still with us, but tyrants nowadays have generally learned that rigged trials or laws that trick up descriptions that a targeted minority will satisfy are a necessary concession to moral decency.

The basic constitution of the republic of the *Social Contract* is justified as satisfying the requirements rational men place on the political order, namely the protection of life and property consistently with the preservation of liberty and equality. These are the ideals that Rousseau's version of democracy explicitly serves. The specification of the constitution provides as good a working definition of democracy as any. You may wonder that my account of Rousseau's democratic theory has so far made no mention of his distinctive contribution – the notion of the general will, but as we shall see, all the materials for this are ready to hand.

Rousseau's contractors, which is to say any citizens concerned to discover and put into effect the principles of political right, recognize that the prudential and moral ideals which alone justify the existence and specific democratic form of the sovereign authority must also govern their deliberations when they act as legislators. The principles of political right motivate their political actions – they manifest a general will, which takes a political form when it is expressed as the outcome of the democratic process, as a decision favoured by the majority of voters. The general will is the will of the citizens and the will of the sovereign when it enacts legislation.

Rousseau's notion of the general will has puzzled many readers and has been the subject of vexed interpretative disputes. There would be no problem if the general will were to be understood as the will of people in general as registered in a vote. Any democratic decision procedure would then yield a general will by definition. There is no doubt that this sense of generality is in Rousseau's mind. That is why it is important to him that the constitution is that of a direct democracy. The ideals of Rousseau's contractors do not permit representative institutions; neither an elected assembly, nor, as in Hobbes's description, a monarchy, could assure the appropriate identity over time of the sovereign's will and that of the citizens. The commitment expressed by Hobbes's contractors, to take the sovereign's decisions as their own, would be irrational if the sovereign body were anything less than the whole body of the people. How could an autonomous agent surrender the power of exercise of her rational will in a domain of particular importance, that of political decision-making? So Rousseau wants his readers to be aware that if the will of a republic is general it cannot be issued in the voice of a monarch or elected assembly. This claim is radical; it disqualifies as illegitimate the decisions of all the sovereigns of his day (and to my knowledge, all present-day sovereigns, too).

Radical though this element of generality may be, it still does not capture the heart of Rousseau's doctrine, since it locates the general will in the legislative actions of the sovereign, the whole of which the citizen is a part. The general will is equally manifested in the actions of citizens severally when they participate as law-making members of the sovereign. So how can we characterize that expression of the general will? The central features of it are best brought out by a contrast of the general will and the particular will.

The particular will is best viewed initially as the will of an individual who is pursuing his own interests, as the will of an egoist. It is possible to construct a defence of democracy from this unlikely premise, as Bentham and James Mill, in his reconstruction of Hobbes, revealed later. Each person is in the best position to know how their own best interests are advanced. When each person casts a vote which records that interest, we can be certain that a majority decision will maximize the aggregate interest by satisfying the majority (at the cost of frustrating the minority). This simple utilitarian argument needs massive qualification or outright rejection, not least because the power exerted by each citizen as they pursue their own interests is so small as to make its expenditure inefficient; truly self-interested citizens or citizens concerned to maximize general utility will not vote.[12] But for the moment, let us keep it in place so that we may clearly outline Rousseau's views in contrast to it.

Rousseau insists that we distinguish decisions which express a general will from decisions of the utilitarian sort which register a majority or even a unanimity of particular wills – 'the will of all'.[13] The distinction can best be drawn by considering the questions those who manifest such wills put to themselves when they determine which policies they support. In the case of the particular will, citizens will ask which policies suit them best; given their conception of their own best interests, they will consider how these interests may be advanced in the most efficacious fashion. By contrast, those who wish to form a general will with respect to the policy proposals in hand will ask a different question. They will consider which policy best promotes the interests and values they share with others, interests and values in the light of which they will recognize both the constitution as legitimate and constitutionally enacted decisions as valid. To be specific, they will ask which of the candidate policies best secures the interest everyone shares in their lives and property in a fashion which is consistent with shared values of liberty and equality.

The general will is, in each individual, a pure act of the under-standing which reasons, when the passions are silent, about what a man can ask of his fellows and what his fellows have the right to ask of him. [14]

There is a massive difference between the questions which elicit a particular will and a general will, which demand an answer in the first-person, singular and plural respectively. Imagine a discussion in some political forum, a programme on television, say. The question up for debate is 'Should Scotland continue to have a devolved assembly in Edinburgh?'. Panellists run through the standard arguments for and against. 'Scotland has been a nation since whenever, with independent legal and educational establishments. There will be a democratic deficit without devolved control.' 'Continued devolution is inefficient, costly and a brake on economic growth.' The final panellist announces that she is all in favour, disclosing that her auntie has a newsagents shop near the new parliament buildings which she will inherit and which will continue to prosper mightily. I surmise that we would regard such a bald statement of private interest as a joke, since we expect politicians or pundits, indeed anyone who addresses the public, to appeal to reasons which they believe a good many of their audience share, reasons, perhaps, that they believe all should share. Political questions, many believe, should be asked in the voice of the first-person plural: Does this policy suit *us*, in the light of values *we* share?

This is the grammar of the general will. Its plural voice attests what Rousseau describes as the common (or public) good (or interest). What is the public interest or the common good?[15] In Rousseau's own terms, the answer is easily given. It comprises the purposes of political association and hence the terms on which any association can command authority. To be specific, the public interest is satisfied, the common good promoted, when citizens' votes are motivated by their desire to live (and live well), by their respect for others' aspirations to these things, and by their universal subscription to values of liberty and equality. The sovereign is legitimate only if it serves these ends and those ends can be served only if the sovereign is composed of all of the citizens, each of whom decides policy issues in accordance with this consensus on desires and values.

It is important to recognize that the general will is transformative. Just as natural independence is lost, so is that sharp sense of individual difference which motivates the moral ideal of autonomy. Rousseau's lesson is that individual freedom is a social achievement made possible only in a carefully articulated social structure which enables citizens to act from a common perspective. Democratic institutions are necessary for individual freedom, but individual freedom is not a solitary project. It is witnessed in the activities of public-spirited citizens who fly to the polls. I should emphasize that this is a recognizable phenomenon. The long queues of voters outside polling stations in South Africa, waiting to cast a vote for the first time, singing and dancing together, attest a common project rather than the pursuit of individual aspirations. These people were not daft. They did not think, each of them, that they were casting the vote that would make the difference. Rather they were properly confident that they were registering their subscription to the social values they deemed should govern their lives, most notably perhaps, their equality as citizens.

Rousseau's conclusion is that if you ask the right question, you will get the right answer. 'Whether the general will is infallible' is the problem posed as the heading of Book II, Chapter III, and the solution is that it is. We are used to deriding claims to infallibility. John Stuart Mill teases Christians with examples of the many occasions they have suffered from such claims.[16] Subsequent Popes, speaking on dogma, were to forget the lesson and provoke laughter and scorn. Rousseau's doctrine escapes the contumely that claims to infallibility invite by announcing that, where folks agree on basic principles, and apply such principles in the making of collective decisions, differences between them come out in the wash. We all agree on what everyone wants and we all share a system of values. What best promotes purposes on which we agree may be a matter of dispute, but if the means of decision expresses our agreement, and if the differences between us are the result of carelessness or unavoidable ignorance concerning how policies will work out, we shan't go far wrong if we abide by a majority decision. Majorities, amongst those who evince a general will, will always be right in this sense: their heart is in the right place; they are thinking along the right lines.

Rousseau's general will is infallible in a further sense. It is well-formed and uncorrupted by particularity. There may be honest differences between people who ask themselves which policy option best secures liberty, for example. But the differences will cancel each other out; the majority decision is likely to give the right answer just in case each voter has a better than even chance of getting the answer right.[17] Controversially, Rousseau believes that citizens will tend to get the right answer only if they deliberate the question at issue in a solitary fashion, consulting their own hearts, uncorrupted by intrigues and factions. If parties emerge and citizens have the opportunity to identify with their aims, they will lose sight of the general will of the community, forming a will which is general amongst members of the partial association, yet particular *vis-à-vis* 'the great association' of which all are members.

In recognition of both the quality of argumentation and its influence on subsequent discussions of democracy, I want to take Rousseauian democracy as an ideal type. Students of Rousseau will notice that I have not mentioned much of Rousseau's development of these ideas in Books III and IV of the *Social Contract* – a process of development which many have argued amounts to self-destruction. I will mention some of these subsidiary doctrines as their relevance becomes apparent to what follows. Rousseau would not demur from the judgement that the republic of the *Social Contract* is an ideal construct, since he was quite clear that the only institutions which could embody the principles of political right would be radically unstable, either inefficient or prone to corruption. Rousseau's clear statement of democratic principles and outline sketch of democratic practice throws up plenty of problems for further investigation. We shall begin by discussing his view that the only genuine democracy is a direct democracy.

Direct and representative democracy

Amongst the great modern thinkers on democracy, Rousseau is the odd one out in insisting that the only proper democratic state is a direct democracy. His reasoning was simple. In a representative system, citizens entrust their will to the representative sovereign.

In Hobbes's language, the sovereign is the actor, the citizens who select the sovereign are the authors of the sovereign acts. Representatives are agents of the citizens; there is an identity of will, so that one may recognize the will of the citizens in the actions of the sovereign representative.[18] The citizens' will is expressed through their voting for representatives. The work of the representatives, in enacting legislation and the like, puts into effect the will of the citizens.

'If only ... ', thought Rousseau. This condition, of identity of interest, is impossible to secure, not least because the representatives, if they form a collective as in a parliament, will swiftly form a will general amongst themselves, and, as in factions or political parties, a will that is particular *vis-à-vis* society at large, that will fail to procure the common good. As a result it would be quite irrational for citizens who value equality and liberty to put these values under threat by giving up their sovereign power.

The institutional consequences of this inference were drastic. Republics should be small, of such a size that 'every member may be known by every other'.[19] He clearly has in mind communities like the ancient Greek city-states, though in some moods he would commend his native Geneva and, in the *Social Contract*, he describes Corsica, for which, in his latter years, he prepared an (incomplete) draft of a constitution, as one of the few states capable of achieving democracy. This severe constraint on the possible size of a genuinely democratic community was a practical implication of Rousseau's philosophical views – and it has been judged, almost universally, to be impractical. This charge would not have worried Rousseau: too bad for the modern nation-state if it cannot meet the conditions necessary for it to be judged legitimate. The *critical* point is not impugned.

Defenders of democracy have not been satisfied to establish principles which license strong critical judgements against non-democratic states. Their prime concern has been to show how democratic values can be implemented in some measure, so they have taken the route of examining the possibilities of representative institutions. Broadly, they have accepted the Hobbesian principle of identity of will between sovereign and people and have sought to design institutions which preserve this. James Mill is the clearest advocate of this strategy. Agreeing with Hobbes that the representatives will be self-interested, and accepting with Rousseau that this is a dangerous and corrupting tendency, he is explicit that the central design problem is that of keeping the representatives on the straight and narrow path of promoting citizens' interests, of establishing institutional conditions that will ensure the coincidence of their own interests with those of their constituents. This is 'the doctrine of checks. It is sufficiently conformable to the established and fashionable opinions to say that upon the right constitution of checks all goodness of government depends.'[20] The most important check is that of limited duration. Representatives who realize that they will be replaced just as soon as they cease to pursue the interests of their constituents will be solicitous of those interests.

The thought that direct democracy is impossible in the modern nation-state prompts the joint efforts of political theorists and political scientists to seek out optimal representative institutions. Noting that in practice there are almost as many representational forms as there are nation-states, and recognizing that the number is multiplied as soon as we take local government procedures into account as well, and accepting that the unimplemented constitutional designs of theoreticians should be included in any review, we shall abandon the task of examining models of representative institutions. This is just as well since the thought that direct democracy is impossible in a modern nation-state needs revisiting.

So far as many practicalities are concerned, Rousseau's insistence that the republic be small (and his critics' rejection of direct democracy on that score) is evidently anachronistic. He was not aware of the power of modern technology. If we thought that direct democracy was the ideal form of political decision-making, we could implement appropriate decision procedures swiftly enough. We could give everyone a telephone and, if necessary a modem, linked up to a central computer designed to register votes. If we can run the Eurovision Song Contest in this way – no longer 'Norway: *nul points* !' – surely we can decide between political options using similar methods. At any rate we can fairly assume that such an exercise would be possible, were we to bend our wills to it.

It can fairly be objected that the procedures are still too sketchy to focus sharply the philosophical question of whether we should implement a technologically driven direct democracy. Who would set the agenda? How could they ensure that only two policies come up for decision? (If there are more than two alternatives, there may be no mathematically decisive way of ranking them.) Who would control the executive as it puts policies into effect? Nonetheless, we should not assume that answers cannot be found to settle these questions, for it is certain that we have not begun to take them seriously.[21]

So that we don't get bogged down in technical perplexities, we can focus the issues even more sharply. Some nations already have a tradition of deciding many a political question by referendum, the Swiss notably. Why shouldn't we have more of it in the UK? There is a tradition in the British parliament of taking votes on questions which are recognized to raise matters of conscience out of the arena of party dispute and giving members of parliament a free vote unconstrained by party discipline. Capital punishment, abortion legislation, fox-hunting – issues of these sorts have been the subjects of free votes. How can democrats resist the claim that such questions should be decided not by representatives but by the people directly? The case is interesting because these are acknowledged to be issues raising moral concerns which should be isolated from party interest. Members of parliament who decide them do, in Rousseauian fashion, consult their consciences. Only the weaker members, or those with slender majorities, consult their constituencies instead, and none, to my knowledge, polls them to seek a mandate. More likely, they seek to find out what local party officers or members favour, with a sharp eye to impending problems of reselection.

So far as I can see, the only objections to taking such decisions by referendum concern the qualities of judgement likely to be exercised by the general public compared with those of members of parliament. It may be suggested that members of the public are likely to be ignorant of crucial matters of fact; in the case of capital punishment for murder, for example, they may believe that this works as a strong deterrent. Their ignorance may be reinforced by the efforts of gifted orators (a.k.a. newspaper editors) who whip up support with an eye to increased circulation or their proprietor's instructions. No doubt there are difficulties here, but no doubt equally, many of them could be eased by the provision of information. What is interesting about such doubts is that they reproduce just about exactly some of Plato's arguments against democracy as a mechanism of public decision-making. They suggest that arguments for representative forms in circumstances where direct democracy is perfectly feasible are at bottom elitist. The people, it is suggested, as against their representatives, are not fit to govern. To put the same point more politely, the people are likely to govern less well than the representatives they appoint.

There is an oddity in this thought. Plato's distrust of popular decision-making fuelled his criticism of democracy and his endorsement of rule by a self-perpetuating elite of philosopher-kings. He would have distrusted representative democracy on much the same grounds as he distrusted direct democracy: if citizens are too ignorant and easily swayed to make the correct policy choices, how can we expect them to choose the best representatives? This would be akin to passengers on a cruise liner selecting the captain as soon as they got on board – too many may select the fellow they judge most charming to dine with. As soon as one accepts that representatives working as professional politicians have special skills which enable them to make better decisions than their constituents would do if left to themselves, one is forced to ask whether voting by the ignorant is the best way to select them.[22]

The question may be less important than it seems. No representative system to my knowledge imposes entry qualifications on the profession of representative politician, though theorists have proposed educational qualifications for the electorate. No regime insists on a doctorate in economics or political science, or proficiency in a foreign language, or knowledge of the constitution, or even spelling tests. Any potatoe (sic!) can aspire to be Vice-President of the United States. This is no bad thing. If, as I am suggesting, democrats should recognize a problem in systems which grant legislative powers to a sub-group of the population, this problem would be exacerbated if qualifications other than electability were required of representatives. The problem of the ignorant selecting the wise or the crafty may in practice be solved, as J.S. Mill saw, by the mechanisms of a political culture which weed out clever rogues and charlatans, mechanisms, for example, which select those with a record of public service. Political parties, for all their chicaneries and infighting, can achieve similar results where the weight of party policy and accountability, as well as requirements of personal integrity, inhibit strategies of personal aggrandizement. That said, political culture is a precious achievement. It is a miracle of political science that the major *a priori* weakness of immature systems of representative democracy – their liability to legitimize the power-seeking antics of nature's commissars – has been exposed in so few of the new democracies of Eastern Europe.

If in the spirit of Rousseau we value democracy because of the ways it advances citizens' freedom and equality, we shall place a particular premium on opportunities for citizens to participate in ruling. We should not take it for granted that the efficiency which is purchased by having decisions taken by a few people outweighs the particular kinds of freedom and equality which direct democracy embodies. And yet we so often do. Experience shows us that no sooner does any collective body set itself up for the pursuit of some interest than a committee is formed to expedite the business. We start off with a convener, a secretary, a treasurer; we add a few members with special enthusiasm and expertise ... and, 'Hey Presto!', we have a decision-making body as well as a secretariat. No group or club seems so small that it cannot establish a council, executive, or assembly with powers to decide policy.

The practical objections to direct democracy look formidable, and none are as weighty as the desire of subjects to have a quiet time and leave the exercise of self-government to others. Who wants to be casting votes in front of a television set every evening? So the greatest danger is probably the tendency of citizens to show respect for those of their fellows who have aspirations to leadership and to acquiesce deferentially in ploys to achieve unequal decision-making power. The checks on the exercise of such powers are rarely as effective as the resources representatives find for circumventing them. It is against this background that citizens should seek out every opportunity for taking decisions out of the hands of representatives and placing them directly in the hands of the community at large. Representation may often be necessary, but that necessity very quickly becomes the occasion of collective bad faith. To make a judgement on the issue which I raised at the start of this discussion: I can think of plenty of reasons that may be offered for having free votes by representatives rather than referenda involving all voters. All of them are working against the core values of democracy.

I doubt whether it is a good reason for choosing representative rather than direct democracy that those selected as represented are wiser than a random sample of the population. Given the career paths of typical politicians, they are likely to be cleverer, I suppose, and given the machinery that needs to be exploited in order to become a representative, they are likely to be more adept than most in the skills of personal manipulation and political manouevring. They will certainly have a greater interest in political affairs and a stronger desire to exercise political power than most of their fellows. They may well be more strongly motivated towards public service. This is guesswork on my part, based on limited personal experience. But whatever the distinctive personal qualities (if any) of the political classes, we have no reason to think they will get things right more frequently or more reliably than other citizens faced with the same problems and given the same information.

It is a feature of representative democracy that governments get things wrong, spending much of their effort seeking solutions to problems of their own causing. It is not a noticeable or striking feature, because it is an inexorable characteristic of the modern nation-state however constituted. No political system can get the trains to run on time. Plato thought that a class of rulers – the philosopher-kings – could be selected, educated and motivated to govern successfully,[23] an ancient version of the elite institutions of the systems of higher education that have developed in France and the United Kingdom over the last hundred and fifty years and supplied the state with most of its leading politicians and civil servants. But there is no reason why anyone should believe him. Politics may be a highly skilled craft, but government is not. It is the most fallible of human activities; because its business is change, it can't settle down into good habits. This is the truth behind conservative thinking: Utopia would be ruled, not by philosopher-kings, but by prophets – but there aren't any. 'The best Prophet naturally is the best guesser',[24] Hobbes cautions us wisely. What the conservative gets wrong is the amount and degree of change that is forced, so that resistance to change becomes just another active political stratagem, no less fallible than any other.

I have been labouring the obvious in emphasizing the fallibility of government. But this has not been without purpose, since despite Rousseau's claims of infallibility, fallibility has been sign-posted as the distinctive failing of democracy. Everyone knows that majorities can make mistakes, that a policy isn't the correct one just because a majority of citizens or representatives endorses it, not least because everyone can think of examples of policies which the majority supports and which are plain wrong. (Needless to say, we won't agree on any list of such political blunders.)

There are different reasons for this. Thus far I have suggested that the major reason is ignorance of matters of fact, in particular ignorance of the future, of how things will turn out. Many political debates are like this. They hinge on prediction and voters on both sides of major issues decide on the basis of guesswork. Everyone is either a prophet or a false prophet, since every voter is a guesser.

A very different reason for the common judgement that majorities go wrong is that unsettled value conflicts are involved. Should the state permit abortion, voluntary euthanasia, capital punishment or the ritual slaughter of animals? Please add your own candidate moral issue to the list. Let me add one from today's newspapers: should schoolteachers be able to give sex education lessons to children which promote the social tolerance of homosexual behaviour? These appear to be questions which elicit fundamental moral disagreement. Of course, questions of these two very different sorts get entangled. Prophecies concerning matters of fact are adduced as decisive in what are at bottom conflicts of values. We shall return later to the implications of deep moral disagreement. For the moment, I want to emphasize that one of the virtues of democracy is its ways of coping with errors.

If representatives err badly, for whatever reason, citizens can vote them out and try a different bunch. If they are wise they will apportion some measure of blame to themselves, the electorate, and hope to learn something from their errors. In a direct democracy, citizens have only themselves to blame – which is a great thing. The wider blame is spread and acknowledged the more chance there is of a constructive response. By contrast, when the

Five-Year Plans or the Great Leaps Forward, so favoured by gangs of tyrants, go wrong, they either keep digging the same hole or launch a hunt for plausible culprits, exacerbating the suffering. Democracy is not infallible in the common-or-garden sense of the term, but it has mechanisms for limiting the damage which should be prized.

Democracy and majority tyranny

I have been drawing attention to the failures of government and suggesting that although failure is ubiquitous, democracy is in a better position than most systems to recoup the losses, and in any case, citizens only have themselves to blame. This is an appropriate point at which to re-examine what has been adduced as the distinctive failing of democracy – its capacity to exercise majority tyranny. As we have seen, the tyranny of the majority was remarked on by de Tocqueville in his study of *Democracy in America* and was held to be of the first importance by John Stuart Mill in requiring a harm principle to protect citizens' liberties. The phenomenon demands careful description.

One who votes in a democratic procedure is expected to abide by the result even if their cause is defeated. They are in a minority but the majority has the day. They must conform to the winning policy although they voted against it. They may be forced to comply with the decision of the majority. This not tyranny; it is just defeat. Those who are defeated should look forward to their next opportunity for decision-making. They may then find themselves in a majority, and depending on the issue at stake in the voting – a representative, a government, a specific policy – they may be able to reverse the decision which went against them on the first occasion. An important assumption behind the practice of majority decision-making is that 'You win some; you lose some'. Most citizens can expect to be in a majority on a majority of occasions, although it is technically possible (but unlikely) that things may work out differently if a large consolidated minority can succeed in attracting just sufficient unattached (but different) voters to tip them into a majority most of the time. This is an important assumption, since if a significant minority of citizens thought that their participation never gained a result, they would be unlikely to regard democracy as securing the political liberty of self-government or being the enactment of political equality.

Majority rule does not entail majority tyranny. Majority tyranny is most conspicuously witnessed in a society which is riven by antecedent divisions:

> Suppose the majority to be whites, the minority negroes, or *vice versa*; is it likely that the majority would allow equal justice to the minority? Suppose the majority Catholics, the minority Protestants, or the reverse; will there not be the same danger? Or let the majority be English, the minority Irish, or the contrary; is there not a great probability of similar evil?[25]

Mill's continuation is disappointing because the division which worries him most is the class division of rich and poor, and in *Representative Government* he fails to take up the problem in the manner in which it is posed in *On Liberty*. It is certain that the contours of the problem are more familiar to ourselves than they were to Mill, given the adoption (or imposition) of broadly democratic regimes in many societies (often postcolonial or postwar settlements) which have strong racial, ethnic or religious divisions. Where such divisions are firmly in place, democracy can entrench them further. The majority party will consider proposals in the light of whether they promote the interests of their group, whether they damage the interests of a group to which they are hostile, often both of these together. The agenda of politics may be manipulated so that issues which are of no interest to the majority rarely arise for discussion and decision. The minority will be permanent and impotent. Worse still, the majority will more recognizably act like a tyrant if it promotes policies or enacts legislation that violate the rights or liberties of members of the minority community. This is the modern phenomenon of the tyranny of the majority, and sadly, it is a staple of current affairs.

The problem that worried Mill in *On Liberty* was subtly different. He believed, accepting de Tocqueville's sociological study of America, that when all citizens regard each other as equals, a spirit of conformity will develop from the uniformity of power and status. Citizens will take a close interest in each other's character and habits as displayed even in the sphere of private life and be disposed to change through prohibition personal qualities of which they disapprove. Indeed, if the forces of conformity are strong enough, prohibition will hardly be needed. Citizens will be anxious to conform and even the odd, bloody-minded eccentric will be vulnerable to social pressures. For Mill, the tyranny of the majority was a product of self-reinforcing homogeneity rather than division. The threat to liberty is the greater the more deeply the spirit of democracy suffuses the decision-making institutions of a society. If there is democracy all the way down, from Parliament or Congress to community council and town meeting, the tendency towards busy intervention in pursuit of conformity will be strengthened.

How real are these threats? How far do they compromise the ideals of democracy? Let us discuss them in turn. The first type of majority tyranny, which is caused by antecedently formed social divisions, is very serious indeed. In fact the problem for democracy may be worse than I have suggested since democracy may serve as the mechanism for quickening as much as expressing social conflict. One explanation of the incredible surfacing of internecine hatreds in the territory of the former Yugoslavia is that the politicians who emerged from the ruins of Tito's regime found it impossible to carve out competing political manifestos within the available space of political dispute without bringing back to life religious and cultural divisions that many citizens had forgotten, or in the case of the young, barely experienced. (It has been claimed that over twenty-five per cent of marriages in Bosnia were mixed marriages between citizens of different faiths.) This did not prevent aspirant politicians in pursuit of a constituency calling up old hatreds in order to gain electoral support and then cultivating those hatreds to the point of civil war when that was judged necessary for political success. I accept that the details of the case are disputed and would not wish to defend this interpretation of events from a standpoint of ignorance. But the point should be clear: democracy can be a powerful source of the sort of strife that the state is supposed to adjudicate and resolve.

Such examples would not have fazed Rousseau. They are after all the consequence of the sort of representative institutions that he held in contempt and would amount to yet another reason for promoting direct democracy. As we have seen, he was hostile to all parties and factions and would have banished sectional organizations from his republic. His citizens do not consult religious or cultural leaders; they appeal merely to their own hearts, to a conscience that does not recognize partial group interests. This is interesting, but hopeless for the democrat who wishes to defend some form of representative institution.

But Rousseau has another argument which should be of wider appeal. We should remember that democracy is an ideal but not a value. It is an ideal precisely because it actualizes the prudential requirement of self-concern together with the (complex) moral values of liberty and equality. He himself recognizes one source of the problem we have been addressing and points towards a solution. Citizens, he emphasizes, accept 'the total alienation of each associate, together with all his rights, to the community . . . each gives himself absolutely . . . the alienation being without reserve'.[26] In this respect he is as absolutist as Hobbes. But this *de jure* absolutism is far from tyranny, since, as we have seen, each subject, in effect, cedes to the sovereign only the rights the sovereign deems it important to control. What looks to be a contradiction is disarmed because the sovereign is the whole body of citizens and the general will of the sovereign is directed towards the maintenance of equality and the protection of each person's liberty. What would be a contradiction would be to suppose that citizens whose strong value of liberty includes a concern for civil liberty would put that liberty under threat, that citizens who value the equality of all could tolerate the powerlessness of a minority of fellow citizens. One true lesson of Rousseau's doctrine of the general will is that democracy is not merely a decision procedure, it is a way of taking decisions informed by specific values shared by all citizens. If it becomes the vehicle of particular sectional interests, it is 'acting no longer as a Sovereign, but as a magistrate'[27] and its decisions no longer carry authority.

It has often been claimed that democracy can institutionalize the structure of values which justify it in so far as they express the general will. What is necessary is that we 'distinguish clearly between the respective rights of the citizens and the Sovereign, and between the duties the former have to fulfil as subjects, and the natural rights they should enjoy as men'.[28] The standard constitutional means of effecting this distinction (as against the moral constraint of a harm principle) is to identify natural or human rights and entrench these in a Bill of Rights which effectively constrains the citizens along the track of respecting rights and liberties. Such a procedure is unobjectionable if the Bill of Rights operates as a statement of principle, a standing reminder of (some of) the principles of association which comprise the general will. If we think of a Bill of Rights as something like the preamble to all legislation, as a mission statement, to use the jargon, for communities and their legislatures to adopt, its use will be clear and no democrat could object. Subscription to international statements of human rights has worked in this fashion, as have international courts of human rights wherein adverse judgements are viewed as political embarassments rather than the striking down of legislation. It is a different story if the Bill of Rights is a constitutional device which opens up decisions of the democratic legislature to judicial review, for now we have the prospect of democratic decisions being overturned by judges.

The objections to this process are perfectly straightforward. It transfers debates about rights and liberties, debates which we can expect to be endemic, from a democratic forum to a courtroom. Decisions will be made by judges who are often selected rather than elected, and who may well exhibit views characteristic of a particular class or gender or ethnic background. Judges will often disagree amongst themselves for reasons which reproduce the leading features of popular debate and then they will generally settle the question by majority decision. 'The citizens may well feel that if disagreements on these matters are to be settled by counting heads, then it is their heads or those of their accountable representatives that should be counted.'[29] A self-confident democracy should not need to hand over some of its most important decisions to a self-selecting profession.

On the other hand, Bills of Rights and processes of judicial review may be vitally important in political cultures which do threaten majority tyranny because of deep antecedent social divisions or, indeed the pressure to conformity. Legislators may fear an unholy alliance of media campaigns and popular prejudice and simply avoid decision-making in controversial areas where they reckon a moral majority may take offence. Judges, who do not fear future elections and who have to decide only on the cases brought before them, may turn out to be the only persons willing to assert individuals' rights where the status quo is oppressive. On the other hand, the availability of a judiciary to take such decisions may well encourage politicians to avoid public discussion in areas of controversy concerning citizens' liberties.

This is not an issue to be settled here, but before we leave it it would be useful to remind ourselves how far the political world we are describing is distanced from the republic of Rousseau's *Social Contract*. The citizens he envisages may well disagree on the minutiae of what their rights require by way of legislation, but their disputes would be informed by a common concern for liberty and equality. Critics of Rousseau are on stronger ground when they consider the threats to liberty from the tendency towards conformity.

It is a strange convergence of opinions that John Stuart Mill and Rousseau agree on a leading feature of the social psychology of democracy. Rousseau's utopian republic is a strange, and for many, an abhorrent place. There are no lively discussions or lengthy debates, or, if there are, these indicate the (inevitable) degeneration of the institution. On matters of the highest importance, it is supposed that there will be near unanimity amongst the electorate. Rousseau is almost Platonic in his disgust for eloquence and the political arts. He supposes deep agreement about values and is disposed to recommend institutions like the civil religion which reinforces that consensus. (Critics of Rousseau are right to deplore these tendencies. It is unlikely that he thought of the civil religion as a version of the Church of England, a unique sociological achievement which effected conformity through its ubiquity together with the emptiness of its theological commitment. The Church of England does not advocate the death penalty for convicted hypocrites or apostates – Rousseau does.[30]) When Rousseau's citizens decide what legislation to enact, they listen, not to each other, but to the voice of conscience speaking to them as they contemplate the issues, and conscience says much the same to each of them.

This quality of consensus of beliefs about values is recognized by Mill as the effect of democracy, rather than the condition of its success. In effect, as they used to say, Mrs Grundy rules.

Eccentricity and idiosyncracy vanish as the hard edges of beliefs in conflict are rubbed away. Democracy levels down and dumbs down, Mill might have said. These processes he saw as the inevitable downside of democracy and they necessitated a lively apprehension of the harm principle if they were to be kept in check.

It is just as well that both Rousseau and Mill were wrong. Democracy does not need the rigid and stifling homogeneity that Rousseau described in order to flourish and it need not produce the conformity Mill deplored. To establish these points, we need to recognize that democracy assumes both agreement and disagreement. It assumes disagreement since, at the limit, if everyone were agreed about what is the right way to behave, barring weakness of will and tricky co-ordination problems, there would be no need of a state at all. Moral disagreement is the evident reality of modern states and moral disagreement is quickly transformed into political dispute as conflicting parties seek to coerce or neutralize the opposing point of view. Democracy assumes agreement with respect to the principles that vindicate it as the best decision procedure (roughly, liberty and equality, as outlined above) and it can fairly presuppose agreement on exactly the same principles when they are germane to the settling of disputes.

There is an old philosophical problem in the offing here, and its persistence in generating practical problems arouses lively debate about the limits of toleration within a democracy. This surfaces most conspicuously when anti-democratic parties put themselves up for election or when those who would limit freedom of speech and association demand the opportunity to campaign publicly and collectively for these objectives. No doubt stable democracies can, in practice, tolerate a good deal of such anti-democratic behaviour. It may be a correct judgement that a public display of idiotic beliefs is not likely to gain them support whereas suppression will do more harm than good. But these are matters of fine political judgement rather than philosophical principle. So far as philosophical principles are concerned, the assertion of rights to equal political powers does not entail that equal political powers should be granted to those who advocate stripping some members of the community of the opportunity to participate. A representative democracy should have a clear eye to the dangers of constitutional subversion carried by different schemes of representation in particular political circumstances. It is well known (but the lesson was recently re-learned in France) that systems of proportional representation which are likely to grant representative status to a small minority of anti-democrats may undermine the application of the very principles that are used to defend them. If, for example, there exist parties which advocate the repatriation of immigrant citizens, or any variety of religious or racial discrimination, a democracy should seek opportunistic remedies to defend its founding principles. It is worth remembering that democracy is not itself a value. Its characteristic practices are justified only to the degree that they express and promote the values of liberty and equality. If, in specific circumstances, democratic processes threaten these values, constitutional change that can protect and strengthen them should be implemented.

Democracy, deliberation and disagreement

The Rousseauian perspective that we have been exploring and modifying stresses agreement with respect to the basic principles which motivate the adoption of a democratic constitution and further agreement concerning the application of those principles in the processes of decision-making. Rousseau assumes that the foundational principles will yield a right answer to questions brought forward for decision and he believes that a majority of right-thinking citizens will register that right answer as required by the general will. In what follows, I want to examine two criticisms of these assumptions. The first concerns the space for disagreement; the second concerns the mechanisms of citizens' deliberations.

Rousseau's citizens recognize prudential goods, and recognize, too, that fellow citizens have similar prudential concerns which deserve their respect. They value liberty in the domains of autonomy, civil liberty and political participation. They value equality of political power, rough material equality and the equality enshrined in the rule of law. For Rousseau, this characterizes a powerful measure of agreement. I propose that universal acceptance of these values is just as readily seen as a recipe for widespread disagreement. Disagreement is possible in the following circumstances, amongst others:

(1) A policy decision may affect the self-interest of different citizens in different fashions when nothing else is at stake. The council wishes to build a road bypassing a village. Farmer A to the north of the village would like the road to cross his land so that he can sell up for a favourable price. Farmer B, having land to the south of the village, disagrees. He would like to sell up, too, looking forward to retirement on the basis of his compensation payments. Farmers C and D, to the north and south of the village respectively, disagree with their immediate neighbours because they do not want the land they farm to be covered in asphalt.

(2) A policy dispute may concern the general welfare. Citizens who may or may not have a personal stake in the outcome may differ in their judgement of the consequences of alternative policies in point of welfare. Should the country protect a nascent industry by the application of favourable tariffs? Two economists disagree as to the likely effects – one predicting retaliation which will cause irrecoverable damage to export industries, the other believing that long-term gains will outweigh the imminent costs.

(3) Citizens may broadly agree on specific elements of the value conspectus but disagree on the contents or applicability of the constituent principles. They may agree on the importance of civil liberty, yet disagree over whether e.g. the right to private property is an element of it. (Indeed this is one of the great problems of political philosophy since many believe, following Hegel, that freedom is the most plausible justification of private property. Philosophers who discuss distributive justice without examining the basis of private property sweep it under the carpet. Rawls is a conspicuous example.) Or they may agree on the importance of a particular liberty, but disagree on the application of the principle. Accepting the importance of freedom of expression, citizens may disagree as to whether this licenses the sale of pornography. Accepting the importance of religious freedom, citizens may differ as to the legitimacy of forced marriages or ritual animal slaughter.

(4) Elements of the complex value of liberty may conflict with each other. Citizens who value liberty in each of these forms may disagree when conflicts between different aspects of liberty arise. That measure of autonomy which is gained through mechanisms of social self-control may infringe civil liberties. Paternalist policies may be an example of this. Prudent but weak-willed citizens will endorse them. Strong-willed libertarians will dissent. Civil liberties, as we have seen, may be compromised by majority decisions taken by citizens exercising rights of political participation. Citizens may disagree on the best policy to adopt in these circumstances, whether to accept the cost in liberty or restrain the powers of the majority.

(5) Conflicts between liberty in its different forms and commitment to the different types of equality will be endemic, particularly if private property is included amongst the list of civil liberties. Liberty to dispose of earned income may not be the noblest cause, as we saw when discussing Nozick's views on taxation, but it should carry some weight in our deliberations. Policies which limit contributions to political parties and, in compensation, direct government funds to party organizations, doubly constrain liberty in the pursuit of equality of political power.[31] Policies which enforce the disclosure of sources of party funding (common democratic wisdom in the United States, but a novelty in the United Kingdom) are deemed to offend privacy in the service of political equality according to spokesmen for the Conservative Party. Since each of the conflicting views in these debates is not obviously ridiculous, we can expect citizens who subscribe to the conflicting values to take different views on how the conflict is to be resolved.

(6) The values of liberty and equality will conflict (again, endemically) with both prudential values and general welfare. Readers are invited to give their own examples.

All of the disagreements we have considered so far have been based on conflicts within, because between the elements of, Rousseau's value consensus. They could be solved if there was an explicit ordering of these values, but I see none, other than the submergence of prudential (particular) interests under the direction of the general will, nor any prospect of a systematic ordering in the face of unflinching and conscientious contrary intuitions. Fundamental disagreement is the fate of even those who agree to a prospectus of values which is promoted as a list of independently justifiable principles. No doubt hard philosophical work can reduce the possibilities of conflict – and we have tried to advance this prospect in our discussions of liberty and distributive justice – but the likelihood of a plausible and practically implementable synthesis of all good things should not be judged promising, as Isaiah Berlin insisted.[32]

The potential for disagreement concerning policies which demand legislation, or, by default, endorsement of the status quo, is magnified as soon as we consider controversies which do not engage the political values we have canvassed thus far. As philosophers, we *know* that disagreement over the legitimacy of abortion is likely to be premissed (in part) on such values as the sanctity (or otherwise) of human life or moral personhood as embodied in the foetus, that disagreement over capital punishment reflects a contested valuation of the evil of the irremedial punishment of the innocent, that disagreement over voluntary euthanasia is based on differing judgements over the locus and subjects of rational consent. We cannot force debates about these issues, which demand political resolution by way of a judgement as to the permissibilty or illegality of alternative actions, into the strait-jacket of the general will where that has the content that Rousseau prescribed.

Disagreement, we have found, is endemic even amongst those who agree on political principles. It is deepened when we acknowledge a range of moral problems which cannot be isolated from the political process, since partisans of the moral views in conflict demand that the regime either permit or forbid the actions in dispute. Disagreement is judged to be even more pervasive when the moral conflict which grounds political disagreement is the product of religious or cultural differences.

We have been contesting Rousseau's assumption that political differences can be resolved by the application of agreed political principles and have noticed that disagreement in respect of fundamental moral principles cannot be bracketed from the political process. If we look beyond the staples of philosophical controversy to the reality of life in the modern nation-state, we see that the position, in point of disagreement, is even worse. We find that the modern nation-state is a multicultural phenomenon, either because a political settlement has integrated distinctive historical cultures into a contingent political unity, or because patterns of immigration have introduced alien cultures into a previously monocultural state, or, most likely, because over time both of these processes have been working together. Where, as in the United States, the dominant culture is that of the immigrants, we find competing metacultural ideologies, commending on the one hand, the 'melting-pot', an integrative process whereby prior allegiances are dissolved through common acceptance of a novel social settlement, on the other hand, multiculturalism, wherein the distinctive constituent cultures are to be preserved as valuable contributory elements of a dynamically innovative way of life. Whatever the historical story, whatever the metacultural establishment or controversy, we can expect that the sociological reality will reveal moral differences which are ineliminable. If, as is usual, they are based on differences of religious belief which cultural ancestry imports, the moral disagreements will often be aggressively divisive.

Disagreement may come about because of *value pluralism*, where folks agree about a range of values but not how they should be ordered or applied in conditions of conflict, and *value difference*, where there is conflict on seemingly basic ethical commitments.[33] Incredibly, given his idiosyncratic views on all manner of ethical issues, ranging from the proper education of children to the regulation of the theatre, and his quick sense of persecution from those of opposing views, Rousseau never sensed the implications of his stance as a self-acknowledged controversialist – such was his assurance that he was right. But on the bottom line he was wrong. Democracy is not the ratification of agreement so much as the means of resolving disagreement.

This immediately raises a problem, since no one believes (or no one should believe) that in matters of controversy of the sort I have described moral disputes are settled by counting heads. Democratic processes give us a decision rather than a definitive answer to a tricky question. Put to one side the thought, which Rousseau would have endorsed, that there must be a right answer to disputes about matters of moral principle. (We can agree with him that there must be; in which case we should be humble about our capacity for reaching it. We can disagree for all sorts of respectable philosophical reasons. Either way, the problem of ethical objectivity can be bracketed.) If democratic procedures are not to serve as tests of rectitude in decision-taking (though to give Rousseau his due, they may witness good intentions – to serve the general will), what is their point in a world of conspicuous disagreement?

The most straightforward justification of democracy in the face of disagreement is that offered by the utilitarians. As we saw above and in Chapter 1, in its simplified Benthamite form, this requires each citizen to work out which of alternative policies suits them best and then to register their preference in a ballot, overall satisfaction being maximized by a majority decision. If all that is stake is the self-interest of the contesting parties, this method looks reasonable. Imagine a village which has received a bequest of £200,000 from a local worthy on condition that it be used for the provision of sporting facilities. Two proposals emerge; villagers can afford the construction of a swimming pool or a gymnasium, but not both. It is hard to think of any satisfactory way of settling the dispute other than by taking a majority decision. It is hard to think of any considerations other than self-interest that might contribute to the villagers' deliberations.

Put to one side the general theoretical questions which utilitarianism raises. Practical disagreements of the sort characterized by this example call for preferences to be consulted and aggregated in accordance with the mathematics of the ballot box. In which case, we can generalize the problem and consider whether all disagreements of the kinds we have distinguished can be resolved in this fashion. There are strong reasons for believing we cannot. Anne, Betty and Christine all agree on the importance of freedom of speech, and all agree that freedom of speech is necessary for the preservation of the democracy they prize. They have to decide whether the National Fascist Party should be allowed to meet in the village hall. Although they each of them detest the views of the NFP, they disagree over whether the planned meetings pose a threat to the values to which they subscribe. This is a reasonable disgreement, and we can all reconstruct the leading points of the debate they conduct. Perhaps one or other of them changes their mind in the course of discussion, but they still do not reach a consensus. At the end, they settle the matter in the only way available to them as democrats – they vote.

The utilitarian would represent the decision process as one wherein the voters register their preferences. Finding that Betty and Christine agree that the meetings should go ahead, Anne dissenting, the outcome is reported as optimal because two of them are suited by it, one of them not. The oddity of this analysis of the proceedings is that none of them believed that they were registering their preferences; neither of the winning pair sought the satisfaction which the victory in the ballot produced. What both of them sought was the freedom which they judged should be permitted the NFP. Likewise with Anne the loser: her concern was not to avoid the dissatisfaction which the ballot produced; it was to prevent the meeting. We can quite understand all the parties acknowledging the satisfaction and dissatisfaction attributed to them, yet insisting that this played no role whatsoever in the decision-making process (how could it?) and is irrelevant to judging the outcome. They don't care about their state of mind when this is put in the balance with the success or otherwise of their policy proposals in the light of what they judged their values required. In which case, it is misleading or philosophically misjudged to identify the value of the solution they reach by the employment of a democratic procedure with the balance of satisfaction over dissatisfaction which is derived.

To reinforce this conclusion, think of the psychological strangeness of one who votes *in order to* achieve the satisfaction of being on the winning side. Such a person would evaluate alternatives not in accordance with their intrinsic merits but in respect of their probability of success. She would be in the curious position of the football fan who shifts her allegiance to whichever side she predicts will be on top of the league. She would be asking which policy is most likely to gain majority support so that she can position herself adroitly. Curiously, if Anne thought like this and knew that Betty and Christine disagreed with each other, she would be delighted. She could toss a coin and still be assured of the satisfactions of success. The thought of all three of them trying to second-guess each others' moves in order to find at least one ally is plainly preposterous.

We know, as a matter of fact, that many voters do not consider their self-interest when they vote in elections or referendums. Indeed it is wise of them not to do so. As we noticed above, if they are clear-sightedly self-interested they would not vote at all as members of a large electorate. They vote because voting expresses their sense of themselves as active citizens who participate with the moral purpose of expressing their values in a decision-making forum. A democratic forum enables them to claim respect and recognize others as free and equal. They do not see it as a vehicle for achieving the satisfaction of their desires, and hence would not justify it in these terms. Again, as a matter of fact, Rousseau's account of the general will fits the rationale for voters' behaviour that we have reconstructed. Even if it were true that majority decisions maximize voter satisfaction, and thereby welfare or utility, this would present a justification for voter behaviour that most voters would disavow – and not because they are ignorant of their own purposes or state of mind.

This conclusion is not decisive against utilitarianism, since the utilitarian can detach the aims or motivation of those who engage in a practice from the justification of that practice. They will urge, plausibly, general claims to the effect that democracies do not suffer famine nor go to war with each other. They may seek to justify the foundational values of democracy, freedom and equality, in utilitarian terms. What they cannot claim is that direct utilitarian reasoning can vindicate the outcome of all democratic decisions. The satisfaction of the winners is too short-term a phenomenon to register strongly in the scales. It may well turn sour if it turns out that the defeated minority were right on a crucial factual issue.

I do not wish to claim that there is no place for utilitarian reasoning in the practices of democracy. As we have seen there may be policy issues where the self-interest of the voters is the only thing that is at stake. It may well be true that more issues should be settled by this sort of calculation than conventional civic virtue dictates. We would often be better off keeping a narrow focus on our own interests or those of our constituency, and constructing coalitions of like-minded self-seekers rather than succumbing to appeals on behalf of a nebulous common good, especially, *pace* Rousseau, when the decision-making group is small. (This is my dismal experience of the politics of university administration, having listened to too many eloquent appeals that one should ignore narrow departmental concerns and address the wider interests of the Faculty or the University as a whole.) The poor, the unemployed, the ill-paid and the sick would do better from national governments if they could co-ordinate effectively to pursue self-interested agendas.

We can listen sympathetically when the utilitarian tells us, in the case of democracy as of other values (rights, liberty, justice), that he is going back to the drawing-board to find deeper, subtler arguments or, what is needed most of all, some convincing facts. Let us move on to consider alternative accounts of democracy as the optimal method of solving the disagreements that inevitably arise from moral pluralism and moral difference.

In recent years, a neo-Rousseauian movement has emerged under the label of 'deliberative democracy'.[34] Deliberative democracy moves beyond Rousseau in the specific respect that it is premised on the fact of disagreement, and so instead of modelling the reflections of solitary thinkers who work out what conscience demands, emphasizes the necessity of social processes which allow citizens to come to terms with their disagreements, to find agreement or to settle the differences *pro tem* as practical exigencies dictate.

In a sense, as I have already claimed, the fact of disagreement is an obvious premiss of democracy. If everyone agreed in respect of values and preferences and their respective and comparative orderings and if all judgements were based on the same available basis of factual information there would be little to dispute and nothing to decide. But as we have seen, there are plenty of sources of disagreement, hence plenty of practical political disputes which need to be settled. This problem is judged more serious in the modern world because of the fact of reasonable pluralism. Reasonable pluralism is a sociological phenomenon with religious and philosophical roots. The term itself derives, to my knowledge, from John Rawls who uses it to characterize the variety of what he describes as comprehensive doctrines which citizens may reasonably avow.[35]

Deliberative democracy is a process of seeking consensus amongst parties who disagree on values and policy yet agree that the pursuit of agreement is the only way forward, that conflict must be resolved through mechanisms of collective deliberation.

When consensus is not possible (which surely must be just about all of the time) the second-best resolution is achieved by using some system of majority voting. Deliberative democracy is a useful idea because it focuses attention on procedures other than majority voting. In particular, it directs us to the nature and quality of the arguments that are to be employed in the process of settling disagreement, to the claims parties to the discussion can fairly make on their own behalf, and to the claims of others that they must reciprocally respect.

Parties to the deliberative process are free and equal, just as Rousseau insisted, although the kinds of freedom and equality differ from his in their different specifications by different writers. In what follows I shall assume conventional values of freedom and equality since these can be adapted to the requirements of social deliberation. Thus free citizens should be able to put issues on a social agenda for decision, should have wide freedom of speech to advance their causes, should be able to associate with each other in pursuit of their objectives, as well as participate as equals in the deliberative process. The key to these processes is what Gutmann and Thompson describe as reciprocity. In seeking fair terms of social co-operation, citizens 'offer reasons that can be accepted by others who are similarly motivated to find reasons that can be accepted by others'.[36] Public debate is a matter of seeking out principles which are shared by parties who disagree about other things and then using this common fund of values to settle the differences. Sometimes – proponents of deliberative democracy tend to be optimistic about these things – the magic works. The Protestant accepts that the Catholic will never accept his religious beliefs, the Catholic acknowledges that the Protestant will never accept hers. Neither of them will be able to procure the salvation of the other, but both can be led to see the importance to each of them of being able to confess their creed. And on the basis of this agreement, they can agree further not to burn down each other's churches or attempt forced conversion, accepting a principle of religious liberty and promoting a policy of religious toleration. On other occasions the magic does not work, consensus is not reached. Pro-life and pro-choice opponents over the question of abortion may bracket off their religious differences but still find that they disagree over the moral status of foetal life. At this point, respecting each others' different points of view amounts to a commitment to adopt a decision procedure which respects their freedom and equality (democracy) and to abide by the majority view – whether it is to permit or forbid abortion.

One proponent of deliberative democracy, Joshua Cohen, claims that democracy itself is 'a fundamental political ideal and not simply . . . a derivative ideal that can be explained in terms of the values of fairness or equality of respect'.[37] We can see why this view is mistaken. Deliberative (and all other?) conceptions of democracy sit on the back of principles of freedom and equality; these may be spelled out in the manner of our reading of Rousseau or they may themselves be derived from deeper intuitions concerning autonomy, equality of respect and a conception of the common good. Such principles are put to work at two stages in the dialectic: first, in deriving the procedural norms which comprise the democratic deliberation and decision procedure, second, in establishing the values which direct arguments and furnish decisions when the democracy is operative.

I recall an old chestnut examination question: 'Is democracy merely a political decision-making procedure?'. We can see clearly now why the answer is 'No'. The principles which serve to generate the procedure, making democratic decisions a fair basis for systems of social co-operation and coercive regulation, also serve to govern the conduct of debate and the justification of decisions. They constitute 'public reason', again Rawls's term,[38] demarcating a stock of principles to which all may be deemed to subscribe and which thereby constrain the terms of the public debates engaged by those who seek to settle disagreement on terms everyone can accept. They mark the premises from which arguments in the public forum must proceed if they are to secure the acceptance of those to whom they are directed. Public reason should be instantly recognizable as a contemporary version of Rousseau's general will.

Does deliberative democracy resolve the problem of disagreement? The first point to notice is that we cannot expect all citizens to accept it as a basis for settling conflict, since it is evident that not all citizens accept the values on which the ideal is constructed. Once again the liberal encounters the usual culprits – those whose religious or philosophical views lead them to deny the foundational values, however unspecified or provisional these may be considered. Gutmann and Thompson describe a group of parents who objected to a basic reading text adopted by the board of education in Hawkins County, Tennessee, on the basis that the reading material conflicted with some of their Christian fundamentalist convictions.[39] Amongst the offending passages was one that described 'a central idea of the Renaissance as "a belief in the dignity and worth of human beings," because such a belief is incompatible with true religious faith' (this is Burns's Holy Willie speaking up again). As Gutmann and Thompson argue, 'the parents' reasoning appeals to values that can and should be rejected by citizens of a pluralist society committed to protecting the basic liberties and opportunities of all citizens'. But of course the objecting parents do not acknowledge a reasonable plurality of ethical beliefs, and, denying the dignity and worth of human beings, they are unlikely to value the protection of basic liberties and opportunities of all citizens.

Straight off we can see that there will be irresolvable conflicts with those who do not think that the search for agreement is worthwhile or do not believe that it demands more than active proselytizing. There will be irresolvable conflicts with those who dismiss the foundational values of freedom or equality as inconsistent with revealed doctrine. We can call such divisive moral perspectives unreasonable on the grounds that their proponents have no interest in resolving the conflicts their beliefs cause. But then they would call the deliberative democrat unreasonable because she cannot acknowledge the only basis on which they believe agreement could be constructed – endorsement of the revealed truth. Deliberative democracy has to recognize that neither its procedures nor the currency of its policy debates can command the acceptance of all elements of the moral plurality to which it commends itself.

The persistence within the polity of individuals and groups who just do not accept the founding values of democracy, values as fundamental as equal respect and freedom for independent judgement, would be more of an embarrassment if we were not comfortable with the claim that such views are plain wrong. It is a weakness, not a strength, of their positions that they do not grant opposing views even the logical space for an argument with them, if they systematically disbar any attempt to seek common ground beyond the literal acceptance of their claims.

So far as I can see, there are only three ways of dealing with serious disagreement concerning policy or principle. First, one can seek substantive agreement, finding arguments which force or seduce one of the opposing parties into changing their mind. Failing that, and accepting that the scale of the disagreement may be much reduced if not altogether eliminated by concerted deliberation, the parties may find sufficient agreement to accept a decision procedure. Turn-and-turn-about or tossing a coin may serve for couples who wish to go out with each other but systematically disagree over whether to go to a concert or a play. Some form of democracy is the only realistic political equivalent. Failing agreement on procedures, the parties must fight, seeking a dominant position which enables them to impose their judgement on continually recalcitrant opponents.

As Hobbes saw, fighting will be endemic where parties to irresolvable conflicts are roughly equal or equally vulnerable to shifting alliances. The best we can wish for, in a world where the prospect of fighting is not so much the nightmare scenario as the condition of conflict portrayed regularly on the TV news, is that *our own* societies have a powerful enough majority committed to the resolution of disputes by majority decision where substantive agreement cannot be achieved. Then, paradoxically, they can impose by coercion decisions which the commitment to agreement at some level cannot secure.

It has been useful to identify the limitations of democracy in point of the ineliminability of first-water, ground-level disagreement and to establish that its credentials will not be established to the satisfaction of all parties to all conflicts. The democrat as well as the tyrant has to display his credentials even as he accepts that not all will accept them. He needs to be able to display his ethical commitments even when he knows they will be rejected. His saving grace – and it is a real grace, of character and manners as well as conduct – is that he attributes to his opponents an equality of respect, if not quite liberty, that they would refuse to him.

Does deliberative democracy fare any better as a response to other sources of disagreement? I categorized earlier value pluralism as that condition wherein citizens agree on a list of values but disagree as to their respective priorities, either in general or in respect of their applicability to different circumstances where a judgement of priorities is required. Betty and Alf can agree that liberty and equality are important values, but Alf insists that liberty trumps equality whereas Bert disagrees. Christine and Denis may have no views as to the systematic ordering of these values, but in respect of rights to private property, Christine may believe that freedom trumps equality whereas Denis disagrees. Denis may believe that freedom of expression and association vindicate unlimited contributions to candidates seeking election, Christine may disagree. All four of them may confess that they find no systematic fashion of justifying the pattern of judgements they avow when freedom and equality as articulated in the contexts of a range of policy disputes come into conflict. They follow their intuitions and can tell a good story, confident that they draw upon respectable traditions of thinking and can find plenty of fellow travellers.

In these sorts of circumstances of dispute, settlement, as ever, demands a basis of agreement, and it is hard to think of parties who advance the cases sketched above not agreeing to the application of the values of freedom and equality which they avow as being relevant to the issue of appropriate decision procedures. I accept that this is possible but believe that it is implausible. Some (the charge has been made against Hayek) may think of freedom as entirely a matter of freedom of exchange plus a list of privileged civil liberties, but they are hard put to deny that the citizen who insists on opportunies for effective political participation claims a liberty which their exclusion from the political process forecloses. (This was one modest conclusion from our discussion of the value of liberty in Chapter 3.) To emphasize the conclusion of many of the arguments that have gone before, freedom and equality, together with some conception of the general good which invokes utilitarian considerations, open up a space for disagreement about policies within an agreement about its practical resolution through the use of democratic processes.

Granted the extent of agreement about core values and recognizing the scope for disagreement which the elaboration of these values permits, it is likely that subscribers will agree along lines of traditional consensus and disagree at points of familiar fracture.

The pluralism I have characterized will both focus the points of disagreement and direct us towards its practical resolution in procedures of democratic decision-making. We can both agree to disagree and agree on a majority settlement.

Matters are different in respect of what we designated as value difference. Here we must accept that there may be no possibility of accommodation through argument. No amount of deliberation will get the pro-life and pro-choice advocates to accept premises from which they can construct an agreement. Agree as they might on political values – they each love liberty, prize equality and value democracy for its capacity to fairly settle political debate – they deny that the rights and wrongs of abortion are a matter of political settlement. There are plenty of other moral questions which reveal striking differences in values and which need some measure of political resolution. In Britain of late much attention has been directed to issues concerning homosexuality. Parliament has had to decide on the age of consent, on whether or not homosexual relations may be permitted between members of the armed forces, whether it is right to forbid the promotion of homosexuality by schoolteachers. These debates raise important questions of liberty and equality but they have also brought into the open ostensibly non-political questions concern the value of marriage and family life as well as discussions of whether homosexual relations are natural or perversions of human nature, questions which, incredibly, seem the stuff of religious dispute. As ever, spokesmen (generally *men*) for the churches have intervened reminding a kingdom of atheists of the principles of divine law, and in fairness, their pronouncements have supported both sides in the debates.

It might look as though opposing parties to moral disputes of this depth and irresolvability stand to each other in the manner of those for whom fighting or the exercise of unauthorized power is the only way forward. But this would be a hasty conclusion. Public reason, the applicability of principles of the general will, cannot be expected to frame the terms of argument in which citizens engage when substantive questions of these sorts are raised for decision. It can be recognized as making a weighty (and for many a decisive) contribution to debate, but its values cannot be expected to trump deep moral beliefs which participants will inevitably assert in pressing a dissenting case.[40] But the principles of the general will do find a place in vindicating a decision procedure to establish a legally binding solution.

Procedural conceptions of democracy, which rest the case for democracy on the fairness of the democratic way of reaching decisions, in particular, on citizens' rightful claims to equal respect as autonomous agents, have been criticized by theorists of deliberative democracy for failing to acknowledge the reach of democratic principles into questions of substance which a democracy deliberates.[41] Procedural considerations come into their own where deliberative democracy overreaches itself, claiming philosophical resources which turn out to be impotent in the resolution of conspicuous and divisive disagreement. One cannot disbar citizens from applying idiosyncratic or narrowly religious principles in matters of political controversy. One cannot get all parties to a democratic decision to respect the moral content of a democratic decision. But one may be able to convince some of them that the decision should be respected on procedural grounds – that it is the only fair way to settle the issue.

For the rest, be on your guard. Ominously, your salvation is their business.

Notes

Preface

1 G.W.F. Hegel, *The Phenomenology of Spirit*, trans. A.V. Miller, Oxford, Clarendon Press, 1977, ¶590, p. 360.

1 Introduction

1 The term could be dreadfully misleading, since particularism is often construed as the moral view that normative ethics concerns the assertion of particular judgements in specific contexts rather than the application of general principles, e.g. it is unjust to punish the innocent. I could find no better term. 'Empiricist' and 'inductivist' seem far too general. I welcome suggestions for an alternative and caution readers that the term is not in widespread use and should be employed with discretion.
2 G.W.F. Hegel, *Elements of the Philosophy of Right* (henceforth *Philosophy of Right*), ed. A.W. Wood, trans. H.B. Nisbet, Cambridge, Cambridge University Press, 1991, §132 and Remark.
3 I. Kant, *Critique of Pure Reason*, trans. and ed. P. Guyer and A.W.

Wood, Cambridge, Cambridge University Press, 1998, note at pp. 100–1.

4 The phrase is Hobbes's. See T. Hobbes, *Leviathan*, ed. C.B. Macpherson, Harmondsworth, Penguin, 1985, Ch.13, p. 188.

5 Remember, I haven't argued for this. I've just asserted it and will proceed to review the implications of this claim as if it were true.

6 J. Rawls, *A Theory of Justice*, Oxford, Clarendon Press, 1972, pp. 48–50. Rawls distinguishes *narrow* and *wide* reflective equilibrium. A reader reminds me that the process of reflection I describe is more akin to the first than the second. I am assuming the pursuit of a wide reflective equilibrium since I am supposing that the philosopher will review candidate moral theories in the light of other available theories as well as in the light of the judgements and principles specific theories reject or endorse.

7 These are not straw targets. No traditionalist practice is so awful that it can't find a trendy apologist. See Martha Nussbaum's report of a conference on 'Value and Technology', in M. Nussbaum, *Sex and Social Justice*, Oxford, Oxford University Press, 1999, pp. 35–7.

8 For a strong defence of utilitarianism as an ethical theory signally apt for political employment, see R.E. Goodin, *Utilitarianism as a Public Philosophy*, Cambridge, Cambridge University Press, 1995.

9 Examples include M. Sagoff, *The Economy of the Earth*, Cambridge, Cambridge University Press, 1988 and J. O'Neill, *Ecology, Policy and Politics*, London, Routledge, 1993.

2 Utilitarianism

1 John Rawls, Robert Nozick, Ronald Dworkin, to name three. John Rawls contrasts his own theory of justice with utilitarianism partly 'because the several variants of the utilitarian view have long dominated our philosophical tradition and continue to do so', J. Rawls, *A Theory of Justice*, Oxford, Clarendon Press, 1972, p. 52.

2 Bentham, upon finding that his proposals for reform were ignored, became incensed by the disregard of government for the welfare of its subjects and railed against its evident pursuit of *sinister* (i.e. sectional or minority) interests. Recently, Robert Goodin has stressed the aptness of utilitarianism as a *public* philosophy. See R. Goodin, *Utilitarianism as a Public Philosophy*, Cambridge, Cambridge University Press, 1995.

3 See Anscombe's reference to Gareth Evans in G.E.M. Anscombe,

'On the Frustration of the Majority by the Fulfilment of the Majority's Will', *Analysis*, 1976, vol. 36, pp. 161–8.

4 For Bentham's misgivings, see B. Parekh (ed.), *Bentham's Political Thought*, London, Croom Helm, 1973, pp. 309–10.

5 J.S. Mill, *Utilitarianism*, in *Utilitarianism, Liberty, Representative Government*, London, Dent, 1968, Ch. 5, p. 58.

6 I take the distinction that follows from D. Lyons, *Forms and Limits of Utilitarianism*, Oxford, Oxford University Press, 1965.

7 There is an important wrinkle here. Do we judge actions (or agents) in the light of what consequences transpire or in the light of what consequences agents believe will transpire (expected utility) or in the light of what a rational agent, possessed of whatever information we expect such agents to gather, would predict should transpire? See J.J.C. Smart, 'An Outline of a System of Utilitarian Ethics', in J.J.C. Smart and B. Williams, *Utilitarianism: For and Against*, Cambridge, Cambridge University Press, 1973, for a survey of the issues.

8 Since agreement should never be taken for granted, it's worth pointing out that Friedrich Nietzsche would not endorse compassion and sympathy as dispositions which should be valued. But he wasn't a utilitarian, either.

9 The *Nautical Almanac* is a famous example used by J.S. Mill, *Utilitarianism*, Ch. II, pp. 22–3.

10 See Bentham's outline of the 'felicific calculus', in J. Bentham, *An Introduction to the Principles of Morals and Legislation*, ed. J.H. Burns and H.L.A. Hart, London, Methuen, 1982, pp. 38–41.

11 In the discussion of rules that follows, I rely heavily on John Rawls, 'Two Concepts of Rules', *Philosophical Review*, 1955, vol. 64, pp. 3–32, repr. in *Collected Papers*, ed. S. Freeman, Cambridge, Mass., Harvard University Press, 1999, pp. 20–46 and P. Foot (ed.), *Theories of Ethics*, Oxford, Oxford University Press, 1967.

12 Ideal rule utilitarianism has been supported most conspicuously by R.B. Brandt. See his *Ethical Theory*, Englewood Cliffs, N.J., Prentice Hall, 1959, and *A Theory of the Good and the Right*, Oxford, Clarendon Press, 1979.

13 The best known criticisms are those of J.J.C. Smart and David Lyons. In what follows I adapt the examples dicussed by Lyons in *Forms and Limits*.

14 The term 'rule-worship' was introduced in this context by J.J.C. Smart in 'Extreme and Restricted Utilitarianism', *Philosophical Quarterly*, 1956, vol. 6, pp. 344–54, repr. in P. Foot (ed.), *Theories of Ethics*.

15 The distinction between internal and external perspectives on institutional rules is made in H.L.A. Hart, *The Concept of Law*, Oxford, Clarendon Press, 1961, pp. 55–6.

16 But notice: I have not mentioned the 'institution' of promising. There is something conventional (as Hume saw) about institutions which is grist to the utilitarian's mill, i.e. we can always ask which institution is best or which form of this institution is best – and use utility to weigh different answers. Since I don't think that promising is up for assessment in these ways, I don't think of it as an institution (cf. J. Rawls, 'Two Concepts of Rules').

17 As Hegel, *contra* Kant, clearly recognized. See G.W.F. Hegel, *Philosophy of Right*, §75 and I. Kant, *The Metaphysics of Morals*, trans. M. Gregor, Cambridge, Cambridge University Press, 1991, §§23–7, for an apt and interesting *contretemps* on the ethical nature of family life.

18 To keep matters simple, I am assuming in my discussion of these examples that goods are distributed equally amongst the population.

19 For a discussion of all of the issues I survey as problems of maximization, see James Griffin, *Well-being*, Oxford, Clarendon Press, 1986, especially Chs v – vii.

20 The proof – as much proof as is possible in the nature of the subject, which is not to say the kind of proof established by strict deduction from true premises – is given in *Utilitarianism*, Ch.2. It has prompted an enormous amount of interpretation, criticism and defence. For a hostile account, see G. E. Moore, *Principia Ethica*, Cambridge, Cambridge University Press, 1903, Ch. 1; for sympathetic defence of elements of the proof, see John Skorupski, *John Stuart Mill*, London, Routledge, 1989, pp. 283–8.

21 J. Griffin, *Well-being*, p. 8.

22 This point is also illustrated by Nozick's famous example of the experience-machine. See R. Nozick, *Anarchy, State and Utopia*, New York, Basic Books, 1974, pp. 42–5.

23 See M. Sagoff, *The Economy of the Earth*, for a strong critique of these techniques in the field of environmental policy.

24 Griffin believes such an account can be given. He claims clear-sighted, straight-thinking sadists would wish to give up their practices, which are costly and risky. See *Well-being*, pp. 25–6. Maybe . . . I opine, from a stance of total ignorance. But the newspapers tell me that practitioners devise consensual arrangements and the punitive institutions of society, from schools to prisons, offer the sadist a variety of career structures in the public service.

25 Other elements should not be discounted in a full treatment, notably the sceptical challenge to assumptions of infallibility.
26 J.S. Mill, *On Liberty*, in *Utilitarianism, Liberty, Representative Government*, Ch. III, p. 114.
27 Many readers have identified non-utilitarian themes in Mill's argument in this chapter, in particular the perfectionist account of human flourishing. In what follows, I shall ignore these.
28 J.S. Mill, *On Liberty*, Ch. I, p. 73.
29 J.S. Mill, *Utilitarianism*, Ch.V, pp. 49–50.
30 The utilitarian position is defended capably by R. Brandt, *A Theory of the Good and the Right*, Ch. XVI.
31 Hume's account is given in the *A Treatise of Human Nature*, Oxford, Oxford University Press, 1965, III, ii, 1–4, the *Enquiries, Concerning Human Understanding and the Principles of Morals*, Oxford, Oxford University Press, 1902, pp. 183–4 and is explicit in many of his essays. It has been widely discussed. David Miller, *Philosophy and Ideology in Hume's Political Thought*, Oxford, Clarendon Press, 1981, pp. 60–77 and J.L. Mackie, *Hume's Moral Thought*, London, Routledge and Kegan Paul, 1980, pp. 76–96, provide accessible discussions. The subject is treated exhaustively in J. Harrison, *Hume's Theory of Justice*, Oxford, Oxford University Press, 1981.
32 This interpretation of Hume has been challenged. For contrary views, see D. Gauthier, 'David Hume, Contractarian', *The Philosophical Review*, 1979, vol. LXXXVIII, pp. 3–38 and R. Hardin, *Morality within the Limits of Reason*, Chicago, University of Chicago Press, 1988. These readings are rejected in D. Knowles, 'Conservative Utilitarianism', *Utilitas*, 2000, vol. 12, pp. 155–75.
33 The law of diminishing marginal utility of income is rejected firmly as unscientific by R. Lipsey, *Introduction to Positive Economics*, London, Weidenfeld and Nicolson, 1965, pp. 149–51. Lipsey's arguments support those of Lionel Robbins in *The Nature and Significance of Economic Science*, London, Routledge and Kegan Paul, 1932.
34 A very full discussion of the difficulties in this area and the implications of them for politics can be found in Raymond Plant, *Modern Political Thought*, Oxford, Blackwell, 1991, pp. 184–218.
35 T. Hobbes, *Leviathan*, Ch.13, p. 186.
36 This interpretation of Hobbes is contested. See Bernard Gert, 'Hobbes and Psychological Egoism', *Journal of the History of Ideas*, 1967, vol. XXVIII, repr. in B.H. Baumrin (ed.), *Hobbes's Leviathan*, Belmont, Calif., Wadsworth, 1969, and T. Hobbes, *Man and*

Citizen, ed. B. Gert, Brighton, Harvester Press, 1978, 'Introduction', pp. 5–10. I believe the issue is settled by a couple of sentences in *Leviathan* where Hobbes insists that persons act only to procure some good *for themselves*. T. Hobbes, *Leviathan*, pp. 192, 209.

37 D. Hume, 'Of Passive Obedience', in *Essays*, Oxford, Oxford University Press, 1963, pp. 474–5.

38 D. Hume, 'Of the Origin of Government', in *Essays*, p. 35.

39 D. Hume, 'Of the Original Contract', in *Essays*, p. 67.

40 D. Hume, 'Of the First Principles of Government', in *Essays*, p. 29. See n. 32 above for sources which challenge this utilitarian reading of Hume.

41 This thumbnail sketch of anarchism derives from many authors. The most celebrated utilitarian anarchist is William Godwin, *Enquiry concerning Political Justice*, Oxford, Oxford University Press, 1971. Good general accounts of the anarchist literature can be found in George Woodcock, *Anarchism*, Harmondsworth, Penguin, 1963 and April Carter, *The Political Theory of Anarchism*, London, Routledge and Kegan Paul, 1971. The most sophisticated modern defence of anarchism is Michael Taylor, *Community, Anarchy and Liberty*, Cambridge, Cambridge University Press, 1982.

42 My presentation of this argument is much more simple than anything to be found in Bentham's writings. The crucial premiss, that individuals are the best judges of their own interests, is obviously false in respect of many individuals. Bentham excludes females, non-adult males, those who fail a reading test and alien travellers from the constituency of democratic participants. See B. Parekh (ed.), *Bentham's Political Thought*, p. 208. He was also well aware that, where ignorance and superstition are rife, voters may make disastrous mistakes. But he also believed that education and full information will tend over the long run to produce social conditions which validate the assumption of wide competence. For a careful discussion of Bentham's views, see Ross Harrison, *Bentham*, London, Routledge and Kegan Paul, 1983, pp. 195–224.

43 Bentham himself thought direct democracy evidently impractical and advocated a form of representative democracy designed to secure an identity of the interests of the representatives and the interests of the people. See excerpts from Bentham's *Constitutional Code* in B. Parekh (ed.), *Bentham's Political Thought*, pp. 206–15. James Mill, Bentham's follower and John Stuart Mill's father, made a most effective defence of representative democracy in his *Essay on Government*, Indianapolis, Liberal Arts Press, 1955, a

tract which nicely summarizes the central elements of Bentham's thought. He argues that, since all potential legislators are rogues, representative institutions with powers of regular recall are the best safeguard against their pursuit of self-interest.

44 See G.E.M. Anscombe, 'On the Frustration of the Will of the Majority'.

45 These objections are most familiar from the work of John Rawls, Robert Nozick, Ronald Dworkin, Bernard Williams and Samuel Scheffler. See the collection of papers, *Consequentialism and its Critics*, ed. S. Scheffler, Oxford, Oxford University Press, 1988, for a review of the most influential recent literature.

46 Peter Railton, 'Alienation, Consequentialism, and the Demands of Morality', *Philosophy and Public Affairs*, 1984, vol. 13, pp. 134–71, repr. in Scheffler (ed.), *Consequentialism* and Shelly Kagan, *The Limits of Morality*, Oxford, Clarendon Press, 1989, have proved stout defenders.

47 J.S. Mill, *Utilitarianism*, Ch. 1, p. 3.

48 Ibid., Ch. II, p. 22.

49 J.-J. Rousseau, *Discourse on the Origins of Inequality*, in *The Social Contract and Discourses*, London, Dent, 1973.

50 Incredibly, economists have attempted to do so. For a description (and severe criticism) of the 'Wyoming experiment', see M. Sagoff, *The Economy of the Earth*, pp. 74–98. See also John O'Neill, *Ecology, Policy and Politics*, pp. 102–22.

51 James Griffin believes this. See his *Well-being*, pp. 75–124.

3 Liberty

1 I shall use the terms 'liberty' and 'freedom' interchangeably.

2 I. Berlin, 'Two Concepts of Liberty', in *Four Essays on Liberty*, Oxford, Oxford University Press, 1969, p. 121. Berlin goes on to claim that historians of ideas have recorded 'more than two hundred senses of this protean word'. I believe him, although he offers no evidence for this.

3 J. Locke, *Two Treatises of Government*, Cambridge, Cambridge University Press, 1960, *Second Treatise*, §§ 6, 22, 57.

4 I. Berlin, 'Two Concepts', pp. 121–2.

5 Ibid., p. 131.

6 T. Hobbes, *Leviathan*, Ch. 21, p. 262.

7 'The existence of an invariably enforced legal rule prohibiting the doing of B does not imply that persons subject to it are unfree

to do B', H. Steiner, *An Essay on Rights*, Oxford, Blackwell, 1994, p. 32. See also H. Steiner, 'Individual Liberty', *Aristotelian Society Proceedings*, 1975, vol. LXXV, pp. 35–50.

8 I. Berlin, 'Two Concepts', p. 122, n. 2.

9 I. Berlin, 'Two Concepts', pp. 124–7 and 'Introduction', pp. liii–lv.

10 Ibid., p. lvi. At p. l, Berlin describes his opponents as 'philosophical monists who demand final solutions'. This careful choice of words embraces both theoretical absurdity and practical barbarity.

11 Ibid., p. xlviii. Earlier he tells us that the 'absence of such [negative] freedom is due to the closing of such doors or failure to open them, as a result, intended or unintended, of alterable human practices, of the operation of human agencies', p. xl.

12 Here I parody the ideological history of the British Labour Party, 1983–94.

13 See Ralph Wedgwood, 'Why Promote People's Freedom?', unpublished. Wedgwood links his account of freedom to those provided in G.A. Cohen, 'Capitalism, Freedom and the Proletariat', in Alan Ryan (ed.), *The Idea of Freedom*, Oxford, Oxford University Press, 1979, and C.B. MacPherson, *Democratic Theory: Essays in Retrieval*, Oxford, Clarendon Press, 1973, Ch.V. He distinguishes freedom as social empowerment from Sen's notion of freedom as opportunities or abilities in general. Thus one's health may impair one's opportunities, but if poor health is not caused by social conditions nor is it remedial by social improvement, it is not a social condition which limits one's liberty. By contrast, 'access to health care ... is a social condition, and – since a standard likely consequence of access to health care is the power that comes with reasonably good health and long life – it is an important constituent of social empowerment. So if two people have equal access to equally good health care, then that will make an equal contribution to their social freedom, regardless of their actual levels of health. On the other hand, even if they are equally advantaged in terms of social freedom, if one is debilitated by ill health and the other is not, then the first person is worse off with respect to power or capabilities than the second', p. 5. For Sen's account, see A.K. Sen, *Inequality Re-examined*, Oxford, Clarendon Press, 1992, Ch. 3 and 'Capability and Well-being', in M.C. Nussbaum and A.K. Sen (eds), *The Quality of Life*, Oxford, Clarendon Press, 1992, pp. 30–53.

14 R. Wedgwood, 'Why Promote People's Freedom?', p. 5.

15 I. Berlin, *Four Essays*, p. 131.

16 J. Locke, *Essay concerning Human Understanding* (many editions), II, XXI, §48; J.-J. Rousseau, *Discourse on the Origin of Inequality*,

1st Part, p. 54; *The Social Contract*, Bk. I, Ch. VIII, p. 178; I. Kant, *Groundwork of the Metaphysics of Morals*, trans. as *The Moral Law* by H.B. Paton, London, 1969, pp. 93–5; G.W.F. Hegel, *Elements of the Philosophy of Right*, ed. A.W. Wood, trans. H.B. Nisbet, Cambridge, Cambridge University Press, 1991, 'Introduction'. H. Frankfurt, 'Freedom of the Will and the Concept of a Person', *Journal of Philosophy*, 1971, vol. LXVII(1), pp. 5–20, repr. in G. Watson (ed.), *Free Will*, Oxford, Oxford University Press, 1982; C. Taylor, 'What is human agency?', in *Philosophical Papers*, Cambridge, Cambridge University Press, 1985, vol. I, pp. 15–44.

17 J.-J. Rousseau, *The Social Contract*, Bk I, Ch. VIII, p.178: 'We might, over and above all this, add, to what man acquires in the civil state, moral liberty, which alone makes him truly master of himself; for the mere impulse of appetite is slavery, while obedience to a law which we prescribe to ourselves is liberty.'

18 G.C. MacCallum, Jr, 'Negative and Positive Freedom', *Philosophical Review*, 1967, vol. 76, pp. 312–34.

19 J. Feinberg, *Social Philosophy*, Englewood Cliffs, N.J, Prentice Hall, 1973, pp. 12–13.

20 J. Gray, *Isaiah Berlin*, London, Harper Collins, 1995, pp. 18–19.

21 Ibid., p. 19.

22 For Rousseau's definition of moral liberty, see note 17 above.

23 Quentin Skinner, most conspicuously in 'The Idea of Negative Liberty', in R. Rorty, J.B. Schneewind and Q. Skinner (eds), *Philosophy in History*, Cambridge, Cambridge University Press, 1984; Philip Pettit, *Republicanism: A Theory of Government and Freedom*, Oxford, Clarendon Press, 1997, which cites the earlier work on which this monograph builds; Jean-Fabien Spitz, *La Liberté Politique*, Paris: Presses Universitaires de France, 1995.

24 P. Pettit, *Republicanism*, p. 52.

25 The phrase is Harrington's, cited by P. Pettit, *Republicanism*, p. 39. James Harrington, *The Commonwealth of Oceana and A System of Politics*, ed. J.G.A. Pocock, Cambridge, Cambridge University Press, 1992, p. 8.

26 J.-J. Rousseau, *Discourse on the Origin of Inequality*, 2nd Part, p. 86.

27 G.W.F. Hegel, *The Phenomenology of Spirit*, trans. A.V. Miller, Oxford, Clarendon Press, 1977, 'Independence and Dependence of Self-consciousness: Lordship and Bondage', §§178–96.

28 J.S. Mill, *On Liberty*, Ch. 1. For 'tracking', see P. Pettit, *Republicanism*, pp. 52–8.

29 J.S. Mill, *On Liberty*, p. 73.

30 J. Raz, *The Morality of Freedom*, Oxford, Clarendon Press, 1986. See especially Chs 1, 14–15.

31 G.W.F. Hegel, *Philosophy of Right*, 'Introduction'. S.I. Benn, *A Theory of Freedom*, Cambridge, Cambridge University Press, 1988.

32 This distinction of first- and second-order desires is the nub of H. Frankfurt's thesis in 'Freedom of the Will'. What follows is best understood as a development of Frankfurt's thesis constructed from a range of critical material.

33 An objection raised by G. Watson, 'Free agency', *Journal of Philosophy*, 1975, vol. 72, pp. 205–20, repr. in G. Watson, *Free Will*. Frithjof Bergmann offers a lovely philosophical redescription of Dostoyevsky's malevolent clerk in *Notes from the Underground* as a sort of contrary wanton, a wanton of the third-order, perhaps. See F. Bergmann, *On Being Free*, Notre Dame, University of Notre Dame Press, 1977, pp. 17–22.

34 For the notion of free action as produced in accordance with ideas of the good and the true, see S. Wolf, *Freedom within Reason*, Oxford, Oxford University Press, 1990. For the notion of 'strong evaluation', see C. Taylor, 'Responsibility for Self', in A.O. Rorty (ed.), *The Identities of Persons*, Berkeley, University of California Press, 1976, pp. 281–99, repr. in G. Watson, *Free Will*. Also, C. Taylor, *Sources of the Self*, Cambridge, Cambridge University Press, 1989, Ch. 3.

35 J.S. Mill, *On Liberty*, Ch. V, p. 152.

36 J.S. Mill, *On Liberty*, p. 116.

37 F.D. Schier, 'The Kantian Gulag', in D. Knowles and J. Skorupski (eds), *Virtue and Taste*, Oxford, Blackwell, 1993, pp. 1–18, cited at pp. 1–2.

38 The account of autonomy I shall develop draws on a range of sources. Prominent amongst them have been J. Raz, *The Morality of Freedom* and S.I. Benn, *A Theory of Freedom*.

39 See, for an influential discussion, P.F. Strawson, 'Social Morality and Individual Ideal', *Philosophy*, 1961, vol. XXXVI, repr. in Strawson, *Freedom and Resentment*, London, Methuen, 1974, pp. 26–44.

40 A typical example is John Rawls' defence of 'the Aristotelian Principle': 'other things equal, human beings enjoy the exercise of their realized capacities (their innate or trained abilities), and their enjoyment increases the more the capacity is realized, or the greater its complexity', *A Theory of Justice*, pp. 424–33, cited at p. 426.

41 This is Schiller's quip, loosely rendered by Hegel. See Hegel,

Philosophy of Right, §124, and the accompanying note by Allen Wood.

42 B. Williams, 'Toleration: An Impossible Virtue?', in D. Heyd (ed.), *Toleration*, Princeton, N.J., Princeton University Press, 1996, p. 18.

43 The classical discussion of this problem, alternatively characterized as incontinence, or, in the Greek, *akrasia*, is Aristotle, *Nichomachean Ethics* (many editions), Bk VII.

44 W. Kymlicka, *Multicultural Citizenship*, Oxford, Clarendon Press, 1995, is an excellent survey of the range of the modern problem of toleration.

45 The pros and cons of this debate are rehearsed more fully in G. Graham, 'Freedom and Democracy', *Journal of Applied Philosophy*, 1992, vol. 9, pp. 149–60 and D. Knowles, 'Freedom and Democracy Revisited', *Journal of Applied Philosophy*, 1995, vol. 12, pp. 283–92.

46 Brian Barry reports that 'Those ordinary people who say in response to the surveys asked by political scientists that they personally could do things to change a national or even a local political decision which they disapprove of are not so much fine unalienated examples of the democratic citizen as – if they mean it – sufferers from delusions of grandeur on a massive scale', 'Is it Better to be Powerful or Lucky?', in B. Barry, *Democracy, Power and Justice*, Oxford, Clarendon Press, 1989, p. 301.

47 J.S. Mill, *On Liberty*, pp. 72–3.

48 J.J. Thomson, *The Realm of Rights*, Cambridge, Mass., Harvard University Press, 1990, pp. 259–71.

49 Defended in full detail in J. Feinberg, *Harm to Others*, vol. 1 of *The Moral Limits of the Criminal Law*, New York, Oxford University Press, 1984.

50 J. Feinberg, *Harm to Others*, p. 37, quoting Nicholas Rescher, *Welfare: The Social Issue in Philosophical Perspective*, Pittsburgh, University of Pittsburgh Press, 1972, p. 6.

51 Lord Justice James Fitzjames Stephen, *Liberty, Equality, Fraternity*, London, Smith, Elder, 1873, new edn, Cambridge, Cambridge University Press, 1967 (a direct riposte to Mill's *On Liberty*), is the classical source of this objection.

52 For a discussion of these questions, see D. Knowles, 'A Reformulation of the harm principle', *Political Theory*, 1978, vol. 6, pp. 233–46.

53 G. Graham, *Contemporary Social Philosophy*, Oxford, Blackwell, 1988, pp. 123–4.

54 As full a list as anyone could usefully employ is found in J. Feinberg, *Harm to Others*, at pp. 16–17.

55 P. Devlin, *The Enforcement of Morals*, Oxford, Oxford University Press, 1965.

56 H.L.A. Hart, *Law, Liberty and Morality*, Oxford, Oxford University Press, 1963.

57 Report of the Committee on Homosexual Offences and Prostitution (CMD 247) 1957 (*The Wolfenden Report*).

58 *Bowers* v. *Hardwick*, 478 U.S. 186.

59 The strongest claims to this effect have been made by M. Sandel, *Liberalism and the Limits of Justice*, Cambridge, Cambridge University Press, 1982.

60 The term is Ronald Dworkin's, used in 'Liberal Community', *California Law Review*, 1989, vol. 77, pp. 479–504, to characterize one argument of his communitarian opponents.

61 Ibid., p. 497. (I confess: this reader's imagination runs riot in contemplation of Dworkin's simile. Is he teasing his opponent? His po-faced prose makes it hard to tell.)

62 L.B. Schwartz, 'Morals Offences and the Model Penal Code', *Columbia Law Review*, 1963, vol. LXIII, pp. 680, cited in J. Feinberg, *Social Philosophy*, p. 43.

63 J. Waldron, 'Rushdie and Religion', in *Liberal Rights*, Cambridge, Cambridge University Press, 1993, p. 142, first published in the *Times Literary Supplement*, March 10–16, 1989, pp. 248, 260, as 'Too Important for Tact'.

64 Ibid., pp. 140–1.

65 J.S. Mill, *On Liberty*, Ch. 1, p. 73.

66 Ibid.

67 Ibid., Ch. V, p. 152.

68 Ibid.

69 One can't conduct this sort of discussion without giving offence. Readers who are fond of these pastimes, please accept my apologies, and note, appropriately for a discussion of paternalism, that the list contains at least one self-inflicted wound.

70 W. Burroughs, *Junkie*, Paris, The Olympia Press, 1966.

71 I accept that this is a caricature of the poorly understood phenomena of addiction.

72 J.S. Mill, *On Liberty*, Ch. 1, pp. 65–72, for his account of the 'tyranny of the majority'.

73 Ibid., Ch. 5, pp. 164–70.

4 Rights

1 In recent years a modern version of natural law theory has been worked out by John Finnis, *Natural Law and Natural Right*, Oxford, Clarendon Press, 1980.
2 J. Bentham, 'A Critical Examination of the Declaration of Rights', in B. Parekh (ed.), *Bentham's Political Thought*, pp. 258–69. Also 'Anarchical Fallacies', in J. Waldron (ed.), *Nonsense upon Stilts. Bentham, Burke and Marx on the Rights of Man*, London, Methuen, 1987.
3 H.L.A. Hart, *Law, Liberty and Morality*, pp. 17–25.
4 W.E. Hohfeld, *Fundamental Legal Conceptions as Applied in Judicial Reasoning*, New Haven, Yale University Press, 1923. Hohfeld's classification is discussed usefully in J. Feinberg, *Social Philosophy*, Ch. 4, and J. Waldron (ed.), *Theories of Rights*, Oxford, Oxford University Press, 1984, 'Introduction'. Scholars of jurisprudence have refined Hohfeld's analysis in an ever more sophisticated fashion.
5 T. Hobbes, *Leviathan*, Ch. 14, p. 189.
6 'Rights of action' is D.D. Raphael's terminology. They are contrasted, in his analysis, with 'rights of recipience'. See D.D. Raphael, *Problems of Political Philosophy*, London, Macmillan, 1970, pp. 68–9.
7 Joseph Raz defines rights in terms of their constituting a sufficient reason for holding some other person(s) to be under a duty. See *The Morality of Freedom*, p. 166 and Ch. 7 generally.
8 Raz claims, plausibly, that there is no closed list of duties corresponding to each particular right. 'This dynamic aspect of rights, their ability to create new duties, is fundamental to any understanding of their nature and function in practical thought', *The Morality of Freedom*, p. 171.
9 J. Waldron, *The Right to Private Property*, Oxford, Clarendon Press, 1988, Ch. 4. Waldron is sharpening a similar distinction drawn initially by H.L.A. Hart, in 'Are there any Natural Rights?', *Philosophical Review*, 1955, vol. LXIV(2), pp. 175–91, repr. in J. Waldron (ed.), *Theories of Rights*.
10 H.L.A. Hart, 'Natural Rights', in J. Waldron (ed.), *Theories of Rights*, pp. 77–8.
11 This line of criticism is taken by Maurice Cranston, *What are Human Rights?*, London, Bodley Head, 1973. The discussion that follows echoes arguments from Henry Shue, *Basic Rights*, Princeton, N.J., Princeton University Press, 1980. A digest of

Shue's central arguments is available in R.E. Goodin and P. Pettit (eds.), *Contemporary Political Philosophy*, Oxford, Blackwell, 1997, pp. 341–55.

12 Jeremy Waldron argues along these lines in 'Participation: The Right of Rights', *Proceedings of the Aristotelian Society*, 1998, vol. XCVIII, pp. 307–37.

13 J. Waldron, *Theories of Rights*, 'Introduction', p. 7.

14 J. Waldron, *The Right to Private Property*, Ch. 2.

15 An account of the different elements of the right to private property is given in A.M. Honoré, 'Ownership', in A.G. Guest (ed.), *Oxford Essays in Jurisprudence*, Oxford, Oxford University Press, 1961.

16 G.W.F. Hegel, *Philosophy of Right*, §§40, 46, 63, R. Tuck, *Natural Rights Theories*, Cambridge, Cambridge University Press, 1979.

17 G.W.F. Hegel, *Philosophy of Right*, §36.

18 R. Nozick, *Anarchy, State and Utopia*, p. 57.

19 The Marxist case against human rights is presented in J. Waldron (ed.), *Nonsense upon Stilts*. The socialist critique of rights is discussed (and a socialist defence of rights mounted) in Tom Campbell, *The Left and Rights*, London, Routledge and Kegan Paul, 1983.

20 Canonical texts of modern communitarianism include Charles Taylor, 'Atomism', in *Philosophical Papers*, vol. II, Cambridge, Cambridge University Press, 1985; Alasdair MacIntyre, *After Virtue*, London, Duckworth, 1981; Michael Sandel, *Liberalism and the Limits of Justice*, Cambridge, Cambridge University Press, 1982. It is fair to say that the variety of forms taken by modern communitarian writings developed as criticisms of modern liberalism. The main contours of these debates are usefully reviewed in S. Mulhall and A. Swift, *Liberals and Communitarians*, Oxford, Blackwell, 1992.

21 The phrase comes from Michael Sandel, 'The Procedural Republic and the Unencumbered Self', *Political Theory*, 1984, vol. 12, pp. 81–96, repr. in R.E. Goodin and P. Pettit (eds), *Contemporary Political Philosophy*, pp. 247–55.

22 The distinction of exclusive and inclusive rights has been put to interesting use in the interpretation of Locke's views on property by James Tully, *A Discourse on Property*, Cambridge, Cambridge University Press, 1980.

23 The cases that follow are discussed in W. Kymlicka, *Multicultural Citizenship*, pp. 158–70. A useful survey of the philosophical problems concerning group rights may be found in A. Buchanan,

'Liberalism and Group Rights', in J.L. Coleman and A. Buchanan (eds), *In Harm's Way: Essays in Honor of Joel Feinberg*, Cambridge, Cambridge University Press, 1994, pp. 1–15.

24 J. Locke, *Second Treatise*, Ch. 2, §6. For the theology underpinning this argument, see J. Dunn, *The Political Thought of John Locke*, Cambridge, Cambridge University Press, 1969.

25 J. Locke, *Second Treatise*, §27.

26 R. Nozick, *Anarchy, State and Utopia*, pp. 169–70.

27 G.A. Cohen, 'Self-ownership, World-ownership, and Equality: Part II', *Social Philosophy and Policy*, 1986, vol. 3.

28 This debate was one of the sub-texts of the development of liberalism. Rousseau, to take one classical example, savages Grotius, arguing that no rational agent would choose slavery (*Social Contract*, Bk 1, Ch. IV). Robert Nozick, to select a modern thinker, believes the opposite (*Anarchy, State and Utopia*, p. 331).

29 H.L.A. Hart, 'Are there any Natural Rights?', p. 175.

30 I argued in Ch. 3 that any account of autonomy which explains why it is valuable must be a good deal more cluttered than this – and I will return to the point in what follows.

31 This 'Choice Theory' of rights was advanced (and subsequently retracted) by H.L.A. Hart in 'Are there any Natural Rights?' It is discussed in Tom Campbell, *The Left and Rights*, pp. 87–9 and J. Waldron, *The Right to Private Property*, pp. 95–8.

32 Richard Dagger, *Civic Virtues: Rights, Citizenship and Republican Liberalism*, Cambridge, Cambridge University Press, 1997, p. 31.

33 Ibid.

34 J.L. Mackie (not a Kantian) tentatively advanced a thesis similar to this in 'Can there be a Rights-based Moral Theory?', in P.A. French, T.E. Uehling, Jr and H.K. Wettstein (eds), *Studies in Ethical Theory*, Midwest Studies in Philosophy, 1978, vol. 3, repr. in J. Waldron (ed.), *Theories of Rights*, pp. 168–81. In the latter volume, pp. 182–200, 'Rights-based Moralities', J. Raz rejects this claim.

35 Mill, *Utilitarianism*, Ch. 5, p. 50.

36 Ibid.

37 L.W. Sumner, *The Moral Foundation of Rights*, Oxford, Clarendon Press, 1987, pp. 8–9.

38 Can one have an interest one doesn't recognize or even disavow? Such issues are canvassed, with further references, in J. Waldron, *The Right to Private Property*, pp. 87–92 and J. Raz, *The Morality of Freedom*, pp. 180–3.

39 Aristotle, *Politics*, trans. E. Barker, Oxford, Clarendon Press, 1946, I, 2, 1253a3, 1253a7, III, 6, 1278b19.

40 T. Hobbes, *Leviathan*, Ch. 13, p. 188.

41 G.W.F. Hegel, *Philosophy of Right*, §§182–7, for a summary.

42 The agreement to establish this court was signed by 120 nations. Seven nations opposed the institution. The blacklist included the governments of Algeria, China, Iran, Iraq, Libya, Sudan and the United States. For details, and a discussion of American policy ('an embarrassing low point for a government that portrays itself as a champion of human rights'), see K. Roth, 'The Court the US Doesn't Want', *The New York Review of Books*, November 1998, vol. XLV(18), pp. 45–7, cited at p. 45.

43 Consequentialist defences of moral rights are advanced in L.W. Sumner, *The Moral Foundations of Rights*, Ch. 6 and T.M. Scanlon, 'Rights, Goals and Fairness', *Erkenntnis*, 1977, vol. II, pp. 81–94, repr. in J. Waldron (ed.), *Theories of Rights*, pp. 137–52.

44 J. Rawls, *A Theory of Justice*, p. 191.

45 R. Nozick, *Anarchy, State and Utopia*, p. 33. On 'side-constraints', see pp. 29–35.

46 J.S. Mill, *Utilitarianism*, Ch. V, p. 58.

47 R. Dworkin, 'Rights as Trumps', in J. Waldron (ed.), *Theories of Rights*, pp. 153–67, adapted from R. Dworkin, 'Is there a Right to Pornography?', *Oxford Journal of Legal Studies*, 1981, vol. 1, pp. 177–212, repr. in R. Dworkin, *A Matter of Principle*, Cambridge, Mass. and London, Harvard University Press, 1985, pp. 335–72.

48 David Lyons, 'Utility and Rights', in J.R. Pennock and J.W. Chapman (eds), *Ethics, Economics and the Law: Nomos XXIV*, New York, New York University Press, 1982, pp. 107–38, repr. in D. Lyons, *Rights, Welfare and Mill's Moral Theory*, Oxford, Oxford University Press, 1994, pp. 147–75 and J. Waldron, *Theories of Rights*, pp. 110–36.

49 Alan Gewirth defends this position in 'Are there any Absolute Rights?', *Philosophical Quarterly*, 1981, vol. 31, pp. 1–16, repr. in J. Waldron, *Theories of Rights*, pp. 91–109. Nozick hopes to avoid the issue of whether rights may be violated 'in order to avoid catastrophic moral horror' (*Anarchy, State and Utopia*, p. 30 n.). Lyons accepts that moral rights may be outweighed by *very substantial* utilities or disutilities (*Rights, Welfare*, pp. 156–8).

50 Arthur C. Danto, 'Constructing an Epistemology of Human Rights: A Pseudo-problem?', in E.F. Paul, J. Paul and F.D. Miller, Jr. (eds), *Human Rights*, Oxford, Blackwell, 1984, p. 30. Danto is criticizing Gewirth's attempt to found rights in the neccessities of human agency. I believe this no-theory theory is central to Hegel's discussion of rights in the 'Abstract Right' section of the *Philosophy of*

Right – for countless historical reasons, folk nowadays just claim them as consequent on the moral status of *person* that they have insisted on conferring on themselves and others whose moral status they recognize. But I expect this reading to be controversial.

5 Distributive justice

1 G.W.F. Hegel, *Philosophy of Right*, §185.
2 For a utilitarian approach, see P. Singer, *Practical Ethics*, Cambridge, Cambridge University Press, 1979. For a Kantian approach, see O. O'Neill, *Faces of Hunger: An Essay on Poverty, Justice and Development*, London, Allen and Unwin, 1986. For contractualist approaches, see C.R. Beitz, *Political Theory and International Relations*, Princeton, N.J., Princeton University Press, 1979, and T. Pogge, *Realising Rawls*, Ithaca, N.Y., Cornell University Press, 1989.
3 R. Nozick, *Anarchy, State and Utopia*, p. 151.
4 Ibid., p. 153.
5 Ibid., p. 153.
6 To use Waldron's language, a legitimate property holding always requires the validation of some *special* rights claim. If so, a theory of distributive justice necessarily grounds such claims. If so, one of Waldron's major theses: that special rights arguments cannot be appealed to in the defence of a specific allocation of private property since it is vulnerable to the claims of *general* rights, cannot be defended, since it is a proper requirement of an acceptable general rights argument that it detail which special rights claims are legitimate. Nozick assumes, wrongly, that the dialectic begins with the vindication of special rights claims. Waldron concludes, wrongly, that special rights-based arguments have no distinctive place in the justification of a system of property holdings. See J. Waldron, *The Right to Private Property*, Chs 4, 7.
7 R. Nozick, *Anarchy, State and Utopia*, p. 161.
8 Ibid., p. 163.
9 Ibid., p. 169.
10 This point is stressed by J. Waldron, *The Right to Private Property*, pp. 266ff., and endorsed by Leif Wenar in 'Original Acquisition of Private Property', *Mind*, 1998, vol. 107, pp. 799–819.
11 J. Locke, *Second Treatise*, §25.
12 R. Nozick, *Anarchy, State and Utopia*, pp. 174–5.
13 In what follows, I reproduce the argument of D. Knowles, 'Autonomy and Side-constraints', *Mind*, 1979, vol. LXXXVIII, pp. 263–5.

14 I. Kant, *Groundwork*, pp. 90–3, Academy edn., Kritik der Reinen Vernunft (I. Auflage), ed. B. Erdmann, Kant's gesammelte Schriften, herausgegeben von der Königlich Preußischen Akademie der Wissenschaften, Band IV (edited by the Royal Prussian Academy of Sciences, vol. IV), pp. 428–31.

15 For a discussion of Kant's view of non-human nature see papers by Allen W. Wood and Onora O'Neill, 'Kant on Duties Regarding Nonrational Nature', *Proceedings of the Aristotelian Society*, 1998, Supp. vol. LXXII, pp. 189–228.

16 G.W.F. Hegel, *The Philosophy of Right*, §§34–69. For discussion, see D. Knowles, 'Hegel on Property and Personality', *Philosophical Quarterly*, 1983, vol. 33, Allen W. Wood, *Hegel's Ethical Thought*, Cambridge, Cambridge University Press, 1990, Ch. 5 and J. Waldron, *The Right to Private Property*, Ch. 10.

17 In a work like this which concentrates on the topics and puzzles that comprise the agenda of political philosophy, it is hard to detach Hayek's views on the problems in hand in a way that does not distort them through abstracting from their linkages to his positions elsewhere. The discussion that follows will amount to crude surgery, so I remedy the injustice to Hayek by recommending that readers follow up his other writings. Brief but well-judged accounts of Hayek's contribution to political philosophy can be found in R. Plant, *Modern Political Thought*, pp. 80–97 and M.H. Lessnoff, *Political Philosophers of the Twentieth Century*, Oxford, Blackwell, 1999, pp. 146–75. The most important primary sources are *The Road to Serfdom*, London, Routledge and Kegan Paul, 1974, *The Constitution of Liberty*, London, Routledge and Kegan Paul, 1960 and *Law, Legislation and Liberty*, Routledge and Kegan Paul, 1982 (published in three vols, 1973, 1976 and 1979).

18 F.A. Hayek, *Law, Legislation and Liberty*, pp. xv–xvi. and vol. 2, throughout.

19 *Ibid.*. vol. 2, pp. 35–42.

20 F.A. Hayek, *The Constitution of Liberty*, Ch. 19.

21 T. Hobbes, *Leviathan*, Ch. 18, p. 234. Michael Lessnoff has argued, intriguingly, that *all* property is social property in a genuine democracy, because it is subject to the powers of the (democratic) sovereign. M.H. Lessnoff, 'Capitalism, Socialism and Democracy', *Political Studies*, 1979, vol. XXVII, pp. 594–602.

22 K. Marx, *1844 Manuscripts*, in *Early Writings*, trans. R. Livingstone and G. Benton, Harmondsworth, Penguin, 1975, pp. 328–9.

23 Centrally but not always. Intellectual property, e.g. patents and copyright, is an exception.

24 D. Hume, *Treatise*, Bk III, Part II; *Second Enquiry*, Section III. Hume believed that a system of rules governing property amounted to a system of justice so long as both the system and its constituent rules promoted utility.
25 G.W.F. Hegel, *Philosophy of Right*, §§190–5. Hegel's terminology is not careless. He regards the transformation of natural needs into 'social' needs as a distinctive (and liberating) feature of the modern world.
26 The argument is taken from A.R. White, *Modal Thinking*, Oxford, Blackwell, 1971, pp. 110–14. It is widely used. See also D. Wiggins, 'The Claims of Need', in *Needs, Values, Truth*, Oxford, Blackwell, 1987, p. 6. My adjudication of this argument agrees with the chief lines of R. Plant's discussion in *Modern Political Thought*, Oxford, Blackwell, 1991, Ch. 5.
27 This objection is put by Brian Barry in *Political Argument*, London, Routledge and Kegan Paul, 1965, pp. 47–9. The reply I offer draws on D. Wiggins, 'Claims of Need', in *Needs, Values, Truth*, pp. 6–11.
28 Ibid., p. 10.
29 Ibid.
30 These categories summarize crudely Wiggins's discussion, Ibid., pp. 11–16.
31 Griffin, *Well-being*, pp. 41–7, 51–3.
32 For the principle, see D. Braybrooke, *Meeting Needs*, Princeton, N.J., Princeton University Press, 1987, pp. 60–75. Further references are given at p. 314.
33 Or what the author describes as (a suggestive, though tentative and incomplete) list of course-of-life needs. The list that follows is cited from Braybrooke, *Meeting Needs*, p. 36. Another list – of central human functioning capabilities – is provided by Martha Nussbaum, *Sex and Social Justice*, pp. 41–2.
34 Notable contributions to these debates include Peter Singer, 'Famine, Affluence and Morality', *Philosophy and Public Affairs*, 1992, vol. 1, pp. 229–43 and *Practical Ethics*, Cambridge, Cambridge University Press, 1979, Onora O'Neill, *Faces of Hunger*, London, Allen and Unwin, 1986.
35 A.K. Sen, *Inequality Re-examined*, Oxford, Clarendon Press, 1992, p. ix.
36 A.K. Sen, 'Equality of What?', in S.M. McMurrin (ed.), *The Tanner Lectures on Human Values*, vol. 1, Cambridge, Cambridge University Press, 1980, pp. 195–220, repr. in Robert E. Goodin and Philip Pettit (eds), *Contemporary Political Philosophy*.

37 J. Rawls, *A Theory of Justice*, p. 62. I shall discuss Rawls's theory in more detail later.

38 Ibid., p. 76. The quotation is amended from the two-person case Rawls describes.

39 A.K. Sen, *Inequality*, p. 20.

40 A.K. Sen, 'Equality of What?', p. 478.

41 *Hymns, Ancient and Modern*, No. 573, 'All things bright and beautiful'.

42 This phenomenon, whereby individuals shape their desires in accordance with the options realistically available, has been dubbed 'adaptive preference formation' by John Elster. It is discussed in John Elster, *Sour Grapes*, Cambridge, Cambridge University Press, 1983. Sen discusses the impact of these considerations on the metric of equality in *Inequality*, pp. 6–7, 54–5. Martha Nussbaum refers to this material in discussing the condition of women in 'American Women: Preferences, Feminism, Democracy', *Sex and Social Justice*, pp. 130–53.

43 A.K. Sen, *Inequality*, p. 44.

44 For a sensitive and clear-sighted discussion of these difficulties, see Thomas Nagel, *Equality and Partiality*, Oxford, Oxford University Press, 1991, esp. Chs 10–11.

45 J.-J. Rousseau, *Social Contract*, Bk 1, Ch. IX, footnote.

46 J. Rawls, *Political Liberalism*, New York, Columbia University Press, 1993.

47 Rawls disavows such a wide ambition, but I believe his practice belies his explicit modesty. See *Theory of Justice*, pp. 7–11.

48 R. Dworkin, 'The Original Position', in N. Daniels (ed.), *Reading Rawls*, Oxford, Blackwell, 1975, pp. 16–53, cited at p. 18.

49 See Rawls, *Theory of Justice*, Ch. VI.

50 Ibid., pp. 130–4.

51 Ibid., p. 18.

52 Ibid., p. 19.

53 T. Hobbes, *Leviathan*, Ch. X.

54 Rawls steps carefully round these questions in *Political Liberalism*, New York, Columbian University Press, 1993, pp. 182–6.

55 J. Rawls, *Theory of Justice*, p. 137.

56 Ibid.

57 Such claims have been developed at book length by William A. Galston, *Liberal Purposes*, Cambridge, Cambridge University Press, 1991 and George Sher, *Beyond Neutrality*, Cambridge, Cambridge University Press, 1997. Rawls's statement of the priority of the right over the good is found at *Theory of Justice*, pp. 31–2. He

articulates, some would say amends, his view at length in *Political Liberalism*. See especially Lecture V, pp. 173–211.

58 Thomas Nagel, 'Rawls on Justice', *Philosophical Review*, 1973, vol. LXXXII, pp. 220–34, repr. in N. Daniels (ed.), *Reading Rawls*. See the latter at pp. 6–10.

59 The general conception and the two principles are cited in their final versions from *Theory of Justice*, pp. 302–3.

60 This formal statement (*Theory of Justice*, p. 152), conceals some dreadful social choices which have been the occasion of anguished historical judgement. Isaac Deutscher, considering whether Russia could have emerged from barbarism by using less barbarous means, is a celebrated example. See in particular the final two chapters of I. Deutscher, *Stalin: A Political Biography*, rev. edn, Harmondsworth, Penguin, 1966.

61 Rawls, *Political Liberalism*, p. 187.

62 Those wishing to take the matter further should note the significant alterations in the principle as stated in *Political Liberalism*, Lecture VIII (at p. 291), in response to the criticisms of H.L.A. Hart, in particular. See H.L.A. Hart, 'Rawls on Liberty and its Priority', *University of Chicago Law Review*, 1973, vol. 40, pp. 534–55, repr. in N. Daniels (ed.), *Reading Rawls*, pp. 230–52.

63 Rawls deploys a battery of arguments against average utility, as a principle one might select in the original position. See *Theory of Justice*, §§ 28–9. The case for average utility is made by J.C. Harsanyi, 'Cardinal Utility in Welfare Economics and the Theory of Risk Taking', *Journal of Political Economy*, 1953, vol. 61, and, discussing Rawls, 'Morality and the Theory of Rational Behaviour', in A.K. Sen and B. Williams (eds), *Utilitarianism and Beyond*, Cambridge, Cambridge University Press, 1982.

64 Is envy a feature of human nature that can't be eradicated by honest and careful reflection? Perhaps it is, but so too, one might think, is the docile and unquestioning acceptance of traditional inequalities, the poor-man-at-the-gate syndrome noted earlier.

65 Rawls, *Theory of Justice*, p. 440.

66 Ibid., p. 4.

67 T. Scanlon, 'Contractualism and Utilitarianism', in A.K. Sen and B. Williams (eds), *Utilitarianism and Beyond*. So far as I can see, specific questions concerning justice are not addressed in Scanlon's recent book, *What We Owe to Each Other*, Cambridge, Mass., Harvard University Press, 1999.

68 This point is made by T. Nagel, *Equality and Partiality*, pp. 38–40. Does Rawls accept Scanlon's version of contractualism, which

NOTES

rejects the apparatus of the original position, the veil of ignorance, and consequently, maximin reasoning governing choice under conditions of uncertainty? In *Political Liberalism*, despite commendatory remarks, he doesn't say.

69 To my knowledge, Rawls does not express a clear view as to whether private ownership of the means of production or some variety of socialism (common ownership by the community or by workers in firms are two different models) is best. The contours of the property system will be dilineated by 'the traditions, institutions, and social forces of each country, and its particular historical circumstances', *Theory of Justice*, p. 274. He *does* argue for a market system of fixing prices (ibid., pp. 270–4) and favours a property-owning democracy wherein property includes 'productive assets'. If 'productive assets' mean tools and raw materials, the idea is quaint; if it means stocks and shares, the ideal is underdescribed. So far as the *powers* of private shareholders in public companies are concerned, they may as well be given cash. See J. Rawls, 'Preface for the French Edition of *A Theory of Justice*', in J. Rawls, *Collected Papers*, ed. S. Freeman, Cambridge, Mass., Harvard University Press, 1999, p. 419.

70 So I claim. Rawls himself distinguishes the idea of the 'welfare state' from that of the 'property-owning democracy', endorsing the latter and rejecting the former: the welfare state may allow such 'large and inheritable inequalities of wealth [as are] incompatible with the fair value of equal liberties . . . as well as large disparities of income that violate the difference principle' (ibid.). Would that these terms were so well defined that such distinctions could be confidently drawn!

71 This objection is put by R. Nozick, *Anarchy, State and Utopia*, pp. 213–27, David Miller, *Social Justice*, Oxford, Clarendon Press, 1976, pp. 46–8 and Ronald Dworkin, 'What is Equality? Part I: Equality of Welfare; Part II: Equality of Resources', *Philosophy and Public Affairs*, 1981, vol. 10, pp. 185–246, 283–345.

72 For a full-length treatment, see George Sher, *Desert*, Princeton, N.J., Princeton University Press, 1987.

73 J. Rawls, *Theory of Justice*, p. 101.

74 Ibid., pp. 303–10.

75 Important contributions to this literature include: A. MacIntyre, *After Virtue*, London, Duckworth, 1981; C. Taylor, 'Atomism', in *Philosophy and the Human Sciences*, vol. 2 of *Philosophical Papers* and 'Cross-purposes: The Liberal–Communitarian Debate', in N. Rosenblum (ed.), *Liberalism and the Moral Life*, Cambridge, Mass.,

Harvard University Press, 1989; M. Sandel, *Liberalism and the Limits of Justice*, Cambridge, Cambridge University Press, 1982; M. Walzer, *Spheres of Justice*, Oxford, Blackwell, 1983. Valuable reviews of these debates are found in W. Kymlicka, *Liberalism, Community and Culture*, Oxford, Clarendon Press, 1989 and S. Mulhall and A. Swift, *Liberals and Communitarians*, Oxford, Blackwell, 1992. The classical source of communitarianism is Aristotle's *Politics*, of modern communitarianism, G.W.F. Hegel, *Philosophy of Right*, §§ 142–57.

6 Political obligation

1 I introduce the qualification here to avoid the implication of legal positivism that any formally authoritative legal prescription gives rise to a legal obligation. Thus, in the case of an unjust law one may have a legal obligation, but no moral obligation, to comply. The issue is too large to broach. Classic modern sources include H.L.A. Hart, *The Concept of Law*, Oxford, Clarendon Press, 1961, L. Fuller, *The Morality of Law*, New Haven, Yale University Press, 1969 and R. Dworkin, *Taking Rights Seriously*, London, Duckworth, 1977.

2 Leslie Green distinguishes the questions of whether the state has legitimate authority from the question of whether citizens have a political obligation by claiming that political obligation is an obligation held by *all* citizens to obey *all* laws. It is 'doubly universal'. By contrast the state may have authority under limited conditions which do not require it to have authority over all persons. See L. Green, *The Authority of the State*, Oxford, Clarendon Press, 1988, pp. 228–40, cited at p. 228. Likewise, Joseph Raz argues for the 'separateness of the issues of (1) the authority of the state; (2) the scope of its justified power; (3) the obligation to support just institutions; (4) the obligation to obey the law', J. Raz, *The Morality of Freedom*, Oxford, Clarendon Press, 1986, p. 104. I judge these matters to be controversial, but have tried not to beg any questions by my use of this range of terminology. Where a substantial philosophical conclusion is at stake, I try to argue the point. Thus, for example, I reject the claim that political obligation is 'doubly universal'.

3 We shall examine this assumption later.

4 Poor Shaw published the quaintly named *Ladies Directory*, giving names, addresses, photographs and listing the special skills of prostitutes. There's an Internet fortune awaiting Shaw's successor.

His case is discussed in H.L.A. Hart, *Law, Liberty and Morality*, pp. 6–12, citing the judgements at (1961) 2 A.E.R. 446 and (1962) A.C. 223.

5 The importance of this purpose to civil disobedience is stressed by Peter Singer, *Democracy and Disobedience*, London, Oxford University Press, 1974, pp. 72–84.

6 T. Hobbes, *Leviathan*, Chs 17–18, quoted at pp. 227 and 230.

7 I ignore the complications introduced in Ch. 29 of *Leviathan*, where Hobbes discusses the dissolution of the sovereign power and the consequent dissolution of citizens' duties. See also Ch. 21, pp. 272–4, where Hobbes discusses cases in which subjects are absolved of their obedience to the sovereign.

8 J. Locke, *Second Treatise*, §6.

9 This matter is well discussed in J. Hampton, *Hobbes and the Social Contract Tradition*, Cambridge, Cambridge University Press, 1986.

10 T. Hobbes, *Leviathan*, Ch. 13, p. 186.

11 Ibid., Ch. 18, p. 238.

12 I. Kant, *The Critique of Pure Reason*, trans. and ed. P. Guyer and A.W. Wood, Cambridge, Cambridge University Press, 1998, pp. 100–1, p. Axii.: *Kritik der reinen Vernunft* (1. *Auflage*), ed. B. Erdmann, *Kant's gesammelte Schriften*, herausgegeben von der Königlich Preußischen Akademie der Wissenschaften, Band IV (edited by the Royal Prussian Academy of Sciences, vol. IV), Berlin, Georg Reimer, 1911.

13 For a useful compendium of anarchist writings, see G. Woodcock, *The Anarchist Reader*, London, Fontana, 1977. For a history of anarchism, see G. Woodcock, *Anarchism*, Harmondsworth, Penguin, 1963. Two useful philosophical discussions of this tradition are A. Carter, *The Political Theory of Anarchism*, London, Routledge and Kegan Paul, 1971 and D. Miller, *Anarchism*, London, J.M. Dent, 1984.

14 M. Weber, *From Max Weber: Essays in Sociology*, trans. and ed. H.H. Gerth and C.W. Mills, London, Routledge and Kegan Paul, 1946, p. 78.

15 J.-J. Rousseau, *A Discourse on the Origin of Inequality*, in *The Social Contract and Discourses*, p. 45. See also pp. 65–6.

16 S. Milgram, *Obedience to Authority*, London, Tavistock, 1974. This work is summarized in S. Milgram, article on 'Obedience', in Richard L. Gregory (ed.), *The Oxford Companion to the Mind*, Oxford, Oxford University Press, 1987.

17 J.S. Mill, *On Liberty*, Ch. 3. Mill may be the wrong authority to invoke here. A critic (Pat Shaw) suggests that the Milgram effect

may be worse in liberal regimes than authoritarian ones. In the latter, folks may obey only when they have to! A dismal, but cautionary thought.

18 Michael Taylor's books defend anarchism in a fashion that is both philosophically sophisticated and sociologically alert. See *Anarchy and Cooperation*, London, Wiley, 1976, 2nd edn published as *The Possibility of Cooperation*, Cambridge, Cambridge University Press, 1987 and *Community, Anarchy and Liberty*, Cambridge, Cambridge University Press, 1982.

19 I remember from my youth (the reference long vanished) an anarchist tract which compared two postwar refugee camps in East Anglia, one anarchic, the other controlled by a local version of Colonel Blimp. Guess which was the happier, healthier and more productive!

20 R.P. Wolff, *In Defense of Anarchism*, 2nd edn, New York, Harper, 1976, p. 15.

21 Wolff's striking thesis was immediately challenged by J. Reiman, *In Defense of Political Philosophy*, New York, Harper and Row, 1972. Wolff replied in the 2nd edn of *In Defense of Anarchism*. The issue is carefully reviewed in L. Green, *The Authority of the State*, pp. 24–36.

22 The bones of the communitarian application of social metaphysics to the relationship of citizens to the state is presented in M. Sandel, 'The Procedural Republic and the Unencumbered Self', *Political Theory*, 1984, vol. 12, pp. 81–96, repr. in R.E. Goodin and P. Pettit (eds), *Contemporary Political Philosophy: An Anthology*. In *Liberalism and the Limits of Justice*, Sandel advances his views indirectly by way of criticism of Kant, J.S. Mill and Rawls. What story does he tell of allegiance or patriotism – of whatever we may identify as the sentiment distinctive of identification with a *political* community? On my reading: none. He tells us about family life, supposing this to be analogous to the state in respect of the relation of member to association – a hopeless strategy in the absence of an argument that the state is a natural association. G.W.F. Hegel, *Philosophy of Right*, should be the canonical source, explaining the metaphysics of social life in terms of existent normative orders being structures of the free will.

23 G.W.F. Hegel, *Philosophy of Right*. In respect of ethical life generally see §149, 'The individual finds his *liberation* in duty'. Applying this thought to family life, he writes of marriage partners, that 'In this respect [they give up "their natural and individual personalities"] their union is a self-limitation, but since they attain their

substantial self-consciousness within it, it is in fact their liberation.' (§162).

24 Ibid., Preface, p. 20.
25 T. McPherson, *Political Obligation*, London, Routledge and Kegan Paul, 1967, p. 64.
26 H. Pitkin, 'Obligation and Consent', *American Political Science Review*, 1965, vols LIX(4), and LX(1), repr. in P. Laslett, W.G. Runciman and Q. Skinner (eds), *Philosophy, Politics and Society, Fourth Series*, Oxford, Blackwell, 1972, cited at p. 78.
27 I stress: 'those I have dubbed "communitarians".' As I have remarked several times before, I don't purport to identify a specific school of thinkers, nor implicate specific authors beyond those to whom I refer explicitly.
28 For readers who are sceptical of my invocation of Hegel, I recommend that they study §§129–35 of the *Philosophy of Right*, noting in particular his claim that 'The *right of the subjective will* is that whatever it is to recognize as valid should be *perceived* by it *as good*,' Hegel, *The Philosophy of Right*, §132.
29 J.-J. Rousseau, *A Discourse on the Origin of Inequality*, pp. 93–4.
30 Ibid., p. 96.
31 T. Hobbes, *Leviathan*, Ch. 17, p. 227.
32 All these phrases are used in the *Second Treatise* at §95.
33 Rousseau may be. Hobbes and Locke are not, on my reading of them. Since large interpretative questions are at stake, I shall suppose that they are describing possible events. The hypothetical version of the argument will be tackled later.
34 John Locke, *Second Treatise*, §119.
35 Ibid., §121.
36 Hume first uses this argument in the *Treatise*, Bk III, §VIII. It is repeated, forcefully, in his essay, 'Of the Original Contract', in D. Hume, *Essays*.
37 J. Locke, *Second Treatise*, §121.
38 D. Hume, 'Of the Original Contract', in *Essays*, p. 462.
39 P. Singer, *Democracy and Disobedience*, pp. 45–59.
40 Ibid., pp. 48–9. As a reading of Locke this is unconvincing. He cannot be supposing that one is thinking of his obligations all the time that he is accepting the benefits of the state, or worse, all the time that he is not dissenting.
41 Ibid., p. 50.
42 This is the theme of Part II of Singer's book.
43 The story is told by P. Singer, *Democracy and Disobedience*, pp. 53–4.

44 According to Jonathan Wolff, this is 'the central problem of political obligation . . . [that of] accounting for the obligations of those
   who do not consent', 'What is the Problem of Political Obligation?',
   Proceedings of the Aristotelian Society, 1990/1, vol. XCI, p. 154. I
   agree. This is the *hardest* and *most important* problem concerning
   political obligation because the onus of justification is placed on
   the state. By contrast, where actual consent of some variety is
   attested, the burden of proof is on those who would deny the normal implications of consent – which is not to say the issue is
   unproblematic, as we have seen.

45 R. Dworkin, 'The Original Position', in N. Daniels (ed.), *Reading
   Rawls*, p. 18.

46 This story has its origins in Hobbes's *Leviathan*, Rousseau's *Discourse on the Origins of Inequality* and James Mill's democratic
   reworking of Hobbes in his *Essay on Government*. It echoes elements of Nozick's argument in *Anarchy, State and Utopia*, Part I. In
   recent times, Jean Hampton has done most to revivify this traditional style of argument, see J. Hampton, *Hobbes and the Social
   Contract Tradition*; Cambridge, Cambridge University Press, 1986
   and *Political Philosophy*, Boulder, Col., Westview Press, 1997, Ch.
   3.

47 H.L.A. Hart, 'Are there any Natural Rights?', cited from J. Waldron
   (ed.), *Theories of Rights*, p. 85; J. Rawls, 'Legal Obligation and the
   Duty of Fair Play', in S. Hook (ed.), *Law and Philosophy*, New York,
   New York University Press, 1964; R. Nozick, *Anarchy, State and
   Utopia*, pp. 90–5; A.J. Simmons, *Moral Principles and Political
   Obligations*, Princeton, N.J., Princeton University Press, 1979, Ch.
   V; G. Klosko, *The Principle of Fairness and Political Obligation*,
   Lanham, Md, Rowan and Littlefield, 1992.

48 J.-J. Rousseau, *Discourse on the Origins of Inequality*, p. 93.

49 Claudia Card notices the inaptness of speaking of debts of grati-
   tude, claiming that the idea is paradoxical, hence metaphorical.
   See C. Card, 'Gratitude and Obligation', *American Philosophical
   Quarterly*, 1988, vol. 25, pp. 115–27.

50 This summarizes the argument of A.J. Simmons, *Moral Principles*,
   pp. 166–7.

51 'We are presumed to have a kind of control over our actions that we
   do not have over our feelings; we can, at least normally, *try* to act in
   specified ways where we cannot try to have certain emotions or
   feelings (in the same way). And surely part of the point of a moral
   requirement is that its content be the sort of thing which we can, at
   least normally, *try* to accomplish', ibid., p. 167.

52 A.J. Simmons, *Moral Principles*, p. 189. This argument is rejected by A.D.M. Walker, 'Political Obligation and the Argument from Gratitude', *Philosophy and Public Affairs*, 1988, vol. 17. Walker's paper is unusual in modern times in that it defends the gratitude argument. Most writers see it as a soft target.

53 This is Walker's view, 'Gratitude', p. 196.

54 T. Hobbes, *Leviathan*, Part 1, Ch. 15, p. 209.

7 Democracy

1 T. Hobbes, *Leviathan*, Ch. XIX, cited at p. 242. Hobbes's famous argument that the sovereign is the representative of the people, the actor who puts into effect the will of the subject authors, is outlined in Ch. XVI and is the major innovation of *Leviathan*. For James Mill's views, see *Essay on Government* (1819), Indianapolis, Liberal Arts Press, 1955, pp. 60–1.

2 J. Locke, *Second Treatise*, §138.

3 J.-J. Rousseau, *Discourse on the Origins of Inequality*, p. 86. This remark, as with so many of the sayings which attest Rousseau's genius, is cast to the swine with an insouciance which defies further elaboration. But Hegel picked it up (characteristically without acknowledgement) in one of the most famous and influential passages of *The Phenomenology of Spirit*, the dialectic of 'Master and Slave', which many believe to have been an enormous influence on Marx. See Hegel's *Phenomenology of Spirit*, trans. A.V. Miller, Oxford, Clarendon Press, 1979, ¶178–96, pp. 111–19.

4 This is the implication of the first sentence of Bk I, Ch. VI, 'The Social Compact', of the *The Social Contract*: 'I suppose men to have reached the point at which the obstacles in the way of their preservation in the state of nature show their power of resistance to be greater than the resources at the disposal of the individual for his maintenance in that state.'

5 Ibid., Bk I, Ch. VI, p. 175.

6 J.-J. Rousseau, *Discourse*, p. 54.

7 J.-J. Rousseau, *Social Contract*, Bk I, Ch. VII, p. 177.

8 Ibid., Bk I, Ch. VIII, p. 178.

9 See the discussion at Bk II, Ch. IV (and the comical footnote), pp. 186–9.

10 Ibid., Bk I, Ch. IX, p. 181.

11 Ibid., Bk II, Ch. XI, p. 204.

12 There is a large modern literature on this topic, beginning with

Anthony Downs, *An Economic Theory of Democracy*, New York, Harper and Row, 1957. There is a useful summary of arguments pro and con in Loren E. Lomasky and Geoffrey Brennan, 'Is there a Duty to Vote?': *Social Philosophy and Policy*, 2000, vol. 17(1), pp. 65–74.

13 J.-J. Rousseau, *Social Contract*, Bk II, Ch. III, p. 185.

14 J.-J. Rousseau, Ch. 2 of the original draft (the 'Geneva Manuscript') of the *Social Contract*, published in *The Social Contract and Discourses* as 'The General Society of the Human Race', cited at p. 160.

15 These and cognate terms excited much interest in the 1950s and 60s. Historians or elderly philosophers should be able to reconstruct the debates without looking up the references: is 'the common good' the familiar and universal nominalization of purposes that politicians commend or attitudes that they express (and if so, which?), or is it descriptive of policy objectives (and if so, what?). These questions should still excite interest (= philosophers' attention). That they don't, is, I suspect, due to the thoroughness of Brian Barry's investigations in *Political Argument*, London, Routledge and Kegan Paul, 1965, Chs X–XV. In political philosophy, careful linguistic analysis is still a valuable technique since its subject matter, political language, is (and will forever remain) a domain ruled by rhetorical techniques. The settling of questions of meaning or the exposure of concepts as essentially contestable is not the end of philosophy since conventional usage may embody falsehoods and contests which seem endemic may turn out to be resolvable.

16 J.S. Mill, *On Liberty*, Ch. II, pp. 80–9.

17 This is Condorcet's result. It is presented as a valuable supplement to Rousseau's argument by Brian Barry, *Political Argument*, Note (A), pp. 292–3. Barry refers to the full discussion in Duncan Black, *Theory of Committees and Elections*, Cambridge, Cambridge University Press, 1958, pp. 164–5.

18 T. Hobbes, *Leviathan*, Ch. 16.

19 J.-J. Rousseau, *The Social Contract*, Bk II, Ch. X, p. 203.

20 James Mill, *Essay on Government*, Ch. VI, p. 66.

21 Benjamin Barber takes the prospect of more direct democracy seriously in *Strong Democracy: Participatory Politics for a New Age*, Berkeley, University of California Press, 1984, though he is not an advocate of telephone voting.

22 John Stuart Mill saw real problems here. He believed firmly that electors should choose representatives who were wiser than

themselves, but 'how are they to judge, except by the standard of their own opinions . . . the tests by which an ordinary man can judge beforehand of mere ability are very imperfect', *Considerations on Representative Government* (1861), Ch. XII, in J.S. Mill, *Utilitarianism, Liberty, Representative Government*, p. 318. Interestingly, one element of his solution to this problem involved qualifications for voting powers among the electorate, the educated having multiple votes.

23 Plato, *The Republic*, trans. H.P.D. Lee, Harmondsworth, Penguin, 1955, Bk 7.

24 T. Hobbes, *Leviathan*, Ch. 3, p. 97.

25 J.S. Mill, *Representative Government*, pp. 249–50.

26 Rousseau, *The Social Contract*, Bk I, Ch. 6, p. 174.

27 Ibid., Bk II, Ch. IV, p. 187.

28 Ibid., Bk II, Ch. IV, p. 186.

29 J. Waldron, *Law and Disagreement*, Oxford, Clarendon Press, 1999, p. 15.

30 As Rousseau does. *The Social Contract*, Bk IV, Ch. VIII, p. 276.

31 This issue was raised by J. Cohen and J. Rogers, in *On Democracy*, Harmondsworth, Penguin, 1983, pp. 154–7. A powerful case in favour of restricting contributions was made by Ronald Dworkin in 'The Curse of American Politics', *New York Review of Books*, October 17, 1996, vol. XLIII(16), pp. 19–25 and the thought that money is a curse on democracy is endorsed by John Rawls in 'The Idea of Public Reason Revisited', in *Collected Papers*, ed. S. Freeman, Cambridge, Mass. and London, Harvard University Press, 1999, p. 580.

32 Berlin's pluralism surfaces in many of his essays and plays a notable role in the argument of 'Two Concepts of Liberty'. For a useful survey, analysis and endorsement of Berlin's views which draws together much of this diffuse material, see John Gray, *Isaiah Berlin*, London, Harper Collins, 1995, esp. Chs 2 and 6.

33 I distinguish value pluralism and value difference, since the distinction signals different strategies for resolving or accommodating the disagreements within the forums of democracy.

34 It is hard to chart the modern ancestry of this movement. Obvious sources include Jürgen Habermas's discourse ethics, notably *The Theory of Communicative Action*, Boston, Mass., Beacon Press, 1984; Rawls's 'Kantian Constructivism in Moral Theory', *Journal of Philosophy*, 1980, vol. 77, pp. 515–72, repr. in *Collected Papers*, ed. Freeman, pp. 303–58; and T.M. Scanlon, 'Contractualism and Utilitarianism', in A.K. Sen and B. Williams (eds), *Utilitarianism and*

Beyond, Cambridge, Cambridge University Press, 1982, pp. 103–28. Notable contributions include Joshua Cohen, 'Deliberation and Democratic Legitimacy', in A. Hamlin and P. Pettit (eds), *The Good Polity*, Oxford, Blackwell, 1989, pp. 17–34; 'Procedure and Substance in Deliberative Democracy', in S. Benhabib (ed.), *Democracy and Difference*, Princeton, N.J., Princeton University Press, 1996, pp. 95–119; and A. Gutmann and D. Thompson, *Democracy and Disagreement*, Cambridge, Mass., Harvard University Press, 1996.

35 Rawls first signals the importance of disagreement in his account of varying 'thick' conceptions of the good in *A Theory of Justice*. In subsequent essays (reconstructed as a monograph in *Political Liberalism*, New York, Columbia University Press, 1993, republished in J. Rawls, *Collected Papers*, Cambridge, Mass., Harvard University Press, 1999, Rawls suggests that the divergent elements of pluralism include both philosophical (normative) theories, including liberalism and utilitarianism, philosophical disputes, e.g. that between values of equality and liberty, and most serious of all, religious doctrines of the sort that generated the sixteenth- and seventeenth-century Wars of Religion in Europe (and fuel present-day conflicts in Afghanistan, Iraq, Algeria, Nigeria, Indonesia, India the former Yugoslavia and on and on . . .).

36 A. Gutmann and D. Thompson, *Democracy*, p. 53.

37 J. Cohen, 'Deliberation', p. 17.

38 J. Rawls, *Political Liberalism*, Lecture VI, pp. 212–54; 'The Idea of Public Reason Revisited', *University of Chicago Law Review*, 1997, vol. 64, pp. 765–807, repr. in *Collected Papers*, pp. 573–615.

39 A. Gutmann and D. Thompson, *Democracy*, pp. 63–9, cited at pp. 64 and 65.

40 John Rawls whistles in the wind in claiming that the right of a woman to an abortion in the first trimester is established by the political value of the equality of women as equal citizens. See the footnote discussion at pp. 243–4 of *Political Liberalism*. This is a strong consideration, but one does not need to look far to find reasonable citizens who accept this value but do not find it decisive in settling the matter.

41 The most impressive statement of a procedural conception of democracy has been Robert Dahl, most fully in *Democracy and its Critics*, New Haven, Yale University Press, 1989. Dahl's views have been criticized by J. Cohen, 'Procedure and Substance in Deliberative Democracy', pp. 97–9 and D. Gutmann and D. Thompson, *Democracy*, pp. 27–33.

Bibliography

Anscombe, E., 'On the Frustration of the Majority by the Fulfilment of the Majority's Will', *Analysis*, 1976, vol. 36, pp. 161–8.

Aristotle, *Nichomachean Ethics* (many editions).

—— *Politics*, trans. E. Barker, Oxford, Clarendon Press, 1946.

Barber, B., *Strong Democracy: Participatory Politics for a New Age*, Berkeley, University of California Press, 1984.

Barry, B., *Political Argument*, London, Routledge and Kegan Paul, 1965.

—— 'Is it Better to be Powerful or Lucky?', in B. Barry, *Democracy, Power and Justice*, Oxford, Clarendon Press, 1989.

Beitz, C.R., *Political Theory and International Relations*, Princeton, N.J., Princeton University Press, 1979.

Benn, S. I., *A Theory of Freedom*, Cambridge, Cambridge University Press, 1988.

Bentham, J., *An Introduction to the Principles of Morals and Legislation*, ed. J.H. Burns and H.L.A. Hart, London, Methuen, 1982.

—— 'Anarchical Fallacies', see J. Waldron (ed.), *Nonsense upon Stilts*.

Bergmann, F., *On Being Free*, Notre Dame, University of Notre Dame Press, 1977.

Berlin, I., 'Two Concepts of Liberty', in *Four Essays on Liberty*, Oxford, Oxford University Press, 1969.

Black, D., *Theory of Committees and Elections*, Cambridge, Cambridge University Press, 1958.

Brandt, R.B., *Ethical Theory*, Englewood Cliffs, N.J., Prentice Hall, 1959.

—— *A Theory of the Good and the Right*, Oxford, Clarendon Press, 1979.

Braybrooke, D., *Meeting Needs*, Princeton, N.J., Princeton University Press, 1987.

Buchanan, A., 'Liberalism and Group Rights', in J.L. Coleman and A. Buchanan (eds), *In Harm's Way: Essays in Honor of Joel Feinberg*, Cambridge, Cambridge University Press, 1994, pp. 1–15.

Burroughs, W., *Junkie*, Paris, The Olympia Press, 1966.

Campbell, T., *The Left and Rights*, London, Routledge and Kegan Paul, 1983.

Card, C., 'Gratitude and Obligation', *American Philosophical Quarterly*, 1988, vol. 25, pp. 115–27.

Carter, A., *The Political Theory of Anarchism*, London, Routledge and Kegan Paul, 1971.

Cranston, M., *What are Human Rights?*, London, Bodley Head, 1973.

Cohen, G.A., 'Self-ownership, World-ownership, and Equality: Part II', *Social Philosophy and Policy*, 1986, vol. 3.

—— 'Capitalism, Freedom and the Proletariat', in A. Ryan (ed.), *The Idea of Freedom*, Oxford, Oxford University Press, 1979.

Cohen, J., 'Deliberation and Democratic Legitimacy', in A. Hamlin and P. Pettit (eds), *The Good Polity*, Oxford, Blackwell, 1989, pp. 17–34.

—— 'Procedure and Substance in Deliberative Democracy', in S. Benhabib (ed.), *Democracy and Difference*, Princeton, N.J., Princeton University Press, 1996, pp. 95–119.

—— and Rogers, J., *On Democracy*, Harmondsworth, Penguin, 1983.

Dagger, R., *Civic Virtues: Rights, Citizenship and Republican Liberalism*, Cambridge, Cambridge University Press, 1997.

Dahl, R.K., *Democracy and its Critics*, New Haven, Yale University Press, 1989.

Daniels, N. (ed.), *Reading Rawls*, Oxford, Blackwell, 1975.

Danto, A.C. 'Constructing an Epistemology of Human Rights: A Pseudo-problem?', in E.F. Paul, J. Paul and F.D. Miller Jr. (eds), *Human Rights*, Oxford, Blackwell, 1984.

Deutscher, I., *Stalin: A Political Biography*, rev. edn, Harmondsworth, Penguin, 1966.

Devlin, P., *The Enforcement of Morals*, Oxford, Oxford University Press, 1965.

Downs, A., *An Economic Theory of Democracy*, New York, Harper and Row, 1957.

Dunn, J., *The Political Thought of John Locke*, Cambridge, Cambridge University Press, 1969.

Dworkin, R., 'The Original Position', in N. Daniels (ed.), *Reading Rawls*, pp. 16–53.

—— *Taking Rights Seriously*, London, Duckworth, 1977.

—— 'Rights as Trumps', in J. Waldron (ed.), *Theories of Rights*, adapted from R. Dworkin, 'Is there a Right to Pornography?', *Oxford Journal of Legal Studies*, 1981, vol. 1, pp. 177–212, repr. in R. Dworkin, *A Matter of Principle*, Cambridge, Mass., Harvard University Press, 1985, pp. 335–72.

—— 'What is Equality? Part I: Equality of Welfare; Part II: Equality of Resources', *Philosophy and Public Affairs*, 1981, vol. 10, pp. 185–246, 283–345.

—— 'Liberal Community', *California Law Review*, 1989, vol. 77, pp. 479–504.

—— 'The Curse of American Politics', *New York Review of Books*, October 17, 1996, vol. XLIII(16), pp. 19–25.

Elster, J., *Sour Grapes*, Cambridge, Cambridge University Press, 1983.

Feinberg, J., *Social Philosophy*, Englewood Cliffs, N.J., Prentice Hall, 1973.

—— *Harm to Others*, vol. 1 of *The Moral Limits of the Criminal Law*, New York, Oxford University Press, 1984.

Finnis, J., *Natural Law and Natural Right*, Oxford, Clarendon Press, 1980.

Fitzjames Stephen, Lord Justice J., *Liberty, Equality, Fraternity*, London, Smith, Elder, 1863, new edn, Cambridge, Cambridge University Press, 1967.

Foot, P. (ed.), *Theories of Ethics*, Oxford, Oxford University Press, 1967.

Frankfurt, H., 'Freedom of the Will and the Concept of a Person', *Journal of Philosophy*, 1971, vol. LXVII(1), pp. 5–20, repr. in G. Watson (ed.), *Free Will*, Oxford, Oxford University Press, 1982.

Fuller, L, *The Morality of Law*, New Haven, Yale University Press, 1969.

Galston, W.A., *Liberal Purposes*, Cambridge, Cambridge University Press, 1991

Gauthier, D., 'David Hume, Contractarian', *The Philosophical Review*, 1979, vol. LXXXVIII, pp. 3–38.

Gert, B., 'Hobbes and Psychological Egoism', *Journal of the History of Ideas*, 1967, vol. XXVIII.

Gewirth, A., 'Are there any Absolute Rights?', *Philosophical Quarterly*, 1981, vol. 31, repr. in J. Waldron (ed.), *Theories of Rights*.

Godwin, W., *Enquiry concerning Political Justice*, Oxford, Oxford University Press, 1971.

Goodin, R.E., *Utilitarianism as a Public Philosophy*, Cambridge, Cambridge University Press, 1995.

—— and Pettit, P. (eds), *Contemporary Political Philosophy: An Anthology*, Oxford, Blackwell, 1997.

Graham, G., *Contemporary Social Philosophy*, Oxford, Blackwell, 1988.

—— 'Freedom and Democracy', *Journal of Applied Philosophy*, 1992, vol. 9, pp. 149–60.

Gray, J., *Isaiah Berlin*, London, Harper Collins, 1995.

Green, L. *The Authority of the State*, Oxford, Clarendon Press, 1988.

Griffin, J., *Well-being*, Oxford, Clarendon Press, 1986.

Gutmann, A. and Thompson, D., *Democracy and Disagreement*, Cambridge, Mass., Harvard University Press, 1996.

Habermas, J., *The Theory of Communicative Action*, Boston, Mass., Beacon Press, 1984.

Hampton, J., *Hobbes and the Social Contract Tradition*, Cambridge, Cambridge University Press, 1986.

—— *Political Philosophy*, Boulder, Co., Westview Press, 1997.

Hardin, R., *Morality within the Limits of Reason*, Chicago, University of Chicago Press, 1988.

Harrington, J., *The Commonwealth of Oceana and A System of Politics* ed. J.G.A. Pocock, Cambridge, Cambridge University Press, 1992.

Harrison, J., *Hume's Theory of Justice*, Oxford, Oxford University Press, 1981.

Harrison, R., *Bentham*, London, Routledge and Kegan Paul, 1983.

Harsanyi, J.C., 'Cardinal Utility in Welfare Economics and the Theory of Risk Taking', *Journal of Political Economy*, 1953, vol. 61.

—— 'Morality and the Theory of Rational Behaviour', in A.K. Sen and B. Williams (eds), *Utilitarianism and Beyond*.

Hart, H.L.A., 'Are there any Natural Rights?', *Philosophical Review*, 1955, vol. LXIV(2), pp. 175–91, repr. in J. Waldron (ed.), *Theories of Rights*.

—— *The Concept of Law*, Oxford, Clarendon Press, 1961.

—— *Law, Liberty and Morality*, Oxford, Oxford University Press, 1963.

—— 'Rawls on Liberty and its Priority', *University of Chicago Law Review*, 1973, vol. 40, pp. 534–55, repr. in N. Daniels (ed.), *Reading Rawls*, pp. 230–52.

Hayek, F.A., *The Constitution of Liberty*, London, Routledge and Kegan Paul, 1960.

—— *The Road to Serfdom*, London, Routledge and Kegan Paul, 1974.

—— *Law, Legislation and Liberty*, Routledge and Kegan Paul, 1982 (published in three vols, 1973, 1976 and 1979).

Hegel, G.W.F., *The Phenomenology of Spirit*, trans. A.V. Miller, Oxford, Clarendon Press, 1977.

—— *Elements of the Philosophy of Right*, ed. A.W. Wood, trans. H.B. Nisbet, Cambridge, Cambridge University Press, 1991.

Hobbes, T., *Man and Citizen*, ed. B. Gert, Brighton, Harvester Press, 1978.

—— *Leviathan*, ed. C. B. Macpherson, Harmondsworth, Penguin, 1985.

Hohfeld, W. E., *Fundamental Legal Conceptions as Applied in Judicial Reasoning*, New Haven, Yale University Press, 1923.

Honoré, A.M., 'Ownership', in A.G. Guest (ed.), *Oxford Essays in Jurisprudence*, Oxford, Oxford University Press, 1961.

Hook, S. (ed.), *Law and Philosophy*, New York, New York University Press, 1964.

Hume, D., *Enquiries, concerning Human Understanding and the Principles of Morals*, Oxford: Oxford University Press, 1902.

—— *Essays*, Oxford, Oxford University Press, 1963.

—— *A Treatise of Human Nature*, Oxford, Oxford University Press, 1965.

Kagan, S., *The Limits of Morality*, Oxford, Clarendon Press, 1989.

Kant, I., *Groundwork of the Metaphysics of Morals*, trans. as *The Moral Law* by H.B. Paton, London, Hutchinson, 1969.

—— *The Metaphysics of Morals*, trans. M. Gregor, Cambridge, Cambridge University Press, 1991.

—— *Critique of Pure Reason*, trans. and ed. P. Guyer and A.W. Wood, Cambridge, Cambridge University Press, 1998. Academy edn, *Kritik der reinen Vernunft* (1. *Auflage*), ed. B. Erdmann, *Kant's gesammelte Schriften*, herausgegeben von der Königlich Preußischen Akademie der Wissenschaften, Band IV (edited by the Royal Prussion Academy of Sciences, vol. IV), Berlin, Georg Reimer, 1911.

Klosko, G., *The Principle of Fairness and Political Obligation*, Lanham, Md, Rowan and Littlefield, 1992.

Knowles, D., 'A Re-formulation of the Harm Principle', *Political Theory*, 1978, vol. 6, pp. 233–46.

—— 'Autonomy and Side-constraints', *Mind*, 1979, vol. LXXXVIII, pp. 263–5.

—— 'Hegel on Property and Personality', *Philosophical Quarterly*, 1983, vol. 33, pp. 45–62.

Knowles, D., 'Freedom and Democracy Revisited', *Journal of Applied Philosophy*, 1995, vol. 12, pp. 283–92.
—— 'Conservative Utilitarianism', *Utilitas*, 2000, vol. 12, pp. 155–75.
Kymlicka, W., *Liberalism, Community and Culture*, Oxford, Clarendon Press, 1989.
—— *Multicultural Citizenship*, Oxford, Clarendon Press, 1995.
Lessnoff, M.H., 'Capitalism, Socialism and Democracy', *Political Studies*, 1979, vol. XXVII, pp. 594–602.
—— *Political Philosophers of the Twentieth Century*, Oxford, Blackwell, 1999.
Lipsey, R., *Introduction to Positive Economics*, London, Weidenfeld and Nicolson, 1965.
Locke, J., *Two Treatises of Government*, Cambridge, Cambridge University Press, 1960.
—— *Essay concerning Human Understanding* (many editions).
Lomasky, L.E. and Brennan, G., 'Is there a Duty to Vote?', *Social Philosophy Policy*, 2000, vol. 17(1), pp. 65–74.
Lyons, D., *Forms and Limits of Utilitarianism*, Oxford, Oxford University Press, 1965.
—— 'Utility and Rights', in J.R. Pennock and J.W. Chapman (eds), *Ethics, Economics and the Law: Nomos XXIV*, New York, New York University Press, 1982, pp. 107–38 and repr. in J. Waldron (ed.), *Theories of Rights*, and D. Lyons, *Rights Welfare, and Mill's Moral Theory*, Oxford, Oxford University Press, 1994.
MacCallum, G.C., 'Negative and Positive Freedom', *Philosophical Review*, 1967, vol. 76, pp. 312–14.
Macintyre, A., *After Virtue*, London, Duckworth, 1981.
Mackie, J.L., 'Can There be a Rights-based Moral Theory?', in P. A. French, T. E. Uehling, Jr and H. K. Wettstein (eds), *Studies in Ethical Theory*, Midwest Studies in Philosophy, 1978, vol. 3, repr. in J. Waldron (ed.), *Theories of Rights*.
—— *Hume's Moral Thought*, London, Routledge and Kegan Paul, 1980.
MacPherson, C.B., *Democratic Theory: Essays in Retrieval*, Oxford, Clarendon Press, 1973.
McPherson, T., *Political Obligation*, London, Routledge and Kegan Paul, 1967.
Marx, K., *1844 Manuscripts*, in *Early Writings*, trans. R. Livingstone and G. Benton, Harmondsworth, Penguin, 1975, pp. 328–9.
Milgram, S., *Obedience to Authority*, London, Tavistock, 1974.
—— 'Obedience', in Richard L. Gregory (ed.), *The Oxford Companion to the Mind*, Oxford, Oxford University Press, 1987.

Mill, James, *Essay on Government* (1819), Indianapolis, Liberal Arts Press, 1955.

Mill, J.S., *Utilitarianism, Liberty, Representative Government*, London, Dent, 1968.

—— *Utilitarianism*, in J.S. Mill, *Utilitarianism, Liberty, Representative Government*.

—— *On Liberty*, in J.S. Mill, *Utilitarianism, Liberty, Representative Government*.

—— *Considerations on Representative Government* (1861) in J.S. Mill, *Utilitarianism, Liberty, Representative Government*.

—— 'M. de Tocqueville on Democracy in America' (1840), repr. in J.B. Schneewind (ed.), *Mill's Ethical Writings*, New York, Collier, 1965, pp. 105–58.

Miller, D., *Social Justice*, Oxford, Clarendon Press, 1976.

—— *Philosophy and Ideology in Hume's Political Thought*, Oxford, Clarendon Press, 1981.

—— *Anarchism*, London, J.M. Dent, 1984.

Moore, G.E., *Principia Ethica*, Cambridge, Cambridge University Press, 1903.

Mulhall, S. and A. Swift, *Liberals and Communitarians*, Oxford, Blackwell, 1992.

Nagel, T., 'Rawls on Justice', *Philosophical Review*, 1973, vol. LXXXII, pp. 220–34, repr. in N. Daniels, *Reading Rawls*.

—— *Equality and Partiality*, Oxford, Oxford University Press, 1991.

Nozick, R., *Anarchy, State and Utopia*, New York, Basic Books, 1974.

Nussbaum, M., *Sex and Social Justice*, Oxford, Oxford University Press, 1999.

—— and A.K. Sen, (eds), *The Quality of Life*, Oxford, Clarendon Press, 1992.

Oakeshott, M., *Rationalism in Politics and Other Essays*, London, Methuen, 1967.

O'Neill, J., *Ecology, Policy and Politics*, London, Routledge, 1993.

O'Neill, O., *Faces of Hunger: An Essay on Poverty, Justice and Development*, London, Allen and Unwin, 1986.

—— 'Kant on Duties Regarding Nonrational Nature', *Proceedings of the Aristotelian Society*, 1998, Supp. vol. LXXII, pp. 211–28.

Parekh, B. (ed.), *Bentham's Political Thought*, London, Croom Helm, 1973.

Pettit, P., *Republicanism: A Theory of Government and Freedom*, Oxford, Clarendon Press, 1997.

Pitkin, H., 'Obligation and Consent', *American Political Science Review*, 1965, vols LIX(4) and LX(1), repr. in P. Laslett, W.G. Runciman and Q. Skinner (eds), *Philosophy, Politics and Society: Fourth Series*, Oxford, Blackwell, 1972.

Plant, R., *Modern Political Thought*, Oxford, Blackwell, 1991.

Plato, *The Republic*, trans. H.P.D. Lee, Harmondsworth, Penguin, 1955.

Pogge, T., *Realising Rawls*, Ithaca, N.Y., Cornell University Press, 1989.

Railton, P., 'Alienation, Consequentialism, and the Demands of Morality', *Philosophy and Public Affairs*, 1984, vol. 13, pp. 134–71, repr. in S. Scheffler(ed.), *Consequentialism and its Critics*.

Raphael, D.D., *Problems of Political Philosophy*, London, Macmillan, 1970.

Rawls, J., 'Two Concepts of Rules', *Philosophical Review*, 1955, vol. 64, pp. 3–32, repr. in *Collected Papers*, pp. 20–46, and P. Foot (ed.), *Theories of Ethics*.

—— *A Theory of Justice*, Oxford, Clarendon Press, 1972.

—— 'Kantian Constructivism in Moral Theory', *Journal of Philosophy*, 1980, vol. 77, pp. 515–72, repr. in *Collected Papers*, pp. 303–58.

—— *Political Liberalism*, New York, Columbia University Press, 1993.

—— 'The Idea of Public Reason Revisited', *University of Chicago Law Review*, 1997, vol. 64, pp. 765–807, repr. in *Collected Papers*, pp. 573–615.

—— 'Preface for the French Edition of *A Theory of Justice*', repr. in *Collected Papers*, pp. 415–20.

—— *Collected Papers*, ed. S. Freeman, Cambridge, Mass., Harvard University Press, 1999.

Raz, J., 'Rights-based Moralities', in J. Waldron (ed.), *Theories of Rights*.

—— *The Morality of Freedom*, Oxford, Clarendon Press, 1986.

Reiman, J., *In Defense of Political Philosophy*, New York, Harper and Row, 1972.

Report of the Committee on Homosexual Offences and Prostitution (CMD 247) 1957 (*The Wolfenden Report*).

Rescher, N., *Welfare: The Social Issue in Philosophical Perspective*, Pittsburgh, University of Pittsburgh Press, 1972.

Robbins, L., *The Nature and Significance of Economic Science*, London, Routledge and Kegan Paul, 1932.

Roth, K., 'The Court the US Doesn't Want', *New York Review of Books*, November 18, 1998, vol. XLV(18), pp. 45–7.

Rousseau, J.-J., *The Social Contract and Discourses*, London, Dent, 1973.

Sagoff, M., *The Economy of the Earth*, Cambridge, Cambridge University Press, 1988.

Sandel, M., *Liberalism and the Limits of Justice*, Cambridge, Cambridge University Press, 1982.

—— 'The Procedural Republic and the Unencumbered Self', *Political Theory*, 1984, vol. 12, pp. 81–96, repr. in R.E. Goodin and P. Pettit (eds), *Contemporary Political Philosophy: An Anthology*, pp. 247–55.

Scanlon, T.M., 'Rights, Goals and Fairness', *Erkenntnis*, 1977, vol. II, pp. 81–94.

—— T.M., 'Contractualism and Utilitarianism', in A.K. Sen and B. Williams (eds), *Utilitarianism and Beyond*.

—— *What We Owe to Each Other*, Cambridge, Mass., Harvard University Press, 1999.

Scheffler, S. (ed.), *Consequentialism and its Critics*, Oxford, Oxford University Press, 1988.

Schier, F., 'The Kantian Gulag', in D. Knowles and J. Skorupski (eds), *Virtue and Taste*, Oxford, Blackwell, 1993, pp. 1–18.

Schwartz, L.B., 'Morals Offences and the Model Penal Code', *Columbia Law Review*, 1963, vol. LXIII.

Sen, A.K., 'Equality of What?', *The Tanner Lectures on Human Values*, vol. 1, ed. S.M. McMurrin, Cambridge, Cambridge University Press, 1980, pp. 195–220, repr. in R.E. Goodin and P. Pettit (eds), *Contemporary Political Philosophy: An Anthology*.

—— 'Capability and Well-being', in M.C. Nussbaum and A.K. Sen (eds), *The Quality of Life*, pp. 30–53.

—— *Inequality Re-examined*, Oxford, Clarendon Press, 1992.

—— and B. Williams, (eds), *Utilitarianism and Beyond*, Cambridge, Cambridge University Press, 1982.

Sher, G., *Desert*, Princeton, N.J., Princeton University Press, 1987.

—— *Beyond Neutrality*, Cambridge, Cambridge University Press, 1997.

Shue, H., *Basic Rights*, Princeton, N.J., Princeton University Press, 1980, excerpted in R.E. Goodin and P. Pettit (eds), *Contemporary Political Philosophy: An Anthology*, pp. 341–55.

Simmons, A.J., *Moral Principles and Political Obligations*, Princeton, N.J., Princeton University Press, 1979.

Singer, P., *Democracy and Disobedience*, London, Oxford University Press, 1974.

—— *Practical Ethics*, Cambridge, Cambridge University Press, 1979.

—— 'Famine, Affluence and Morality', *Philosophy and Public Affairs*, 1992, vol. 1, pp. 229–43.

Skinner, Q., 'The Idea of Negative Liberty', in R. Rorty, J.B. Schneewind, and Q. Skinner (eds), *Philosophy in History*, Cambridge, Cambridge University Press, 1984.

Skorupski, J., *John Stuart Mill*, London, Routledge, 1989.

Smart, J.J.C., 'Extreme and Restricted Utilitarianism', *Philosophical Quarterly*, 1956, vol. 6, pp. 344–54, repr. in P. Foot (ed.), *Theories of Ethics*.

—— 'An Outline of a System of Utilitarian Ethics', in J.J.C. Smart and B. Williams, *Utilitarianism: For and Against*, Cambridge, Cambridge University Press, 1973.

Spitz, J.-F., *La Liberté Politique*, Paris, Presses Universitaires de France, 1995.

Steiner, H, 'Individual Liberty', *Aristotelian Society Proceedings*, 1975, vol. LXXV, pp. 35–50.

—— *An Essay on Rights*, Oxford, Blackwell, 1994.

Strawson, P.F., 'Social Morality and Individual Ideal', *Philosophy*, 1961, vol. XXXVI, repr. in P.F. Strawson, *Freedom and Resentment*, London, Methuen, 1974, pp. 26–44.

Sumner, L.W., *The Moral Foundation of Rights*, Oxford, Clarendon Press, 1987.

Taylor, C., 'Responsibility for Self', in A. O. Rorty (ed.), *The Identities of Persons*, Berkeley, University of California Press, 1976, pp. 281–99, repr. in G. Watson (ed.), *Free Will*.

—— *Philosophical Papers*, 2 vols, Cambridge, Cambridge University Press, 1985.

—— 'What is Human Agency?', in *Philosophical Papers*, vol. I, pp. 15–44.

—— 'Atomism', in C. Taylor, *Philosophical Papers*: 2, pp. 187–210.

—— 'Cross-purposes: the Liberal–Communitarian Debate', in N. Rosenblum (ed.), *Liberalism and the Moral Life*, Cambridge, Mass., Harvard University Press, 1989.

—— *Sources of the Self*, Cambridge, Cambridge University Press, 1989.

Taylor, M., *Anarchy and Cooperation*, London, Wiley, 1976; 2nd edn. published as *The Possibility of Cooperation*, Cambridge, Cambridge University Press, 1987.

—— *Community, Anarchy and Liberty*, Cambridge, Cambridge University Press, 1982.

Thomson, J.J., *The Realm of Rights*, Cambridge, Mass., Harvard University Press, 1990.

Tuck, R., *Natural Rights Theories*, Cambridge, Cambridge University Press, 1979.

Tully, J., *A Discourse on Property*, Cambridge, Cambridge University Press, 1980.

Waldron, J. (ed.), *Theories of Rights*, Oxford, Oxford University Press, 1984.

—— (ed.), *Nonsense upon Stilts: Bentham, Burke and Marx on the Rights of Man*, London, Methuen, 1987.

—— *The Right to Private Property*, Oxford, Clarendon Press, 1988.

—— 'Rushdie and Religion', in *Liberal Rights*, first published as 'Too Important for Tact', in the *Times Literary Supplement*, March 10–16, 1989, pp. 248, 260.

—— *Liberal Rights*, Cambridge, Cambridge University Press, 1993.

—— 'Participation: The Right of Rights', *Proceedings of the Aristotelian Society*, 1998, vol. XCVIII, pp. 307–37.

—— *Law and Disagreement*, Oxford, Clarendon Press, 1999.

Walker, A.D.M., 'Political Obligation and the Argument from Gratitude', *Philosophy and Public Affairs*, 1988, vol. 17, pp. 191–211.

Walzer, M., *Spheres of Justice*, Oxford, Blackwell, 1983.

Watson, G., 'Free Agency', *Journal of Philosophy*, 1975, vol. 72, pp. 205–20, repr. in G. Watson (ed.), *Free Will*.

—— (ed.), *Free Will*, Oxford, Oxford University Press, 1982.

Weber, M., *From Max Weber: Essays in Sociology*, trans. and ed. H.H. Gerth and C.W. Mills, London, Routledge and Kegan Paul, 1946.

Wedgwood, Ralph, 'Why Promote People's Freedom? (unpublished).

Wenar, L., 'Original Acquisition of Private Property', *Mind*, 1998, vol. 107, pp. 799–819.

White, A.R., *Modal Thinking*, Oxford, Blackwell, 1971.

Wiggins, D., 'The Claims of Need', in *Needs, Values, Truth*, Oxford, Blackwell, 1987.

Williams, B., 'Toleration: An Impossible Virtue?', in D. Heyd (ed.), *Toleration*, Princeton, N.J., Princeton University Press, 1996.

Wolf, S., *Freedom within Reason*, Oxford, Oxford University Press, 1990.

Wolff, J., 'What is the Problem of Political Obligation?', *Proceedings of the Aristotelian Society*, 1990/1, vol. XCI.

Wolff, R.P., *In Defense of Anarchism*, 2nd edn, New York, Harper, 1976.

Wood, A.W., *Hegel's Ethical Thought*, Cambridge, Cambridge University Press, 1990.

—— 'Kant on Duties Regarding Nonrational Nature', *Proceedings of the Aristotelian Society*, 1998, Supp. vol. LXXII, pp. 189–210.

Woodcock, G., *Anarchism*, Harmondsworth, Penguin, 1963.

—— *The Anarchist Reader*, London, Fontana, 1977.

Index